INTRODUCTION TO REFERENCE WORK

VOLUME I *Basic Information Sources*

McGRAW-HILL SERIES IN LIBRARY EDUCATION

Jean Key Gates, Consulting Editor
University of South Florida

Boll   INTRODUCTION TO CATALOGING, VOL. I:
DESCRIPTIVE CATALOGING
Boll   INTRODUCTION TO CATALOGING, VOL. II:
ENTRY HEADINGS
Gates   INTRODUCTION TO LIBRARIANSHIP
Heiliger and Henderson   LIBRARY AUTOMATION:
EXPERIENCE, METHODOLOGY, AND TECHNOLOGY OF
THE LIBRARY AS AN INFORMATION SYSTEM
Jackson   LIBRARIES AND LIBRARIANSHIP IN THE WEST:
A BRIEF HISTORY
Katz   INTRODUCTION TO REFERENCE WORK, VOL. I:
BASIC INFORMATION SOURCES
Katz   INTRODUCTION TO REFERENCE WORK, VOL. II:
REFERENCE SERVICES AND REFERENCE PROCESSES

INTRODUCTION
TO REFERENCE WORK

Volume I   **BASIC INFORMATION SOURCES**

Third Edition

William A. Katz

Professor, School of Library and Information Science
State University of New York at Albany

McGraw-Hill Book Company
New York   St. Louis   San Francisco   Auckland   Bogotá
Düsseldorf   Johannesburg   London   Madrid   Mexico
Montreal   New Delhi   Panama   Paris   São Paulo
Singapore   Sydney   Tokyo   Toronto

INTRODUCTION TO REFERENCE WORK, Volume I
Basic Information Sources

    4 5 6 7 8 9 0 D O D O 8 3 2 1

This book was set in Baskerville by National ShareGraphics, Inc.
The editors were Rhona Robbin and Phyllis T. Dulan;
the designer was Anne Canevari Green; the production supervisor was
Milton J. Heiberg. The cover was designed by Andrew W. Roberts.
R. R. Donnelley & Sons Company was printer and binder.

Library of Congress Cataloging in Publication Data

Katz, William A   date
    Introduction to reference work.

    (McGraw-Hill series in library education)
    Includes bibliographies and index.
    CONTENTS: v. 1.   Basic information sources.—v. 2.
Reference services and reference processes.
    1.   Reference services (Libraries)   2.   Reference books.
I.   Title.
Z711.K32   1978   011'.02   77-12539
ISBN 0-07-033331-9 (v. 1)
ISBN 0-07-033332-7 (v. 2)

For Linda and the librarians

CONTENTS

Preface   xi

PART I   INTRODUCTION

1   *The Reference Process*   3
    Reference Service and the Public   5
    Reference Service and the Library   8
    Reference Questions   10
    Information Sources   14
    Evaluating Reference Sources   20
    Suggested Reading   26

PART II   INFORMATION: CONTROL AND ACCESS

2   *Bibliographies: Introduction*   31
    Systematic Enumerative Bibliography   32
    Guides to Reference Books   36
    Current Selection Aids   41
    Indexes to Reviews   46
    Negative Selection   49
    Suggested Reading   52

3 *Bibliographies: National Library Catalogs and*
     Trade Bibliographies   55
     National Library Catalogs   57
     National and Trade Bibliography   63
     United States Retrospective Bibliography   71
     Bibliographies: Periodicals and Newspapers   77
     Bibliographies: Nonprint Materials   84
     Bibliography of Bibliographies   91
     Suggested Reading   93

PART III SOURCES OF INFORMATION

4 *Indexing and Abstracting Services*   97
     Evaluation   99
     Periodical Indexes   104
     Indexes to Current Events   112
     Material in Collections   117
     Abstracting Services   125
     Suggested Reading   132

5 *Encyclopedias: General and Subject*   135
     Evaluating Encyclopedias   139
     Adult Encyclopedias   153
     Popular Adult and High School Sets   157
     Children's and Young Adults' Encyclopedias   159
     Preschool and Children's Encyclopedias   161
     Other Encyclopedias   162
     Encyclopedia Supplements: Yearbooks   164
     One-Volume Encyclopedias   166
     Foreign-Language Encyclopedias   169
     Subject Encyclopedias   173
     Suggested Reading   184

6   *Ready-Reference Sources: Almanacs, Yearbooks,*
     Handbooks, Directories   187
     Almanacs and Yearbooks   188
     Representative Subject Almanacs and Yearbooks   195
     Handbooks and Manuals   203
     Representative Subject Handbooks and Manuals   206
     Directories   213
     Suggested Reading   226

7   *Biographical Sources*   229
     Evaluation   230
     Searching Biographical Sources   234
     Biographical Dictionaries   237
     Indexes to Biography   238
     Current Biographical Sources   243
     Retrospective Biographical Sources   248
     Related Biographical Areas   252
     Professional and Subject Biographies   254
     Suggested Reading   263

8   *Dictionaries*   265
     Evaluation   268
     Unabridged Dictionaries   276
     Desk (Collegiate) Dictionaries   280
     Children's Dictionaries   283
     Historical Dictionaries   284
     Slang   288
     Synonyms and Antonyms   289
     Usage and Manuscript Style   291
     Abbreviations and Acronyms   292
     Subject Dictionaries   293
     Foreign-Language Dictionaries (Bilingual)   294
     Suggested Reading   296

9   *Geographical Sources*   299
     Evaluation   304
     World Atlases   311
     National Maps   315
     Thematic Maps and Atlases   317
     Gazetteers   319
     Travel Guides   320
     Suggested Reading   321

10   *Government Documents*   323
     Guides   325
     Catalogs and Indexes   325
     Organization and Selection   333
     Types of Publications   338
     State and Local Documents   341
     Suggested Reading   342

Index   345

PREFACE

The purpose of this book is to assist librarians, students, and other library users to become familiar with the various information sources and to employ them to best advantage in reference work. Although written with the reference librarian in mind, it introduces basic publications that will help the student and the layperson to use the library effectively, easily, and quickly.

Basic Information Sources is the first volume in the two-volume set, *Introduction to Reference Work.* In this third edition, revision is extensive and all material is updated. Some chapters have been consolidated, and selected materials from the second volume have been incorporated in this volume, as suggested by teachers expert in library reference work.

This volume may be used independently by the student or the layperson. The second volume, *Reference Services and Reference Processes,* provides a far more detailed description of what reference work is all about. Consequently, the serious student of reference work should realize that *Basic Information Sources* is only the beginning and, admittedly, gives a one-sided view of the extremely important profession of librarianship.

Since no book can possibly cover the whole field and meet everyone's needs, only foundation or basic reference works are considered here. Nor is any effort made to cover the vast and growing area of subject specialization and bibliography. This field is left to other texts and other courses. Some major subject forms are noted, but they are primarily illustrative and are not intended to be in any way exhaustive.

Limited attention is given in this first volume to the rapid growth and importance of machine-readable data bases, especially as they relate to indexing and abstracting. However, the new format for reference works is not as yet extensive enough to warrant a separate chapter, at least in this volume. That is left to the second volume, where data bases are considered in more detail.

After a brief introduction on reference work and information sources, the text is divided into chapters on traditional forms, such as bibliographies, indexes, and encyclopedias. Each chapter considers various common attributes of the form and how they relate to answering questions. While it is pointless for students to memorize details about specific reference sources, they should at least grasp the essential areas of agreement and difference among the various forms. To this end, every effort is made to compare rather than to detail. Not all so-called basic titles are included or annotated, because (1) there is no consensus on what constitutes "basic"; (2) more important, the objective of this text is to discuss various forms, and the titles used are primarily illustrative of those forms; and finally, (3) the annotations for a specific title are duplicated over and over again in Sheehy's *Guide to Reference Books* and Walford's *Guide to Reference Materials,* which list the numerous subject bibliographies.

Suggested readings are found (1) at the end of each chapter and (2) in the footnotes. Where a publication is cited in a footnote, the reference is rarely duplicated in the suggested readings at the end of the chapter. For the most part, the readings are limited to publications issued since 1974; thus the citations in the second edition have been updated, and it is easier for the student to find the readings. [Note: A number of the readings will be found in the author's *Library Lit: The Best of . . .* and in *Reference and Information Services, a Reader.* Both are published by Scarecrow Press, the former from 1970 to date (annual), the latter in 1978.]

Prices are noted for most of the major basic titles to indicate the relative expense of each work. This feature was suggested by several readers of the first edition who pointed out that budgetary considerations are sometimes equally as important as selection, particularly in terms of peripheral titles. Prices are as of mid-1977 and, obviously, are subject to change.

Bibliographic details are based on publishers' catalogs, *Books in Print,* and the latest edition of Sheehy's *Guide.* The information is applicable as of mid-1977 and, again, is subject to change.

Finally, despite the traditional arrangement and presentation of materials, this textbook is not a vote for the traditional methods of teaching beginning reference courses. The material is presented in such a way that imaginative teachers will find themselves free to use the text as a base for launching and developing their own style and techniques in teaching. It should serve as background material so that the individual teacher may use any type of presentation or methodology deemed necessary for the particular situation.

I am grateful to many teachers of reference and bibliography for their advice and help. My thanks also go to the students who so kindly made suggestions. I am particularly grateful to Andrea Wasson, my student assistant, who carefully read and corrected the manuscript.

William A. Katz

INTRODUCTION TO REFERENCE WORK

VOLUME I *Basic Information Sources*

INTRODUCTION

CHAPTER ONE

The Reference Process

WHEN LAYPERSONS THINK of reference work, they view it in terms of questions and answers. One has a question. One expects the librarian to provide an answer, or at least to indicate where or how the answer may be found. Disengaged from necessary quantitative and qualitative variables, reference work is the process of answering questions.

The ability of the librarian to translate the query into terms that can be met by a given reference source is known as reference service. A consideration of the communication process between the librarian and the person posing the question moves the definition to the broader context of the total reference process. It is a type of hierarchical scheme with the reference process encompassing reference service, reference work, and, of course, the reference sources.[1] This analytical approach is not simply restating the phrase, "Rose is a rose is a rose is a rose." It serves a purpose. Until such time as the intricacies of the reference process are understood, it will be difficult to plan and organize methods of service intelligently.

---

[1] Throughout the text, the terms "reference process" and "information process," like "reference services" and "information services," are employed synonymously. When librarians wish to differentiate between "traditional" concepts and functions and "nontraditional" services, they tend to substitute "information" for "reference." There are distinct differences between the terms, however, which are discussed in *Reference Services and Reference Processes,* the second volume of this text.

The definitions, or lack of them, mean little in themselves. Yet, in order to define any process properly, it must be understood. It is suggested here that the reference process, throughout its history, has been and is all too little understood. For example, consider the interaction between the librarian and the person posing a question.

This is a familiar communication process learned in childhood. A small child asks, "Why?" He looks to his mother or father for a satisfactory answer. The parent, in turn, draws upon experience, knowledge, or intuition to give the proper reply. The communication elements remain the same whether a person is a child at a parent's knee or a scientist scanning a computer printout. First, there has to be someone to ask the question. Second, there has to be a question or inquiry, whether it be a simple "Why?" or "How do I get special care for my aged parents?" Third, there has to be someone to respond. And, finally, the person responding must have some resources with which to answer the query.

Shera suggests the library is an agency of communication. "But what is the act of communication? How do we communicate? . . . We tend to assume that this is a simple act, when, as a matter of fact, it is very far from being simple."[2] He then illustrates his point by describing the experience of the reference librarian and the individual asking a question. The individual's first problem is to express the question, "to put it in terms [such] that either the organization of the library will reveal it or the intelligence of the reference librarian can comprehend it." This problem and other communication factors "point up the very great need to analyze far more thoroughly than we have ever done, what the (reference) process is, and interpret that . . . process in psychological, neurological, and organizational terms."[3]

In the dialogue between a questioner and the librarian, the question must first be clarified. The woman who wants "something about gardening" may want just that, a general book on the subject; or, more likely, she wants a specific bit of information to assist her in checking the disease of a given plant or in deciding what type of plant to put in a shaded area. The possible *real* questions, quite different from the general questions, are almost as numerous as the users of a library.

When the actual needs of the library patron are understood, the next step is to formulate a search strategy of possible sources. This step requires translating the terms of the question into the language of the reference system. If a basic book on gardening is required, the librarian will find it

[2] Jesse H. Shera, *Sociological Foundations of Librarianship* (New York: Asia Publishing House, 1970), p. 32.
[3] Ibid., pp. 47, 48, 50.

readily enough in the card catalog under a suitable subject heading. At the other specific extreme, the question may involve searching indexes, such as the *Biological & Agricultural Index,* to find the latest information on elm blight, or perhaps checking out various bibliographies, such as *Subject Guide to Books in Print* or a union catalog, to find what may be available on elm blight in general and other libraries. (Note, too, that the subject "elm blight" must be translated into terms used as subject headings in the various indexes and bibliographies to cover works on elm blight.) Once the information is found, it then has to be evaluated. That is, the librarian must determine whether it is really the kind, and at the level, that the woman wants. Is it too technical or too simple? Is it applicable in this geographic area?

Not all searches need be complicated. Much of the reference work in libraries is of the simple fact type which requires direct answers to such questions as: How high is the Empire State Building? What is the world record for long-distance swimming? Who is my state senator? Here, experience and knowledge of reference sources make it relatively easy for the librarian to find the needed fact in a moment or two.

REFERENCE SERVICE AND THE PUBLIC

Whereas the theory of the reference process is difficult to isolate, it does have elemental factors that are easily understood. For example, on a day-to-day level, reference entertains and, to a degree, enlightens millions of magazine and newspaper readers. "Is it true that drinking milk after eating lobster will poison us?" a nervous reader asks. "The Doctor Answers," a daily newspaper column, asserts, "There's no truth in that old wheeze." On another page of the paper, "Dear Abby," everyone's friendly reference librarian, copes with problems of mind, heart, and state. "Household Hints by Heloise" solves the difficulty of a woman who "had a nasty fat fire in her broiler." The Sunday newspaper supplement "Parade" features a page given over to answering queries. A twist of the radio or television dial brings local or national quiz and talk shows based on the question-answer syndrome. Mention of these resources is not to suggest that the library should become a substitute for the popular media, but only that the average man or woman who takes an interest in finding answers to questions has a need, if not always an understanding, of the basic reference process.

The father of the American reference process, Samuel Green, instituted the first formal reference service at the Worcester Public Library in Massachusetts in 1876. He emphasized the importance of personal aid to people requesting information. Until Green made his policy statement, the tendency of librarians was to look upon themselves as keepers of archives rather than as activists in providing information for the public.[4]

Since the end of World War II, information has been a gigantic resource, a major business.[5] The advent of computers, data bases, information networks, and a new generation of information companies in the 1970s has taken reference work out of the familiar library and into the marketplace. Information is appreciated at the highest levels of government. In 1976 Secretary of State Henry Kissinger considered information to be as important as any resource available, and he offered the United Nations General Assembly American services in providing developing nations with scientific and technical information—or, at the level of everyday reference work, answers to queries ranging from how to build roads to how to construct power stations and scientific laboratories. Both the profit-making and the nonprofit segments of the private and public sectors are now involved with information, and despite economic pressures, libraries are making an effort to maintain and expand their place in the information-reference complex.

Nevertheless, there is no totally satisfactory definition or theory of the reference process. Diversity of types of libraries, personal philosophies of reference service, and the complexity of information sources and needs are only some of the factors contributing to the confusion. Of some help are the "guidelines" to information service, prepared by the Standards Committee of the Reference and Adult Services Division of the American Library Association (ALA). After 10 years of discussion and preparation, these guidelines (officially known as "A Commitment to Information Services") were adopted in early 1976.[6]

This document is directed "to all those who have any responsibility for providing reference and information services"; its most valuable contribution is its succinct description of a reference librarian's duties. Defined by function, reference service may be divided into two categories: direct and indirect.

1. The direct category includes:
   a *Reference or information services.* This is the "personal assistance provided to users in pursuit of information." The depth and

---

[4] The standard history of American reference service is Samuel Rothstein's *The Development of Reference Service Through Academic Traditions, Public Library Practice and Special Librarianship* (Chicago: American Library Association, 1955) (ACRL Monograph No. 14).

[5] Susan Wagner, "Wanted More Information about Information," *Publishers' Weekly,* June 7, 1976, pp. 43–44. A report on the annual meeting of the Information Industry Association which briefly outlines present concerns with reference work and information science.

[6] The text of the guidelines appeared in the summer issue, 1976, of *RQ* and, with comments by Bernard Vavrek ("Bless You Samuel Green!") in the *Library Journal,* April 15, 1976, pp. 971–974. Quotes which follow are from the *Library Journal* reprint of the guidelines.

character of such service vary with the type of library and the kinds of users it is designed to serve.

This service may range from answering an apparently simple query to supplying information based on a bibliographical search combining the librarian/information specialist's competence in information-handling techniques with competence in the subject of inquiry.

b *Formal and informal instruction in the use of the library or information center and its resources.* This direct service may consist of various activities ranging from helping the user to understand the card catalog to "interpretative tours and lectures" on how to use the library. In most libraries, the interpretation of "instruction" is showing the user how to find an article, book, or other item by "interpreting" the mysteries of an index, reference work, etc.

2. Indirect services may be summarized thus:

These services reflect user access to a wide range of informational sources (e.g., bibliographies, indexes, information data bases), and may be the extension of the library's information-service potential through cooperation with other library or information centers. This type of service recognizes the key role of interlibrary and interagency cooperation to provide adequate information service to users.

More specifically, the average reference librarian is likely to be engaged in performing a number of indirect services:

Selection of Materials This service consists of the recognition of the various types of materials needed for adequate reference service—not only books, but periodicals, manuscripts, newspapers, and anything else which can conceivably assist the librarian in giving direct service. Another aspect of selection is the weeding of book collections and files.

Organization of References The organization and administration of references are matters of staff coordination of reference service with other services in the library.

Interlibrary Loan With the increasing emphasis on networks and the recognition that the whole world of information should be literally at the command of the user, interlibrary loan may be categorized as an access activity. In recent years, it has become a major element in reference service. Administratively, some libraries now divorce it from reference and maintain it as a separate division.

Evaluation of Reference Section   How well is the reference section serving the public? What has been done and what can be done to improve service? This analysis presupposes a method of evaluating not only the collection, but the organization of the reference section and the library as a whole.

Miscellaneous Tasks   There are a variety of "housekeeping" duties, including such tasks as assisting with photocopying, filing, checking in materials, keeping a wary eye on reading rooms, maintaining records, plus all the chores that are the responsibility of any library department—from budgeting to preparing reports and publicity releases. The extent of this kind of activity depends to a great degree on the size of the library and the philosophy and the financial support of the reference section.

REFERENCE SERVICE AND THE LIBRARY

The reference librarian does not function alone in a library but is part of a larger unit. Briefly, how do reference services fit into the library?

The specific purpose of any library is to obtain, preserve, and make available the recorded knowledge of human beings. The system for doing so can be as intricate and involved as the table of organization for the Library of Congress or General Motors. At the other extreme, it may be as simple as that used in the one-man small-town library or the corner barbershop.

Regardless of organizational patterns or complexities, the parts of the system are interrelated and common to all sizes and types of libraries. They consist of administrative work, technical services (acquisition and cataloging), and reader's services (circulation and reference). These broad categories cover multiple subsections. Still, they are not independent units but parts of larger units; all are closely related. They form a unity essential for library service in general and reference in particular. Let one fail and the whole system will suffer.

Administrative work

The administration is concerned with library organization and communication. The better the administration functions, the less obvious it appears—at least to the user. The reference librarian must be aware of, and often participate in, administrative decisions ranging from budget to automation. Precisely how administration functions effectively is the subject of countless texts and coffee conversations. It is not the topic of this text, although specific administration of reference sections and departments is discussed later.

Technical services: Acquisitions

The selection and acquisition of materials are governed by the type of library and its users. Policies vary, of course, but the rallying cry of the nineteenth-century activist librarians, "The right book for the right reader at the right time," is still applicable to any library. It presents many challenges. For the general collection, it presupposes a knowledge of the clientele as well as personal knowledge of the material acquired and its applicability to the reader. The librarian must cope with publishers, sources, and reviews, and must show an appreciation for cooperation with other libraries. The unparalleled production of library materials over the past 50 years makes the process of selection and acquisition a primary intellectual responsibility.

While reference librarians are responsible for the reference collection, their responsibility extends to the development of the library's entire collection—a collection which may serve to help them answer questions.

Technical services: Cataloging

Once a piece of information is acquired, the primary problem is how to retrieve it from the hundreds, thousands, or millions of bits of information in the library. There are a number of avenues open, from oral communication to abstracts; but when dealing with larger information units, such as books, recordings, films, periodicals, or reports, the normal finding device is the card catalog. The catalog is the library's main bibliographical instrument. When properly used, it (1) enables persons to find books for which they have the author, title, or the subject area; (2) shows what the library has by any given author, on a given subject, and in a given kind of literature; (3) assists in the choice of a book by its form (e.g., as handbook, literature, or text) or edition; (4) assists in finding other materials from government documents to films; and, often most important, (5) specifically locates the item in the library. It is a primary resource for reference librarians; and it is essential they understand not only the general aspects of the card catalog, but also its many peculiarities.

Reader's services: Circulation

Circulation is one of two primary public service points in the library. The other is reference.

After the book has been acquired and prepared for easy access, the circulation department is concerned with (1) charging out the material to the reader; (2) receiving it on return; and (3) returning it to its proper location. Other activities of the circulation department include registration of prospective borrowers, keeping records of the number of books and patrons, and maintaining other statistics pertinent to charting the operation of the library. In small libraries, up to 50 percent or more of the reference work may be centered at the circulation desk. Such a library normally has one or two professionals who must pinch-hit in almost every capacity from administration to cataloging. Also, there simply may be no space for a separate reference desk, and the circulation point is a logical center where people come not only to check out books, but also to ask questions.

Reader's services: Reference

Reference service is part of the library and draws upon all the resources of the library to answer questions. At one time, the availability of material was fairly limited to individual libraries. When a question was beyond the resources of the library (or, for that matter, the abilities of the librarian), the user had no choice but to move on to a larger or different type of library. Accessibility to information was, in a word, provincial. Today, accessibility is considerably more sophisticated. Thanks to technological innovations from microfilm to data bases, the holdings of almost any library can be brought to the individual in any part of the nation.

REFERENCE QUESTIONS

There are various methods of categorizing types of reference questions. By way of an introduction to a complex situation, queries may be divided into two general types:

1. *The user asks for a known item.* The request is usually for a specific document, book, article, film, or other item, which can be identified by quoting certain features such as author, title, or source. The librarian has only to locate the needed item via the card catalog, an index, or similar source.
2. *The user asks for information without any specific knowledge of the necessary source.* Such a query triggers the usual reference interview. Most reference questions usually fall into the second type, particularly in school and public libraries where the typical user has little or no knowledge of the reference services available.

The ease of handling the two broad types of questions may be deceptive. For example, the person who asks for a specific book by author may (1) have the wrong author, (2) actually want another book by the author than the one requested, (3) discover the wanted book is not the one required (for either information or pleasure), or (4) ask the librarian to obtain the book on interlibrary loan and then fail to appear when the book is received. There are other variables which may turn the first type of question into the second type.

A more finely drawn categorization of reference questions is to divide them into four types:

(1) Directional "Where is the card catalog?" "Where are the indexes?" "Is this the library?" The general information or directional question is of the information booth variety, and the answer rarely requires more than a geographical knowledge of key locations. The time required to answer such questions is negligible, but they may account for 30 percent or more of the queries put to a librarian in any day.

(2) Ready Reference "What is the name of the governor of Montana?" "How long is the Nile River?" "Who is the world's oldest person?" Here is the typical ready-reference or data-type query which requires only a single, usually uncomplicated answer. The requested information is normally found without difficulty in standard reference works ranging from encyclopedias to almanacs and indexes. The time to answer this type of question is usually no more than a minute or two. The catch is that while 90 percent of such queries are simple to answer, another 5 to 10 percent may take hours of research because no standard reference source in the library will yield the necessary data. Apparently simple questions are sometimes complicated, e.g., "What are the vital statistics of Venus de Milo?" "What three words in the English language end in -gry?" "What kind of present does one give for an eighteenth wedding anniversary?" Difficult questions of this type are often printed in a regular column in *RQ,* the official journal of reference librarians.[7]

The percentage of ready-reference questions asked in any type of library will differ from place to place, although they constitute a large proportion of all queries (85 to 95 percent, when directional questions are excepted) in public libraries. In academic, school, and special libraries, this type of question may account for 6 to 10 percent of the total. Public libraries, which have a well-developed phone service for reference questions as well as a high percentage of adult users, tend to attract the ready-reference question. Still, this is hardly a constant. The public library serv-

---

[7] The "tricky" questions quoted here are answered or submitted to be answered in the column, "The Exchange," *RQ,* Spring 1976, pp. 249–251. Reference librarians are invited to submit difficult questions to the editor. A glance at a few of these columns is an excellent introduction to ready-reference work.

ing a higher proportion of high school students than adults will probably be more involved with the next type of reference question.

(3)   Specific Search   "Where can I find information on sexism in business?" "What is the difference between the conservative and the liberal view on inflation and unemployment?" "Do you have anything on the history of atomic energy?" "I have to write a paper on penguins for my science class. What do you have?" The essential difference between the specific search and the ready-reference question is the amount of material needed. The latter normally may require no more than a one- or two-line answer; the answer to the former may develop into directing the user to several books, articles, bibliographies, and encyclopedias. More is required because the user is writing a school paper, is preparing a speech, or is simply interested in learning as much about a subject as is necessary for his or her needs.

This type of query is often called a "bibliographic inquiry" because the questioner is referred to a bibliographic aid such as the card catalog, an index, or a bibliography. The user then scans what is available and determines how much and what types of material are needed. At a less sophisticated level, the librarian may merely direct the user to an encyclopedia article, a given section of the book collection, or a newspaper index. Specific search questions constitute the greatest proportion of reference questions in school and academic libraries as well as in many special libraries.

The time taken to answer the question depends not only upon what is available in the library (or through interlibrary loan), but also upon the attitude of the librarian. If the librarian offers a considerable amount of help, the searching may take from 10 minutes to an hour or more. Conversely, the librarian may turn the question into a directional one by simply pointing the user in the direction of the card catalog.

Some types of specific search questions are treated by librarians as reader advisory problems. These are the types of questions that, in essence, ask, "What is the best source of information for my needs?" *The New York Times* noted that in New York these types encompass inquiries for:

> *how-to books, with an emphasis on home appliance repairs, automobile repairs and craft skills . . . books on preparing job résumés or those that could help candidates for Civil Service employment . . . [and books] describing the qualifications for jobs in those segments of the labor market that seem to be doing active hiring.*[8]

Some questioners are seeking everything from fiction and poetry to hobby

---

[8] February 15, 1976, p. 40.

magazines. Depending upon the size and the organizational pattern of the library, their queries may be fielded by subject or reader advisory librarians or handled by reference librarians.

(4) Research Almost any of the types of questions described in the "Specific search" section may be turned into research questions. Research and specific search differ only in the scope and amount of time involved. A research query is usually identified as coming from an adult specialist who is seeking detailed information to assist in specific work. The request may be from a professor, a business executive, a scientist, or anyone else who wishes data for a decision or for additional information about a problem. With the exception of some academic and special libraries, it is safe to say that this type of inquiry is a negligible part of the total reference pattern.

The complete library, as well as resources outside the library, may be used to assist the researcher. There is no way of measuring the difficulty or the average amount of time spent on such questions. If one considers intellectual challenge, research queries are usually more interesting for the reference librarian and certainly suggest that the librarian is more than a directional signal. Fortunately, reference work of the future seems to be turning toward research-oriented situations.

The four types of questions rarely can be so easily classified in terms of effort, sources employed, or ease of determination of search strategies. For example, the librarian may think a question is a simple directional one, only to have it later develop

> *during interrogation into more complex problems. . . . It cannot be assumed that because an inquiry appears to be a simple information direction question, it always permits a rapid answer, or that the training of a professional librarian will be wasted in pursuing the answer.*[9]

The Yale library study from which this statement is quoted observes that 11 percent of the directional questions required not seconds, but 3 minutes or longer to answer; and "of these, 19 required six to ten minutes and three required 11 to 60 minutes."[10] This is to say that a directional query may become a ready-reference question or a specific search problem. And under some circumstances it may change to even a research question. The point is worth stressing that categorization of queries is no more certain than the type of question likely to be asked at this or that library at any given moment.

---

[9] Robert Balay and Christine Andrew, "Use of the Reference Service in a Large Academic Library," *College and Research Libraries,* January 1975, p. 21.
[10] Ibid.

INFORMATION SOURCES

Many inexperienced reference librarians dread the moment someone stands before them and asks: Who, what, when, where, how, or why? No single reference question will incorporate all six of these question categories. One can sometimes be quite enough, or too much. Still, it does not require an expert to know there is usually an answer, even if it is that no answer exists. The secret is to find a reference source with the correct answer.

The rigid concept of a reference source being *only* a book labeled as "reference" and isolated in a special collection is no longer valid. Anything in the library, from periodicals to manuscripts and photographs, is part of the real reference collection, as are the holdings of libraries in the immediate area or at a national or international level. A reference source is any source, regardless of form or location, which provides the necessary answer or answers.

Moving from the general to the specific definition of a reference form, personal experience and technology begin to shade our definition.

(1) Interpersonal Reference Most men and women do not use a library reference service to answer questions. Rather, they tend to depend upon verbal exchanges with friends to assist them in determining the best make of car to purchase, opportunities in employment, or indications of fair rents in a given area. They also rely upon newspapers, television, and radio, as well as blind intuition and experience. At a more sophisticated level, a puzzled doctor may consult with a colleague to solve a problem, and a business executive will discuss probable moves with those who have been through similar crises before.

(2) Technology and Reference The computer and the data base are an integral part of reference service in many large or specialized libraries. Even in the smallest library, it is impossible to ignore present and future potentials of being able to store reference materials in a data bank. Add to this capability various audiovisual media, microforms, and copying machines, and it is evident that reference sources are much more than printed works.

Nevertheless, an implication that the reference book is a thing of the past would be misleading. In the hot pursuit of information, the traditional forms remain the most satisfactory, and they certainly must be mastered before the student or librarian can move on to other forms. One must understand the complexities of a printed index before one may determine whether it is more expedient, not to mention more efficient, to tap the same index via a costly online computer search. It is necessary first to understand basics—in this case, the basic reference book forms.

Information chain

If the ideal reference service, to paraphrase André Malraux, is "reference service without walls," the nature of information does impose certain limitations on that service. This side of tapping experts in the community for "firsthand" information, the library generally must rely upon published data—data which by the nature of publishing may be weeks, months, or even years out of date. A rough way of measuring the usual timeliness of materials is to classify them as primary, secondary, or tertiary.

(1)   Primary Sources   These are original materials which have not been filtered through interpretation, condensation, or often even evaluation by a second party. The materials tend to be the most timely in the library, normally taking the form of a journal article, monograph, report, patent, dissertation, reprint of an article, or some other work. Some primary sources for information are not published, as, for example, the offering of firsthand information ("I was there," or "I discovered," or "I interpreted. . . . ") verbally by one person to one or more others at a meeting or seminar, or in a letter which may be destroyed. Where primary sources are available in a library, the controls to call them up for reference work are usually secondary sources, such as indexes, abstracts, and bibliographies.

(2)   Secondary Sources   If an index is used to locate primary sources, the index itself is a secondary source. A secondary source is information about primary or original information which usually has been modified, selected, or rearranged for a purpose or an audience. The neat distinction between primary and secondary sources is not always apparent. For example, a person at a meeting may not be stating original views, but may simply be repeating what he or she has read or heard from someone else. A journal article is usually a primary source if the article represents original thinking or a report on a discovery; but the same journal may include secondary materials which are reports or summaries of the findings of others.

(3)   Tertiary Sources   These consist of information which is a distillation and collection of primary and secondary sources. Twice removed from the original, it includes almost all the source types of reference, works such as encyclopedias, reviews, biographical sources, fact books, almanacs, and the like.

The definitions of primary, secondary, and tertiary sources are useful only in that they indicate (1) relative currency (primary sources tend to be more current than secondary sources); and (2) the relative accuracy of materials (primary sources will generally be more accurate than secondary sources, only because they represent unfiltered, original ideas; conversely, a secondary source may correct errors in the primary source).

Whenever a reference source has become part of our experience, it requires little thought to match a question with a probable answer form. Those forms may be divided into two large categories: the control-access-directional type and the source type.

The control-access-directional type of source

The first broad class or form of reference sources is the bibliography. This form is variously defined but, in its most general sense, it is a systematically produced descriptive list of records.

Control   The bibliography serves as a control device—a kind of checklist. It inventories what is produced from day to day and year to year in such a way as to enable both the compiler and the user to feel they have a control, via organization, of the steady flow of knowledge. The bibliography is prepared through research (finding the specific source), identification, description, and classification.

Access   Once the items are controlled, the individual items are organized for easy access to facilitate intellectual work. All the access types of reference works may be broadly defined as bibliographies; but for purposes of enumeration, they are subdivided here:

1. Bibliographies of reference sources and the literature of a field either of a general nature or of subject nature. Example: Sheehy's *Guide to Reference Books* or *The Information Sources of Political Science.* Another type of bibliography includes the bibliography of bibliographies and the index to bibliographies.

2. The library card catalog or the catalogs of numerous libraries arranged for easy access via a union list. Technically, these are not bibliographies but are often used in the same manner.

3. General systematic enumerative bibliography which includes various forms of bibliography. Example: *The National Union Catalog.*

4. Indexes and abstracts which are usually treated separately from bibliographies, but are considered a bibliographical aid.[11] They are systematic listings of materials which help to identify and trace those materials. Indexes to the contents of magazines and

---

[11] In a card catalog, an index may be classified as a bibliography, a catalog, or an index. The problem is considered by Archie G. Rough in "Catalog, Bibliography or Index," *RQ,* Fall 1973, pp. 27–30.

newspapers are the most frequently used types in the reference situation. Examples: *The Readers' Guide to Periodical Literature* and *The New York Times Index.*

Direction The bibliography itself normally does not give a definitive answer but serves to direct the user to the source of an answer. To be used effectively, most of these must assume that the items listed are either in the library or available from another library system.

Source type

Works of the source type usually suffice in themselves to give the answers. Unlike the access type of reference work, they are synoptic.

Encyclopedias The most used single source are encyclopedias; they may be defined as works containing informational articles on subjects in every field of knowledge, usually arranged in alphabetical order. They are used to answer specific questions about X topic or Y person or general queries which may begin with, "I want something about Z." Examples: *Encyclopaedia Britannica; World Book Encyclopedia.*

Fact Sources Yearbooks, almanacs, handbooks, manuals, and directories are included in this category. All the types have different qualities, but they share one common element: They are used to look up factual material for quick reference work. Together, they cover many facets of human knowledge. Examples: *World Almanac; Statesman's Year-Book.*

Dictionaries Sources which deal primarily with all aspects of words from proper definitions to spelling are classified as dictionaries. Examples: *Webster's Third New International Dictionary; Dictionary of American Slang.*

Biographical Sources The forms which are self-evident sources of information on people distinguished in some particular field of interest are known as biographical sources. Examples: *Who's Who; Current Biography.*

Geographical Sources The best-known forms are the atlases, which not only may show given countries but may illustrate themes such as historical development, social development, and scientific centers. Geographical sources also include gazetteers, dictionaries of place names, and guidebooks. Example: *The Times Atlas of the World.*

Government documents

Government documents are official publications ordered and normally published by the federal, state, and local governments. Since they may include directional and source-type works, their separation into a particular unit is more one of convenience and organization than of distinct use in a reference situation. Examples: *Monthly Catalog of United States Government Publications* (access type); *United States Government Manual* (source type).

The neat categorization of reference types by access and by source is not always so distinctive in an actual situation. A bibliography may be the only source required if the question is merely one of verification or of trying to complete a bibliographical citation. Conversely, the bibliography at the end of an encyclopedia article, or a statement in that article, may direct the patron to another source. In general, the two main categories—access and source—serve to differentiate between the principal types of reference works.

Reference works formats

Reference works are normally in printed form, and are usually considered as books in the reference section of a library. There are other formats. The beginner should be aware of a new way of packaging and retrieving information.

(1) Data Bases As the name suggests, a data base is a collection of data which is organized for rapid search and retrieval, normally via a computer-linked keyboard. The content of the data base is often similar to the traditional printed reference work. Instead of printing that content, the publisher chooses to issue it in a machine-readable form, usually on reels of magnetic tape. The data base is normally *not* new reference material, but it is a distinctive method of making traditional reference materials available for mechanical rather than manual searching.

Psychological Abstracts is one of scores of services which are in both printed and machine-readable form. Until the advent of data bases, it was necessary to search laboriously through 10 or more volumes of the abstracts for citations on, for example, "depression among teenagers." This meant pulling down volume after volume, turning pages, and copying citations. Thanks to the availability of those same volumes in machine-readable form, the librarian may now command the computer to print out the needed citations in a fraction of the time. Not only is the process of searching faster, but it tends to be more accurate and comprehensive.

Data bases are "control-access-directional" types of reference form. Most of them are conventional bibliographical-abstract-index sources.

Machine-assisted reference service promises to modify and improve the traditional literature search. The use of computers and data bases in reference work has improved the reference interview, not to mention the prestige of the reference librarian who must employ serious intellectual effort to negotiate a search request. The new technology now suggests a practical method of linking even the smallest library with multiple information sources associated only with large libraries.[12]

(2) *Micrographic Technology* Microform is another publishing method; it is older, and better understood by the layperson. Almost every library user knows that many newspapers and periodicals are on microfilm, as well as thousands of books and other information sources from reports to government documents. Both the data base and microform are methods of storing information, and, as with data bases, much of what is on microform is also available in the traditional printed book. In fact, the two new technologies are wed in Computer Output Microfilm (COM), which "prints out" machine-readable data on microfilm, which in turn may be used by itself or for assisting in printing hard copies of reference aids.

Unconventional reference sources

A term frequently seen in connection with reference service at the public library level is "information and referral," or simply "I&R." There are other descriptors such as "community information centers." Essentially, the purpose of this special reference service is to offer the users access to resources that will help them with problems of health, rent, consumer questions, legal queries, etc. While I&R is discussed in the second volume of this text, the beginner should realize that in even the most traditional library, it is now common to (1) call upon individual experts for assistance, and they may include anyone from a local professor to a leader in a local special-interest group; (2) provide files, pamphlets, booklists, etc., which give users information on topics ranging from occupations to local housing regulations; and (3) provide a place which active groups in the community may identify as an information clearinghouse for their needs.

Librarians differ on the amount and the type of such unconventional reference work and reference aids. The irrefutable argument, however, is that no matter what the librarian's attitude,

---

[12] Data bases and automation are discussed in detail in *Reference Services and Reference Process*, the second volume in this text (3d ed; New York: McGraw-Hill Book Company, 1978).

when the patron does need information, it matters little to the patron that the answer to the question posed was not found in one of the respected reference titles. . . . The patron will measure the worth of the library in absolute terms—either the answer was provided or it was not.[13]

EVALUATING REFERENCE SOURCES

A thorough understanding of the day-to-day sources of answers requires some evaluation of those sources. How does the librarian know whether a reference source is good, bad, or indifferent? A detailed answer to the question will be found throughout each of the chapters in this volume. Still, the state of the art can be stated in rather simplistic terms: (1) A good reference source is one that serves to answer questions; (2) a poor reference source is one that fails to answer questions. Constant and practical use will quickly place any source (whether a book or a data base) in one of these two categories.

What follows is primarily concerned with traditional reference books, but much of it is applicable to other reference forms including machine-readable records. Evaluation of data bases is considered in the second volume of this text.

Because of the expense of most reference sources, the typical practice is to read one or more book reviews before deciding whether or not to buy. Given the reviews, large libraries usually request or automatically receive examination copies before purchase. Smaller libraries may have no choice but to accept the word of the reviewer and order or not order. Ideally, the reference source should be examined by a trained reference librarian before it is incorporated into the collection. No review or review medium is infallible.

Help in evaluating reference works may be found in the "terminology report" prepared by the American Library Association's Reference and Subscription Books Reviews Committee.[14] This report gives short definitions for 31 terms "used in the description and evaluation of reference works." While some are technical and therefore more applicable to analytical bibliography than to reviews (i.e., they list the impression, offset, issue, etc.), others are actually keys to what to look for when evaluating a reference source (such as the edition, revision, copyright date, and publication date).

The librarian must ask four questions about any reference work:

[13] Dale R. Schrag and Calvin Boyer, "Nonconventional Information Sources and Services in the Library: Our Credo," *RQ,* Fall 1975, p. 8.
[14] *The Booklist,* November 1, 1974, pp. 301–304.

What is its purpose? Its authority? Its scope? And its proposed audience? Finally, the format of the work must be considered.

(1) Purpose The purpose of a reference work should be evident from the title or form. The evaluative question must be posed: "Has the author or compiler fulfilled the purpose?" An encyclopedia of dance, for example, has the purpose of capturing essential information about dance in encyclopedic form. Fine, but immediately the librarian must ask such questions as: "What kind of dance and for what period? For what age group or experience or sophistication in dance? For what countries? Is the emphasis on history, biography, practical application, or some other element?"

The clues to purpose are found in the following: (a) table of contents; (b) introduction or preface, which should give details as to what the author or compiler expects this work to accomplish; and (c) index. Judicious sampling of the index will tell what subjects are covered. A reference book without an index is usually of little or no value. Exceptions are dictionaries, indexes, directories, and other titles where the index is built into an alphabetical arrangement. This system is suitable for the data type of reference work, but not for running prose. Then an index is absolutely essential.

Another hint as to the purpose of a specific work is often given in the publisher's catalog, in advance notices received in the mails, and in the copy on the jacket of the book. Such descriptions may help to indicate purpose and even relative usefulness, but are understandably less than objective.

(2) Authority The question of purpose brings us close to a whole series of questions which relate to the author:

(a) What are the author's qualifications for the fulfillment of his or her purpose? If the writer is a known scholar, there is no problem with authority. Where the difficulty arises is in the 95 percent of the other reference works that are prepared by experts but not those of the type that make the best-seller list. Here the librarian must rely (1) on the qualifications of the author given in the book; (2) on the librarian's own understanding and depth of knowledge of the subject; and (3) on a check of the author in standard biographical works, such as *Who's Who* or *American Men and Women of Science.*

(b) What were the sources of the author's knowledge? This question, properly answered, may also serve to answer the query about the author's qualifications. Did he or she go to primary source material—or rely on secondary material? If new sources were explored, were they well chosen and sufficient? Answers to these questions may be found by looking for footnotes, citations to sources, and bibliographies. Many reference works are secondary material (encyclopedias, almanacs, yearbooks, etc.) but draw heavily on primary sources. A book based on derivative material is often useful, but the authority is highly suspect if the primary sources are not cited. In collective works, such as encyclopedias and many handbooks, the articles should be signed, or some indication should be given as to who is responsible for the work.

(c)   The imprint of the publisher may indicate the relative worth of a book. Some publishers have excellent reputations for issuing reference works, others are known for their fair to untrustworthy titles. In a few cases, as, for example, encyclopedias and dictionaries, the cost of publishing is so high that the field is narrowed down to three or four firms. Even at their best, publishers are generally less interested in the progress of learning than in making money; a given group of publishers may have a well-deserved reputation for excellent reference books, but they too can slip. A reputable publisher may issue a half-dozen fine reference works, but the seventh may be a "bomb," possibly initiated for commercial purposes. Often these books are written by knowledgeable people and many are fairly informative, but even they are likely to be superfluous.

Authority, then, is a matter of the author and the publisher. But neither is infallible; the best sometimes miss. In the final analysis, authority can be measured only by careful scrutiny of the book by the knowledgeable librarian.

(d)   Although writing style is not usually a major consideration in reference works, there is no excuse for bad writing. In fact, a poor presentation is often indicative of poor thinking or, even worse, a lack of impartiality. No writer, not even the statistician, can be completely objective. Still, reference works more than other books should reflect an independence of mind. They should state both sides of controversial thought, giving a just view of the relevance and comparative merit of various viewpoints. Readers, then, should be able to draw their own conclusions. When a reference work is dealing with any controversial subject, particularly in the areas of religion and politics, bias may be detected not only in the style of presentation, but also in the relative length of articles, the selection of facts, and the sources cited.

(3) *Scope* The first question of major importance in selecting a reference work is: Will this book be a real addition to our collection, and if so, what exactly will it add? The publisher usually will state the scope of the book in the publicity blurb or in the preface, but the librarian should be cautious. The author may or may not have achieved the scope claimed. For example, the publisher may claim a historical atlas covers all nations and all periods. The librarian may check the scope of the new historical

atlas by comparing it against standard works. Does the new work actually include *all* nations and *all* periods, or does it exclude material found in the standard works? If an index claims to cover all major articles in X and Y periodicals, a simple check of the periodicals' articles against the index will reveal the actual scope of the index.

(a)   What has the author contributed that cannot be found in other bibliographies, indexes, handbooks, almanacs, atlases, dictionaries, etc? If the work is comprehensive within a narrow subject field, one may easily check it against other sources. For example, a who's who of education which limits itself to educators in the primary colleges and universities in the Northeast may be easily checked for scope by comparing the current college catalog of P & Q University against the new who's who. If a number of faculty members are missing from the new work, one may safely conclude the scope is not what is claimed.

Most reference works tend to be selective, and in this case the publisher and author should clearly state what is and is not included. What methods were employed for selection or rejection? And does the selection plan fit in with the audience claimed by the reference work. An encylopedia of detection, for example, may or may not include fiction's noble detectives, but if it claims to list the masterminds of detection from novels, are they *all* included? Are the detectives included in keeping with the purpose and the audience of the work?

Other general questions involving scope are almost as numerous as reference works. One might ask the national or political scope of a work; the scope of the bibliographies in terms of numbers, length, language, timeliness, etc.; the inclusion or exclusion of guides, indexes, illustrations, etc.; the number of this or that actually covered or considered, as, for example, the number of entries in a dictionary. Beyond these important general considerations are others a bit easier to pinpoint.

(b)   Timeliness is one of the most important features of any reference work, particularly one used for ready-reference purposes. Data change so quickly that last year's almanac may be historically important but of little value in answering current queries.

Except for current indexes, such as *Facts on File* and *The Readers' Guide to Periodical Literature,* most published reference works are dated before they are even off the presses. The time between the publisher's receipt of a manuscript and its publication may vary from six months to two years. Thus, in determining the recency of a work, some consideration must be given to the problems of production. Normally, a timely reference book will be one that contains information dating from six months to a year prior to the copyright date.

The copyright date in itself may be only a relative indication of timeliness. Is this a new work, or is it based on a previous publication? In these days of reprints, this is a particularly important question. A standard reference work may be reissued with the date of publication shown on the title page as, say, 1978, but on the verso of the same title page, the original copyright date may be 1966. If the work has been revised and updated, the copyright date will usually correspond to the date on the title page. A marked discrepancy should be sufficient warning that content must be carefully checked for currency.

Few reference works, unless entirely new, will not contain some dated information. The best method of ascertaining whether the dated material is of value, of checking the recency factor, is to sample the work. This is a matter of looking for names currently in the news, population figures, geographical boundaries, records of achievement, new events, and almost any other recent fact which is consistent with the purpose and scope of the work. Needless to add, no reference work should be accepted or rejected on a sampling of one or two items.

If the work purports to be a new edition, the extent of claimed revisions should be carefully noted. One can easily do so by checking it against the earlier edition or by noting any great discrepancy between the dates of the cited materials and the date of publication. For example, when an encyclopedia purports to be up to date but has no bibliographies dated within two or three years of the date on the title page, something a bit odd is certainly indicated.

(c) Within the work itself, the scope should be consistent for comparable entries. For example, in a biographical dictionary the reader should be certain to find the same general type of information for each entry: birth date, place of birth, address, achievements, etc.

(d) Can the reference work be used alone, or must it be supplemented by another work? For example, the scope of *Contemporary Authors* is considerably greater than that of *World Authors*. The emphasis on many little-known authors in the former work makes it a valuable finding aid, but the latter reference book is much more useful for detailed biographical sketches. Where a choice must be made, the librarian will have to consider carefully the potential users.

(4)   Audience   With the exception of juvenile encyclopedias, most reference works are prepared for adults. When considering the question of audience, the librarian must ask one major question: Is this for the scholar or student of the subject, or is it for the layperson with little or no knowledge? For example, in the field of organic chemistry, Beilstein's *Handbuch der Organischen Chemie* is as well known to chemists as the "top ten" tunes are to music fans. It is decidedly for the student with some basic knowledge of chemistry. Often the distinction in terms of audience is not so clear-cut, however.

A useful method of checking the reading level of a given reference work is for the librarian to examine a subject well known to him or her and then turn to one that is not so well understood. If both are comprehended, if the language is equally free of jargon and technical terminology, if the style is informative yet provocative, the librarian can be reasonably certain the work is for the layperson.

(5)   Format   The questions which have been discussed are essential, but one of the most meaningful questions of all concerns arrangement, treated here as part of the format. Arrangement is of major importance. There must be a handy form of access to the material.

There are some general rules for arrangement which are significant guides to the relative worth of a particular work as a tool in answering questions. Briefly:

(a)   Wherever possible, information should be arranged alphabetically in dictionary form. The advantage is that there is no need to learn a scheme of organization.

(b)   Where alpabetical arrangement is not used, there should be an author, subject, and title index, or an index covering aspects of content. Even with alphabetical order, it is usually advisable to have an index, particularly where bits of information must be extracted from long articles.

(c)   Where needed (in either the text, the index, or both), there should be sufficient cross-references that lead to other material and not merely to blind entries. For example, a book which refers readers to "archives" when they look up "manuscripts" should have an entry for "archives." This is a simple rule; but too frequently, in the process of editing and revising, the entry for the cross-reference may be deleted.

(d)   In some works another method must be employed, particularly in scientific sources. The classification should be as simple as possible; certainly it should be consistent and logical throughout. If it is difficult to comprehend, this may be sufficient warning about the merits of the work as a whole.

The arrangement can be either hindered or helped by the physical format. Even the best-arranged work can be a nuisance if bound so that the pages do not lie flat, or if there is no clear distinction between headings on a page and subheads within the page. The apparatuses of abbreviation, typography, symbols, and indication of cross-references must be clear and in keeping with what the user is likely to recognize. The use of offset printing from computerized materials has resulted in some disturbing complexities of format. For example, it may be impossible to tell West Virginia, when abbreviated, from Western Virginia. Uniform lower-case letters will be equally confusing. Lack of spacing between lines, poor paper, little or no margins, and other hindrances to reading are all too evident in even some standard reference works.

A word regarding illustrations. When photographs, charts, tables, and diagrams are used, they should be current, clear, and related to the text. They should be adjacent to the material under discussion, or at least clearly identified.

One matter has intentionally been postponed to this point, and this is price. The decision to purchase should always be dictated by need, and not by the cost of the work. If the reference work will serve a number of readers and their interests, is not duplicated by other materials in the library, and meets all criteria for selection, it should be purchased. The librarian whose budget is so limited that the purchase cannot be made is strongly advised to campaign for additional funds and work toward closer cooperation with larger units where cost is a secondary factor to service.

The last word may sound as cynical or as simplistic as the reader cares to interpret it, but—trust no one. The reviewer, the publisher, and the author do make mistakes, sometimes of horrendous proportions. The librarian who evaluates reference sources with the constant suspicion of the worst is less likely to be the victim of those mistakes.

Similar skepticism is necessary when evaluating data bases. The sheer cost of providing computer-assisted searching requires particular attention to duplication among services, variation of electronic devices, incompatibility of one data base with another, etc. Even in the late 1970s there are not sufficient guidelines for evaluating data bases, although it is becoming increasingly evident that at least fundamental standards are being developed, if not by the producers, at least by librarians.

SUGGESTED READING

American Society for Information Science Bulletin, March 1976. "Information Science in America" is the theme of this complete 60-page issue. The 20 articles provide both a historical and a current background on aspects of information science, including a useful bibliography of key publications in the area.

Arntz, Helmut, "Information as a Strategy and the Shock of the Future," *International Forum on Information and Documentation,* Vol. 2, No. 1, 1977, pp. 3–8. A lucid and intelligent overview of the importance of information "in the historical evolution of human society." A useful article to read after Ortega y Gasset.

Day, Alan, "There Is No Bibliography of Theophilus Shepstone," *New Library World,* July 1977, pp. 131–132. A witty view of what is to be learned "from a conscientious reading of the bibliographies provided for our instruction in all kinds of books." An admirable indication, too, of how to evaluate bibliographies.

Draheim, David, "I Never See Him Come into the Library Much Anymore," *Booklegger,* May 1975, pp. 9–11. A parody on what not to do at the reference desk. As the author describes all the worst characteristics of reference service, he indicates by implication the truly good points which every reference librarian should consider.

Hentoff, Nat, "How Publishers Get Away with (Factual Murder)," *The Village Voice,* August 2, 1976, p. 31; and "Hey, Ralph, How Many Errors in a Book Constitute Consumer

Fraud?" ibid., September 6, 1976, pp. 33–34. The popular journalist asks the question: "When you're reading a nonfiction book, how do you know it is accurate?" He claims that the book reviewer should carry the responsibility for telling the reader whether or not the book is accurate. However, he points out that too many reviewers are as inaccurate as the books they read. Good points for evaluation of reference titles.

Katz, William, and Andrea Tarr, *Reference and Information Services, A Reader.* Metuchen, N.J.: Scarecrow Press, 1978. A collection of close to 40 articles, selected from the "Suggested Readings" or footnotes throughout the present text. The purpose is to bring together in one volume a convenient, representative selection of articles which may be used by readers of this text.

Library Journal, January 1, 1976. Close to 300 pages of this centennial edition are devoted to 23 perceptive articles on the past, present, and future of library service, including reference work. The issue offers an excellent, timely overview of what it means to be a librarian in the last quarter of the twentieth century.

Lynch, Mary Jo, and George W. Whitbeck, "Work Experience and Observation in a General Reference Course—More on 'Theory vs. Practice'," *Journal of Education for Librarianship,* Spring 1975, pp. 271–280. A survey of what students found while working at a reference desk as compared with what they were taught. A good introduction for the beginner to the realities of the profession.

Murfin, Marjorie, and Lubomyr Wynar, *Reference Service: An Annotated Bibliographic Guide.* Littleton, Colorado: Libraries Unlimited, 1977. The publisher claims this is "the first comprehensive attempt to collect and describe the literature on reference work in the United States." Includes over 1200 items from articles and books to theses.

Ortega y Gasset, José, "The Mission of the Librarian," *Antioch Review,* Summer 1961, pp. 133–154. The distinguished philosopher considers the role of the librarian and the bibliographic control of information. The issues presented are still with us, still unresolved, but the writer sees hope in a new intellectual role for reference service.

St. Clair, Jeffrey, and Rao Aluri, "Staffing the Reference Desk: Professionals or Nonprofessionals," *Journal of Academic Librarianship,* July 1977, pp. 149–153. An excellent analysis of the type of reference questions asked "of an undergraduate medium-sized" university library. Includes a useful "Reference Question Analysis Form." For a similar approach in another university, see Cornick, Donna, and Katherine Winslow, "Reference Questions Asked A Humanities Department: A Statistical Analysis," *The Southeastern Librarian,* Summer 1977, pp. 79–84.

Shera, Jesse, *Introduction to Library Science: Basic Elements of Library Service.* Littleton, Colorado: Libraries Unlimited, Inc., 1976. Among the scores of introductory books to library science, this is among the best. The master's literate, sophisticated, and witty appreciation of libraries is matched only by his almost infinite understanding of the field.

Wahba, Susanne, "Job Satisfaction of Librarians: A Comparison between Men and Women," *College and Research Libraries,* January 1975, pp. 45–51. While this article is concerned with librarianship as a whole, much of it will be of interest to the person who wants an overall picture of working conditions in a library.

Winger, Howard (ed.), "American Library History: 1876–1976," *Library Trends,* July 1976. This issue is much like a book. In 400 pages, 19 contributors consider the present status of libraries, the profession, the organization of resources, and aspects of library service.

Witty, Francis J., "Reference Books of Antiquity," *Journal of Library History,* April 1974, pp. 101–119. A well-written history of the beginning of reference works from the Greco-Roman period to the Middle Ages. Arranged by subject and by form, the article gives the student a quick overview of where it all began.

INFORMATION: CONTROL AND ACCESS

CHAPTER TWO

Bibliographies:
Introduction

A BIBLIOGRAPHY IS analogous to a map or a chart. It serves to guide the librarian in the chaotic world of books and other forms of communication. Just as no sensible navigator will put to sea without a chart, no modern library will hope to function without bibliographical guides.

From the viewpoint of the user who may not understand the fine shades of bibliography, it serves one basic need. He or she may have something specific in mind, but is not sure it exists or, more important, where it can be found. The bibliography provides the answers.

A request for a book by title, author, or subject is a common question. Normally, the first logical place to find the answer is the card catalog. For most purposes this serves well enough. It fails when a part of the book is needed, when the book is not in the library, or when it is a type of material, such as an elusive government document, which may not be in the catalog. Then, too, the patron may have the incorrect title or author, or may simply find it impossible to fathom the ambiguities of the cataloging system. At this point, assistance is needed from a librarian who may go to other bibliographic tools to locate the desired material. The provision of solutions to such problems is the practical function of a bibliography, which may be defined as a well-organized list or inventory. There are numerous definitions, and champions of this or that explanation can become heated in their insistence on the true meaning of the word. Still, regardless of form, the bibliography is usually enumerative; that is, some selection process is carried on to determine what will or will not be listed. Also, it is generally systematic in that the material is arranged in a consistent form. Roy Stokes sums up the definitions of bibliography thus:

> *Enumerative bibliography is the easiest of all the particular areas of the study to understand. This is largely because it meets most accurately all that is generally required by the lay public, a straightforward listing of books and without the burdening of over-much detail. Having collected the material, the importance of its systematizing becomes obvious and this area of bibliography is just as happily called "systematic" as "enumerative". . . . The basic idea of enumerative bibliography . . . is clear, the listing of the salient details about a particular group of books which have some kind of coordinating factor.*[1]

SYSTEMATIC ENUMERATIVE BIBLIOGRAPHY

The average librarian, when speaking of bibliography, is probably referring to systematic enumerative bibliography, i.e., a list of books, films, or recordings. If a bibliography is adequately to meet the need for control and access, several elements are presupposed.

Completeness   Either through a single bibliography or a combination of bibliographies, the librarian should have access to the complete records of all areas of interest. This access is in terms not only of what is now available, but also of what has been published in the past and what is being published today or is proposed for publication tomorrow. Also, the net should be broad enough to include the world, not only one nation's works.

Access to a Part   Normally the librarian is apt to think of bibliographies in terms of the whole unit, book, periodical, manuscript, or the like; but an ideal bibliography should also be analytical, allowing the librarian to approach the specific unit in terms of the smallest part of a work.

Various Forms   Books are considered the main element of most bibliographies, but a comprehensive bibliographical tool will include all forms of published communication from reports and documents to phonograph records and data bases.

These three elements are usually referred to as parts of bibliographical control or organization, that is, of effective access to sources of informa-

[1] Roy Stokes, *The Functions of Bibliography* (London: André Deutsch, 1969), p. 26.

tion. No bibliography or set of bibliographies has yet met all these needs. At best, a bibliography is a compromise between completeness, access to parts, and various forms.

With the bibliography ready at hand, how does the librarian use it on a day-to-day basis? Regardless of form, a bibliography is used primarily for three basic purposes: (1) to identify and verify, (2) to locate, and (3) to select.

Identification and Verification The usual bibliography gives standard information similar to that found on most catalog cards: author, title, edition (if other than a first edition), place of publication, publisher, date of publication, a collection (i.e., number of pages, illustrations, size), and price. Another element added to many bibliographies is the International Standard Book Number, abbreviated as ISBN or simply SBN (see the footnote on page 65). In seeking to identify or verify any of these elements, a librarian will turn to the proper bibliography, usually beginning with the general, such as *Books in Print* or *The National Union Catalog,* and moving to the particular, such as a bibliography in a narrow subject area.

Location Location may be in terms of where the book is published, where it can be found in a library, or where it may be purchased. However, from the point of view of the patron's needs, the location is more apt to be in terms of subject. What is available in this subject area, either in a book, periodical, article, report, or some other form of communication?

Selection The primary aim of a library is to build a useful collection to serve users. This objective presupposes selection from a vast number of possibilities. In order to assist the librarian, certain bibliographies indicate what is available in a given subject area, by a given author, in a given form, or for certain groups of readers. Depending on its purpose, a bibliography may give an estimate of the value of the particular work for a certain type of reader.

Forms of systematic enumerative bibliography: Universal bibliography

A true universal bibliography would include everything published, issued, or pressed in the field of communications from the beginning through the present to the future. Such universality is now an impossible dream. In practice, the term is currently employed in a narrower sense. It generally means a bibliography that is not necessarily limited by time, territory, language, subject, or form. National library catalogs, some book dealers' catalogs, and auction catalogs are the nearest thing to a universal bibliography now available.

Forms of systematic enumerative bibliography: National and trade bibliographies[2]

These kinds of works are limited to materials published within a given country. The sieve may be made even finer by limiting the bibliography to a section of the country, a city, or even a hamlet. For ease of use and convenience, national bibliographies normally are divided into even finer parts.

Time   This is a matter of listing works previously published, works being published, or works to be published. Such bibliographies are normally labeled as either retrospective or current.

Form   This classification may be in terms of bibliographical form: collection of works, monographs, components (i.e., essays, periodical articles, poems); in terms of physical form: books, recordings, pamphlets, microfilm; or in terms of published and unpublished works (such as manuscripts, dissertations).

A typical national bibliography will set itself limits of time, form, and, obviously, origin. For example, *Books in Print* is limited to books available for purchase (time); it includes only printed books, albeit both hardbound and paperbacks and some monographs and series (form); and it is a trade bibliography, i.e., issued by a commercial organization (origin).

There is no limit to the possible subdivisions of national bibliography. For example, within the overall area appear bibliographies (works by and about a given author) and anonym and pseudonym listings. Other sieves continue to be devised as needed.

Subject bibliography

The universal and the national bibliographies are the base for any subject bibliography. While the two major forms tend to be used almost exclusively by generalists, such as the book dealer, the librarian, and the publisher, the subject bibliography is intended for the research worker and for others in special areas.

Once a subject is chosen, the sieves common to national bibliographies may be employed—time, form, origin, and others. However, unlike

---

[2] The term "trade" bibliography is often used as synonymous with "national." Trade bibliography refers to a bibliography issued for, and usually by, the booksellers and publishers of a particular nation. Its purpose is identical to that of national bibliography; thus the confusion in terms. The emphasis of a trade bibliography is on basic data. A national bibliography includes basic data, plus much other information used primarily by catalogers.

most national bibliographies, a subject work may use all the sieves. For example, a definitive bibliography on railroad engines may be retrospective, current (at least at date of publishing), inclusive of all forms from individual monographs to government publications, and reflective of various sources or origins.

Guides to reference materials

Theoretically, lists which include the "best" works for a given situation or audience are not bibliographies in the accepted definition of the term. In practice, however, they are normally so considered. They include guides to reference books, special reading lists issued by a library, and books devoted to the "best" works for children, adults, students, business people, and others.

Bibliographies of bibliographies

There are few of this type of bibliography, but they guide the user to other helpful bibliographies, normally by subject, by given place, or by individual.

This description of five types of bibliography does not exhaust the innumerable possibilities for methods of organizing and describing bibliographies. It barely touches on the various combinations. There is no universally accepted method of even approaching parts and divisions of a bibliography. The problem is to bring order out of this chaotic, primarily free-wheeling approach to listing materials.

Analytical and textual bibliography

Analytical bibliography is concerned with the physical description of the book. Textual bibliography goes a step further and highlights certain textual variations between a manuscript and the printed book or between various editions. Often the two are combined into one scientific or art form. This type of research is designed to discover everything possible about the author's ultimate intentions. The goal is to recover the exact words that the author intended to constitute his or her work. In driving toward this goal, one group of bibliographers may be experts, for example, in nineteenth-century printing practices and bookbinding, another group in paper watermarks or title pages.

There are differences between analytical and textual bibliographies—the most basic being that analytical bibliography is more concerned with the physical aspects of the book, and textual bibliography with the author's words, i.e., the exact text as the author meant it to appear in printed form. The two must necessarily work together, but they are not necessarily similar disciplines. In fact, each variety has its experts, as a casual reading of *Studies in Bibliography* (Charlottesville, Virginia: University Press of Virginia, 1947 to date, annual) will reveal. In the world of librarianship, analytical bibliography is best known because of its relationship to descriptive cataloging and its explanation and discussion in library school history of the book courses.[3]

GUIDES TO REFERENCE BOOKS

The basic purpose of a bibliographical guide to reference material is to introduce the user to (1) general reference sources which will be of assistance in research in all fields and (2) specific reference sources which will help in research in particular fields. These guides take a number of forms, but primarily are either (1) annotated lists of titles with brief introductory remarks before each section or chapter or (2) handbooks which not only list and annotate basic sources, but also introduce the user to tools of investigative study by a discursive, almost textbooklike approach. There are numerous subclassifications and types of guides.

Another type of guide is more didactic and is usually limited to a broad or even a narrow subject or area, e.g., *The Literature of Political Science* (broad) or *How to Find Out in Iron and Steel* (narrow). Like the general guides, these guides give an overview of the subject, but they go a step further and consider the core of highly specialized publications which probably are not listed in the more familiar general guides. In addition, they may list textbooks, journals, newspapers, societies, libraries, subject experts, recordings, films—in fact, just about anything which is applicable to an understanding of research and reference in the given field.

The singular contribution of the better subject guides is not so much a rote listing of materials as a discursive discussion of (1) the field as a whole; (2) peculiarities of research (and reference) in the discipline; (3) the place of the subject in the mainstream of knowledge; and (4) various forms which are especially applicable for work in the field, i.e., everything from specialized abstract services, to patent guides, to sources of unpublished research reports.

There are several publications that can be extremely helpful in the selection and use of reference books. The most valuable are the following:

---

[3] An overview of analytical bibliography will be found in Howell J. Heaney's "Bibliographical Scholarship in the United States, 1949–1974: A Review," *College and Research Libraries,* November 1975, pp. 493–510.

Sheehy, Eugene P. *Guide to Reference Books,* 9th ed. Chicago: American Library Association, 1976, 1050 pp., $30.

Walford, Albert John. *Guide to Reference Materials,* 3d ed. London: The Library Association, 1973–1977, 3 vols. $30 each. (Distributed in the United States by American Library Association, Chicago.)

Wynar, Bohdan. *American Reference Books Annual.* Littleton, Colorado: Libraries Unlimited, Inc., 1970 to date, annual. $30.

Ryder, Dorothy E. *Canadian Reference Sources: A Selective Guide.* Ottawa: Canadian Library Association, 1973; 185 pp. *Supplement,* 1975, 121 pp. $10; paper $7.

The two basic guides which tell a reference librarian what reference books are basic in all fields are those by Sheehy and Walford. Most librarians refer to them as "Sheehy" and "Walford." (Prior to Sheehy's ninth edition of *Guide to Reference Books,* the work was compiled by Constance Winchell. Many librarians still refer to the guide as "Winchell.")

The guides list and annotate the major titles used in reference service. Sheehy includes some 10,000 entries, Walford about 12,000. Complete bibliographical information is given for each entry, and most of the entries are annotated.

Arrangement varies in each. Sheehy has five main sections in a single volume. Walford, using the Universal Decimal Classification System, divides his work into three separate volumes: science and technology; social sciences; and generalities, languages, the arts, and literature.

Both works begin with a large subject and then subdivide by both smaller subjects and forms. Sheehy, for example, has a section on economics under the social sciences. This is subdivided by forms: guides, bibliographies, periodicals, dissertations, indexes and abstract journals, dictionaries and encyclopedias, atlases, handbooks, etc. The economics section is later broken down into smaller subjects and often, within the subject, a further division is made by country as, for example, in political science. Walford subdivides economics by bibliographies, thesauruses, encyclopedias and dictionaries, dissertations, etc., thus fairly well following the Sheehy pattern. In practice, the arrangement is not really important. Each volume has an excellent title, author, and subject index, although here Sheehy is better because individual items are keyed, whereas Walford refers the reader only to a page.

Sheehy concentrates on American, Canadian, and English titles, and Walford is stronger on English and European titles. In the second volume of Walford, about 13 percent of the listings are from American publishers, 31 percent from Great Britain, and over 50 percent from predominantly European and Commonwealth nations.

The problem with Sheehy is timeliness. The ninth edition, issued in late 1976, includes titles published only until the end of 1973, with a "disappointingly small" number of 1974 entries. The guide was almost three years in arrears when published. Supplements are issued about every three years but also have a history of being behind. Walford is much more current, and usually no more than 12 to 18 months separates a new edition from current titles.[4]

A partial answer to the time-lapse problems of Sheehy and Walford is suggested by the *American Reference Books Annual* (usually cited as *ARBA*). It differs from either Sheehy or Walford in three important respects: (1) It is limited to reference titles published or distributed in the United States; (2) it is comprehensive for a given year and makes no effort to be selective; (3) the annotations are written by more than 300 subject experts and are both more critical and more expository than those found in Sheehy or Walford. Depending on the extent of American publishing, the annual volume usually available in March or April of the year following the year covered in text analyzes some 1700 to 1800 separate reference titles. The work is well organized and indexed.[5] A useful feature exists in the references to reviews published in periodicals such as *Library Journal, Choice,* and *Wilson Library Bulletin.* The librarian may easily compare the opinion of the subject expert in *ARBA* with a reviewer elsewhere.

General guides to reference books, such as those of Sheehy and Walford, concentrate on the publishing output of their national base, with due emphasis on important reference works published in other countries. But "other" countries rarely think the coverage is adequate, and Canada is no exception. To fill the gap of both Sheehy and Walford, *Canadian Reference Sources* uses much the same arrangement as Sheehy, but annotates materials of interest to the 10 provinces, territories, and major cities. The *Supplement* (1975) adds new works and editions published up to December 1973 and increases the scope to include personal bibliographies and materials dealing with areas smaller than provinces.

Here a special note. The author recognizes the importance of Cana-

---

[4] Of some limited help in the updating of *Guide to Reference Books* is the biannual listing by Eugene P. Sheehy in *College and Research Libraries,* i.e., "Selected Reference Books of 1976–1977" and ". . . 1977–1978." The annotated listings usually appear in the July and January issues. According to correspondence of the author with the American Library Association publishing department, an effort is being made in 1977 to keep the *Guide to Reference Books* more up to date, possibly via computer. For a discussion of this and the history of the current volume, see Art Plotnik, "They Have Created the Ultimate Reference Guide . . . ," *American Libraries,* March, 1977, pp. 129–132.

[5] A cumulative index to the first five years of *ARBA* was issued in 1974: *Index to American Reference Books Annual, 1970–1974: A Cumulative Index to Authors, Titles and Subjects* (Littleton, Colorado: Libraries Unlimited, Inc., 1974).

dian bibliographies and other reference sources. Lack of space, however, prevents a more enthusiastic coverage of those titles. Some works are at least mentioned, but both Canadian and United States readers should keep in mind that for almost every basic reference work devoted exclusively to the United States, there is likely a similar title for Canada, from *Canadian Books in Print* to the *Canadian Periodical Index*. Similar titles, covering national works, are published in almost all English-speaking and other Western countries. A general survey of the situation is given by Irene Martin in her informative "Canadian Books and American Libraries," *PNLA Quarterly*, Winter 1975, pp. 4–12. Also see the irregular annotated listings, "Recent Canadian Reference Books—A Selected List" in the *APLA Bulletin*, as for example, No. 1, 1977, pp. 9–13.

There are scores of listings, guides, and catalogs of reference works which are either smaller, larger, or more specialized than either Sheehy or Walford. Carolyn Peterson's *Reference Books for Elementary and Junior High School Libraries* (2d ed.; Metuchen, New Jersey: Scarecrow Press, 1975, 314 pp.) lists and annotates about 900 titles. Peterson is highly selective and provides a reliable, up-to-date critical analysis of titles from which schools may select appropriate materials.[6] At the other extreme, one has the 638-page *Library of Congress Main Reading Room Reference Collection Subject Catalog*. As an unannotated subject guide to the 44,000 reference volumes (including serials) in the Main Reading Room of the Library of Congress, this is a 1976 guide to one of the largest general reference collections in the world. Still another approach is suggested by *Texas Reference Sources, A Selective Guide* (Houston: Texas Library Association, 1976), which provides subject access to reference works about Texas. And so it goes. One may devise various sizes and forms of guides to reference materials, all of which are ultimately based on a variation of the Sheehy and Walford models.

Subject guides to reference books

There are two outstanding guides to reference books:

> White, Carl M. *Sources of Information in the Social Sciences: A Guide to the Literature*, 2d ed. Chicago: American Library Association, 1973, 702 pp. $25.

> Freidel, Frank. *Harvard Guide to American History*, rev. ed. Cambridge: Harvard University Press, 1974, 2 vols. $45.

Where does the librarian find whether a subject area has its own

[6] Another useful title for school libraries is Christine Wynar's *Guide to Reference Books for School Media Centers*, discussed in Chapter 3.

guide to reference materials? The subject guides are usually listed in the opening sections of particular subject divisions in Sheehy, Walford, or the *ARBA*. The guides are important for four reasons:

1. Specialization, accompanied by overwhelming publication, requires more and more sophisticated methods of getting at particular bits of information. The guides offer such help.

2. The guides offer an overview of the communications process in a given discipline, an overview which the librarian must necessarily understand in order to deal adequately with particulars.

3. The lack of adequate reference staffing requires that more and more students do their own searching. While the librarian can be of some help, the guides afford the student or other layperson a basic introduction to the reference aids in the subject being studied.

4. Finally, the better guides assist the librarian who may be called upon to work in a totally unfamiliar subject area. And, of course, they serve to refresh the memory of even the experienced librarian.

Two representative subject guides to reference works are listed here. The White guide features discursive essays on the social science disciplines from history and geography to economics and political science. (Note: An updated third edition is planned for publication in 1978.) The experts introduce the reader to the basic reference titles in an area, and each of the listed sources is briefly annotated. Some of the listings are to be found in both Sheehy and Walford, but White has the advantage of limiting himself to a much narrower area and, therefore, can include titles considered too specialized for the more general reference aids. Going even further into specialization, Freidel concentrates on only one part of the eight subject areas in White, i.e., American history. The first volume begins with an essay on research methods, moves to biographies, comprehensive and area histories, and histories of special subjects. The second volume is a chronological bibliography of sources, and the whole is united by a detailed author and subject index. Other examples may be found for other disciplines, and a notion of the field may be indicated by the following short list of titles:

Holler, Frederick. *The Information Sources of Political Science.* Santa Barbara, California: ABC-Clio, 1975, 5 vols. In the first volume Holler covers general reference sources: in the others he moves to history, anthropology, government, sociology, and other specialities, giving basic bibliographies, guides, indexes, etc.

Rogers, A. Robert. *The Humanities: A Selective Guide to Information Sources.* Littleton, Colorado: Libraries Unlimited, Inc., 1974, 400 pp.

Here general reference sources are mentioned; then the compiler moves to sections on philosophy, religion, literature, etc.

Then, within each of the larger divisions, there are guides to reference works in subdivisions such as:

Kehler, Dorothea, and Fidelia Dickinson. *Problems in Literary Research: A Guide to Selected Reference Works.* Metuchen, New Jersey: Scarecrow Press, 1975, 160 pp. Here the compilers limit themselves to 36 basic titles for the student doing research in literature, but "as numbers do not necessarily a good reference guide make," the book within its limits is quite adequate.

Burke, John, and Jill Reddig. *Guide to Ecology Information and Organization.* New York: The H. W. Wilson Company, 1976, 292 pp. A general introduction to information sources is provided; then major print and nonprint publications are listed.

This short list indicates the tip of the hundreds of subject guides to reference books, most of which one will find listed and annotated in Sheehy, Walford, or the *ARBA*.

In that the subject bibliographies are relatively selective, the librarian has a guide to the "best" of this or that in reference. An annual list of the outstanding reference titles of the previous year will be found in the April 15 issue of *Library Journal.* Usually limited to fewer than 100 titles, the annotated list is compiled by experts from the Reference and Adult Services Committee of the American Library Association. It is useful as a checkpoint for evaluating library purchases.

The compilations of "Reference and Subscription Books Reviews," discussed on pages 43 and 44, are handy retrospective guides to the "best." Anyone who wishes to use the compilations as a buying guide is urged to check the recommendation, or lack of it, at the end of each review. Another approach is suggested by *Best Reference Books: Titles of Listing Value Selected from "American Reference Books Annual," 1970–1976.* (Littleton, Colorado: Libraries Unlimited, Inc., 1976). This publication annotates 818 major reference titles from seven volumes of *ARBA,* and as the selection is carefully done, the list can be recommended as a buying guide and as a method of evaluating what the library does or does not have in relatively current reference titles.

CURRENT SELECTION AIDS

The librarian who wants to build a collection in a given subject need only consult a guide of personal preference for basic titles. Beyond that, one runs into the problem of currency. The ninth edition of *Guide to Reference*

Books has a cutoff date of late 1973, and the *American Reference Books Annual* is of limited help for a title issued between publication of the annual volumes. The reference librarian with an interest in current titles must study reviews in periodicals. Most of the periodicals to be discussed review other types of books ranging from fiction to technical publications.[7]

The selection of reference sources is a highly individualized process. No two libraries are alike. The character and the distribution of the elements which constitute the needs of users differ from library to library. Consequently, the first and most important rule when considering the selection of reference materials, or anything else for the library, is to recognize the needs of the users. Attention should be given to them in terms of both known and anticipated demand.

What constitutes a satisfactory selection policy? First and foremost, there must be a librarian who has some subject competence, that is, one who knows the basic literature of a field, or several fields, including not only the reference works, but also the philosophy, jargon, ideas, ideals, and problems that make up that field. There is no substitute for substantive knowledge. Second, the librarian must be aware in some depth of the type of writing and publishing done in that special field. Where is there likely to be the best review? Who are the outstanding authors, publishers, and editors in this field? What can and cannot be answered readily in this or that type of work?

Selection is charted, rather than dictated, by the following:

1. Knowing as much as possible about the needs of those who use the reference collection.

2. Calling upon expert advice. In a school situation the expert may be the teacher who is knowledgeable in a certain area. In a public library it may be the layperson, skilled practitioner, or subject specialist who uses the library. Most people are normally flattered by a request that draws upon their experience and knowledge, and one of the best resources for wise selection of reference materials is the informed user.

3. Keeping a record of questions. This is done to determine not only what the library has in the way of materials, but what it does not have. Most important, a record of unanswered queries will often be the basis for an evaluation of the reference collection.

4. Knowing what other libraries have, and what resources are available. For example, the small library contemplating the purchase

---

[7] These periodicals are therefore employed for book selection at every level of library service. They are used, too, in readers' advisory services.

of an expensive run of periodicals or a bibliography would certainly first check to see whether the same materials may be readily available in a nearby library.

These four points only begin to suggest the complexity of selection. Many libraries have detailed selection policy statements which consider the necessary administrative steps only hinted at here.

Once a title has been determined for purchase, the material is normally ordered through the regular channels. In large libraries, the process consists of turning over the order with full bibliographical citation to the acquisitions department. In smaller libraries, the reference librarian (who also may be the head librarian and the only professional on the staff) may go through the whole ordering process singlehandedly.

Reference book reviews

Library Journal. New York: R. R. Bowker Company, 1876 to date, semimonthly. $19.

Choice. Chicago: American Library Association, 1964 to date, monthly. $35.

RQ. Chicago: American Library Association, 1960 to date, quarterly. $15; members, $7.50.

The Booklist. Chicago: American Library Association, 1905 to date, semimonthly. $24.

Wilson Library Bulletin. New York: The H. W. Wilson Company, 1914 to date, monthly. $14.

Reference Services Review. Ann Arbor, Michigan: Pierian Press, 1972 to date, quarterly. $25.

The most exhaustive, essay-type reviews appear in *The Booklist* in "Reference and Subscription Books Reviews," a separate section at the back of each issue of *The Booklist.*[8] Prepared by a committee of librarians and teachers, the reviews are detailed, highly critical, and primarily involved with the subscription type of reference works, in this case encyclopedias, dictionaries, atlases, and major bibliographies and guides. Be-

---

[8] The reviews are now compiled annually (previously they were compiled every two years) and published in a separate paperback by the American Library Association. As the reviews are extensively used in evaluating expensive encyclopedias, atlases, etc., they should be purchased in the compilation form for the permanent reference collection. (Although "Reference and Subscription Books Reviews" is a physical part of *The Booklist*, it is a separate entity administratively. Formerly two separate magazines, they were combined in 1956. *The Booklist* is a general review medium for all types of books and has nothing to do with the reference reviews.)

ginning in 1975, the service shortened many of its reviews and considered more titles each year (there were 43 percent more reviews in 1976 than in 1975). It also developed a more current service than theretofore. It is now the best single source of reviews of reference titles, and would be the first choice in any library.

Other current sources are:

1. *Choice.* While specifically geared to college libraries, the magazine evaluates a number of reference titles of value to all libraries. The reference books lead off the main section of general reviews. Also, from time to time bibliographical essays in the front part of the magazine highlight reference titles. Reviews are not signed. There are approximately 6000 reviews a year, of which about 500 are of reference books. The reviews are usually 150 to 200 words in length. Almost all reviewers make an effort to compare the title under review with previously published titles in the same subject area, a feature which is particularly useful.

2. *Library Journal.* Again, the general book review section leads off with "Reference." (To be more precise, it follows "The Contemporary Scene" section.) Reviews are 100 to 150 words in length and are usually written by librarians or teachers. All reviews are signed. Approximately the same number of reviews appear annually in *Library Journal (LJ)* as in *Choice.* From time to time, other reference works are discussed in the "Professional Reading" section of *LJ.* Also, *School Library Journal* includes reviews of reference titles.

3. *RQ.* The last section of this quarterly magazine is given over entirely to the review of reference books. A few other related titles are considered, but, unlike *Library Journal* and *Choice, RQ* makes no effort to review general books.

4. *Wilson Library Bulletin.* One section is devoted to "Current Reference Books," and all the reviews are written by the section editor, Charles Bunge. Some 20 to 30 titles are noted in each issue, and each is graded with an "A," "B," or "C" rating.

5. *Reference Services Review.* This quarterly provides a current index to reviews of new reference books. Some 100 journals are analyzed, and the reviews are indexed by title and by author. Many of the reviews are indexed elsewhere (see pages 46 to 49). However, the service is useful as a single source of all new reference books as they appear. Furthermore, in the issues of April/June 1976 and thereafter, the publisher includes brief excerpts from reviews as well as one- or two-line descriptive annotations of books which

have not yet been reviewed. Beginning with the Spring 1977 issue, the quarterly listings are cumulated in an annual which not only serves as an index to reviews, but is a type of abbreviated *American Reference Books Annual.*

The review sources listed here concentrate on the major English-language titles issued by American publishers. They do not include foreign-language titles and more esoteric works. Estimates vary, but about one-quarter to one-third of the reference books associated with highly specialized subjects are not reviewed in these magazines. Here the reference librarian must turn to reviews found in subject journals.[9]

The services hardly exhaust the possibilities of finding reference book reviews. Among other useful places to look are the general reviewing titles from *The New York Times Book Review* to *Saturday Review* to *The Times Literary Supplement.* Aside from the index in *Reference Services Review,* the librarian may find the reviews by consulting the book review indexes listed and discussed in the section "Indexes to Reviews."

Evaluating reviews

With the "Reference and Subscription Books Reviews" in *The Booklist* as the recognized best, the choice of "next-best" and "better" reviewing services is a matter of opinion. For quantity of reviews, *Library Journal* and *Choice* would be first selections. *RQ* and *Wilson Library Bulletin,* although not necessarily in that order, are good choices for smaller libraries, with the *Reference Services Review* an index aid for a large library.

There is no end to the studies of the various reviewing services as to amount of coverage of total output, timeliness, objectivity, critical tone, etc. Still, Covey concludes that:

> *There is no single tool, nor a combination of tools in existence today, that enables the conscientious reference librarian systematically and efficiently to select the best reference books for her or his particular library. . . . In view of the continuing importance of reference books, there should be further and periodic study of the media that review them.*[10]

Covey's assumption is based upon the magazines mentioned here (plus the *School Library Journal*), and she may just be right. The solution to

[9] For a study of specialized reviews, see Geza A. Kosa, "Book Selection Tools for Subject Specialists in a Large Research Library: An Analysis," *Library Resources & Technical Services,* Winter 1975, pp. 13–18.

[10] Alma C. Covey, *Reviewing of Reference Books* (Metuchen, New Jersey: Scarecrow Press, 1972), pp. 129, 130.

call for further study seems relatively pointless, however. The fact remains that there is no single, totally satisfactory source of reference book reviews any more than there is a single satisfactory source of trade book reviews. And this condition will continue until such time as all librarians begin to act and think alike. There is, certainly, a variety of review media, and if they do not cover all reference titles, perhaps it is just as well that a few be lost. If not all the reviews are as scholarly or as critical as they might be, consider that the reviewers are librarians and teachers, not omniscient statisticians. Finally, in any evaluation of the review, the choice must be made by the librarian, not a reviewer.[11]

INDEXES TO REVIEWS

Book Review Digest. New York: The H. W. Wilson Company, 1905 to date, monthly, service. *Author/Title Index, 1905–1974,* 4 vols. $245.

Book Review Index. Detroit: Gale Research Company, 1965 to date, bimonthly. $68. (Annual cumulations, $68.)

Current Book Review Citations. New York: The H. W. Wilson Company, 1976 to date, monthly (except August). $75.

Reference librarians seeking reviews of reference books will use the indexes considered here—plus the aforementioned *Reference Service Reviews.* They will use them more often to give direct answers to reference queries. Those questions are from students or other laypersons seeking background information on a given title or an author. The student has to write a paper on a modern author, wants to find out what the critics said about that author's book, and turns to the reference librarian for help. The librarian, in turn, goes to one of the review indexes.

All the indexes rely upon an author and/or title entry. Only the *Book Review Digest* offers a subject approach as well. In most cases it is necessary to know not only the correct author or title, but the approximate date of when the book was published. The fastest method is simply to search the *Book Review Digest Author/Title Index, 1905–1974.* For reviews published after 1974, one needs to go to the annual index volumes or other services. If the date cannot be found in these indexes, the librarian should turn to the card catalog where the title may be entered, or to one of the national or trade bibliographies such as *Books in Print.*

[11] The fascination with reviews and reviewers is reflected in almost every American Library Association meeting—as well it might be! For a short summary of the 1976 meeting, see "Reviews: Who Needs Them," *Library Journal,* September 1, 1976, p. 1711.

The indexes to reviews are of two basic types. Most list the citation to a review after the author and title entry. A few include the citation and passages from selected reviews.

(1) *Book Review Index (BRI)* and *Current Book Review Citations (CBRC)* list sources of book reviews. Titles are listed under the author or other main entry, and each listing gives a full review citation. Both have title indexes.

The two are competitive; they frequently index the same periodicals and therefore include references to the same reviews; i.e., both analyze the major sources of reference reviews, including *Library Journal, Choice,* and *The Booklist.*

They differ in that (a) *BRI* analyzes nearly 300 widely read periodicals. *CBRC* analyzes more than 1000 periodicals, which are indexed in the various H. W. Wilson indexes.[12] Also, *CBRC* includes reviews from major book reviewing periodicals not usually indexed by Wilson, for example, *The Booklist, Choice, Kirkus, The New York Times, Library Journal,* and *School Library Journal.* (b) *BRI* has the distinct advantage of ease of use in that it is cumulated three times during the year, and annually. *CBRC* has only an annual cumulation, which means each issue must be searched—a nuisance. (c) *BRI*'s second advantage is currency: review citations frequently appear here faster than in *CBRC.* (d) *CBRC* has the edge of indexing more titles, and listing names of reviewers, a feature not found in *BRI.*

If a choice has to be made, *BRI* would come first for ease of use and timeliness, but second for coverage and cost. The bimonthly and annual cumulation run $136 as against $75 for *CBRC.* Both services are needed for larger libraries.

(2) *Book Review Digest* is not only an index of book reviews, but has the added feature of including excerpts from reviews. Hence the user often does not have to consult the reviews, and can make judgments about a title by merely reading the excerpts. Titles are arranged by author, and a valuable addition is not only a title index, but also a subject index which gives subject access not available in the other indexes. Found in almost every library, the *BRD,* going back to 1905, has the added advantage of being the first of its kind, has a 70-year cumulative index, and often serves the scholar as an invaluable key to contemporary reviews.

The catch is in the limitations exercised by the *BRD.* It analyzes only 75 periodicals, and even more unfortunately, it includes reviews of nonfiction only when there have been a minimum of two reviews, and of fiction

[12] The development of this index has meant an added feature for other Wilson indexes. They now all have a separate section, "Book Reviews," which is arranged alphabetically by author.

only when four or more reviews have appeared. The result is that the *BRD* is a bastion of conservatism, and is about the last place anyone might hope to find a review of a book by a beginning author. Therefore, for most purposes it is best first to check out the *Book Review Index* or the *Current Book Review Citations*.

Book Review Index lists approximately 78,000 reviews for 38,000 titles each year. *Current Book Review Citations* covers about the same number of titles but lists almost twice as many reviews. Still, larger libraries have need for even more specialized indexes.[13] There are several, among which the most frequently used are:

1. *Index to Book Reviews in the Humanities.* Detroit: Phillip Thomson, 1960 to date, annual. A good backstop for hard-to-find reviews of architecture, drama, literature, music, philosophy, and the wide range of the other humanities in several hundred specialized periodicals.

2. *Technical Book Review Index.* Pittsburgh: JAAD Publishing Co., 1935 to date, monthly. A type of *Book Review Digest* for scientific, technical, and trade journal reviews. Excerpts from reviews are included and many libraries use it as a reliable buying guide. Since January 1977, it has been published by the author. Up until then it was issued by the Special Libraries Association.

3. *Canadian Book Review Annual.* Toronto: Peter Martin Associates Ltd., 1976 to date, annual. The first edition, published in 1976 covered 682 Canadian published titles for 1975. Arranged by subject with author and title indexes. Each title includes an original 250-word or so excellent, evaluative review.

4. *Children's Literature Review.* Detroit: Gale Research Company, 1975 to date, biannual. A type of *Book Review Digest* for children's books. It differs in that it includes both current and retrospective titles and reviews. For example, it will list and annotate titles by an author over 5- or 10-year period or even longer. To cover current citations but not excerpts from reviews, the same publisher issues *Children's Book Review Index*, 1975 to date, irregular, with annual cumulations. This is a spin-off of *Book Review Index* and is arranged in much the same fashion, but is limited, as the title suggests, to children's works.

---

[13] *Note: The Index to Scientific Reviews* (Philadelphia: Institute for Scientific Information, 1975 to date, annual), a spin-off of *Science Citation Index,* considers reviews from some 2400 journals. The important point is: Here, "review" is used in the sense of an overview of a scientific situation, and while it may refer to specific books and periodicals, this type of review is not a specific review of a book, but rather of scientific findings.

The two best retrospective sources for book reviews, *Book Review Digest* aside, are: (1) *The New York Times Book Review Index, 1896–1970* (New York: Arno Press, 1973, 5 vols., $600). The five volumes are really five indexes; i.e., one volume is an author approach to the book reviews, another volume is an index by title, a third by "by-lines," the fourth by subject (excluding fiction), and the last by category which includes fiction, anthologies, drama, etc. The *Index* may be used with either the microfilm issue of *The New York Times Book Review* or with the reprint of the 136 volumes. Both the *Index* and the reprint volumes are to be updated and supplemented. (Incidentally the cost for the reprint set of *The New York Times Book Review* is $6885. Most libraries will have the much less expensive microfilm edition.) (2) *A Library of Literary Criticism* (New York: Frederick Ungar Publishing Company, 1966–1975, 4 vols.). Unlike the *Times Index,* this set can be used by itself because it includes sometimes lengthy excerpts from reviews, as well as added comments. Coverage is from the Middle Ages through the twentieth century.

NEGATIVE SELECTION[14]

The term "negative selection" is attributed by Margaret Hutchins to James Wyer, and seems as good as any to replace the more horrendous word "weeding." By any name, this is the process of eliminating from the reference collection certain materials. It is a delicate process.

"Delicate" is used advisedly. Conceivably any book, pamphlet, magazine, newspaper, or what you will can have reference value—particularly for the historian or anyone else concerned with social mores and records of the past. To discard such a work is little short of destroying the past. For example, one of the most difficult research problems is to locate materials in local newspapers of the nineteenth century. Thanks to some enterprising "weeders," a vast number of these newspapers (including many of the larger ones) were completely destroyed, or, at best, only certain issues were saved.[15]

Anyone who has sought contemporary opinion, or a biography of a

---

[14] Stanley J. Slote, *Weeding Library Collections* (Littleton, Colorado: Libraries Unlimited, Inc., 1975). The basic handbook on the subject. Includes objectives, methods, and examples of weeding. Not limited to reference works, but most of the material is applicable.

[15] "How I Made $17,500 Robbing a Library" (advertisement for a periodical in *The New York Times,* September 13, 1975, p. 11). The detailed advertisement tells how one man "hauled away hundreds of volumes (of newspapers), some nearly 200 years old," which had been discarded by Columbia University. They were given to him for nothing. His appraisal of value: $17,500.

little-known figure, or statistical data knows that there is no limit to the type of material that may be found in older reference works, certainly in books from both the general and the specific reference collections. Many, such as the early editions of the *Encylopaedia Britannica,* are now classics, invaluable sources of material found nowhere else.

From a purely pragmatic, mercenary point of view, a number of the books discarded because they were worn, outdated, or generally of "poor" content have, over the years, become much-sought-after rarities. Antiquarian bookdealers' catalogs and records of book auctions are made up of books which at one time were considered to be no longer of use. Many of those that now command high prices are frequently described as "ex-library"; that is, they were discarded and carefully stamped (too often on the title page) as being discharged from this or that library.

Guidelines for discarding

In view of these past losses, why then discard titles from the reference collection? Large libraries rarely do; at best they may move the little-used, outdated works from the reference collection into the main collection. Smaller libraries, of course, do not have the alternative. Thus, the telling argument for discarding is lack of space. Other considerations for all sizes of libraries, regardless of what is eventually done physically with the work, include:

Timeliness Most of the reference books that are used for ready reference have to be up to date. Older ones may be helpful historically, but are of little value for current material.

Reliability Data and viewpoints change, and the changes must be reflected in the reference collection. Yesterday's reliable explanation of a given event or phenomenon may no longer be applicable.

Use Needs change from generation to generation, and yesterday's valued reference work may no longer be used by today's reference librarian or the public.

Physical Condition Some of the books do wear out and must be either discarded or replaced with new editions.

None of the arguments is particularly strong except, perhaps, lack of adequate space. Nevertheless, discarding is usually carried out, and to select the discards wisely requires:

Thorough Knowledge of the Collection   The librarian should know how it is used and by whom. Should X work be totally eliminated, or should a new edition be purchased, or should a similar work be considered? These are all questions that vary from situation to situation and can be answered only by the librarian working closely with the collection and the public.

Knowledge of Other Resources   An understanding of the collections of regional and national librarians is needed. Is at least one copy of what you propose to discard in a local or national collection for use at some later date? Obviously a much-used work, such as a 10-year-old copy of the *World Almanac,* need not be checked. But any material that is purely local (particularly pamphlets and ephemera) or anything more than 50 years old, or any items about which there is any question at all regarding use or value, should first be cleared with the larger libraries in the region. Such an item may appear shabby and of little use, but may prove to be a unique copy.

Older Works Worth Keeping   One should have an appreciation that age does not necessarily dictate discarding. No worthwhile reference collection, for example, lacks the much-dated *Encyclopedia of the Social Sciences* or the mass of bibliographies and other guides that were published a number of years ago and are still basic works.

Some general guidelines for reference works may be suggested, but only as just that. Specific rules for discarding depend upon use, not upon any arbitrary set of rules.

Encyclopedias   Maintain as many older editions as possible, *but* a new edition is needed at least every five years, and preferably every year.

Almanacs, Yearbooks, Manuals   These are usually superseded by the next edition or the succeeding volume. Nevertheless, as the information in each is rarely duplicated exactly (new material is added, old material deleted), it is wise to keep old editions for at least 5 years, preferably 10.

Dictionaries   In a sense, these are never dated and should never be discarded unless replaced by the same editions. An exception might be the abridged desk-type dictionaries. The unabridged works and those devoted to special areas are of constant value.

Biographical Sources   Again, the more of these and the more retrospective the sources, the better. Only in a few select cases should any be discarded.

Directories   Like yearbooks, almanacs, and other such works, these are frequently updated, and the older ones (5 to 10 years) can generally be discarded safely.

Geographical Sources   Inexpensive atlases may be safely discarded after 5 to 10 years. More expansive, expensive works are invaluable. In fact, many gain in both research and monetary value over the years.

Government Documents   Never discard these if they are part of a permanent collection. Discards should be considered where material is used only peripherally for pamphlet files. However, be particularly careful to check local and state materials before discarding.

In the subject areas, it is relatively safe to assume that except for botany and natural history, science books are generally dated within five years. The recurrent yearbooks, manuals, and encyclopedias may be discarded as new editions are obtained. In the humanities, discarding should rarely take place unless the material is quite obviously totally and unreservedly dated and of no historical or research value. In the social sciences, timely or topical material may be considered for discard after 10 to 15 years.

SUGGESTED READING

Aiyepeku, Wilson O., "Ground Rules for the Study and Teaching of Subject Literatures," *Journal of Librarianship,* April 1974, pp. 80–90. When one speaks of subject bibliography, what are the criteria for determining the scope of that bibliography? The author attempts an answer, using geography as an example.

Bates, Marcia J., "Rigorous Systematic Bibliography," *RQ,* Fall 1976, pp. 7–26. A detailed argument for the "technically subtle" aspects of systematic bibliography, with an explanation of "requirements for a good systematic bibliography."

Boodson, K., "Subject Bibliographies in Information Work," *The Indexer,* April 1976, pp. 15–23. A clear analysis on the history and development of various types of bibliography, with sections on abstracting and indexing and a short history of the subject.

Brenni, Victor J., *Essays on Bibliography.* Metuchen, New Jersey: Scarecrow Press, 1975. A collection of 50 essays on various aspects of bibliography and bibliographical control from 1919 to 1974. The selection is good and much of the material is yet relevant.

Freides, Thelma, "Bibliographic Gaps in the Social Science Literature," *Special Libraries,* February 1976, pp. 68–75. Like Aiyepeku, Freides discusses "the problem of identifying the literature of a discipline" and duplication in bibliographic services.

McPherson, William G., Jr., "Ezra Pound Meets the Reference Librarian," *Oklahoma Librarian,* April 1975, pp. 13–19. An example of a reference search which begins "by employing the reference works access to which is provided either directly or indirectly by [Winchell . . . and Walford]." The class project indicates the imaginative possibilities of bibliographic searching.

Mangouni, Norman, "An International Style for Bibliographic References," *Scholarly Publishing*, April 1974, pp. 239–245. In discussing proper citations with other publishers, the author gives some insights into the problems of standard bibliographic reference style and bibliographical works.

Public Library of Youngstown and Mahoning County, Ohio, "Serials: Standing Order Suggestions—How Often to Purchase and How Long to Keep," *The Unabashed Librarian*, No. 22, 1977, pp. 11–14. An alphabetical listing of primarily annual directories, guides, almanacs, etc., with specific instructions as to how long to keep. One may argue with some decisions, but a good example of how to handle weeding.

Scott, Edith, "The Evolution of Bibliographic Systems in the United States, 1876–1945," *Library Trends*, July 1976, pp. 293–310. Both a history and an explanation of major American bibliographic developments. This solid overview is updated in the same issue of *Library Trends* by Barbara E. Markuson, "Bibliographic Systems, 1945–1976," pp. 311–328.

Tanselle, G. Thomas, "Bibliographers and the Library," *Library Trends*, April 1977, pp. 745–762. An essay on how scholars use (or do not use) bibliographical aids. Incidentally, this whole issue of *Library Trends*, ably edited by Don Krummel, is devoted to "trends in the scholarly use of library resources," and is an excellent introduction to scholarly research.

Young, Arthur P., "Scholarly Book Reviewing in America," *Libri*, No. 3, September 1975, pp. 174–182. An analysis of reviews and indexes with suggestions for further research. Useful for its author's choice of leading book reviews in scholarly journals.

CHAPTER THREE

Bibliographies: National Library Catalogs and Trade Bibliographies

 **T** HERE IS NO universal bibliography. No single source will give bibliographical details on all books published in the world.[1] Nor is there such a bibliography for films, periodicals, recordings, and the like. Despite the lack of such a master control, there are methods whereby the serious researcher can be reasonably certain that the work being undertaken has not been duplicated. Furthermore, when seeking material in almost any subject area from the sciences to the humanities, the researcher is at no loss for locating more than sufficient sources. This is not to say duplication and loss of material (for lack of proper bibliographical control) are not problems. They are, but the situation is far from hopeless. In many ways, the various national library catalogs do serve as an interlocking type of universal bibliography. They are not absolutely complete, but they are inclusive enough for most practical situations.

[1] While it is utopian at this time to think of a single record of all the world's publications, a worldwide cooperative system of bibliographical control is possible. Under the title "Universal Bibliographic Control" (UBC), several national and international agencies are working toward a global bibliographic network whose end result would be close to the much dreamed-of universal bibliography. See A. H. Chaplin, "Basic Bibliographic Control: Plans for a World System," *Aslib Proceedings,* February 1975, pp. 48–56; and Dorothy Anderson, "Universal Bibliographic Control and the Information Scientist," *The Information Scientist,* March 1976, pp. 11–12.

As a national library catalog is not limited by time, territory, language, subject, or many forms of communication, it does come close to the ideal universal bibliography. And although none of the national library catalogs claims to be universal in scope, collectively they do offer a relatively comprehensive record of international publishing. The Library of Congress, for example, catalogs materials from around the world, and a good proportion of its holdings are books, magazines, music, and the like from international publishers. Numerically, a notion of the idea of the scope of the Library of Congress holdings may be gathered from the fact that the Library "contains more than 72.3 million discrete items and, on the average, adds from 1 to 1.5 million new items each year. More than five million authors are represented among the 20.2 million cards in the Library's complete catalogue."[2] Comparatively speaking, the average number of books published in America each year hovers around 35,000 titles, a small part of the overall annual acquisitions of the Library's net which sweeps in titles from around the world, as well as other published items. Quite similar figures are true for the British Museum.

Union catalogs

A term associated with national catalogs is "union catalog," for example, the Library of Congress's *National Union Catalog* and *Union List of Serials*. Interlibrary cooperation on local, regional, and international scale makes a union list of particular importance. In fact, wherever two or more libraries band together, there is apt to be a by-product of that cooperation—a union list. The utilization of the union list and bibliography is considered in the chapter on The Search in the second volume of this text (pp. 81–120); but because the term appears through this volume, it is well to define it clearly, if only briefly at this point.

A union catalog indicates who has what. A fuller, often repeated definition is: an inventory common to several libraries and listing some or all of their publications maintained in one or more orders of arrangement. The user turns to a union list to locate a given book, periodical, or newspaper in another library, which may be in the same city or thousands of miles away. Given the location and the operation of an interlibrary loan or copying process, the user can then have the particular book or item borrowed from the holding library for personal use.

When each library in the bibliographical network or bibliographic center knows what fellow members have purchased, a union list can be

[2] Norman Mangouni, "An International Style for Bibliographic References," *Scholarly Publishing*, April 1974, p. 240.

helpful in acquisitions. Expensive and little-used items, for example, need be purchased by only one or two of the cooperating libraries because those items are always on call for members.

Some, although not all, of the union lists will give pertinent bibliographical information to help the library trace and identify a given item. When the sole purpose of the union catalog is location, the descriptive entry is normally kept to a minimum, e.g., *New Serial Titles*. Conversely, when it serves numerous other purposes as well (e.g., *The National Union Catalog*), the description will be relatively complete. In most cases, arrangement is in alphabetical form by title or author.

NATIONAL LIBRARY CATALOGS[3]

U.S. Library of Congress. *The National Union Catalog: A Cumulative Author List.* Washington, D.C.: Library of Congress, Card Division, 1956 to date. Nine monthly issues and three quarterly cumulations. $1025.

The National Union Catalog: Pre-1956 Imprints. London: Mansell, 1968 to date. (Approximately 610 volumes, the set to be completed by mid-1979 or early 1980.) £6336.

U.S. Library of Congress. *Library of Congress Catalogs: Subject Catalog* (formerly: *Library of Congress Catalog. Books: Subjects*). Washington, D.C.: Library of Congress, Card Division, 1950 to date. Three quarterly issues with annual cumulations, $800. Quinquennial cumulations from 1950, various prices.

The two ongoing book catalogs of the Library of Congress are essentially no different from the familiar card catalog found in the local library. This is important to recognize. Sometimes the prepossessing sets which run to many hundreds of volumes confuse the novice.

First, what is the scope of *The National Union Catalog?* One will note that each page photographically reproduces catalog cards—the same familiar cards found in many libraries. Each card represents an item cataloged by the Library of Congress or by one or more than 750 libraries in the United States and Canada. This feature makes it a union catalog in that it shows the holdings of more than one library.

---

[3] Discussion here is necessarly limited to space to the printed *National Union Catalog (NUC)*. For a discussion of other forms of the *NUC* (*Library of Congress* depository sets and proofsheets, MARC distribution service), and microform versions of the *NUC,* see Nancy H. Knight, "Microform Catalog Data Retrieval Systems: A Survey," *Library Technology Reports,* May 1975, pp. 1–10. Also, see Chapter 7 of the second volume of this text for more on MARC.

What is cataloged? Almost every communication medium. In this case, the entries are primarily for books, maps, atlases, pamphlets, and serials, including periodicals. The magazines are listed by title; only those cataloged by the Library of Congress are included, and for this reason, *New Serial Titles* is a much better bibliographical catalog of magazines. This aside, *The National Union Catalog* is a basic tool for working with books and pamphlets, as well as music and film.

The various forms are in separate sets, i.e., books and periodicals in one set, music and recordings in another set, etc. See the foreword to any issue of *The National Union Catalog* for an explanation of the parts. What follows is limited to a discussion of the basic book sets.

How is it arranged and what information is given? The volumes are arranged alphabetically by author or main entry. (Generally, the heading of a main entry is an author's name, but, lacking such information, it may be a title. It is never both author and title.) There is no subject approach in the main *National Union Catalog* and cross-references are minimal.

The reproduced card varies in the quantity and type of information given; but in almost all cases, it includes the typical bibliographical description in this order: full name of author, dates of birth and death; full title; place, publisher, and date; collation (e.g., paging, illustrations, maps); series; edition; notes on contents, history; tracing for subject headings and added entries; the Library of Congress and, usually, the Dewey classifications; and The International Standard Book Numbers (see the footnote on page 65).

How is *The National Union Catalog* used in reference work?

1. Since this is a union catalog, showing not only the holdings of the Library of Congress but also titles in over 750 other libraries, it allows the reference librarian to locate a given title quickly. Hence, users who need a work not in their library may find the nearest location via *The National Union Catalog*. For example, the first edition of a mystery, *The Man Who Followed Women* by Hurbert Hitchens, is identified as being in eight other libraries. Location symbols for the eight are: OOxM, TxU, OCU, OCL, MnU, NIC, ViBibV, and WU. The initials stand for libraries in various parts of the country. Initials are explained in the front of cumulative volumes. Depending on the policy of the holding library, the librarian may or may not be able to borrow the title on interlibrary loan. Failing a loan, it may be possible to get sections copied.

2. *The National Union Catalog* virtually amounts to a basic, full author bibliography. Anyone wanting to know everything (magazine articles and other such items aside) that author X has published has

only to consult the author's name under the full *National Union Catalog* set.

3. The full cataloging not only gives details on a book (e.g., when it was published, by whom, and where), but helps the reference library to verify it does exist—an important matter when there is a question on whether X actually did publish this or that. Verification, however, is even more important when the reference librarian is attempting to straighten out the misspelling of a title or an author's name. In other words, *The National Union Catalog* sets the record straight when there is doubt about the validity of a given bit of information.

4. In terms of acquisitions, particularly of expensive or rare items, *The National Union Catalog* permits a library to concentrate in subject areas with the assurance that the less-developed areas may be augmented by interlibrary loan from other libraries.

5. In terms of cataloging (which is basic to reference service), *The National Union Catalog* offers a number of advantages (and headaches). The primary asset is central cataloging, which should limit the amount of original cataloging necessary.

6. The sixth advantage of *The National Union Catalog* is as psychological as it is real. Its very existence gives the librarian (and more involved users) a sense of order and control which would otherwise be lacking in a world that cries for some type of order.

The National Union Catalog is primarily an approach via the author. What does one do when one wants to find books in a given subject area? The user turns to the *Library of Congress Catalogs: Subject Catalog*. Here *The National Union Catalog* entries are rearranged by subject. There is one important catch. The subject approach can be used only for material published since 1945. (The set begins in 1950, but cataloging goes back to books published in 1945.) Prior to that date, there is no subject avenue to *The National Union Catalog* titles.

The subject catalog includes all works cataloged by the Library of Congress, but not necessarily by libraries who contribute location data to *The National Union Catalog*. Hence, it is not a complete *National Union Catalog*. When in doubt, and the author's name is known, *The National Union Catalog* should be double-checked. Also, some, but not all, *National Union Catalog* location symbols are given; again, the main *National Union Catalog* set must be checked for location.

So far, the discussion has concerned only ongoing copies of *The National Union Catalog*, i.e., those published monthly and cumulated annually. But how does one locate a title published, say, in 1950, or for that matter, any one of 10 million retrospective entries not in the current *National Union Catalog?* The answer requires a brief historical sketch of *The National Union Catalog.*

The National Union Catalog in card form began in 1901. By 1926, the *NUC* had over 2 million cards, physically located in the Library of Congress. If anyone wanted to consult the *NUC,* one had to query the Library of Congress or go there in person. The problem was solved, or so it was thought, by sending duplicate cards of the *NUC* to key research libraries throughout the United States. This procedure proved as costly as it was inefficient. So, beginning in the early 1940s, work started on the printed book catalog; the individual cards were reproduced in the familiar *NUC* book form instead of being sent to libraries card by card. However, it was not until January 1, 1956, that it was decided that the book catalogs should be expanded to include not only Library of Congress holdings, but also the imprints of other libraries.

So, since July 1956, the book catalog has borne the new name: *The National Union Catalog.* This means that most large libraries have several sets of book catalogs from the Library of Congress, but the catalogs issued prior to 1956 represent books cataloged only by the Library of Congress, not the entire *National Union Catalog.* What was to be done with *The National Union Catalog* prior to 1956, that is, with the card catalog in the Library of Congress which was not in book form? The answer came in 1968 when *The National Union Catalog: Pre-1956 Imprints* began to be published.

The largest printed bibliography ever undertaken, the *Pre-1956 Imprints* will be completed in 1979 or 1980. As of 1977, approximately 500 of the 600-plus volumes had been published, taking the set well through the alphabet. If the librarian needs to trace a title in the latter part of the alphabet, not yet covered by the printed *Pre-1956 Imprints,* one of three series of catalogs—catalogs which are now replaced by the *Pre-1956 Imprints*—may be consulted; naturally, they will be used for only that portion of the alphabet not yet available in the master set. The series that one may consult until the *Pre-1956 Imprints* is complete are these:

1. 1898–1942. *A Catalog of Books Represented by Library of Congress Printed Cards Issued to July 31, 1942.* Ann Arbor, Michigan: Edwards Brothers, Inc., 1942–1946, 167 vols. This series consists of printed catalog cards produced only by the Library of Congress from 1898 to 1942, and *not* by member libraries. Therefore, it is not properly a union catalog, although some of the cards printed at the Library of Congress do represent scattered holdings of member libraries.

2. 1942–1947. *A Catalog of Books Represented by Library of Congress Printed Cards: Supplement: Cards Issued August 1, 1942–December 31, 1947.* Ann Arbor, Michigan: Edwards Brothers, Inc., 1948, 42 vols.

3. 1948–1952. *Library of Congress Author Catalog: A Cumulative List of*

Works Represented by Library of Congress Printed Cards, 1948–1952. Ann Arbor, Michigan: Edwards Brothers, Inc., 1953, 24 vols.

4. 1953–1957. *National Union Catalog . . . , 1953–1957.* Ann Arbor, Michigan: Edwards Brothers, Inc., 1958, 28 vols.

For subsequently published titles, the librarian may consult the following:

5. 1958–1962. *National Union Catalog . . . , 1958–1962.* New York: Rowman & Littlefield, 1963, 54 vols.

6. 1963–1967. *National Union Catalog . . . , 1963–1967.* Ann Arbor, Michigan: Edwards Brothers, Inc., 1969, 72 vols.

7. 1956–1967. *National Union Catalog . . . , 1956–1967.* Totowa, New Jersey: Rowman and Littlefield, 1970–1972, 125 vols. (A 12-year compilation which eliminates need for (5) and (6) above.)

Considering that one had to search many series before publication of the *Pre-1956 Imprints,* and that they gave only a partial entrance to a true national union catalog before 1942, it is little wonder librarians have greeted the comprehensive set with enthusiasm. However, this is only the "beginning." By 1978 the Library of Congress is planning "a prospective series of new catalogs to trim publication costs, streamline the size of the catalogs themselves and improve access to information."[4]

Which library has X collection?

A major use of *The National Union Catalog* is to discover which library has what title. But how does the reference librarian answer such a question as, "What library has the best *collection* of books—or perhaps manuscripts—on waffle irons or the history of science?" Experts know where primary collections are to be found without consulting librarians. Still, it is useful to realize there are several guides to collections.

The best is Lee Ash's *Subject Collections* (4th ed.; New York: R. R. Bowker Company, 1975, 908 pp.). Arranged under Library of Congress subject headings, data are given for collections in 15,000 libraries in the United States, Canada, and Puerto Rico. The libraries are arranged alphabetically by state with name, address, and an indication of the number

[4] "New Bibliographic Tools Proposed by LC," *Library Journal,* September 1, 1977, pp. 1701–1702. See also Margaret Porter Smith, "*The National Union Catalog Pre-1956 Imprints:* A Progress Report," *Library Resources & Technical Services,* Winter 1976, p. 48. A short article which gives students the necessary background on not only the catalog, but also the history of the development of *The National Union Catalog* concept from 1901.

of volumes within the subject area. Robert Collison's *Published Library Catalogues: An Introduction to Their Contents and Use* (New York: R. R. Bowker Company, 1974, 184 pp.) is more discursive in that essays on collections are included under 11 broad subject areas. It has the advantage of being international in scope and features a detailed index to 756 subject catalogs.

The library catalogs listed in Collison[5] and elsewhere take many forms, although for major library holdings they usually resemble *The National Union Catalog* in format; in other words, they consist of multiple volumes of the card catalog of that library printed in book form. Many are published by the G. K. Hall Company of Boston, for example, *Dictionary Catalog of the G. Robert Vincent Voice Library at Michigan State University . . . ,* 1975, a listing by speaker of tapes, discs, and recordings; and *Harvard University Dictionary Catalogue of the Byzantine Collection . . . ,* 1975, 12 vols., a listing of some 172,000 main, subject, and added entries.

Library catalogs in Great Britain

British Museum. Department of Printed Books. *General Catalogue of Printed Books.* London: Trustees of the British Museum, 1959–1966, 263 vols. *Ten-Year Supplement, 1956–1965,* 1968, 50 vols. *Five-Year Supplement, 1966–1970,* 1971–1972, 26 vols. Prices on request.

————. *Subject Index of the Modern Works Added to the Library of the British Museum in the Years 1881–1900.* London: Trustees of the British Museum, 1903. Five-year supplements have been published to date since the initial three-volume work was issued. Prices on request.

The Library of the British Museum is roughly equivalent to our Library of Congress, and its various catalogs are similar in purpose (if not in scope) to *The National Union Catalog.*[6] The essential differences are:

1. The British Museum is much older than the Library of Congress and has a considerably larger collection of titles dating from the fifteenth century up to the all-out embrace of world publications by the Library of Congress in the 1960s.
2. The British Museum's catalog is not a union catalog and shows holdings only of the Museum.
3. The data for titles are somewhat more brief than those in *The National Union Catalog.*

[5] Robert L. Collison, *Abstracts and Abstracting Services* (Santa Barbara, California: American Bibliographical Center—Clio Press, 1971).

[6] Under reorganization, the British Museum Library is now known as the British Library, but the basic bibliographies still retain the British Museum authorship in 1977.

4. Conversely, larger amounts of analytical material and cross references are included. For example, considerable attention is given to the analysis of series, and there are numerous cross references from names of editors, translators, and other names connected with a title.

5. Catchword title entries are used; and in some ways this approach is useful because of the lack of a satisfactory subject catalog. The problem, of course, is that the title must reveal something of the contents.

6. Whereas *The National Union Catalog* can be considered very much as a current bibliographical aid, the *General Catalogue,* because of its approach and its infrequent publication, is more retrospective.

How much duplication is there between the massive British catalog and *The National Union Catalog?* Walford did a sampling and found that 75 to 80 percent of the titles in the British work are not in the American equivalent; for titles published before 1800, the percentage is 90 percent. With increased interest in capturing worldwide titles in *The National Union Catalog,* the amount of duplication is bound to increase in the years ahead. Meanwhile, no large research library can afford to be without the British Museum's *General Catalogue.*

The *Subject Index* is considerably less useful than its American counterpart. It is not issued until several years after the main entries in the *General Catalogue,* and large, rather than definitive, subject headings are used.

NATIONAL AND TRADE BIBLIOGRAPHY

Most of the enumerative bibliographies found in libraries can be classified as national and trade bibliographies. The distinction between the types is not always clear, if indeed there is a distinction (see the footnote on page 34). There are estimated to be 9600 basic types of bibliography and 147,000 possible combinations. Consequently, innumerable possibilities exist for defining, categorizing, and argument. The important consideration is not so much where the bibliography falls in the sometimes esoteric reference scheme, but rather, how it is used.

The pragmatic function of a national bibliography is to tell the librarian what was, what is, and what will be available either by purchase or (via other aids) by possible loan from another library. The bibliographies help to give necessary bibliographical information (e.g., publisher, price, author, subject area, Library of Congress or Dewey numbers), which is used for a number of purposes ranging from clarifying proper spelling to locating an item in terms of its subject area. Also, the national bibliography is a primary control device for bringing some order to the 35,000 or more books published in the United States each year, not to mention similar staggering figures for pamphlets, reports, recordings, films, and other items.

The process of compiling national bibliographies differs from country to country, but there is a given basic pattern. Effort is made, first, to give a current listing of titles published the previous week, month, or quarter. These data are then cumulated for the annual breakdown of titles published; and beyond that step are other forms to indicate what is in print, what is out of print, and what is going to be published. (The same process, and this statement bears repeating, is applicable to forms other than books.)

United States national and trade bibliography: Weekly and monthly

Publishers' Weekly. New York: R. R. Bowker Company, 1872 to date, weekly. $30.

Weekly Record. New York: R. R. Bowker Company, 1974 to date, weekly. $12.50.

American Book Publishing Record. New York: R. R. Bowker Company, 1961 to date, monthly, $19. The annual cumulation, $45. *Five-Year Cumulative 1970–1974,* 1977, 4 vols., $110.

Cumulative Book Index. New York: The H. W. Wilson Company, 1898 to date, monthly, with three-month, annual, and five-year cumulations. Service basis.

Forthcoming Books. New York: R. R. Bowker Company, 1966 to date, bimonthly. $25. *Subject Guide to Forthcoming Books,* 1967 to date, bimonthly. $15. Combined subscription, $35.

United States: Annual and biannual

(All titles published by the R. R. Bowker Company)

Publishers' Trade List Annual, 1873 to date, annual. 6 vols., $50.

Books in Print, 1948 to date, annual. 4 vols., $86.50.

Books in Print Supplement, 1973 to date, annual. $42.50.

Subject Guide to Books in Print, 1957 to date, annual, 2 vols., $65.

Paperbound Books in Print, 1955 to date, biannual (Jan. and Oct.), 2 vols., $62.50.

Children's Books in Print, 1969 to date, annual. $25.

Subject Guide to Children's Books in Print, 1970 to date, annual. $25.

Booksellers call the national and trade bibliographies listed here "the tools of the trade." Librarians also regard them as such, and their purpose is self-evident from the titles. Essentially, the bibliographies list the books that can be purchased from American publishers (i.e., are in print), in what forms (hardback, paperback, text), and at what prices. Depending on the individual trade bibliography, additional information is given as to the date of publication, the number of pages, the subjects covered, and other data necessary for proper and easy use of the bibliography.

Retrospective titles

The most frequently consulted titles are *Books in Print (BIP)* and *Subject Guide to Books in Print.* More than 480,000 in-print books of all kinds (hardbounds, paperbacks, trade books, textbooks, adult titles, juveniles) are indexed by author and by title in *Books in Print.* The trade bibliography tells the user whether the book can be purchased, from whom, and at what price. It also answers such questions as: What books by Richard Brautigan are in print, including, it should be noted, both hardbound and paperbound editions at various prices? Who is the publisher of *Psychic War in Men and Women?* Is Laurie John's book still in print? (The fact that sometimes the inquiry cannot be answered is not always the fault of the questioner's spelling of the title or because the author's name is not correct or even close. *Books in Print,* either through filing errors or misinformation from the publishers, may fail to guide users to a title which they otherwise know to be correct.)

Almost every entry in *BIP* includes the author, co-author, editor, price, publisher, year of publication, number of volumes, Library of Congress card number and the International Standard Book Numbers (ISBN).[7] The names and addresses of the nearly 5300 U.S. publishers represented in *BIP* are included, as they are in most trade bibliographies. The listings provide the source of answers to queries about publishers,

[7] ISBN is employed by publishers to distinguish one item from another, and is of considerable assistance when two works have the same title or when confusion arises over the author. Most American publishers now include the ISBN on the verso of the title page and use it as a method of identifying invoices. A similar system, the International Standard Serial Numbers (ISSN), is employed for identifying serials.

although the librarian who needs more detail should consult reference works specifically geared for information about publishers.[8]

Issued in November or December of each year, *Books in Print* is supplemented by a single volume in the spring of the following year. Here publishers list titles newly published and not included in the basic *BIP*, as well as titles which are out of print or which they plan to issue before the next annual *BIP* volumes. These listings are arranged by author and by title as well as by subject; thus the *Books in Print Supplement* is also a supplement to *Subject Guide to Books in Print*. For normal purposes, *BIP* is enough for most questions. When the original publishing date is more than one or two years old, when there has been a spurt of inflation, or when the librarian cannot find a title, a double check in the *Books in Print Supplement* is wise.

The majority of titles listed in *BIP* are similarly found in *Subject Guide to Books in Print*. In the subject approach, no entries are made for fiction, poetry, or bibles. (Note, though, that the guide does list books about fiction under the author's name; criticism of Henry James, for example, is found under James.) The use of the subject guide, which virtually rearranges *BIP* under 62,000 subject headings, is self-evident. It is not only a help in locating books about a given subject, but it also may be used to help expand the library's collection in given areas. If, for example, books about veterinarians are in great demand, the guide gives a complete list of those available from American publishers. An important point: The list is inclusive, not selective. No warning sign is given to differentiate the world's most misleading book about veterinarians from the best among, say, 20 titles listed. The librarian must turn to other bibliographies and reviews for judgment and evaluation of titles in any subject area.

The massive *Publishers' Trade List Annual (PTLA)*, while less frequently used by reference librarians, fits in here because it is part of the bibliographical apparatus for tracing books in print. The *PTLA* is a collection of United States publishers' catalogs in book form. The catalogs conform to a certain physical cut size, but may be in hundreds of various typefaces, arrangements, and lengths. For convenience, the catalogs are bound in alphabetical order in six volumes. The first volume of the set, which will vary in number of volumes from year to year, contains the index and a section reserved for small publishers who may not have enough titles to warrant a separate bound catalog. *PTLA* contains the listings or catalogs

---

[8] There are two standard works. *American Book Trade Directory* (New York: R. R. Bowker Company, 1915 to date, biannual) gives a comprehensive listing of United States publishers as well as retail booksellers and wholesalers. More detailed information on types of materials favored by specific publishers is found in *The Literary Market Place* (New York: R. R. Bowker Company, 1940 to date, annual). The 82 sections answer a great many of the queries asked by a would-be writer.

of 1600 publishers represented in *Books in Print*. It is not complete, as some 5300 publishers have titles in *BIP*. The actual number of separate, bound catalogs in the 1977 edition was 1400. Other publishers are represented in the green section list at the front of the first volume. It is useful in answering questions like: What are the titles in the St. Martin's Press series on motion pictures? What are the prices of various dictionaries published by Random House? Who are the mystery writers published by Simon and Schuster? Also, the publisher may give a brief description of a title or a series not included in *Books in Print*.[9]

New titles

How does one discover facts about books published last week, or a month ago, or, for that matter, books which are not yet out but are promised in the next few months? To put it another way, how does the librarian answer such questions as, "What recent books—I mean in the past few weeks or months—has Y written? I saw a review of Y's last book somewhere, but I can't remember the title." Or, "I can't remember the author, but there is a good book recently on John Coltrane." Or, "What is the price, publisher, subject, and so on, of the X or Y title?"

If the question concerns a popular title such as Leon Uris's *Trinity*, Woodward and Bernstein's *The Final Days*, or Alex Haley's *Roots* (to name some 1977 best sellers), the librarian has no difficulty because the book is familiar and, furthermore, it is probably in the library or on order. The problem is with lesser-known titles, and here the librarian must turn to certain basic aids. The two most often used are the *Cumulative Book Index (CBI)* and the *American Book Publishing Record (ABPR)*. Both are monthly publications and both list or index books recently published. A year's cumulation of either one will give the librarian a record of titles published that year in the United States (which is *ABPR*'s limited scope), or for the United States *and* the rest of the English-speaking world (which gives the *CBI* a quantitative edge over its competitor).

Beginners sometimes have difficulty in differentiating between the *CBI*, the *ABPR*, and *Books in Print*. The basic difference is that *Books in Print* gives information on available books that have been published in the previous year, or 5 or even 100 years ago. *CBI* and *ABPR* are concerned only with recording and indexing books as they are published. Their monthly

---

[9] Until *Books in Print* was computerized in the mid-1970s, *Publishers' Trade List Annual* was the base from which the information for *BIP* was drawn. In fact, *BIP* was a type of index to *PTLA*. This is not now true. Data found in *BIP* are no longer taken from the still manually produced *PTLA,* but from information received directly from the publishers on advance book-information forms. One result of this new approach is that there is no standard form for an author's name, and it may appear in several forms in *BIP*.

or annual cumulations tell the librarian what books were issued last month or last year, but do not indicate whether they are still available from the publisher, that is, are still in print. (For working purposes, of course, consultation of either the *CBI* or *ABPR* on a monthly or quarterly basis is usually a safe indication that the reported book is still in print. A dependence on the annual cumulation may be more hazardous, and checking out the five-year volumes of the *CBI* or the *ABPR* for information on in-print titles is plain foolish.)

Although the *CBI* claims to be a "current index to books published in the English language," it hardly claims "all" English-language titles. Therefore, larger libraries will rely on more specific bibliographical aids for a wider sweep of English titles. Conversely, for most libraries the *CBI* coverage of American books, which is impressively complete for the majority of publishers, as well as of English-language titles, is quite enough to answer almost all reference queries.

Published since 1898, the familiar brown-covered *CBI* is to be found in almost all libraries, as are the monthly and annual cumulations. It has the advantage of being well known, accurate, and easy to use. Books are listed in one alphabet by author, title, and subject. The author, or main, entry includes pertinent bibliographic information, as well as useful data for catalogers and acquisitions librarians. The subject headings, which follow those established by the Library of Congress, are exhaustive. Although fiction is not included as a subject, one does find headings on science fiction, short stories, mystery and detective stories, etc. There is also a good directory of publishers.

The publisher of *CBI* is able to list new titles monthly because "most publishers in the United States and Canada send copies of their books to the H. W. Wilson Company promptly," to quote a Wilson Company brochure, "and these are processed quickly and appear in the earliest possible issue of *CBI*. Therefore books are frequently listed in *CBI* before they appear in any other major bibliography." There is an understandable "sales pitch" here which is of interest because the rival to *CBI* does much the same thing in terms of listing new titles each month. One would not want to argue that *CBI* is faster to the mark with new titles than the *ABPR*, but only that the librarian who cannot find a title in *CBI* has the advantage of being able to check another source in *ABPR*, or vice versa.

ABPR covers much the same ground as *CBI,* but differs in that (1) it limits listing to titles published in the United States; (2) it is arranged by the Dewey Decimal System, that is, by subject, and it has an author and title index; (3) it includes separate sections on juvenile and adult fiction. The information is much the same as found in *CBI*. Why take both services? Some librarians do not, giving preference to the long-established *CBI*. Larger libraries do take both, primarily as a double check of one

against the other for titles missed, for the different arrangements of mate
rial, or for the more inclusive coverage of English-language titles by *CBI*.

The monthly issues of *ABPR* lead back to another service, the *Weekly
Record*. While more important to catalogers and acquisitions librarians, the
Weekly Record is interesting to reference librarians in that it records on a
weekly basis what is published in the United States. Until 1974 it was part
of the periodical *Publishers' Weekly,* but it is now issued as a separate publication. The same information as found in *ABPR* appears here, differing
only in that the arrangement is by author or main entry, not by subject.
The arrangement limits its use by reference librarians. Every four weeks,
the contents of the *Weekly Record* are rearranged and cumulated as, yes, the
ABPR.

When the "Weekly Record" was a department in *Publishers' Weekly
(PW)*, the periodical was found in most reference departments. Now that
the department has been converted to a separate publication, *PW* is more
a piece of necessary reading than a direct reference aid. The weekly gives
essential notes and articles on all aspects of publishing (both here and
abroad) and libraries. It is difficult to imagine an involved reference librarian not at least thumbing through the weekly issues, if only for the
"PW Forecasts." Here the critical annotations on some 50 to 100 titles give
the reader a notion of what to expect in popular fiction and nonfiction to
be published in the next month or so.

A more definitive approach to what is going to be published is found
in *Forthcoming Books*. Again, this periodical is likely to be of more value to
acquisitions and cataloging than to reference, but it does answer queries
about a new book, or possibly about a book which the patron may have
heard discussed on a radio or television program before it is actually published. The bimonthly lists by author and by title (not by subject) books
due to be published in the next five months.[10] For a subject approach, one
must consult the bimonthly *Subject Guide to Forthcoming Books.* One need not
be an expert to realize that the two works would be much easier and faster
to use were they combined.

While *Books in Print* lists paperbound titles, *Paperbound Books in Print*
rearranges these same listings in a single volume which is nicely divided
into three separate indexes: title, author, and subject.[11] The 1976 compila-

---

[10] In *Books in Print* as well as in some standard bibliographies which have borrowed from *Books
in Print* or *Forthcoming Books,* one may find "ghost titles," i.e., books which were supposed to be
published but were never issued. Such errors come from *BIP* and *Forthcoming Books* policy
which depends on publishers' early announcements—announcements which may be later
amended but not always corrected in *BIP*.

[11] A major problem with the subject headings is their limited number, slightly over 450.
Although an improvement over the 26 major categories in earlier volumes, the headings are

tion includes more than 140,000 books with full bibliographical information about each. Beginning in 1978, the annual and two supplements change to a schedule of two volumes a year (January and October). Only the latest volume is needed for reference. As a guide to a particular form, *Paperbound Books in Print* is invaluable in bookshops, although it may be of more limited use in libraries. Librarians tend to use it as a double check against *BIP*, particularly as not all new paperbound titles are in *BIP*.

Using the same information as gathered from publishers for the compilation of *BIP*, *Paperbound Books in Print* is, in essence, a publisher's spin-off of the basic volume. It adds not only convenience for users and librarians but, it is hoped, profits from the publisher. Librarians must ultimately decide whether, once the basic volumes are acquired, the spin-offs are really necessary. The answer for a large or special library is usually yes, because of added convenience. Small libraries might think again. Another fallout of *Books in Print* is *Children's Books in Print* and *Subject Guide to Children's Books in Print*. Over 40,000 titles are included with full bibliographical information, including grade levels. (If one wonders why *Books in Print* developed grade levels for some titles, the answer is here: Gather as much information as possible from the publisher for possible use in another bibliographical form at a later date, or so the publisher's reasoning goes. Add a machine-readable data base and computer to the compilation, as is the case for *BIP* and its spin-offs, and the process becomes relatively easy.)[12]

Separating out the 40,000-plus titles at the kindergarten through high school levels from *BIP* for the children's version is of some value for schools. Of considerably more use, however, is the subject arrangement because here the book is really new in that the *Subject Guide to Books in Print* headings (Library of Congress–based) are deleted in favor of over 8000 *Sears,* headings, i.e., those found in *Sears List of Subject Headings,* 11th ed. (New York: The H. W. Wilson Company, 1977) which are subject headings based on the Library of Congress system, but modified for small libraries. *Sears* offers subjects closer to the needs of children. As more than one reviewer has noted, however, the *Subject Guide to Children's Books in Print* has a major flaw—lack of adequate cross-references, i.e., via *see* and *see also* suggestions.

---

still too general for most libraries, e.g., there are almost 30 pages of titles, without any subheadings, under United States history, here indicated, by the way, as "History—United States."

12 Other R. R. Bowker Company spin-offs from *Books in Print: Bowker's Medical Books in Print, Business Books in Print, El-Hi Textbooks in Print, Scientific and Technical Books in Print,* etc. Modifications, changes, and additions are made, but the base is the same for all. Other publishers, it should be stressed, follow much the same procedure—a procedure which is expanding with the automation of bibliographical records.

From bibliography to bibliography

While the preceding discussion has been limited to two American publishers, the bibliographical apparatus for recording published titles and those still to be published is much the same throughout the United States and the rest of the world. The English, for example, have *British Books in Print,* a weekly *British National Bibliography, Whitaker's Cumulative Book List,* etc.[13] Differences exist in scope and in emphasis between British and American efforts, but essentially the purpose is the same, as one finds when one explores the current and retrospective bibliographies of France, West Germany, and other countries.

Just because there are numerous bibliographies, the beginner sometimes tends to forget the obvious. For example, having become involved with the trade bibliographies, one may overlook that old standby, *The National Union Catalog,* which, thanks to its complete record, is a favored place to look for retrospective titles. Asked to compile a bibliography of novels by Anthony Powell, an English writer, the librarian would first turn to *Books in Print,* then to *CBI* and *ABPR,* to name only three sources which would list American and some English editions of Powell. Just to be certain, the librarian would then go to the English bibliographies. This procedure would be right and proper for a definitive list, but for a general rundown of Powell novels, it would be much simpler to consult the ongoing *National Union Catalog* and the *Pre-1956 Imprints,* with a double check over the past six months or so in *CBI.* The librarian seeking books on a subject would accomplish much the same by looking into *Books: Subject. A Cumulated List of Works . . . ,* again with an update in *CBI* and/or *ABPR* and *Subject Guide to Books in Print.*

One can see the advantage of the yet-to-be automated system which would incorparate all these bibliographies into a number of related data bases. The librarian might then sit at a computer keyboard, type in the query regarding an author (or a subject), and have the results printed out or flashed on a television screen. The potential of such a data base for searching and saving valuable time and effort is literally limitless.

UNITED STATES RETROSPECTIVE BIBLIOGRAPHY

Most daily reference work is carried on with relatively current national and trade bibliographies. There are times when one or more of the retrospective bibliographies are needed as when trying to answer the following

---

[13] An interesting comparison between the scope of *Whitaker's Cumulative Book List,* the American *CBI,* and the *British National Bibliography* will be found in "Reference and Subscription Book Reviews," *The Booklist,* April 15, 1975, p. 875.

type of question: What is the original price of John Jenkin's *Lives of the Governors of the State of New York,* published in 1851? Who is the author of *The Ballad of the Abolition Blunder-buss,* published in 1861? What is the correct title of a work on rattlesnakes by S. W. Mitchell, published in 1860? The person asking this type of question is likely to be a historian, literary scholar, librarian, or anyone else deeply involved in research of a given subject, place, or person.

In trying to fathom a retrospective bibliography, which is not always easy to do because of erratic arrangement, coverage, and purpose, the librarian is apt to overlook other approaches which are somewhat simpler. The first one is *The National Union Catalog* which, when the pre-1956 set is complete, will supply answers to all but the most elusive and esoteric titles.

Retrospective bibliography is not limited to the United States. In fact, it has reached scholarly, awesome proportions in England and on the Continent. Examples of the basic foreign retrospective bibliographies will be found in Sheehy and Walford. Regardless of national origin, retrospective bibliographies tell what was published where and by whom. They are a source of information about national, state, and local history and thus trace the cultural and scientific development of people in a given place and time.

In chronological order, the leading American retrospective bibliographies are:[14]

1500–1892　　Sabin, Joseph. *Bibliotheca Americana. Dictionary of Books Relating to America from Its Discovery to the Present Time.* New York: Sabin, 1869–1892; Bibliographical Society of America, 1928–1936, 29 vols.

Molnar, John. *Author-Title Index to Joseph Sabin's Dictionary of Books Relating to America.* Metuchen, New Jersey: Scarecrow Press, 1974, 3 vols.

1639–1800　　Evans, Charles. *American Bibliography: A Chronological Dictionary of All Books, Pamphlets and Periodical Publications Printed in the United States of America From the Genesis of Printing in 1639 Down to and Including the Year 1800.* Chicago: Printed for the author, 1903–1959, 14 vols. (Vols. 13 and 14 published by the American Antiquarian Society.)

Shipton, Clifford. *National Index of American Imprints Through 1800; The Short Title Evans.* Worcester, Massachusetts: American Antiquarian Society, 1969, 2 vols.

---

[14] Original publishers are given for these titles, but most have been reprinted by one or more publishers and a number are available on microform.

1801–1819   Shaw, Ralph, and Richard Shoemaker. *American Bibliography: A Preliminary Checklist.* Metuchen, New Jersey: Scarecrow Press, 1958–1965, 22 vols.

1820–1861   Roorbach, Orville. *Bibliotheca Americana.* New York: O. A. Roorbach, 1852–1861, 4 vols.

1820–1875   Shoemaker, Richard H., and others. *A Checklist of American Imprints, 1820+,* Metuchen, New Jersey: Scarecrow Press, 1964 to date. (Shoemaker died in 1970, and the plan is now to continue the series through 1875 with editors Scott Bruntjen and Grace Bruntjen. As of 1977, the series was up to 1832.)

1861–1870   Kelly, James. *American Catalogue of Books, Published in the United States from January 1861 to January 1871, with Date of Publication, Size, Price, and Publisher's Name.* New York: John Wiley & Sons, Inc., 1866–1871, 2 vols.

1876–1910   *American Catalogue of Books, 1876–1910.* New York: *Publishers' Weekly,* 1880–1911, 13 vols.

1899–1927   *United States Catalog: Books in Print.* 4th ed. New York: The H. W. Wilson Company, 1928, 3164 pp.

The following titles are still being published and are discussed elsewhere. They are listed here by their beginning publishing date as an indication of what can be used for retrospective searching from 1928 to the present.

1872–   *Publishers' Weekly*
1873–   *Publishers' Trade List Annual*
1898–   *Cumulative Book Index*
1948–   *Books in Print*
1957–   *Subject Guide to Books in Print*

Sabin differs from all the other bibliographies listed here in that he includes books, pamphlets, and periodicals printed in the United States *and* works printed about America in other countries. The others are limited to titles published in the United States. An Oxford scholar, Sabin was an authority on rare books about America. He began his ambitious project (often called *Bibliotheca Americana*) in the early 1860s, lived long enough to see 13 volumes published by 1881. The next seven volumes were by Wilberforce Eaames. R. W. G. Vail ultimately called a halt to the proceedings with the final volumes in 1936. Arrangement is by author, with some title entries and other entries by names of places. Entries include collation, usually the location of a copy, and a note on contents. There is no subject index. Each volume contains entries for one section of the alphabet up to the date of publication; hence, it is uneven in chronological coverage, particularly since cutoff dates of acceptable publications moved further and further back as the work continued. There is no guarantee that a work published in 1870, say, is apt to be listed here. The author must be known or the set is virtually worthless. However, once the author is identified, the information found is enough to warrant searching. Thanks to Molnar's index, it is now a relatively simple thing to consult the otherwise badly organized Sabin. The massive author-title index includes 270,000 entries. (NOTE: A completely revised Sabin is the goal of a project to begin in the late 1970s.)

A work of love and considerable hardship for Charles Evans, *American Bibliography* is a classic. It is considered the keystone upon which all retrospective American bibliography is built and is basic to any large collection. Arrangement is not alphabetical by author. It is chronological by dates of publication. If one does not know the date, or approximate date, there is an author, subject, and printer and publisher index to help. For each entry, there is the author's full name with birth and death dates, a full title, place, publisher, date, paging, size, and usually the location of one or more copies in American libraries.

The *National Index* is a required addition for anyone using Evans. It serves to eliminate nonexistent titles, or "ghosts" which Evans dutifully recorded without seeing a copy of the actual item. Furthermore, it adds over 10,000 titles discovered since Evans's set was published. The 49,197 entries are arranged alphabetically by author and short title, and there is reference to the original entry in Evans—if it is listed there. (The *National Index* is particularly valuable for use with the microcard reproduction of all nonserial titles listed in Evans and elsewhere, and published in America before 1801. It is virtually an index to the tremendous set of nearly 50,000 individual books on microform.)

Shaw and Shoemaker continued Evans's initial efforts to 1820 and the gap between Evans and Roorbach is filled only partially. Each volume covers one year and gives the briefest author citation, along with a location for some copies. Addenda volumes include a title and author index for the full series.

Another set in the same series is *A Checklist of American Imprints*, which was to carry the same type of listing down to 1875 and the beginning of Kelly. From the 1821 volume on, this series differs from the 1801–1819 set in that locations are given for most of the copies and the compiler did check out the books listed. (In the earlier compilation, titles were primarily from secondary sources with little attention given to checking the accuracy of those sources.) Since Shoemaker's death in 1970, the series has been carried on by Scott and Grace Bruntjen and the publisher. There is a title and author index to the 1820–1829 series.

Until the *Checklist of American Imprints* is taken down through 1875, the Roorbach and Kelly bibliographies must be used. Roorbach is a contemporary bibliography similar in its intent to *Books in Print,* but done with considerably less care. The arrangement is alphabetical by author and title with information on the publisher, size, and usually, but not always, the price and date. Entries are frequently incomplete. From 1861 to 1870, Kelly serves the same purpose as Roorbach and succeeds in giving the same type of incomplete information. Both Roorbach and Kelly, for example, list less than one-half as many titles per year as Evans, who was recording a much less productive period in American publishing. Although inaccurate and incomplete, the two bibliographies are the only reference aids of their kind.

In terms of retrospective searching, then, there is something less than a blank period from the time of the last Shoemaker volume to the beginning of the *American Catalog of Books* in 1876, i.e., from 1830 to 1876. Begun by Frederick Leypoldt as a trade bibliography of books in print, the *American Catalog* was published annually and later cumulated. Arrangement is by author and title with subject supplements. The information is generally reliable and comprehensive—but no more so than the publisher's catalogs from which the information came.

Competition from The H. W. Wilson Company's *United States Catalog* caused cessation of the *American Catalog* in 1910, and it did not begin publishing again until 1948 as *Books in Print.* The *United States Catalog* is really a cumulation of the *Cumulative Book Index* which began in 1898 as a type of *Books in Print* in competition with the *American Catalog.* There are four editions of the *United States Catalog,* but the most often used is the last, which lists all the books in print published in English in the United States and Canada in 1928. (Earlier volumes must be consulted for finding books out of print by 1928 and for fuller information on other titles.) By 1928, the increase in the number of titles published forced Wilson to abandon the *United States Catalog* in favor of cumulative issues of the *CBI.*

While this discussion may be too detailed for the beginner, it is an important part of bibliographic history and is included here to indicate the tremendous range of bibliographies needed when one becomes involved with other than current titles. For those who wish additional information in a pleasant, yet scholarly fashion, nothing could be better than George Tanselle's *Guide to the Study of United States Imprints* (Cambridge: Harvard University Press, 1971).

Book prices

American Book Prices Current. New York: Bancroft-Parkman, 1895 to date, annual. Publisher and price vary. (1975 vol., $53.50.)

Book Auction Records. Folkestone, England: Wm. Dawson & Sons, 1903 to date, annual. Publisher and price vary.

Bookman's Price Index. Detroit: Gale Research Company, 1965 to date, annual. $58.

The average layperson's contact with retrospective bibliography is indirect, usually taking the form of trying to find a long out-of-print book or, more likely, the answer to a question about the value of a book printed years ago. "What is my book, map, or broadside worth?" This is a familiar enough question in many libraries. The three guides listed here are the most often used for an answer. The larger library will have them, not only to help the user, but to assist in acquisitions where a very real question about a used-book dealer's asking price may arise. Should the library pay X dollars for a title which last year cost Y dollars less at an auction? There are many variables for both the user and the library, but the guides indicate the logical parameters of pricing.

American Book Prices Current and *Book Auction Records* are collections of book prices paid at various auctions.[15] The third, *Bookman's Price Index,* is based on prices garnered from antiquarian dealers' catalogs. The two first titles are frequently indexed over a period of a number of years. Hence, it is not always necessary to search each volume for a given title.

The American work lists items sold for $20 or more and includes books, serials, autographs, manuscripts, broadsides, and maps. Arrangement is alphabetical by main entry with cross-references. Each of the forms is treated in its own section. Sales run from the fall to the spring, and hence each volume is usually numbered with two years, e.g., 1976–1977. Some 14 major auction firms, from Parke-Bernet Galleries to Christie, Manson & Woods Ltd., are included, as are a number of large individual sales of private libraries. The entries are cumulated about every five years, e.g., *American Book Prices Current. Index, 1970–1975* (New York: Bancroft-Parkman, 1976, 2 vols.). The cumulations give a quick overview of prices, but it should be noted that the two-volume set sells for $175.

Book Auction Records is the English equivalent of the American title, and while it duplicates some of the information found in that work, it includes a number of European auctions not covered elsewhere. Arrangement and form are similar to the *American Book Prices Current* and there are periodic cumulations. Both titles suffer a time lag, and normally are at least one year, and usually two years, behind the sales reported.

---

[15] For a comparison of these two annual works, see Robert Vaughan, "Pounds, Dollars and Deutschmarks," *The Times Literary Supplement,* January 30, 1976, p. 119.

Bookman's Price Index differs from the other two titles in that it includes prices in catalogs of some 60 booksellers. Entries are listed in a standard main-entry form. Volume 11, issued in 1976, in includes over 35,000 titles—almost twice the number found in the auction price lists. It also has the advantage of representing retail prices which may be somewhat higher than those at an auction where book dealers themselves are bidding.

The guides give only relative indications of price. The price requested by a book dealer or at an auction often represents the maximum. Someone selling the same copy of the book to a dealer must expect a lower price in order for the dealer to realize a profit. Other variables, such as condition and the demands of the current market, enter into pricing. On the whole, a librarian should refer such matters of pricing to an antiquarian book dealer. The most the librarian should do is show the price lists to the inquirer, who can then reach his or her own conclusions.

BIBLIOGRAPHIES: PERIODICALS AND NEWSPAPERS

To this point, the primary focus has been on books, but national and trade bibliographies are also concerned with other physical forms of information. Library materials include not only books but periodicals, recordings, films, data bases, etc.

Periodicals

Titus, Edna Brown (ed.), *Union List of Serials in Libraries of the United States and Canada,* 3d ed. New York: The H. W. Wilson Company, 1965, 5 vols., $120.

New Serial Titles. Washington, D.C.: Library of Congress, 1961 to date, eight issues per year, cumulated quarterly and annually, $170.

New Serial Titles, 1950–1970. New York: R. R. Bowker Company, 1973, 4 vols., $220. *New Serial Titles, 1950–1970. Subject Guide.* New York: R. R. Bowker Company, 1975, 2 vols., $138.50.

Ulrich's International Periodical Directory, 17th ed. New York: R. R. Bowker Company, 1977, 2300 pp., $5750. *Ulrich's Quarterly,* 1977 to date, $24.

The approximate equivalent of *The National Union Catalog* for periodicals is the *Union List of Serials . . .* and its continuation in *New Serial Titles. The National Union Catalog* lists catalog serials, including periodicals, but only those acquired by the Library of Congress.[16] The series for serials is a better guide, if only because more than one source is indicated for location and, more important, the serials, bibliographies, and union lists are limited solely to that single form.

The base of the American series of union lists is the *Union List of Serials in Libraries of the United States and Canada,* which includes titles published before 1950. It is continued by *New Serial Titles* on an eight-times-a-year basis. *New Serial Titles* is cumulated not only annually, but every 21 years, e.g., *New Serial Titles, 1950–1970.* Given the basic volumes and the almost monthly updating, the librarian is able to (1) locate one or more libraries that have almost any periodical published from its beginning until today; (2) learn the name and location of the publisher; (3) discover the name, and various changes in the name, of a magazine; (4) check the beginning date of publication and, where applicable, the date it ceased publication and possibly the date it began publication again. This information is valuable for interlibrary loan purposes and for determining whether a library has a complete run of a magazine, whether the magazine is still being published, whether it has changed its name, and so on.

When someone finds an article through one of the library indexes in a journal or magazine which the library does not have, the librarian turns to one of the union lists to find the closest library where the magazine may be borrowed or the article copied. However, not all locations are given for a magazine. This has led to the development of regional, state, and even citywide periodical union lists. A regional list is composed of holdings of libraries in the immediate vicinity. Borrowing is easier and faster from a neighbor than from a distant library located via *New Serial Titles.* Ongoing and older local and regional union lists are found in Sheehy, Walford, and the *American Reference Books Annual.* The most frequently used lists are those published at the local, regional, or state level. These are known to any librarian who is in the least involved with periodicals.

Dealing with distinctive bits of data, union lists are a favorite target of computer-assisted systems. For example, the *Berkeley Serials Union List* (Berkeley, California: University of California) includes 210,000 titles of 41 libraries on the Berkeley campus. It is updated and published every month on some 40 microfiche cards. There is also a frequently revised 10-volume *Serials Keyword Index,* again made possible by automation of records.

---

[16] There is no entirely satisfactory definition of "serial." Generally, it can be considered an umbrella term for any publication issued in parts published over an indefinite period of time. The two basic types of serials are periodicals and newspapers, but there are many other varieties which are considered. For a discussion of this point, see William Katz and Peter Gellatly, *Guide to Magazine and Serial Agents* (New York: R. R. Bowker Company, 1975), pp. 4–7.

The librarian searching for a periodical published before 1950 will turn to the basic unit in the periodical union lists, the *Union List of Serials in Libraries of the United States and Canada*. Here, alphabetically listed by title, are 156,499 serial titles held by 956 libraries in the United States and Canada. As defined by the compilers of this reference work, as with *New Serial Titles*, the primary meaning of "serial" is a periodical. Newspapers are not included nor are government publications, except for some periodicals and monographic series. As many serials change name, numerous cross-references to the main entry give complete bibliographical information on the title. Serials published in all countries are included.[17]

If a serial has been issued after 1950 but before 1971, the next place to look is *New Serial Titles, 1950–1970*. The 21-year cumulation contains the same type of basic bibliographic data as found in the basic *Union List*. The number of serials listed for only 21 years is almost half again the number of the basic list—220,000 titles held by 800 United States and Canadian libraries, with the addition of International Standard Serial Numbers (ISSN) and country codes. There is, also, a separate listing of cessations.

For information after 1970, the librarian should turn to the monthly, quarterly, and annual *New Serial Titles*. Here the full address of the publisher is usually given. (In the cumulations only the place of publication is generally indicated.) Also, the annual sales price is usually indicated.

Just as *The National Union Catalog* cannot be used for subject approach to books before 1950 (when a separate subject service began), neither can it be used with periodicals. There is no subject entry to the *Union List of Serials*. However, there is a subject guide to *New Serial Titles*, and the 1950–1970 set arranges the 220,000 titles in a modified Dewey Decimal order of about 255 broad subject headings.[18] Bibliographical information is given for each entry (usually the title, name of publisher, and ISSN number), although locations are not given. For this information, one must turn back to *New Serial Titles*.

The ongoing *New Serial Titles* also has a separate and twin publication to help with subjects, *New Serial Titles—Classed Subject Arrangement*, which begins with 1955. Lack of cumulations after 1970 makes this a difficult tool to use, and it would be much more valuable if it were combined with *New Serial Titles* as a subject index.

Turning from union lists to trade bibliographies, one finds that the approximate equivalent to *Books in Print* for periodicals is *Ulrich's Interna-*

---

[17] This sometimes confuses beginners. The list shows *holdings* of only American and Canadian libraries. The list *includes* titles *published* in most, but not all, countries and languages.

[18] The introductory material to *New Serial Titles, 1950–1970: Subject Guide* is worthwhile reading because it gives specific data on problems of compiling such a work as well as techniques employed in the compilation of bibliographies.

tional Periodical Directory. Revised and updated every two years or so, it provides bibliographical information to close to 60,000 periodicals. Unlike *Books in Print,* it is not limited to American publishers, but includes titles from around the world. The titles are arranged alphabetically under about 250 broad subject headings, and there is a title index. A separate listing is provided for titles which have ceased publication since the last edition of the directory.

Reference librarians use *Ulrich's* to locate such basic information about a periodical as the address of the publisher, frequency of issue, year first published, and price. The problem is that information is dated almost as soon as the volume is published—a fault which of course cannot be overcome as long as periodical publishers change prices, names, locations, etc., with alarming frequency.[19] A related title which lists 62,500 American and Canadian periodicals is *The Standard Periodical Dictionary* (New York: Oxbridge Communications, 1977, 5th ed.). While limited to the United States and Canada, it includes thousands of house organs, newsletters, descriptive notes, etc., not listed in *Ulrich's.*

In addition to using *Ulrich's* for bibliographical data about a title, or *New Serial Titles* for location of a serial, there are several reference questions related to these and other serial aids:

(1) What are the *basic* periodicals in chemistry, geography, art, needlework, etc.? Since *Ulrich's* and *New Serial Titles* have a subject approach, one can at least isolate old and new titles in subject areas. However, in both cases the lists are no more selective than *Subject Guide to Books in Print* and therefore are questionable selection aids, particularly as neither has annotations. For more specific results the librarian should turn to selection tools such as *Magazines for Libraries* (W. A. Katz and Berry Gargal, New York: R. R. Bowker Company, 1978, 3d ed.) or other annotated specialized lists, such as *Periodicals for School Libraries* (Chicago: American Library Association, 1977, 2d ed.) and Darlene Arnold's and Kenneth O. Doyle's *Education/Psychology Journals: A Scholar's Guide* (Metuchen, New Jersey: Scarecrow Press, 1975).

(2) Where is *Time,* or *Ocean Engineering,* or *Indiana Slavic Studies* indexed? Such a question may be asked when the librarian or the user knows a particular periodical title is likely to give an answer to a query. For example, someone asks about current prices of antique bottles. The librar-

---

[19] A considerable help is the new quarterly supplement to *Ulrich's,* issued in March, June, September, and December. The supplement follows the same pattern as the main volume. Related to *Ulrich's* is another R. R. Bowker publication, *Irregular Serials and Annuals,* which is updated every two or three years. The 1976 fourth edition, following the pattern of *Ulrich's,* lists 30,000 titles which are published irregularly.

ian either knows, or discovers through checking *Ulrich's,* that an answer is likely to be found in *The Antique Trader, Hobbies,* or *Antique Monthly,* to name only three possibilities. (Of course, one could look for a book on the subject via the card catalog, *Subject Guide to Books in Print,* etc.) Given this much of a lead, the librarian has to know where one or all of the periodicals are indexed. Sources:

(a) The traditional source is *Ulrich's,* which lists one to four indexes or abstracting services for many, although not all, titles. However, *Ulrich's* analyzes only the basic services, and then not always well.[20]

(b) A useful addition to *Ulrich's* is Joseph Marconi's *Indexed Periodicals* (Ann Arbor, Michigan: Pierian Press, 1976). This volume lists, in alphabetical order by title, some 11,000 periodicals which have been indexed in major services. Usually two to four basic indexes are cited for each entry. No effort is made to be comprehensive (only 33 basic indexes are analyzed), and as a result, numerous indexes and abstracting services are not listed—particularly those of a specialized nature. On the other hand, within its scope the service is excellent, and of tremendous value in most libraries.

(c) *Chicorel's Index Abstracting and Indexing Services* (New York: Chicorel Library Publishing Corporation, 1974, 2 vols.) lists in alphabetical order 3 times the number of periodicals found in *Indexed Periodicals* and indicates, again, basic abstracts and indexing services in which they are listed. Scientific and technological titles are covered only if they are indexed in standard social science and humanities services.

Aside from lack or even near total coverage of indexes and abstracts, none of the above indicates whether the service indexes the title on a selective or on a complete basis.[21] Aside from more esoteric, specialized titles, the librarian who is familiar with the indexes and abstracts in her or his library can at least hazard a safe guess that a query dealing, for example, with education will be in an education index, a query on business in *Business Periodicals Index,* etc.

---

[20] Elliot S. Palais, "References to Indexes and Abstracts in *Ulrich's,* . . ." *RQ,* Fall 1974, pp. 34–35. In the fifteenth edition (1973–1974), the author found "a total of seventy-one index references for twenty-five journals," but *Ulrich's* missed 101 references to indexes for the 25 as well as 107 to indexes which *Ulrich's* did not analyze. Lesson: If *Ulrich's* does not include an index for a title, this does not necessarily mean the title is not indexed or abstracted.

[21] Lack of truly adequate coverage of where periodicals are indexed or abstracted may dismay librarians, although the reason for the lack is economical. To do a complete listing of services and titles listed would result in a massive, expensive volume (or volumes) of limited interest to all but the largest general libraries. The problem may be overcome via a machine-readable data base, or in another nonprint format.

Newspapers

> *American Newspapers, 1821–1936* . . . reprint. Millwood, New York: Kraus Reprint Company, 1970, 791 pp. $75.
>
> *Ayer Directory of Publications* (Formerly *N. W. Ayer & Son's Directory of Newspapers and Periodicals*). Philadelphia: Ayer Press, 1880 to date, annual. $54.

As neither the *Union List of Serials* nor *New Serial Titles* includes newspapers, how does one locate American newspapers in a given library? The answer before 1936 is *American Newspapers*. After 1936, and assuming the wanted newspaper is still being published, one may turn to the *Ayer Directory* to locate the city or town likely to have a run of the newspapers, usually in the local library.

The lack of a national union list may be accounted for as follows:

1. In the United States at least, the number of newspapers has tended to decrease. There were 2461 dailies in 1916; today, there are no more than 1750 and the number is shrinking. The control problem, therefore, is nowhere near the control problem regarding magazines which, worldwide, now number over 100,000.

2. Current newspapers are filed, often indexed, and microformed by the state and by larger cities; therefore, locating them, or parts of them, for interlibrary loan is usually a simple matter.[22]

3. Lacking indexes to all but the largest newspapers, access is limited and demand is small for given newspapers of a given date on any national or international scale. (The local newspapers may be indexed and used locally or regionally, but seldom nationally.) For these and other reasons, the need for an up-to-date newspaper union list has never been pressing.

The location of American newspapers prior to 1821 is found in Clarence S. Brigham's *History and Bibliography of American Newspapers, 1690–1820* (Worcester, Massachusetts: American Antiquarian Society, 1947, 2 vols.). The list is not chronologically complete; where research is being done in a given geographical area, it is wise to check with libraries for local union lists of holdings of newspapers not included in the two major union lists.

The approximate equivalent to *Books in Print* and *Ulrich's* for newspa-

---

[22] A type of union list in that it locates microform masters of newspapers, both domestic and foreign, is: U.S. Library of Congress, *Newspapers in Microform, 1948–1972* (Washington, D.C.: Library of Congress, 1974; 1973 to date, annual). In addition to reporting on new titles, the annual series lists additional library locations for numerous items previously reported in the base set. Also, three times a year the Library of Congress issues *Newspaper and Gazette Report* on various aspects of newspapers, microform, and collections.

pers is the *Ayer Directory of Publications*. It gives relatively complete information (from circulation and price to names of writers and editors) on daily, weekly, monthly, and less frequently published newspapers in the United States and Canada, as well as Puerto Rico, the Virgin Islands, the Bahamas, Bermuda, Panama, and the Philippines. Arrangement is geographical, first by state or province, then by city or town. Preceding each geographical section there is valuable reference material, including 69 clearly printed maps showing where the newspapers are published, market and economic data for each city and town, plus summaries of population, agriculture, industry, etc. This "bonus" makes *Ayer* a popular reference aid where the library (1) needs up-to-date information on a state or community that is not found in an almanac, encyclopedia, etc.; or (2) does not have the much more detailed *Rand McNally Commercial Atlas and Marketing Guide*. Classified indexes provide ready access to the publications by subject, type, name, editors, etc.

In addition to newspapers, *Ayer* lists periodicals geographically by state, province, and territory. The reference librarian thus has a handy way of answering questions about the magazines and newspapers published in X community, the interests they represent, the existence of any foreign-language publications in the area, etc. (Also, for the would-be writer who wants to find a local publication, *Ayer* is of help.) Listing close to 23,000 titles of both newspapers and periodicals, *Ayer* is a good backup reference work for *Ulrich's*, at least for United States, Canadian, and some territorial titles.[23]

A useful guide for the reference librarian working with newspapers is: Grace D. Parch, *Directory of Newspaper Libraries in the U.S. and Canada* (New York: Special Libraries Association, 1976, 336 pp.). The directory provides data on 297 newspaper libraries arranged geographically. When a reference librarian has to refer someone to a newspaper library, the guide is a must in that it describes the collections and indicates the services available to outsiders.

Pamphlets

Vertical File Index. New York: The H. W. Wilson Company, 1935 to date, monthly. $14.

---

[23] Basic guides for newspapers (and some periodicals) outside of America are: *Newspaper Press Directory, Benn's Guide to Newspapers and Periodicals of the World* (London: Benn Brothers, 1846 to date, annual) and *Willing's Press Guide* (London: Willing, 1874 to date, annual). There are, also, special press directories covering everything from black newspapers to alternative newspapers listed in Sheehy, *ARBA*, etc.

A pamphlet is understood to be a publication of a few printed leaves, normally bound in paper. *The Weekly Record* does not list pamphlets "under 49 pages," and such works are rarely included in the standard trade bibliographies.

Individual libraries tend to classify pamphlets in terms of those important to rebind and catalog separately and those ephemeral enough to warrant no more than placement in a vertical file under an appropriate subject.

Recognizing the failure of most general trade bibliographies to list pamphlets, the Wilson Company has a bibliography devoted solely to this form. Issued monthly except in August, *Vertical File Index* is a subject approach to a select group of pamphlets. Selection is based on their probable use for the general library, not for the special, technical library.

Each entry includes the standard bibliographical information and a short descriptive note of content. A title index follows the subject list. Wilson does not recommend any of the works, many of which are distributed by companies and organizations for advertising and propaganda purposes.

One of the headaches of ordering pamphlets is that they must be purchased from the publisher. No general book jobber will bother handling them. A free pamphlet may involve many dollars' worth of paperwork and time on the part of a librarian or clerk.[24]

BIBLIOGRAPHIES: NONPRINT MATERIALS

Nonprint is not a precise descriptor. It has come to mean any communication material other than the traditional book, periodical, and newspaper. Nonprint is closely associated with linked terms such as the "new media," "multimedia," "nonbook," and other expressions which indicate new approaches to reference work in particular, and library service in general.

A good deal of this byplay with descriptors is trendy and fashionable, so much so that one can never be sure that today's descriptor will be tomorrow's acceptable term. Be that as it may, in the late 1970s nonprint materials are an essential part of reference service, particularly in school libraries, or, as they are called, "school media centers" or "learning centers."[25]

---

[24] Information on vertical files is sparse, but articles do appear from time to time, e.g., Kathryn Schultz, "The Development of a Vertical File," *California School Libraries,* Summer 1977, pp. 16–25.

[25] Terms used to describe this service in schools may vary from "school library" to "instructional materials center," "learning resources center," "instructional media center," "library media center," "system media center," and "audio-visual center," but these names do not exhaust the terminology.

When working with resources other than books, the reference librarian functions much as when working with the traditional media:

1. In schools, universities, and colleges, the librarian will be called upon by the teacher for information on media that are available not only in the library, but also that may be ordered, or even borrowed from other libraries.
2. The students will want information and advice about multimedia for the primary learning process.
3. The layperson's needs will be somewhat similar, although here one suspects most of the emphasis will be on advice about likely films, recordings, etc., within the library which may extend one's knowledge (or recreational interests) beyond the traditional book.

The reference librarian should be at least conversant with the basic bibliographies and control devices for the new media. Knowledge of bibliographies and sources is important for answering questions directly dealing with audio-visual materials: "Where can I find such and such a catalog of films, records, tapes?" "Do you have anything on film that will illustrate this or that?" "What do you have pertaining to local history on recordings or film?" In large libraries such questions might be referred to the proper department, but in small and medium-sized libraries, the questions usually will have to be answered by the reference librarian.

In a breakdown of what constitutes nonprint materials, Jean Weihs offers the following designations:

Audiorecord	Includes sound recordings of all types: disc, tape, wire, roll.
Chart	Includes flip chart, wall chart.
Computer record	Includes all machine-readable data files (quite possibly, this designation will be changed shortly to machine-readable data file).
Diorama	
Filmstrip	Includes filmslip.
Flashcard	
Game	
Globe	
Kit	Consists of two or more media, all significant but not fully interdependent.
Map	
Microform	Includes aperture card, microfilm, microfiche, micro-opaque.

Microscope slide

Model   May include relief model, though relief model may be included under "Map." The final decision has not been made.

Motion picture   Includes motion picture loop.

Picture   Includes photograph, art original, art print, art reproduction, study print.

Realia   Includes specimen, sample. This medium designation may be changed to "Specimen."

Slide   Includes stereoscope slide.

Transparency

Videorecord   Includes videotape, videocassette, videodisc, electronic video recording.[26]

The divisions indicate the range of possibilities of nonprint materials.[27] Each medium has its own bibliographies, guides, indexes, reviews, annuals, etc. A glance at the basic overall guides and bibliographies which consider all the media as a whole, not just as single, distinct parts, is sufficient for the beginner. If one wishes more detail, with subject bibliography, one must specialize.

Guides and bibliographies[28]

Wynar, Christine, L. *Guide to Reference Books for School Media Centers.* Littleton, Colorado: Libraries Unlimited, Inc., 1973, 473 pp. Paper, $10. *1974–1975 Supplement,* 1976, 131 pp. $8.

Rutsvold, Margaret. *Guides to Educational Media.* 4th ed. Chica-

[26] Jean R. Weihs, "The Standardization of Cataloging Rules for Nonbook Materials: A Progress Report—April 1972," *Library Resources & Technical Services,* Summer 1972, pp. 313–314.

[27] See also *Media Programs: District and School* (Chicago: American Library Association, 1975). The official standards give specific recommendations for types of materials, personnel, facilities, etc. In so doing, they offer a concise overview of elementary through secondary school media programs. The ALA has similar standards for public libraries. See, too: *Nonprint Media in Academic Libraries* (Chicago: American Library Association, 1975), a collection of articles on the subject.

[28] There are numerous texts about nonprint materials and the library. Among the titles are: F. E. Kaiser (ed.), *Handling Special Materials in Libraries* (New York: Special Libraries Association, 1974); Emanuel Prostano, *The School Library Media Center,* 2d ed. (Littleton, Colorado: Libraries Unlimited, Inc., 1977). A useful annual summary is given in *Educational Media Yearbook* (New York: R. R. Bowker Company, 1973 to date) which also includes directory data.

go: American Library Association, 1977, 125 pp. Paperback, $5.

Wellisch, Hans. *Nonbook Materials: A Bibliography of Recent Publications.* College Park, Maryland: University of Maryland, College of Library and Information Services, 1975, 131 pp. Paperback, $5.

National Information Center for Educational Media. *NICEM Media Indexes.* Los Angeles: University of Southern California, National Information Center, 1967 to date. Various services, prices.

Audiovisual Market Place. New York: R. R. Bowker Company, 1964 to date, annual. $19.95.

There are no entirely satisfactory bibliographies for all nonprint materials—no *Books in Print,* no *Cumulative Book Index,* no *National Union Catalog.* And even the by-now standard bibliographies leave much to be wanted in organization and in coverage. Lacking overall bibliographical control the materials are difficult to track. The lack of such tools accounts in no small way for the development of media experts who are familiar with the many access routes, routes which the average harrassed reference librarian has neither the time nor the inclination to follow.

There are guides which at least indicate the dimensions of the materials available. One is Wynar's *Guide to Reference Books for School Media Centers.* Most of the guide is given over to critical annotations of reference books suitable for kindergarten through grade 12. However, the first section on "media sources" is useful for both school and nonschool libraries, as are the scattered annotations of "media selection" aids throughout the work. Moreover, this guide has the advantage of biennial supplements and analytical annotations as well as frequent references to reviews of the titles being examined.

Another guide with annotated listings of titles useful in media centers is Carolyn Sue Peterson's *Reference Books for Elementary and Junior High School Libraries,* 2d ed. (Metuchen, New Jersey: Scarecrow Press, 1975). While there is no separate section on media sources, many of the titles, arranged by broad subject and form, are suitable for the grades served by this quite good compilation. Media titles may be located through the index.

The best single guide to bibliographies and media publishers' catalogs in this field is *Guides to Educational Media.* Arranged alphabetically by title of a published catalog, the guide clearly identifies each of the catalogs and annotates it in such a way to indicate audience, scope, number of entries, and special features. Close to 300 bibliographies on films, instructional materials, slides, videotapes, and the like are included. Entries are listed in an author, subject, and title index.

There are other general guides which profess to guide but generally only list with less than critical consideration everything in sight. During the past 10 years there has been a mass of bibliographies and guides. Few of them are worth mentioning. The librarian should be careful in purchasing such titles. The amount of rubbish and duplication is amazing.

There are partial guides, and *Nonbook Materials* has the advantage of relative currency, useful descriptive annotations to both books and periodical articles, and a good arrangement of citations under subject headings. However, this publication is more a background reading list compiled by students than it is a true guide. A useful collection of 45 articles will be found in Deidre Boyle's *Expanding Media* (New York and Phoenix: Neal Schuman/Oryx Press, 1977, 340 pp.).

When one turns to bibliographies, the closest thing to *Books in Print* for audio-visual materials is the *NICEM Media Indexes.* The purpose of these indexes, which are really bibliographies, is to provide noncritical information on what is available in nonprint materials. And, although directed at elementary and secondary school needs, a good deal of the data is applicable for other types of libraries. Hence, it can be used to answer such queries as: What transparencies are available for geography? What educational films are here on animals? Environmental studies? And so on.

The *NICEM Indexes* are really a series of individual bibliographies, and *not* a single alphabetical subject/title index to the media. In early 1978 the indexes listed over a half-million items in the following fields: 16 mm films (4 vols.); 35 mm filmstrips (2 vols.); audio tapes; video tapes; records; 8 mm motion cartridges; overhead transparencies (2 vols.); and slides. In addition to listings by form, the indexes include subject approaches with multimedia listings (recordings, films, etc.) for psychology, health and safety education, vocational and technical education, environmental studies, and free educational multimedia materials.

The volumes are arranged in different ways, although essentially each has separate subject and title indexes. Some volumes include directories of producers and distributors, and a separate volume is given over entirely to this type of directory information. Each entry gives essential information for tracking or ordering. While this is the single best bibliographical guide available to all the nonbook media, it has several drawbacks: (1) The lists are usually two or more years behind; (2) the subject headings are less than satisfactory and there are not enough cross-references; (3) the items are usually annotated, but the information is noncritical and of little help in selection; (4) the data are not always accurate. The reason for much of the difficulty is familiar enough: lack of funds.[29] The indexes are a product of the nonprofit National Information Center for Educational Media.

[29] And lack of profit. There have been several private efforts to index nonbook materials, but none has succeeded, e.g., *Educational Media Index* (New York: The McGraw-Hill Book Company, 1964, 14 vols.) failed to continue.

A more limited bibliography often found in libraries is the *Educator Guides* (Randolph, Wisonsin: Educators Progress Service, 1934 to date, annual, various prices). The unique feature is that all items listed are free. Each annual edition is totally revised and carries descriptive annotations for most items. The formats include film, filmstrips, and tapes; among the topics are guidance, social studies, science, and health curriculum materials. The guides are an accurate, valuable source of answers to queries put by teachers as well as members of the community seeking free support materials for talks, lectures, or programs.

The *NICEM Indexes,* and especially the volume on producers and distributors, give information on who sells what. A more thorough listing is offered in the annual *Audiovisual Market Place,* which claims some 4500 listings under 25 subject headings.[30] The librarian looking for information, say, on overhead projector manufacturers, distributors of films, or sources of slides will find the needed data under the subject or via a detailed index. A third section, of less use, includes periodicals, reference books, and a calendar of events. A related title is the *North American Film and Video Directory* (New York: R. R. Bowker Company, 1976, 400 pp.), which geographically lists 2000 libraries and gives vital information on types, size, budgets, personnel, etc., of their media collections.

Indexes to reviews

> *Media Review Digest.* Ann Arbor, Michigan: The Pierian Press, 1970 to date, annual. 2 vols. $79.50.

A type of *Book Review Index* for films, videotapes, filmstrips, records, tapes, and other miscellaneous media, *Media Review Digest (MRD),* until 1974 called *Multi Media Reviews Index,* analyzes reviews of the media appearing in over 150 periodicals. The 50,000 or so reviews are then indexed, with full citations, by type of medium reviewed. Some excerpts from reviews are given and an evaluative sign shows whether the review was favorable or not. Its use by a librarian is almost the same as for the indexes to book reviews, i.e., to check out reviews, probably for purposes of buying or renting a given item. The information provided is full, and often includes descriptions of the material as well as cataloging information. The service has the major drawback of lack of timeliness. While one supplement a year is provided, it is late and the time lag is considerable. More timely is the *International Index to Multi-Media Information* (Pasadena, Califor-

---

[30] *Index to Instructional Media Catalogs* (New York: R. R. Bowker Company, 1974, 272 pp.). Revised frequently, this is an index to catalogs issued by some 650 publishers or producers frequently listed in the *Audiovisual Market Place.* It is broken down under 150 subject headings with some 30,000 items listed in total.

nia: Audio Visual Associates, 1970 to date, quarterly), but this includes reviews from only 110 periodicals. It has a subject index, gives prices not found in the *MRD,* and includes more review extracts. It lacks the full bibliographical information of the *Media Review Digest.*

Microform

> *Guide to Microforms in Print.* Weston, Conn.: Microform Review, 1961 to date, annual. $35.
>
> *Books on Demand.* Ann Arbor, Michigan: University Microfilms, 1975 to date, annual. 3 vols., $73.50.

Although the nonprint media are normally associated with schools, many years ago microform established itself as a major nonprint source for all types of libraries and situations. Microfilm, microfiche, and printouts are as familiar to library users as the books, periodicals, and newspapers which often find their way to being preserved and/or republished as microform.

It is unlikely that in answering queries, the librarian will look for microform per se as might be done for films, recordings, etc. So why is it necessary to have a bibliography of microforms? Primarily for purposes of acquisition of out-of-print titles, works published in no other form, or those possibly issued in both a printed form and a microform.

The *Books in Print* of microform is the ever expanding *Guide to Microforms in Print.* It alphabetically lists over 60,000 titles from some 200 publishers, including international firms. Not all microforms are listed, as, for example, theses and dissertations. Another approach by the same company is *Subject Guide to Microforms in Print.*

For ongoing microforms the publisher issues *Microform Review* (1972 to date, quarterly), which includes news of the field and detailed, critical reviews of more expensive microform publications. This publication is augmented by *Microlist* (1975 to date, monthly), which updates *Guide to Microforms in Print* with an alphabetical listing of new microforms.

Microform is employed in a library for many reasons, one of the most frequent being its use as a substitute for book or other form of printed material which is no longer in print, no longer available from a used-book dealer, or so prohibitive in cost as to make microform perferable. It would require a chapter alone to explain how librarians find out-of-print materials, but one approach is suggested by *Books on Demand.* This is a multivolume author, title, and subject catalog of about 100,000 out-of-print titles which may be purchased literally "on demand." The titles are available on microfilm or as hard copy xerographic prints of the microform at an average cost of $6 to $15, depending on the number of pages.

Other companies offer similar services as well as standard reprints of titles which the publisher thinks will be in sufficient demand. The reprints usually are listed in *Books in Print* as well as in a number of specialized guides, such as *International Bibliography of Reprints* (New York: R. R. Bowker Company, 1976–1977, 2 vols.). The first volume is an author and title listing of reprints; the second is a title list of annuals and periodicals.

BIBLIOGRAPHY OF BIBLIOGRAPHIES

Bibliographic Index: A Cumulative Bibliography of Bibliographies. New York: The H. W. Wilson Company, 1937 to date, triannual with cumulations. Service basis.

A bibliography of bibliographies is, as the name suggests, a listing of bibliographies. One may find a bibliography on dogs at the end of a periodical article, an encyclopedia essay, or as part of a book on pets. If one lists these three bibliographies and adds a dozen to a thousand more, one has a bibliography of bibliographies—in this case a listing of bibliographies, from various sources, about dogs. (In turn, each of the bibliographies constitutes a subject bibliography.)

The primary example of a bibliography of bibliographies is *Bibliographic Index*. Under numerous headings, one may find bibliographies about subjects, persons, and places. The entries represent (1) separate published books and pamphlets which are normally bibliographies in a specific subject area, e.g., *East European and Soviet Economic Affairs: A Bibliography* . . .; (2) bibliographies which are parts of books and pamphlets, such as the bibliography which appears at the end of David Kunzle's book *The Early Comic Strip*; and (3) bibliographies which have been published separately or in articles in some 2200 English- and foreign-language periodicals. Emphasis is on American publications, and to be listed, a bibliography must contain more than 50 citations.

The inevitable catch to many reference works is applicable here: (1) the bibliographies are not listed until from six months to a year after they are published, and (2) while books, and to a lesser degree pamphlets, are well covered, the index cannot be trusted to include many periodical bibliographies. Why? Because there are over 55,000 periodicals issued, often with bibliographies, and the index includes only 2200.[31] The result is that the *Bibliographic Index* is usually a beginning point for the subject expert, or,

---

[31] There are two other difficulties with this aid when used by experts: It is primarily limited to English-language works; and there is no indication as to whether the bibliography is selective or comprehensive, or whether annotations are included. Experts, particularly those

most likely, a way for the expert to check to see whether anything has been missed in the mining of more detailed sources. The general user is likely to find all that he or she needs in the way of bibliographies in the card catalog, *Subject Guide to Books in Print,* a subject index such as *Music Index,* or other general sources in the library. For the person between the expert and the generalist, *Bibliographic Index* is useful for finding hard-to-locate materials on lesser known personalities and subjects.

A point to remember about any bibliography of bibliographies is that it is twice removed from the subject. Once a bibliography is located in *Bibliographic Index,* the next step is to find the bibliography itself. After that, still another step is required: the location of the particular article or book listed in the bibliography. At any point along the way, the user may be frustrated by not finding what is listed in the index, of if finding it, by not being able to locate the desired information in the bibliography. With these stumbling blocks, it is no wonder that many reference librarians favor more direct sources.

Types of materials listed, along with the frequent difficulty in locating the final needed title, tend to restrict more limited bibliographies of bibliographies to specialists. The classic case in point is Theodore Besterman's *A World Bibliography of Bibliographies,* 4th ed. (Lausanne: Societias Bibliographica, 1965–1967, 5 vols.). This fourth edition examines 17,000 separately collated volumes of bibliography in 40 languages published from the fifteenth century through 1963. Material is arranged alphabetically under 16,000 subject headings.[32] Besterman's bibliography is being updated through a series of augmented reprints, for example, *A World Bibliography of African Bibliographies.* Revised and brought up to date by J. D. Pearson (Totowa, New Jersey: Rowman and Littlefield, 1975), Pearson includes the 1136 bibliographies on Africa from the original set and adds about as many more published from 1963 to 1973. Similar volumes are planned for other sections of the world.

Library bibliographies

Librarians and those who work in related organizations, from library schools to information centers, seem constantly to be preparing bibliographies on subjects of interest to their users. Some of these are no more than

---

familiar with other languages, tend to use *Bibliographic Index* in conjunction with *Bibliographische Berichte* (Frankfort Main: Klostermann, 1959 to date, quarterly).

[32] Edward Carter, "Historical Studies in Documentation," *Journal of Documentation,* March 1977, pp. 79–87. An informative sketch of the life and work of Besterman.

short reading lists of the "best of" type; others are specialized bibliographies generated by a search or series of searches for users. An ongoing three- to five-page title listing of such bibliographies (with sources for ordering) will be found in "Bibliography Bargains," a quarterly feature of *RQ*, the American Library Association's journal for reference librarians. A more ambitious effort is *Library Bibliographies and Indexes* (Detroit: Gale Research Company, 1975, 301 pp.). Organized under some 1500 subject headings, it lists bibliographies and indexes compiled by libraries, information centers, library schools, and library associations in the United States and Canada. "As a rough rule of thumb, works are included normally when they cover 40 or more entries. Materials of only local concern are excluded, as are generalized readings lists." The subject headings are often too broad and the compiler chose to include bibliographies from such massive organizations as the National Library of Medicine (ably represented in many other places). Despite the flaws, it is a useful addition to the literature of bibliographies of bibliographies.[33]

SUGGESTED READING

Brown, James, "New Media in Public Libraries," *Wilson Library Bulletin*, November 1976, pp. 232–240. A well-written summary of media programs from videotapes to other nonbook materials is highlighted. The article points up the necessity for having up-to-date bibliographies which cover the various media.

Carter, Edward J., "Theodore Besterman: A Personal Memoir," *Journal of Documentation*, March 1977, pp. 79–87. A tribute to the compiler of the *World Bibliography of Bibliographies*, who died in 1976. Good because it illustrates that there is more than a computer behind the world's standard bibliographies.

Diaz, Albert (ed.), *Microforms in Libraries: A Reader*. Weston, Connecticut: Microform Review, 1975. Collection of 41 articles about microforms under six broad categories: introduction, organization, bibliographic control, applications, standards, user reactions. Contains nothing on computer output microfilm, ultrafiche, or library catalogs on microform.

Foskett, D. J., "Theory and Practice in the Presentation of Information," *International Federation for Documentation*, December 1975, pp. 5–9. A clear analysis of the difficulties with the control of information via the standard bibliographic forms. The author considers various types of information and knowledge.

Francis, Frank, "The American Record," *The Times Literary Supplement*, February 6, 1976, p. 141. A history and description of the *NUC—Pre-1956 Imprints*. The concise, clear explanation is ideal for beginning students and for laypersons.

---

[33] Librarians as publishers and/or compilers of bibliographies of bibliographies, union lists, catalogs, etc., are the central concern of Robert Downs's *American Library Resources: A Bibliographical Guide, Supplement, 1961–1970* (Chicago: American Library Association, 1972). This lists and annotates more than 3400 library catalogs, union lists, archives, bibliographies, and other library-produced listings, including numerous library school and classroom guides to reference works.

Kane, Leslie, "Reference Sources in Film, Television and Radio," *Reference Services Review*, January/March 1977, pp. 11–19. Introductory material, 22 titles with long critical annotations, and a bibliography make up this review article. A useful checklist for libraries with media collections.

Olson, Paul E., "The Union Catalog—Its Cost versus Its Benefit to a Network," *Special Libraries*, May/June 1976, pp. 251–255. While a cost analysis of a 43-library Midwest Medical Union catalog, the study is equally valuable for its insights into union catalogs and interlibrary loan operations, and particularly for its recommendation that the catalog eventually be replaced by computerized data bases.

Rogers, David, "The Revision of the STC," *The Times Literary Supplement*, August 27, 1976, p. 1061. A lengthy review of the *Short Title Catalogue of Books Printed in England, Scotland. . . .* begun by Pollard and Redgrave, carried on by Wing, and under revision. The reviewer considers problems with this and all such reference works.

Scott, Edith, "The Evolution of Bibliographic Systems in the United States, 1876–1945," *Library Trends*, July 1976, pp. 293–310; and Markuson, Barbara, "Bibliographic Systems, 1945–1976," ibid., pp. 311–328. The two articles not only trace the history of bibliography, but point up the problems of bibliographical control and discuss some of the basic works in the field. *Library Trends*, January 1977, is devoted to "Trends in Bibliographic Control: International Issues."

U.S. Department of Health, Education, and Welfare, Education Division, *A Handbook of Standard Terminology . . . About Educational Technology*. Washington, D.C.: Government Printing Office, 1975. "Provides assistance in the form of standardized terms and definitions," and in 275 pages (including an index) shows the relationship among those terms. An extremely useful dictionary and guide for anyone trying to get through the mush of nonprint terminology.

SOURCES OF
INFORMATION

PART

III

CHAPTER FOUR

Indexing and
Abstracting Services

 T HERE IS NO more familiar reference form than the index. Used daily by all librarians and numerous laypersons, it is truly the heart of any information retrieval system. The index, whether it be a separate guide to periodical articles or part of a book, is used to locate specific pieces or bits of information in a larger unit. Most indexes are easy enough to understand, and the beginner's primary challenge is to isolate and identify those most commonly used in the reference process.

Abstracting services are an extension of indexes. They perform the same function as an index in locating and recording the contents of a periodical, book, and various types of documents. They differ from an index in that (1) by definition, they include a summary of the material indexed; (2) they tend to be confined to relatively narrow subject areas; and (3) the arrangement rarely follows the single author, subject, and sometimes title alphabetical arrangement of an index. Usually an abstracting service is arranged by subject, or by accession numbers, or by issuing bodies, or by some other system. The whole is tied together by various separate indexes. Abstracting services sometimes require the use of a thesaurus or separate subject listing when available in machine-readable form for computer-assisted retrieval.

Leaving aside the individual book index, a reference librarian is most likely to be concerned with the following types of traditional indexes:

1. Periodicals

   a. General indexes, covering many periodicals in a wide or specific subject field. *The Readers' Guide to Periodical Literature* is the most widely known of this type of index.

   b. Subject indexes, covering not only several periodicals, but also other material found in new books, pamphlets, reports, and government documents. The purpose is to index material in a narrow subject field. Examples of this type of index are the *Applied Science & Technology Index* and *Index Medicus.*

   c. Indexes to single magazines, either at the end of a volume or as separately published works. *The National Geographic Magazine Cumulative Index* is an example.

2. Newspapers

   There is limited newspaper indexing in the United States. Normally, this scarcity of indexing is made up for by individual libraries indexing local papers. Still, the best-known newspaper index is *The New York Times Index.*

3. Material in collections

   These indexes cover collections of poems, plays, fiction, songs, and so on. The *Speech Index* and *Granger's Index to Poetry* are examples.

4. Other indexes

   Here one might include everything from concordances to indexes of various forms from *Book Review Index,* to collections of quotations, to indexes to patents or music. Usually these indexes are treated by reference librarians in terms of the subject covered rather than as indexes per se.

Physical format

Among indexes found in libraries, the greatest number are in the familiar printed format. As one moves into abstracting services and more specialized indexes, the format changes. Several of the subject works are produced as hardbound books from machine-readable data bases. These computer-produced indexes and abstracts may differ in arrangement from the traditionally arranged index or abstract—often to serve the needs of the computer-aided production as much as to help the user.

There are two important points about indexes on machine-readable data bases: (1) Publishers who offer both printed and computer-based services are, in fact, offering two versions of the same index or abstract. What comes out at the computer terminal or on the television screen is drawn from the same data base as the published version of the index or abstract. Some data bases have added features not found in the printed version, particularly additional subject headings, but essentially the two forms are one and the same. (2) However, the computer-aided search of the index or abstract has the advantage over the manual search of the printed version in that (*a*) it is faster; (*b*) the search is usually more comprehensive; (*c*) important, "linked" subjects are not likely to be overlooked; (*d*) it is probably more up to date; and (*e*) in terms of effort and time, it may be less expensive, although this is debatable. The major drawback of the computer search of a data base is the same as for the manual search: Once a citation is located, the user must still find the full document text, usually in an elusive periodical.

Examples and a much more detailed analysis of what is sometimes called the electronic reference service will be found in Part II of the second volume of the text. Within this chapter, the reader should keep in mind that several of the printed indexes and abstracts are available also as data bases, e.g., ERIC (*Resources in Education* and *Current Index to Journals in Education*), *Psychological Abstracts, The New York Times Index,* and *America: History and Life,* to name only a few. On the other hand, as of now, the traditional and much-used H. W. Wilson indexes, from *The Readers' Guide to Periodical Literature* to *Art Index,* are available only in printed form, as are most of the generalized indexing services.

A combination of technology, jargon, and downright erroneous information has confused the issue of the electronic and the standard index or abstracting service. The librarian who hopes to search an index or an abstract with the help of a computer must learn the techniques of such searching, both intellectually and manually, that is, what keys to punch. On the other hand, the basic reference objective is precisely the same as when the librarian searches an abstract or index volume by volume, issue by issue, and that objective is maximum performance for the user.

EVALUATION

With the understanding that computer-based index and abstracting services (i.e., bibliographic data bases) should be evaluated as carefully as the traditional printed forms, although such evaluation is outside the scope of the present chapter, the reader is asked to move to consideration of standard printed sources.[1]

---

[1] Data-base format aside, much of what follows is equally applicable to machine-readable index or abstract services. Notes on evaluation of data bases will be found in the second volume of this text, *Reference Services and Reference Processes* (New York: McGraw-Hill Book Company, 1978).

There are some relative constants in the evaluation of indexes and abstracting services. They are:

1 The publisher

The most used indexes in all but special libraries are issued by The H. W. Wilson Company. The firm has an excellent reputation for producing easy-to-use, accurate indexes. One may argue with what is or is not included in one of these indexes, but the format and the depth of indexing are excellent. At the other extreme are the publishers of time-tested specialized and technical indexes such as *Science Citation Index*. In between are publishers about whom the librarian may know nothing, and who seem to be offering *(a)* a duplication of another service or *(b)* a questionable adventure into a new area. The librarian should check out the publisher, preferably by talking to subject experts and to other librarians, whose talents may not be mutually exclusive, and by reading reviews. Any or all of these safety checks will quickly reveal whom to trust and whom not to trust.

2 Scope

The most essential evaluative point about an index or an abstract is that of coverage. Neither the librarian nor the user will consult an index unless he or she thinks it adequately covers the periodicals—or other materials—in the field of interest. Here one must consider obvious points: *(a)* the number and kind of periodicals indexed, especially whether the number is adequate for the field, and whether the titles represent the best in the United States and, if necessary, abroad; *(b)* the inclusion of other material, since in some disciplines it will be necessary to consider not only periodicals, but reports, books, monographs, etc.

Few librarians or users are ever entirely contented that index or abstract X or Y is totally satisfactory in scope. In general or in large, undivided disciplines, there is always the nagging doubt that this or that journal (or type of book, or report, or other item) should be indexed rather than P or Q. In narrow, specialized subject areas, the question is usually resolved for the so-called core titles which everyone tends to agree are necessary, but arguments arise over what should be indexed in the fringe areas or in closely related disciplines.

3 Duplication and gaps

A decade or so ago, users complained of the lack of proper indexes or abstracts; but in the 1970s the same people are complaining about too many services. "The user is handicapped at present by the large number of abstracting services currently available—with a good deal of overlap in some areas and large gaps in others."[2] The key phrase is "large gaps" because each new index or abstract is published in the hope of filling those gaps, although, in the process, it tends to duplicate much of what is offered in an existing service. For example, two basic indexes for educators are *Education Index* and *Current Index to Journals in Education.* Of the titles indexed, close to 80 percent are found in both services. Timeliness, subject headings, abstracts or lack of them, and thoroughness of indexing vary among the services.

Ideally, index and abstract publishers would divide the disciplines in such a way that duplication of titles covered would be limited. They do not. Therefore, the librarian must always ask the key evaluative question: How much duplication exists between X and Y service, and is the difference so much (or so little) that X should be chosen over Y?

4   Depth of indexing

Indexing thoroughness varies considerably, and the publisher of a periodicals index should explain (but often does not) whether all articles in the relevant periodicals are indexed. Few indexes include short items, notices, announcements, etc., but reputable ones should at least cite the main articles in terms of subjects covered, authors, and possibly titles. In a survey of 10 political science services, one study found that only 3 of the services actually indexed all possible articles. Depth of indexing for other services ranged from a low of 4.20 percent to a high of 96 percent.[3]

5   Timeliness

The frequency of publication is a fair indication of the timeliness of the service. This yardstick is only fair because there are factors which cancel out publication frequency as a method of evaluation. For example, *The New York Times Index* is always two and sometimes three months behind in indexing the newspaper. For example, the December 29 issue of *The New York Times* will not be in index form and available for library use until at least the following March. Other indexes may be as much as a year or more behind.

In another situation, the index or abstract does reach the library within the calendar period announced on its cover. When one turns to the contents, one finds the material indexed is several weeks or months in

---

[2] Maurice Line, quoted in Elliot S. Palais, "The Significance of Dispersion for the Indexing of Political Science Journals," *The Journal of Academic Librarianship,* May 1976, p. 72.

[3] Palais, ibid., p. 75. The Palais study is a good example of necessary procedures for evaluating indexes and abstracts.

arrears of the date on the cover. For example, "the mean time lag for papers abstracted in *Library and Information Science Abstracts* was 3.8 months while that for *Library Literature* was 6.7 months." As they are both issued bimonthly, the difference is difficult to understand, particularly as the former must include time-consuming preparation for abstracts and is published in England. What may be an understatement was made by the authors of a study on the two services: "It was of some interest that it took longer to index domestically published articles in *Library Literature* than to abstract them abroad in *Library Science Abstracts*."[4]

The lag between the time the periodical appears and the time it is picked up in the index is easy to check. Compare a few dates of indexed articles with the date on the cover of the index or abstract.

How often, if at all, is the index cumulated? Is there an annual volume which cumulates the weekly, monthly, quarterly, or other issues? Are there 5-year, 10-year, or other cumulations? For purposes of retrospective searching, the necessity for frequent cumulations is apparent to anyone who has had to search laboriously through, say, the bimonthly issues of *Library Literature* before the annual or the two-year cumulation appears.

Infrequently issued indexes sometimes are a year or several years behind. They do not seem to have any consistent publishing pattern; for example, *The Middle East Record* published the 1968 index in 1973.

6 Format

Employing "format" as a grab-bag term, the index or abstract must be considered in terms of *(a)* arrangement, easy or difficult to understand or to use; *(b)* arrangement by alphabet, by subject, a classed form, or a citation form; *(c)* form, whether in dictionary form or in separate divisions by subject, author, title, etc.; *(d)* readability of format, a particularly important point when one considers indexes published via a computer printout; *(e)* completeness of the citation, with enough bibliographical information to identify the material and to locate it in the material indexed; and *(f)* accuracy of the bibliographical information.

7 Subject headings

The type, number, and form of subject headings used in an index or

---

[4] Mary R. Turtle and William C. Robinson, "The Relationship between Time Lags and Place of Publication . . .," *RQ*, Fall 1974, p. 28. The authors offer a methodology for checking time lags in indexes.

abstract are important. Many standard indexes rely upon the Library of Congress subject headings, or Sears. Conversely, indexes for specific disciplines may develop their own subject headings, rely upon key words in the title, or adopt a plan suitable for the material being indexed or abstracted. Regardless of what type of subject-heading system is employed, there should be adequate *see* and *see also* references, a thesaurus of subject terms, or both.

This brief paragraph only skims the most vexing problem of indexers, and one which has resulted in a considerable body of theoretical and practical literature. (See, for example, any issue of *The Indexer,* the official journal of The American Society of Indexers.)

8   Readability

When one turns to abstracts, there is the added dimension of their readability. One must ask whether the abstract adequately describes the document. The readability factor may be high or low, depending on how the abstracts were prepared (by the author of the indexed item, by the publisher, or by both—in other words, whether the author's abstract has been edited judiciously or by "automatic" methods such as key word scanning). Another consideration: Sometimes abstracts for the nonexpert "were more difficult to read than their source documents."[5]

In order truly to test an index for inclusion or exclusion in a library, a considerable amount of time and effort is required, as well as some expertise in comparative analysis. Consequently, the majority of librarians rely upon reviews, the advice of experts, or both—particularly when considering a specialized service. The benefit of learning evaluation techniques is as much to show the librarian how indexes or abstracts are (or should be) constructed as it is to reveal points for acceptance or rejection.

The best evaluative summary is suggested by users' attitudes toward indexes. Among the preferences shown by users:

(a) accuracy; *(b)* ease of use; *(c)* layout and presentation; *(d)* choice of subject index headings; *(e)* optimum use of cross references; *(f)* overall effectiveness in practical use; *(g)* minimum amount of "noise."[6]

[5] Rosemary King, "A Comparison of the Readability of Abstracts with their Source Documents," *Journal of the American Society of Information Science,* March/April 1976, pp. 118–121.

[6] K. Boodson, "Subject Bibliographies in Information Work," *The Indexer,* April 1976, p. 21. This is a good summary article on abstracts and indexes.

PERIODICAL INDEXES

General indexes

The Readers' Guide to Periodical Literature. New York: The H. W. Wilson Company, 1900 to date, semimonthly (September–June), monthly (July and August). $50.

Popular Periodical Index. P.O. Box 739, Camden, New Jersey: Popular Periodical Index, 1973 to date, semiannual. $15.

Humanities Index. New York: The H. W. Wilson Company, 1974 to date, quarterly. Service.

Social Sciences Index. New York: The H. W. Wilson Company, 1974 to date, quarterly. Service.

British Humaniites Index. London: Library Association, 1962 to date, quarterly and annual cumulations.

Canadian Periodical Index. Ottawa, Ontario: Canadian Library Association, 1948 to date, monthly. Rates on request.

A large proportion of periodical indexes used in small and medium-sized American libraries, as well as in the largest research library but on a more limited scale, originate from The H. W. Wilson Company. The Wilson indexes are celebrated for their ease of use and have become a model of the best in indexing. Many of the company's publications are sold on a service basis. Since the larger, better-financed libraries often use more services, they usually pay more than the small libraries for the same index.[7]

Since 1952, the selection of works to be indexed has been determined by a group of librarians, the Committee on Wilson Indexes. In addition to deciding what should or should not be included in an index, the committee also advises on needs for new indexes or approaches to materials. How the committee operates is explained in full by Edwin R. Colburn in an article in the *ALA Bulletin* (January 1965, pp. 35 +). The committee, whose membership is rotated periodically, draws upon advice and suggestions from subscribers to the Wilson indexes. Major changes in titles included and excluded were made, for example, in 1977, as a comparison of a list of titles for 1976 and 1978 will show.

Discussion of general periodical indexes becomes more and more outmoded. Emphasis is now on specialized indexes; and with the exception of the *Readers' Guide,* the day of attempting to cover a general field is about past. Because of its wide scope, the *Readers' Guide* is by far the most popular general index in the United States, followed only by its smaller brother,

---

[7] For a complete explanation of this system, see the latest Wilson Company catalog of publications.

the *Abridged Readers' Guide.* Some 156 magazines of general interest are indexed in the larger work, approximately 44 in the junior edition. In covering subjects, they range from *Art in America* to *Ms.* The assumption is that the wide coverage will ensure that most users will find something about the subject that interests them.

The main work is issued twice a month and thus is one of the best guides to recent literature. It is frequently the only guide to current material on some out-of-the-way point raised at a reference desk. Cumulations serve the retrospective needs of many patrons.

Remember, too, that now the Wilson indexes, including the *Readers' Guide,* include citations to book reviews. Reviews are arranged alphabetically by author in a separate section of the indexes.

The abridged version, issued monthly from September to June, is geared to smaller libraries and schools. There is some debate as to the wisdom of more than halving the coverage, particularly if a user can secure indexed material from a larger library. Its low price (less than half that of the full-sized work) and its selection of periodicals primarily for students seem to ensure its popularity.

The great advantage of the indexes for general use is the arrangement. Author and subject entries are in a single alphabet. The subject headings, as in all the Wilson indexes, are consistent and easy to locate. Furthermore, numerous cross-references make the indexes a model for rapid use. Each entry contains all necessary information to find the article. Abbreviations are held to a minimum, and they are clearly explained in the front of the index.

Although the general periodical index is no longer a viable publishing venture, there are three other indexes which augment the *Readers' Guide.* "Augment" is perhaps the wrong word, as the raison d'être of these indexes is the inclusion of periodicals which for one reason or another have been excluded by the selection committee for the *Readers' Guide.* The earliest of the indexes of omission is the *Popular Periodical Index,* which includes 27 titles not found in the Wilson index. Some examples: *Playboy, Crawdaddy, Rolling Stone, Washington Monthly, TV Guide,* and *Essence.* The librarian publisher, Robert Bottorff, includes subject headings for reviews, motion pictures, recordings, etc. Where a title does not describe content, the editor often adds a word or line or two explaining what the article is about. While this is hardly a full abstract, enough information is given to make the index particularly useful.

Access (Syracuse, New York: Gaylord Bros., Inc., 1975 to date, triannual, $75) is another general index. This includes over 160 titles, with particular emphasis on popular music, travel magazines, science fiction, and arts and crafts titles. The index has separate subject and author indexes. Many of the titles appear to be more suitable for popular reading than for reference (*Oui, Viva, Modern Bride,* etc.), although the indexing of numerous regional and city magazines will be of considerable use to local libraries. A third general entry, *The New Periodicals Index* (Boulder, Colorado: The Mediaworks Ltd., 1977 to date, semiannual, $25), includes a subject-author index to 68 titles with a particular emphasis on "alternative" culture periodicals, e.g., *Mother Earth News, CoEvolution Quarterly, Country Woman.* Although there is some limited duplication between *Access* and *Popular Periodical Index, The New Periodicals Index* does offer distinctive new coverage. However, only the largest library needs all these services; in order of probable importance (and considering cots), librarians will want *The New Periodicals Index* and *Popular Periodical Index* first, with *Access* next.

Another service promises to give an added dimension to research in popular magazines. This is *Abstracts of Popular Culture* (Bowling Green, Ohio: Bowling Green University Popular Press, 1976 to date, quarterly). The service selectively abstracts articles from over 600 scholarly journals, and includes almost anything which deals with comics, soap operas, westerns, adventure stories, television, and other popular interests. Although the emphasis is "about" culture rather than a reflection of that culture as found in the other indexes, the abstracting service offers such a wide variety of subjects that it seems essential for larger public, academic, and even high school libraries.

Having suffered a division, the *British Humanities Index* is somewhat less ambitious than *The Readers' Guide to Periodical Literature.* From 1915 on, it was called the *Subject Index to Periodicals,* but after 1962, it omitted titles in the fields of education (taken up by *British Educational Index*) and technology (now in *British Technology Index*). Medical sciences and business were also cut out. What remains is a serviceable and relatively general guide to British journals covering such subjects as politics, economics, history, and literature. Unlike the *Readers' Guide,* it is of limited use in the area of current materials because it is published only quarterly with annual cumulations. By the time the *British Humanities Index* and the corresponding periodicals reach North America, the timeliness factor is nil.

The *Canadian Periodical Index* is an approximate equivalent to the *Readers' Guide.* It is an author-subject index to about 96 Canadian magazines including 14 French titles. Owing to an added interest in Canadian periodicals among Canadian readers and libraries, the *Index* has tried to increase the scope of its analysis. It includes special sections for poems and short stories as well as book and motion picture reviews.

After these general indexes, the closest to a general approach to large areas of interest is the *Humanities Index,* followed by the *Social Sciences Index.*[8] (Until 1974, the two were issued as a single index, called *Social Sciences and*

---

[8] Background on these two indexes, as well as a detailed analysis of content and use, will be found in "Reference and Subscription Book Reviews," *The Booklist,* April 15, 1976, pp. 1211–1214. The review serves as a model of evaluating an indexing service.

Humanities Index. It was then divided to allow wider coverage of the two areas.) The *Humanities Index* covers 260 periodicals, and the *Social Sciences Index* includes 265.

Areas covered in the *Social Sciences Index* include anthropology, economics, environmental science, psychology, public administration, sociology, and related subjects. The *Humanities Index* considers archaeology and classical studies, folklore, history, language and literature, literary and political criticism, performing arts, philosophy, religion and theology, and related subjects. The wide net for both indexes makes them general indexes for the social sciences and humanities.

There is one general index which is consulted by those with a knowledge of foreign languages. This is *IBZ, Internationale Bibliographie der ZeitschriftenLiteratur; Aus Allen Gebieten des Wissens* (Osnabrück, West Germany: Felix Dietrich Verlag, 1965 to date, cumulated semiannual). While this index has a long publishing history, going back to 1896 under a different name and publisher, today it is, as the translated title indicates, an "International Bibliography of Periodical Literature Covering All Fields of Knowledge." Approximately 8000 periodicals are indexed by subject in one set of cumulations, and by author in a companion set.[9] Although emphasis is on German-language titles, there is coverage of a large number of "foreign" periodicals, including those in French and English. Subject headings are in German, but there are often cross-references to these from English or French forms. The *Bibliographie* is not difficult to use, although the major problem for other than large research libraries is that few collections have even a small number of the 8000 periodicals indexed.

Subject indexes

All the following titles are published by The H. W. Wilson Company:

> *Applied Science and Technology Index.* 1958 to date, monthly. Service.
>
> *Art Index.* 1929 to date, quarterly. Service.
>
> *Biological and Agricultural Index.* 1964 to date, monthly. Service.
>
> *Business Periodicals Index.* 1958 to date, monthly. Service.
>
> *Education Index.* 1929 to date, monthly. Service.
>
> *Index to Legal Periodicals.* 1908 to date, monthly. Service.

[9] Confusion arises in using this index, as it is first issued in some 30 parts before it is cumulated semiannually. Cumulations are advised for all but the experts. The same publisher also issues an *International Bibliography of Book Reviews of Scholarly Literature,* which is often found on the shelves next to the periodical index, sometimes adding confusion to confusion for the beginner.

> *Library Literature.* 1934 to date, bimonthly. Service. (Note: Cumulative volume, 1921–1932, published in 1934.)

The following are non-Wilson Company publications:

> *Public Affairs Information Service Bulletin.* New York: Public Affairs Information Service, 1915 to date, twice a month, $180, including cumulations and annual. (The four cumulations and annual, $125, the annual alone, $80.)
>
> *The Catholic Periodical and Literature Index.* Haverford, Pennsylvania: Catholic Library Association, 1930 to date, bimonthly. Service.
>
> *Index to U.S. Government Periodicals.* Chicago: Infordata International, 1974 to date, quarterly. $175. (Cumulations back to and including 1970, 1971, 1973, available at $150 each.)

The basic subject indexes found in most American and Canadian libraries are published by The H. W. Wilson Company, and follow much the same format and approach as do Wilson's aforementioned general indexes. There are several hundred subject indexes and abstracting services from other publishers. They concentrate on more specialized areas than those covered in the Wilson entries.

When considering subject indexes, three facts must be kept in mind:

1. Many are broader in coverage than would be indicated by such key title words as "Art" or "Education." Related fields are often considered. Therefore, anyone doing a subject analysis in depth often should consult indexes which take in fringe-area topics.
2. Most of the subject indexes are not confined solely to magazines. They often include books, monographs, bulletins, and even government documents.
3. A great number are not parochial, but tend to be international in scope. True, not many foreign-language works are listed, but anything in English is usually noted, even if issued abroad.

Because of this wider base of coverage, many libraries are doubtful about including such indexes. What good is it to find a particular article in a specialized journal and then be unable to obtain the journal? The library should be in a position either to borrow the journal or to have a copy made of the article. If it is not, it had better look to improving its services. Also, even without the pertinent items indexed, the indexes do serve to give readers a broader view of the topic than they might get from only a general index.

There is little point in describing each of the Wilson subject indexes. For the most part, their titles explain their scope and purpose. The user may be either the specialist or the generalist—journals and periodicals for both are indexed. Most indexed titles are American, but there are representative selections from other countries in other languages. The number indexed ranges from 185 to over 300. Beginning in 1976, the Wilson Company expanded coverage in many of their indexes, e.g., the *Business Index,* and added 126 new periodicals. Expansion is to continue for other indexes. Also, from time to time new indexes are added to the dozen or so now published by The H. W. Wilson Company; e.g., plans were being considered in 1977 for a general science index (for laypersons) to augment the more specialized *Applied Science and Technology Index.*

The approach is much the same; that is, the author and subject entries are in a single alphabet and there are the usual excellent cross-references. Subject headings are frequently revised and in most services book reviews are listed in a separate section. Each index has its peculiarities, but a reading of the prefatory material in each will clarify the finer points.

One non-Wilson subject-type index which is found in most libraries is the *Public Affairs Information Service Bulletin.* This has the advantage of relative currency. The *Bulletin* (or *PAIS,* as it is usually called) is issued twice a month and cumulated four times a year, with a final annual volume which may be purchased separately. Coverage is primarily of material in political science, government, legislation, economics, and sociology. Periodicals, government documents, pamphlets, reports, and some books in such areas as government, public administration, international affairs, and economics are indexed. Valuable additions are a "key to periodical references" and a list of "publications analyzed." Both serve as a handy checklist and buying guide for the library.

While works analyzed are limited to those in English, coverage is international. Arrangement is alphabetical, primarily by subject. A few of the entries have brief descriptive notes on both contents and purpose. Beginning in 1972, *PAIS* issued a second index, *Foreign Language Index,* which does much the same service as the *Bulletin.* The essential difference is that the quarterly index considers the same subject areas in a number of foreign-language journals, books, reports, pamphlets, and the like.

One of the advantages of searching indexes in machine-readable form is that the reader need not go through countless individual volumes to search out everything pertinent on a given subject. The data base, linked to the computer keyboard or television screen, rapidly searches the index file. *PAIS* has been an online data base since 1976 (the *Foreign Language Index,* since 1972). However, another approach in printed form is possible. For example, *The Cumulative Subject Index to the PAIS Annual Bulletin 1915–1974* (Arlington, Virginia: Carrollton Press, Inc., 1975, 15 vols.) arranges almost 60 years of *PAIS* in a single subject index, thereby accomplishing in printed form one of the same services of a machine-readable data base. It is similar to machine-readable indexes for retrospective searching, although it has the disadvantage of not being updated monthly as a data base would be. If the publisher should want to keep the set up to date, it would have to be republished each year with the preceding year's subjects integrated into the main set. This appears economically prohibitive. Also, the user of the index still must go to the original *PAIS* index to find specific entries. The cumulative index indicates only issues of the *PAIS* where the subject is covered, not the precise citation itself.

Almost all the aforementioned titles, and particularly *PAIS*, index government periodicals.[10] The *Index to U.S. Government Periodicals*[11] is geared solely to that form. This is a subject and author approach to some 120 periodicals issued by various bureaus and agencies of the federal government. It is particularly useful for the social sciences and, for an extensive search, should be employed along with *PAIS* and the *Social Sciences Index*. It includes only about 10 to 15 percent of the government periodicals listed in the February issue of the *Monthly Catalog of United States Government Publications*. The service is nevertheless invaluable for larger libraries. Note, too, it may be used along with the *American Statistical Index*, which analyzes over 800 government periodicals for statistical data.

Where does the librarian find whether or not a discipline has an indexing or abstracting service? The first places to look are Sheehy, Walford, and *American Reference Books Annual*. After checking there, one will find indexes and abstracts in the listing, alphabetical by title, in *Ulrich's International Directory of Periodicals*. Look, also, for guides such as Dolores B. Owen and Marguerite Hanchey's *Abstracts and Indexes in Science and Technology: A Descriptive Guide* (Metuchen, New Jersey: Scarecrow Press, 1974); and, of course, check current reviews of new reference sources. Since publishers depend almost solely upon libraries to support indexes and abstracts, the librarian is usually bombarded with notices of such new services.

Some notion of the extent of available indexes and abstracts available in 1978 may be provided by simply listing a few whose titles are self-descriptive. (Note: Several other basic titles are discussed in detail in

[10] For a list of where government periodicals are indexed as of 1976, see Elizabeth A. McBride and Mary L. Morgan, "Guide to the Indexing of U.S. Government Periodicals," *Special Libraries*, February 1976, pp. 76–83. A more detailed listing of 704 titles, plus the indexing policies for 54 services, will be found in Rebekah Harleston and Carla J. Stoffle, "Government Periodicals: Seven Years Later," *Government Publications Review*, no. 4, 1975, pp. 323–343.

[11] Of the numerous reviews of this index, a useful one which shows problems faced by all index publishers is Kathleen Heim's review in *Documents to the People (Dttp.)*, May 1976, pp. 67–69.

the second volume of this text.[12]) The list includes *Index to Free Periodicals* (Ann Arbor, Michigan: Pierian Press, 1976 to date, semiannual); *Women Studies Abstracts* (Rush, New York: S. S. Whaley, 1972 to date, quarterly); *Alternative Press Index: An Index to Alternative and Underground Publications* (Baltimore: Alternative Press Centre, 1969 to date, quarterly); *Film Literature Index* (Albany, New York: Filmdex, 1973 to date, quarterly) *Sociological Abstracts* (San Diego, California: Sociological Abstracts, 1953 to date, 6 times a year); and *Hospital Literature Index* (Chicago: American Hospital Association, 1945 to date, quarterly). And so it goes. The lesson of so many of these indexes, which vary in usefulness and worth, is that the librarian should rarely say no to an inquiry about the availability of an index or abstract in a subject field. Look first!

Retrospective periodical indexes

> *Poole's Index to Periodical Literature*, 1802–1906. Vol. 1, 1802–1881, Boston: Houghton, 1891; vols. 2–6 (supplements 1–5), 1882–1907, Boston: Houghton Mifflin Company, 1888–1908 (6 vols. reprinted in 7 vols., Gloucester, Massachusetts: Peter Smith Publisher, 1963).

This was the first general magazine index, and the forerunner of the *Readers' Guide*. It was the imagination of William Frederick Poole, a pioneer in both bibliography and library science, that made the index possible. Recognizing that many older periodicals were not being used for lack of proper indexing, he set out, after one or two preliminary starts, to index 470 American and English periodicals covering the period 1802 to 1881. Having completed this work, he issued five supplements which brought the indexing to the end of 1906.

The modern user is sometimes frustrated upon realizing that the total approach is by subject of an article. The author index to some 300,000 references in the main set and the supplements is supplied by C. Edward Wall's *Cumulative Author Index for Poole's Index* . . . (Ann Arbor, Michigan: Pierian Press, 1971, 488 pp.). The index is computer-produced and not entirely easy to follow, but it is a great help to anyone seeking an author entry in *Poole*.

With all its faults, Poole's work is still a considerable achievement and an invaluable tool for the man or woman seeking some key to nineteenth-century periodicals. The last decade of the century is better treated in *Nineteenth Century Readers' Guide to Periodical Literature*, 1890–1899, with

[12] Katz, op. cit.

supplementary indexing 1900–1922 (New York: The H. W. Wilson Company, 1944, 2 vols.). Limited to 51 periodicals (in contrast with Poole's 470), this guide thoroughly indexes magazines by author and subject for the years 1890 to 1899. Some 14 magazines are indexed between 1900 and 1922.

The term "retrospective" in this section is fairly well limited to nineteenth-century periodicals, although it should be remembered that when one speaks of a retrospective index, one indicates any index which covers a period other than the present. In this sense, all indexing is retrospective. But to stay with nineteenth- through twentieth-century retrospective indexes, there are three computer-generated guides which are suitable for tracing periodicals in history, political science, and sociology. These are: *Combined Retrospective Index to Journals in History, 1838–1974,* an index to 234 history journals in the English language arranged by subject, with two author index volumes; *Combined Retrospective Index to Journals in Political Science, 1886–1974,* an index to 179 journals; and *Combined Retrospective Index to Journals in Sociology, 1895–1974,* an index to 118 titles. All are published by the Carrollton Press, Arlington, Virginia, and range in price from $550 to $985. (The combined price in 1977: $2075.) As these are computer-generated, the page format is quite different from that of The H. W. Wilson Company indexes. Subjects are indicated by a key word in the left-hand margin, followed by the full title of the article, followed by the author's name, and the year, volume, journal name, and page. The primary difference is that the journal is given a code number, and to find the full title, one must turn to that number at the end of each volume.

Although this set of indexes has extreme retrospective value, it should be noted that the cutoff date is 1974. Therefore, many of the titles already have been and are being indexed in standard indexes. Hence, there is duplication of much of the material. The Carrollton sets are "to be kept current with *Annual Supplement* volumes." The supplements will "also include entries from the backfiles of other journals," thus making them, again, probably of value for retrospective searching.

INDEXES TO CURRENT EVENTS

In any reference library, one of the most time-consuming, sometimes futile, types of search is for current material on recent events. How is one to answer the question concerning a Presidential appointment of a week or a month ago, trace current sporting records, or find information on a prominent woman who died only last week?

The first general index source is *The Readers' Guide to Periodical Literature* (discussed earlier), which is issued every two weeks and may be no more than four to six weeks behind actual indexing of some current news periodicals. A subject rather than a general aid, with somewhat more of a time lag, is the semimonthly *Public Affairs Information Service Bulletin.* The natural inclination is to turn to a newspaper index, but even the semimonthly *New York Times Index* is usually several months behind its actual publishing schedule. (A solution to the problem of timeliness and current events is suggested by linking the indexes to data bases for computer retrieval; and this is discussed in the third section of the second volume of this text. What follows is limited to traditional forms.)

How, then, does one locate material published yesterday, or a week or a month ago, if the average index is so far behind? There are several approaches: (1) The least satisfactory is simply to go through current issues of magazines related to the subject or to examine the latest issues of newspapers; (2) a somewhat more rewarding step is to consult the weekly summaries of events, such as *Facts on File,* which, if nothing more, give the date of the event; and (3) one may consult with the local newspaper, radio, or television news bureau. There is always the "expert" in the community who may have exactly the information needed. The last suggestion, and ultimately the best solution of all, is (4) for the librarian to keep advised of current events via a careful reading of at least one newspaper each day and of the weekly news magazines, and also to keep an ear open for community events.

Sources for last week's events

Facts on File, a Weekly World News Digest, with Cumulative Index. New York: Facts on File, Inc., October 30, 1940, to date, weekly. $270.

Keesing's Contemporary Archives. London: Keesing's, July 1, 1931, to date, weekly (represented in the United States by Charles Scribner's Sons). $120.

Canadian News Facts. Toronto: Canadian News Facts, January 1, 1967, to date, biweekly. $115.

Congressional Quarterly Service Weekly Report, 1943 to date. Washington, D.C.: Congressional Quarterly, Inc., 1943 to date, weekly. Price varies; query publisher.

Of all the services, *Facts on File* tends to be the most prompt (the United States mails permitting), and normally only a few days elapse between the last date covered and receipt of the publication. Emphasis is on news events in the United States, with international coverage related for the most part to American affairs. Material is gathered mainly from the major newspapers and condensed into objective, short, factual reports. The index is arranged under broad subject headings, such as "World affairs," "Finance," "Economics," "National affairs," and so on. This is a bit confusing; but fortunately, every two weeks, each month, and then quarterly and annually, a detailed index is issued which covers previous issues. There is also a *Five-Year Master News Index,* published since 1950. The latest edition, covering 1971–1975, was published in 1976.

In *Keesing's Contemporary Archives,* emphasis differs from *Facts on File* in two important respects. The scope is primarily that of the United Kingdom, Europe, and the British Commonwealth. Detailed subject reports in certain areas are frequently included (the reports are by experts and frequently delay the weekly publication by several days), as are full texts of important speeches and documents. Conversely, *Keesing's* does not cover in any detail many ephemeral events, such as sports, art exhibitions, and movies, which may be included in *Facts on File.* Arrangement is by country, territory, or continent, with some broad subject headings, such as "Religion," "Aviation," and "Fine arts." Every second week, an index is issued which is cumulated quarterly and annually.

Following much the same procedure and format as *Facts on File, Canadian News Facts* differs in its scope and its frequency; it appears every two weeks rather than weekly. The news digests vary from 8 to 12 pages, and are concerned almost exclusively with Canada. While it would be a first choice for Canadian libraries, *News Facts* would be well down the selection scale for all but the largest libraries in the United States.

While both *Keesing's* and *Facts on File* are sources of information on general news events, there are some specialized weekly services which assist the reference librarian. Among the best of those giving detailed reports on government activities is the *Congressional Quarterly Weekly Report.* Issued by a private firm, not by the government, it presents in condensed form all congressional and political activities of the previous week—not only those relating to Congress. Bills, acts, names of members of congress, how they voted, committee action, major legislation, and related subjects are covered in full and are competently indexed and summarized in a "fact sheet" procedure. Since the service is indexed in *Public Affairs Information Service Bulletin,* it may be approached via two indexes.

Another approach is *News Bank* (Greenwich, Connecticut: News Bank Inc., 1970 to date, monthly), which selects articles from some 200 American newspapers and indexes them by subject. The subscriber receives the articles on microfiche cards and a monthly index to each of the series. Series topics cover business and economic development to social relations to review of the arts. The library may subscribe to one or all of the series.

Newspaper indexes

The New York Times Index. New York: The New York Times, 1851 to date, semimonthly. $125. Annual cumulation, $125. Combined, $225.

Newspaper Index. Wooster, Ohio: Bell & Howell, 1972 to date, monthly. $695. Individual sections for individual papers, $225.

Christian Science Monitor Index. Wooster, Ohio: Bell & Howell, 1960 to date, monthly. $55.

Wall Street Journal Index. Princeton, New Jersey: Dow Jones Books, Inc., 1950 to date, monthly. $90. Annual vol., $90. Combined monthly and annual, $150. (Note: 1957 vol. published in 1975.)

National Observer Index. Princeton, New Jersey: Dow Jones Books, Inc., 1969 to date, annual. $21.

The Times. London: Index to the Times, 1906 to 1977, bimonthly and quarterly; 1977 to date, monthly, $250. (Distributed in the United States by Research Publications, Woodbridge, Connecticut.)

A distinct advantage of *The New York Times Index* is its wide scope and relative completeness. Although the United States does not have a truly national newspaper, the *Times,* in its effort to cover all major news events, both national and international, comes close to being a daily national paper The *Times Index* provides a wealth of information and frequently is used even without reference to the individual paper of the date cited. Each entry includes a brief abstract of the news story. Consequently, someone seeking a single fact, such as the name of an official, the date of an event, or the title of a play, may often find all that is needed in the index. Also, since all material is dated, the *Times Index* serves as an entry into other, unindexed newspapers and magazines. For example, if the user is uncertain as to the day ship X sank and wishes to see how the disaster was covered in another newspaper or in a magazine, the *Times Index* will narrow the search by providing the date the event occurred.

The New York Times Index is arranged in dictionary form with sufficient cross-references to names and related topics. Events under each of the main headings are arranged chronologically. Book and theater reviews are listed under those respective headings.

Some libraries subscribe only to the annual cumulated *Index.* This volume serves not only as an index but also as a type of guide to the activities of the previous year. Thanks to the rather full abstracts, maps, and charts, one may use the cumulated volume as a reference source in itself. But two problems exist: First, the semimonthly indexes are not cumulated until the end of the year, and the librarian must search each issue, a time-consuming task unless an approximate date is known. The second problem is lack of timeliness. The regular index is usually two to three months behind, and the annual may be published six to seven months after the end of the year.

The Bell & Howell *Newspaper Index* is really six indexes to six geographically important newspapers—*Houston Post, San Francisco Chronicle,* the *Chicago Tribune, Los Angeles Times, The New Orleans Times Picayune,* and *The Washington Post.* Originally published as a single index, it now consists of one index per newspaper. Each index is in two parts. The first part is a subject index, the second an index to personal names. There are no abstracts, but the entries are descriptive enough to give the drift of the article. The reader can soon see how six newspapers view events from a story on the President to a story on a tennis star. The computer-printout format is clear and the subject approach is easy to follow. Again, though, as there is only an annual cumulation, each issue must be searched separately, and the indexes, like *The New York Times Index,* are two to three months in arrears.

Issued since 1958, the index to *The Wall Street Journal* is in two parts, "Corporate News" and "General News" with brief summaries of the events. As in *The New York Times Index,* enough information is usually found in the summaries to cancel the need to go to the newspaper. While of primary interest in business and economic studies, the paper is more general in its news coverage than the title or its previous history indicates. It frequently carries articles in depth about national problems other than those linked to economics.

The monthly *Christian Science Monitor Index* has been issued since 1960, but retrospective indexing to 1950 is available (the paper began publishing in 1908). Although the newspaper is biased on its editorial page, its reporting of the general news is considered to be extremely objective. In fact, many libraries that draw the line at subscribing to any religion-supported newspapers make an exception of the *Monitor.* Consequently, the index is extremely useful as an adjunct to *The New York Times Index.*

The *Monitor Index* cites stories carried in its three editions: Eastern, Western, and Midwestern. The approach is primarily by subject, and no effort is made to annotate the items as the *Times Index* does. It has one distinct advantage over the other indexes—a much lower price.

The annual *National Observer Index* is in two parts: subjects and personal names. There is a statement on content and amount of text, and an indication of illustrations. The subject headings are well chosen, and there are a number of cross-references. Although the infrequency of publication limits use of the *Index* to retrospective searching, it is nevertheless valuable for that, particularly since the weekly *National Observer* resembles *Time* or *Newsweek* in its coverage of the week's events.

The index published by *The Times* of London is in dictionary form with sufficient cross-references to names and related topics. It has had a varying publishing schedule, but on January 1, 1977, it became a monthly. At the same time, it added brief abstracts (somewhat on the order of *The New York Times Index*) which provide dates, facts, and, often enough, material for ready-reference work which does not require the user to consult the newspaper itself. Note: In addition to indexing the newspaper, it indexes related *Times* publications, including *The Times Literary Supplement, The Times Educational Supplement,* and *The Times Higher Educational Supplement.* It, too, appears several months after the publications have been issued and cannot be used for really current searching.

The need remains for individual libraries to index local publications. To quote a recent survey: "We would like to suggest that librarians across the country take on as their responsibility the provision of indexes to the newspapers in their communities."[13]

More and more librarians have acted on this suggestion. As a result, there are now such local indexes as those of the *Atlanta Constitution, The St. Paul Dispatch and Pioneer Press,* and *The Minneapolis Tribune Services,* all prepared by librarians. *Newspaper Indexes: A Location and Subject Guide* (Metuchen, N.J.: Scarecrow Press, 1977) is a state-by-state listing of local newspaper indexes by Anita Milner.

Beginning in 1976, a new type of index became available, namely, *CBS News Index* (New York: Microfilming Corporation of America, 1976, quarterly to date). Access is offered on microfilm or microfiche to verbatim transcripts of daily television broadcasts. The index, arranged alphabetically by subject and personal name, includes a one- or two-phrase description of the item and a citation to the microform transcriptions. The quarterly index to the file is cumulated annually, and only time will tell if it will be any more prompt than *The New York Times Index.*

MATERIAL IN COLLECTIONS

Essay and General Literature Index. New York: The H. W. Wilson Company, 1900 to date, semiannual. $30. (Five-year cumulations, $75.)

Short Story Index. New York: The H. W. Wilson Company, 1975 to date, annual. $20. (Irregular, 1953 to 1973; basic volume, 1953, plus five supplements, 1956 to 1974, various prices.)

Granger's Index to Poetry. 6th ed. New York: Columbia University Press, 1973, 2223 pp. $90.

[13] "Survey of Local Newspapers in California," *California Librarian,* January 1975, p. 7.

Play Index. New York: The H. W. Wilson Company, 1953 to date. (Irregular; basic volume, 1953, plus three additional volumes. $23 to $24.)

Anthologies and collections are a peculiar blessing or curse for the reference librarian. Many of them are useless, others are on the borderline, and a few are worthwhile in that they bring the attention of readers to material which otherwise might be missed or overlooked. Regardless of merit, all collections may serve the reference librarian who is seeking a particular speech, essay, poem, play, or other literary form. In reference, the usefulness of anthologies is dependent upon adequate indexes.

This type of material is approached by the average user in one of several ways. He or she may know the author and want a play, a poem, or other form by that author. The name of the work may be known, but more than likely it is not. Another approach is, "I want something about X subject in a play, poem, short story. . . ."

Consequently, the most useful indexes to material in collections are organized so they may be approached by author, subject, and title of a specific work. Failure to find a particular title in an anthology or collection usually means it has been published independently and has still to find its way into a collective form. The card catalog certainly should be checked; if it fails to produce an answer, standard bibliographical tools, such as the *Cumulative Book Index* and *Books in Print,* should be consulted.

Indexes to materials in collections serve two other valuable purposes. Most of them cover books or other materials which have been analyzed; and since the analysis tends to be selective, the librarian has a built-in buying guide to the better or outstanding books in the field. For example, the *Essay and General Literature Index* picks up selections from most of the outstanding collections of essays. The library that has a large number of these books in its collection will have a good representative group of works.

The second benefit, particularly in these days of close cooperation among libraries, is that the indexes can be used to locate books not in the library. Given a specific request for an essay and lacking the title in which the essay appears, the librarian may request the book on interlibrary loan by giving the specific and precise bibliographical information found in the index.

Aside from sharing a similar purpose of locating bits of information from collections, anthologies, and individual books and magazines, this type of reference aid tends to center in the humanities, particularly in literature. There is little need for such assistance in the social sciences and the sciences, or where the need does exist, it is usually met via an abstracting or indexing service. While the titles listed here are the best known, new entries appear each year. They range from guides to science-fiction stories to information on handcrafts, costumes, photographs, and such. Once the form is recognized, the only basic change is in the topics covered and the thoroughness, or lack of it, in arrangement and depth of analysis.

The single most useful work in libraries as an entry into miscellaneous collections of articles is the *Essay and General Literature Index*. It is valuable for general reference questions in that the analyzed essays cover a wide variety of topics. For 1970 to 1974, there are 20,896 analytical subject entries to the contents of 1337 collected works on every subject from art to medicine. While the indexing emphasis is on subjects, the index is useful for approaching an author's work via his or her name, as well as for locating criticism of his or her individual efforts. All librarians have their favorite general reference works, including the late John Waddell of Columbia University School of Library Service. He "often praised the [*Index*], referring to it as 'Waddell's Mania' with a claim that it eventually could solve the toughest reference problems."[14]

The *Essay and General Literature Index* is also a type of buyer's guide to collections in that subscribers each month receive a list of the books to be indexed. (A necessary companion volume for the large library with a complete run of the index is *Essay and General Literature Index: Works Indexed 1900–1969*. This 70-year list cites all the 9917 titles that have been analyzed in the seven permanent cumulations.)

The useful addition to *Essay and General Literature Index* is *Canadian Essay and Literature Index* (Toronto: University of Toronto Press, annual, 1975 to date). This differs from the American title in several ways: (1) In addition to analyzing contents of about 90 books, it indexes some 40 periodicals; (2) all publications are from Canada, although content is not limited to Canadian interests; (3) in addition to essays, the contents of books and periodicals are analyzed for book reviews, poems, plays, and short stories. All material is integrated into a single author-title-subject index, with only essays and book reviews in separate sections. Finally, the indexing lags by about two years—i.e., the 1977 volume covers 1975; the 1976 volume, 1974; etc.

The elusive short story may be tracked down in the *Short Story Index*. Now published annually, the *Index* lists stories in both book collections and periodicals. A single index identifies the story by author, by title, and by subject. The subject listing is a handy aid for the reference librarian attempting to find a suitable study topic for a student who may not want to read an entire book on the Civil War or life in Alaska. The names of the books and the magazines analyzed are dutifully listed. More than 3000

---

[14] *American Libraries,* January 1976, p. 64.

stories are considered each year, and the four annual volumes are cumulated in a permanent hardbound volume. The first, to be issued in 1978, will, according to the publisher, "index approximately 11,000 stories in 800 collections, in addition to approximately 2,500 stories in periodicals." Note, however, that before the annual series was begun in 1975, the earlier volumes analyzed only books, not periodicals.[15]

Indexing both individually published plays and plays in collections, *Play Index* is a standard reference work. The basic part is an author, title, and subject index. The author entry for a play "contains the full name of the author, title of the play, a brief descriptive note, the number of acts and scenes, the size of the cast, and the number of sets required." There are numerous other helpful devices ranging from symbols for plays suitable for elementary school children to prizes a play has won. A cast analysis, making up the second section, helps the reference librarian locate plays by number of players required. The other sections key the plays to collections from which they have been taken. While there is a certain amount of duplication, *Ottemiller's Index to Plays in Collections* (6th ed; Metuchen, New Jersey: Scarecrow Press, 1976) tends to analyze collections not found in the *Play Index*. The 1977 edition of *Ottemiller* includes information on 3686 plays in 1237 collections.

Another index to plays in collections is the multivolume *Chicorel Theater Index to Plays in Anthologies and Periodicals* (New York: Chicorel Library Publishing Corp., various dates). First issued in 1970, the set reached six volumes in late 1977, with promise of a volume almost every year. This index differs from the others in that it includes plays in periodicals as well as in anthologies. Another feature is its lists of plays available on records or tapes. Arranged in one alphabet, the *Index* covers the title of the play, author, editor, translator, etc.

The same publisher offers a similar approach to poetry with the *Chicorel Index to Poetry in Anthologies in Print*. There is an author, title, and first-line approach to the entries in the four volumes. Another four-volume set offers the same approach to poetry in older, retrospective collections.

The sixth edition of *Granger's Index to Poetry* follows previous editions in arrangement and approach. Close to 800 poetry anthologies are analyzed in three sections, each alphabetically arranged, which cover title and first line, author, and subject. Each of the anthologies is listed with full bibliographical information. Not only is *Granger's* useful for tracing elusive poems, but the first-line approach is a resource for quotations which may

---

[15] Another index to short stories in collections: *Chicorel Index to Short Stories in Anthologies and Collections* (New York: Chicorel Library Publishing Corp., 1974, 4 vols.). Although published in 1974, the index lists many out-of-print collections.

not be included in standard quotation books. An equally good reference work in this area is John Brewton's *Index to Poetry for Children and Young People: 1964–1969* (New York: The H. W. Wilson Company, 1972, 575 pp.). This offers a title, subject, author, and first-line approach to 117 collections, and supplements the original 1942 index. *The Index of American Periodical Verse* (Metuchen, New Jersey: Scarecrow Press, 1973 to date, annual) is an author and title (or first-line, if no title) index to a broad variety of magazine verse by both well-known and lesser-known writers. Actual indexing is about two years behind the date the index is published; for example, the 1975 volume covers 171 periodicals published in 1973.

There are indexes to various types and forms of poetry. One example is Dorothy Chapman's *Index to Black Poetry* (Boston: G. K. Hall, 1974, 541 pp.), which analyzes the contents of 94 current books and pamphlets and 33 anthologies. It has the usual indexes listing title and first line, author and subject.

Concordances

There is one other form of index which is "basic" in most libraries, and that is the concordance. A concordance is an alphabetical index of the principal words in a book, or more likely, in the total works of a single author, with their contexts. Early concordances were limited to the Bible; a classic of its type, often reprinted, is Alexander Cruden's *Complete Concordance to the Old and New Testament . . . ,* first published in 1737. This, as in many Bible concordances since, is equally an index of subjects and topics with citations, as in all concordances, to where the words appear.

The laborious task of analyzing the Bible word by word, passage by passage, is matched only by the preparation of early concordances to Shakespeare. Fortunately, the advent of the computer considerably simplified the concordance effort (both for editorial and production purposes). Today there are concordances to not only the Bible and Shakespeare, but to almost every major writer. Examples for 1975 include concordances to F. Scott Fitzgerald's *The Great Gatsby,* James Joyce's *Finnegans Wake,* the complete poetry of Stephen Crane, and the plays of Federico García Lorca.

A concordance is used in a library for two basic purposes: (1) to enable students of literature to study the literary style of an author on the basis of his or her use of, or lack of use of, given words; and (2) more often, to run down elusive quotations. With one or two key words of a quote, the librarian may often find the exact quotation in the concordance. This approach presupposes that he or she has some knowledge of the author.

Quotations

Bartlett, John. *Familiar Quotations,* 14th ed. Boston: Little, Brown and Company, 1968, 1750 pp. $15.

Stevenson, Burton E. *The Home Book of Quotations, Classical and Modern,* 10th ed. New York: Dodd, Mead & Company, Inc., 1967, 2816 pp. $40.

Indexing who said what is the role of the book of quotations. Actually, these books are not so much indexes as distinctive forms unto themselves, defying ready classification. Having found the quote, for example, the average user is satisfied and does not want to go to the source as might be the case when using the standard index to materials in collections. Be that as it may, a frequent question in any library is either, "Who said the following?" or "What do you have in the way of a quote by or about X subject?" Any of the standard books of quotations may provide the answer. "May" is used here advisedly, for frequently the quotation is not found in any of the standard sources either because it is so unusual or, more than likely, because it is garbled. When the patron is not certain about the actual wording, another approach is via subject.

By far the most famous book of quotations is Bartlett (as *Familiar Quotations* is often called). A native of Plymouth, Massachusetts, John Bartlett was born in 1820 and at sixteen was employed by the owner of the University Bookstore in Cambridge. By the time he owned the store, he had become famous for his remarkable memory, and the word around Harvard was, "Ask John Bartlett." He began a notebook which expanded into the first edition of his work in 1855. After the Civil War, he joined Little, Brown and Company, and he continued to edit his work through nine editions until his death in December 1905.

Although Bartlett and the two other sources frequently contain similar material, many quotation works are needed; often what will be found in one may not be found in the others.

Briefly, the differences between Bartlett and Stevenson (a common identification of *The Home Book of Quotations, . . .*), aside from content, are:

1. *Arrangement.* Stevenson is arranged alphabetically under subject. Bartlett is arranged chronologically by author.
2. *Index.* Both have thorough indexes by subject, author, and key words of the quotations or verses. Stevenson does not repeat the subject words employed in the main text in the index. As more than one critic has pointed out, the indexes to these works are frequently an unconscious source of "modern" poetry. For example, from Bartlett come such memorable lines as:

Sleepless Eremite, nature's patient:
nights, never so many.
soul that perished
to give readers sleep

3. *Other features.* Stevenson has brief biographical data on authors. Bartlett features helpful historical footnotes, sometimes tracing the original quote normally associated with one individual back to another person or time.

Every year, there are half a dozen or so other compilations of quotations, e.g., *The Reader's Digest Treasury of Modern Quotations* (New York: Thomas Y. Crowell, 1975, 810 pp.) and *A Concise Treasury of Bible Quotations* (New York: Jonathan David, 1975, 175 pp.). These vary in quality, but most libraries buy as many as possible for running down an elusive quote not found in Bartlett or Stevenson. Note, too, that questions about quotations make up a major part of the difficult query section in each issue of *RQ.* A run of this section with eventual answers is a good key to hard-to-find sources.[16]

Timeliness normally does not loom so large for indexes of quotations as it does for other reference books;[17] still, a useful up-to-date title covering quotes of the previous year is *What They Said in 197 . . .* (Beverly Hills, California: Monitor Books, 1969 to date, annual). Published about mid-year after the closing year, this compilation includes about 600 pages of "direct quotations from speeches, news conferences, interviews, etc." Quotes are grouped by subject, and there is a detailed subject-author index. Full citations are given and an added bonus is the full identity of the author by position, rank, title, etc.

There is no guarantee that even with a massive set of quotation books, the librarian will be able to trace a given quote. Proof of this will be found by those stalwarts who attempt to master *Nemo's Almanac* (Oxford, England: Sycamore Press, 1892 to date, annual). Actually, the name is deceptive, as the so-called *Almanac* is really a literary contest whose readership "constitutes the most literate body of obsessive compulsives in the world."[18] The pamphlet consists of 73 unidentified quotations from English-language sources, arranged in almanac style, i.e., by month. Each

[16] The popularity of quotations (or trivia) is with us always, and frequently constitutes inspiration for newspaper and magazine articles. See, for example, Frank Giordano, "Quick, Who Said, 'Where is the rest of me?'—and Other Memorable Questions about Forgettable Lines," *The New York Times,* April 11, 1976 (theater section), p. D19.

[17] For example, Bartlett's is revised only about every 10 to 12 years; the next edition is scheduled for 1980.

[18] Veronica Geng, "Nemo's Almanac," *The New York Times Book Review,* September 14, 1975, p. 47. Not only an amusing analysis of this classic, but a source of marvelous steps in how a search is made for an elusive quote.

month's set of quotations fits a theme, and the contestant is asked to identify the quotes. Except for some regulars, who dutifully mail their results to the publisher for confirmation of success or failure, few are able to identify even a small number of the quotations.

A late 1976 entry in the quotation reference field is *Dictionary of Contemporary Quotations* (Syracuse, New York: Gaylord Publications). Issued twice a year and priced at $35 ($15 more than *What They Said in 197. . .*), it is arranged alphabetically by author of the modern quote, and includes a cumulated subject and author index. The service has the advantages of timeliness (a widely quoted remark may be picked up in late August for the November issue), about the same number of quotes as in its annual rival, and an editorial policy which puts emphasis on quotes useful as much for their subject matter as for the names of the people who made the remarks. Librarians welcome any new source of quotes, and despite its being priced higher than *What They Said in 197 . . .*, the *Dictionary* may prove useful in larger libraries—particularly when, after a number of years, a large cumulative index becomes available.

Related index queries

One of the most confusing aspects of periodical citations is the abbreviated title for the journal or magazine. All indexing and abstracting services, in a more or less convenient place, give the meaning of the abbreviations employed. Therefore, when one finds an abbreviated citation in an index, the abbreviation can be deciphered without too much difficulty.

The real reference problem arises when a user is confused by an abbreviation for a periodical which is found in a book or footnote article. Each publisher seems to employ a distinctive style of abbreviating periodical titles.

The most useful guide to periodical abbreviations is Leland G. Alkire and Margaret E. Schultz's *Periodical Title Abbreviations* (2d ed., Detroit: Gale Research Company, 1977, 436 pp.). This lists alphabetically, letter by letter, 20,000 entries. Each entry has the abbreviation followed by the full title of the periodical. (The primary sources for titles are basic indexes that abbreviate periodical titles.) Even with this aid, it is not always clear what an abbreviation means. For example, there are nine "AA" abbreviations for as many titles.[19]

Abbreviations become less of a problem as the literature becomes more specialized. For example, in chemistry, where there is a wide varia-

---

[19] See also Mary R. Kinney, *The Abbreviated Citation* (Chicago: American Library Association, 1969), which considers the whole problem and offers a number of specialized sources to consult.

tion of abbreviated forms for periodical titles, the primary guide is *Chemical Abstracts*. When in doubt, the librarian should turn to the contracted forms as found in the abstracting service, or to the list of contractions issued as a list by the American Chemical Society, publishers of *Chemical Abstracts*. Similar help will be obtained by consulting other specialized indexes and abstracts which list abbreviations.

ABSTRACTING SERVICES

The difference between the traditional index as exemplified by The H. W. Wilson Company groups and abstracting services is that the latter give the user an added feature—a summary of the contents of the item indexed. The "item" can be a periodical article, a book, a research report, an interview, or anything else the abstracting service deems important to recognize. Usually the abstract is short (50 to 150 words), covers major points made in the item indexed, and at its best objectively outlines primary points, methodology, arguments, essential results, and conclusions.[20]

The purpose of an abstract is twofold: (1) It saves time by elaboration of content and thus indicates to the user whether the full article should be read; and (2) it serves as a rapid method of surveying the retrospective literature without actually looking at the material indexed. A survey of United States scientists some years ago found that 48 percent of them used abstracts at least part of the time as a substitute for examining the literature itself.

Most of the abstracting services aim at relatively complete coverage of a narrow subject area. Coverage tends to be worldwide, with abstracts of foreign-language articles in English. The format varies from abstract to abstract, although normally the issues (1) are arranged under broad subject headings with appropriate author and some subject indexing; (2) do not cumulate, but have an exhaustive annual index that includes author, definitive subject headings, report numbers, corporate authors, and any other items that will help the reader locate the initial abstract; and (3) list titles of periodicals and other material abstracted.

The arrangement by broad subject classification sometimes confuses beginners. It is a blessing to experts who need only turn to the classification section of interest. The traditional index uses the specific rather than

---

[20] Technically, there are two types of abstracts. The "indicative" abstract indicates the type of article and the author's approach and treatment, but does not usually include specific data. The "informative," and most often used in works described in this text, summarizes enough of the data and findings to relieve the reader of the necessity of always reading the article. In neither case does the abstractor make any critical assessment.

the broad approach, thus often requiring the searcher to go back and forth in the index to run down related subject headings. Most abstracting services have limited author and subject indexes for the ongoing issues, but prepare exhaustive annual author-subject indexes. The librarian unfamiliar with the subject will save time by turning to the annual cumulated index to discover the subject classifications under which this or that specific subject is likely to appear in the monthly abstracts.

A drawback, even more severe for most abstracting services than for indexes, is the delay time in publication. Whereas an average index may be 1 to 3 months behind material analyzed, the average abstract has a time lag of 9 to 15 months or more. Therefore, while any reasonably important journal may be covered by two or three different abstracting services in the United States, if time is a factor, the librarian should first consult standard indexes which usually include the same titles but analyze them more quickly than the abstracting services.[21]

Representative abstracting services

Library and Information Science Abstracts. London: Library Association, 1969 to date, bimonthly. $72.50.

Psychological Abstracts. Washington, D.C.: American Psychological Association, Inc., 1927 to date, monthly. $240.

America: History and Life; Part A, Article Abstracts and Citations. Santa Barbara, California: American Bibliographical Center-Clio Press, 1974, three issues per year. Service rate, $155 to $560.

Dissertation Abstracts International. Ann Arbor, Michigan: University Microfilms, 1938 to date, monthly. $175.

These four abstracting services are representative of what is available in the humanities, science, and the social sciences. More technical scientific abstracts and indexes are considered in the second volume of this text.

The service most familiar to librarians is *Library and Information Science Abstracts,* which supplements, but does not in any way replace, the standard index, *Library Literature.* Whereas *Library Literature* is in the traditional alphabetical subject-author arrangement, the abstracting service depends upon a classification system for the arrangement of material. Thanks to an author and subject index, even the novice has no real difficulty in locating material.

An even more sophisticated approach is offered in *Information Science Abstracts* (Philadelphia: Documentation Abstracts, Inc., 1966 to date, bi-

---

[21] Computer scanning of texts may shorten the process of preparing the abstract, and this is likely to increase in importance as progress is made in text-scanning technology. On the other hand, some experts question how effective even the best automated scanner will be when compared with the mental, evaluative effort of an abstractor.

monthly, $95). The emphasis is on technical periodicals, books, reports, proceedings, and similar materials. And of the some 4500 abstracts issued each year, a vast proportion deal with aspects of automation, communication, computers, mathematics, artificial intelligence, etc. It is a service particularly suited to the needs of the researcher and the librarian in a large system. Arranged under broad subject headings, the abstracts are well written and complete. Each issue has an author index, and there is an annual subject index. A 1966–1975 cumulative index is available on microfilm, but not in printed form.

One of the most familiar and often used abstracting services in almost any medium-sized to large library is *Psychological Abstracts.* This publication literally covers every major journal and many books in the world involved with psychology and related fields. Foreign-language articles are abstracted in English. Abstracts are arranged under major subject classifications, many of which have subsections. The monthly issues provide access via rather limited subject indexing, and author indexes. Beginners should first consult the annual index for fuller subject headings.

America: History and Life; A Guide to Periodical Literature, first issued in 1964, was subdivided into four parts in 1974–1975. With volume 11, the title became *America: History and Life: Part A, Article Abstracts and Citations.*[22] Covering articles on United States and Canadian history in 2000 scholarly journals throughout the world, the service follows much the same procedure as in the original title.

Approximately 6000 abstracts are published each year, as well as about the same number of brief descriptions from local and specialist historical publications. The classified arrangement ends with a subject and author index.

What is new and welcome is the "subject profile index" which expands the subject approach to the classified abstracts in four areas: subject, geography, biography, and chronology. An article on Cornwallis's campaign for Virginia, for example, would be listed: subject: Revolutionary War; biography; Cornwallis; geography; Virginia; chronology; 1781. Under these and other headings, the article analyzed appears in the subject index an average of four or five times, providing insurance against a user's not finding a work.

This is made possible because the abstracting system is virtually a printout of a machine-readable data base.[23] Computer rotation of the

[22] Part B is *Index to Book Reviews* (covering over 100 scholarly United States and Canadian journals of history): Part C is *American History Bibliography (Books, Articles and Dissertations).* Part D is *Annual Index.* The whole series is often simply called: *America: History and Life.*

[23] The publisher, ABC-Clio, has two other humanities indexes on data bases (as well as in printed form): *ARTbibliographies Modern* and *Historical Abstracts,* which covers world history except for the United States and Canada, which are covered in *America: History and Life.*

various key words in the abstract allows the in-depth indexing. *Psychological Abstracts* is similarly available on a data base, as is *ERIC,* discussed in the next section. (See the second volume of this text, Part III, for a discussion of data bases.)

Most abstracting services not only analyze periodicals and books, but often include dissertations. However, only *Dissertation Abstracts* concentrates exclusively on the form—a form which covers all disciplines and interests. Dissertations are important for the reference librarian seeking specific, often unpublished information about a given subject, place, or person. Since most dissertations contain extensive bibliographies and footnotes, they can be used as unofficial bibliographies for some relatively narrow areas. Before a librarian begins a broad search for bibliographies in any area, these lists should be checked. There is a good chance that some student has already completed the bibliography sought, or at least has done enough work to indicate other major sources.

One problem with dissertations is that most libraries will not lend them. Policy differs, but the excuse for not lending is that (1) there is only one copy and it cannot be replaced or (2) a microfilm copy may be purchased from University Microfilms. The second explanation is most often the case, and today a library requiring a dissertation must usually purchase the microfilm or a printout copy at a slightly additional cost.

Dissertation Abstracts International both locates and gives brief abstracts of works accepted for a higher degree in American and Canadian universities as well as in a number of major European universities. Published monthly, the work arranges the dissertations under major classifications—the humanities and social sciences, and the sciences and engineering—which in turn are broken down into subsections. The material is indexed by author and key words in the titles. Unless the subject is named in the title, the dissertation is likely to be "lost." Hence, it is wise to search under a number of possible entries.

A similar type of search should be made when using the *Comprehensive Dissertation Index, 1861–1972* (Ann Arbor, Michigan: University Microfilms, 1973, 37 vols., plus annual supplements, 1974 to date). This, too, is a computer-generated key word and author index which is an entry not only into *Dissertation Abstracts,* but to other lists which carry the entries back to 1861.[24] The various volumes are arranged by subject area from four volumes for chemistry to a volume for philosophy and religion. The last five volumes are an author index. In most situations the librarian would begin here, consulting the indexes to *Dissertation Abstracts* only for updating. Full

---

[24] For an annotated bibliography of lists which deal with both dissertations and theses, see Michael M. Reynolds (ed.), *Guide to Theses and Dissertations* (Detroit: Gale Research Company, 1975).

information is given for each entry, including availability of the dissertation on microfilm from University Microfilms.

ERIC/IR: Specialized information service

> U.S. Educational Resources Information Center. *Resources in Education* (formerly *Research in Education*). Washington, D.C.: Government Printing Office, 1966 to date, monthly. $42.70.
>
> *Current Index to Journals in Education.* Riverside, New Jersey: Macmillan Information, 1969 to date, monthly, semiannual cumulations. $156.

Many of the current abstracting and indexing systems are only one part of documentation systems. They may be illustrated by ERIC/IR, or, in full, Educational Resources Information Center/ (clearinghouse for) Information Resources. The system includes (1) an index and an abstracting service available both in printed form and on data base for computer retrieval; (2) an ongoing subject vocabulary as represented in the frequently updated *Thesaurus of ERIC Descriptors;* (3) a dissemination system which depends primarily upon reproducing the material indexed on microfiche and distributing that microfiche to libraries; and (4) a decentralized organizational structure for acquiring and processing the documents which are indexed and abstracted.[25] In 1966, ERIC instituted a monthly abstract journal to bring order out of the chaos of reports on education and related areas. These reports, often federally or state financed, tended to be ignored in indexes and abstracting services. Why? Chiefly because there was an almost total lack of control. No one was sure when or by whom they were available for purchase.

As the body of reports grew, some control factor was needed. The first step was to create the Educational Research Information Center. The initial project was to collect and index some 1750 documents on the special educational needs of the disadvantaged. From this grew a national system of 16 clearinghouses designed to gather and to deliver to ERIC reports, monographs, and the like which would otherwise be lost to most of the very people for whom the reports were prepared.

While the Educational Resources Information Center in Washing-

---

[25] ERIC/IR is frequently discussed in library literature, as a glance at *Library Science Abstracts* will show. Two useful, brief summaries of the service will be found in Judith Yarborough's "A Novice's Guide to *ERIC*," *Online,* July, 1977, pp. 24–30; and "ERIC: What It Can Do for You/How to Use It," *Information Reports and Bibliographies,* vol. 4, no. 5, 1975. The 32-page issue is given over entirely to this helpful study. In early 1977, the headquarters for the system was located at Syracuse University, in Syracuse, New York. The move is reported in *Library Journal,* March 1, 1977, p. 529.

ton coordinates the system, the 16 clearinghouses are responsible for information on various disciplines and the abstracting of reports in their areas of interest. Locations change from contractual period to contractual period, but, for the most part, the centers tend to gravitate toward universities that have experts and special collections in the areas controlled. The clearinghouses have four primary responsibilities:

(1) Acquisition, selection, abstracting, and indexing of documents for Resources in Education *and the microfiche collection; (2) reference and information services (including computer searches at some clearinghouses) for the educational community; (3) publication of papers and monographs synthesizing and analyzing the literature; and (4) maintenance of contacts with professional associations and other client groups in their areas of specialization*[26]

There are two ways of retrieving information from the ERIC clearinghouses. The first is the abstracting service, *Resources in Education.* Each year, the monthly service abstracts or lists about 15,000 reports and related materials, including books, conference papers, and other documents. Arrangement is by accession number. The key to access is the subject and the author index in each issue. The index is cumulated semiannually and annually.

The second method of tapping ERIC is through *Current Index to Journals in Education.* This is an index to some 750 periodicals in education, which results in about 20,000 to 25,000 citations each year. Although published by a commercial firm, the indexing is provided by the 16 clearinghouses. The first part of the index is much like *Resources in Education* in form, that is, items are abstracted and arranged numerically by the accession number. The second part is the subject index, which again follows the style of *Resources in Education.* There are also an author index and a fourth section in which the indexed journals are arranged alphabetically by title and the table of contents for each is given, with accession numbers for articles.

One outstanding feature of ERIC, although a usual one among similar documentation systems such as that developed by the National Aeronautic and Space Administration, is that some 80 percent of the documents abstracted in *Resources in Education* are available on microfiche.[27] In most large libraries, the user finds the required citation in *Resources in Education,* and then, instead of laboriously looking for the item abstracted, he or she simply turns to the microfiche collection where the items are

[26] Barbara Booth, "A Look at ERIC after Ten Years," *Education Libraries Bulletin,* Autumn 1975, p. 3.

[27] About 20 percent of the items are copyrighted and must be purchased from the publisher or the author.

arranged by accession number. This, then, is a total information system and not the normal two-step bibliographical reference quest in which one finds the abstract or the indexed item and then must try to find the document, journal, book, or what have you, which the library may or may not have available.

Ideally, the total information system would be offered with the second ERIC finding tool, *Current Index to Journals in Education*. It is not. Why? Because here the index and abstracts are for journal articles and the journals themselves have to be searched. The cost of putting each article on a microfiche card, not to mention copyright problems with publishers, makes the cost of a total information service prohibitive.[28]

It is well to stress the difference between the two searching tools because both of them are integrated into a magnetic tape format which may be searched by computer. The computer printout does not discriminate between the two services. Hence, one may end up with part of the material on the printout being available on microfiche and the other part being available only through finding and searching.

Another feature which is linked to indexes and abstracts available in machine-readable form is individual indexing. Lacking an adequate indexing system when ERIC began, the compilers of *Resources in Education* and *Current Index to Journals in Education* decided to rely on indexing from terms used in the documents themselves. From this "free indexing" developed the *Thesaurus of ERIC Descriptors*, which, as of 1977, included some 6000 terms and approximately 3000 cross-references from synonyms. The advantage of the *Thesaurus* is that it not only quickly gives the user the proper subject heading, but also, like any thesaurus, suggests additional concepts for search. Although it is not absolutely necessary to use the *Thesaurus* for searching, beginners in particular will find it extremely useful.

Also, most librarians and users tend to become at least vaguely familiar with subject headings employed by the Library of Congress or Sears. These headings normally are much broader than those found in a thesaurus for a particular discipline's indexing or abstracting service. The thesaurus gives the wide spectrum of possible headings which will not be found in other services.

The ERIC/IR system offers several additional services, including

---

[28] Here, *Current Index to Journals in Education (CIJE)* is no different from any index which limits itself to analyzing periodicals. The H. W. Wilson Company *Education Index* does just that, and users do not expect microfiche copies of articles. The differences between these two major education indexes are discussed by Alan Schorr in "*Education Index* and *Current Index to Journals in Education:* Do We Really Need Both?" *Journal of Academic Librarianship*, July 1976, pp. 135–136. His answer: No. He thinks *CIJE* is quite enough.

publications and referral services to other information sources. There are nearly 175 publicly and privately operated centers where computer searches may be made of the ERIC files, i.e., where one may find what one seeks, although with a bit more trouble, by searching through *Resources in Education* and/or *Current Index to Journals in Education*. Where this computer search service is offered, it is often normal to find related data bases which will also be searched. For example, *Psychological Abstracts* is one of the data bases quite commonly linked to ERIC.

Last, but not least, ERIC is an invaluable source of information for many types of reference queries. As education is America'a largest "industry," the work done in its name involves almost every field of endeavor. Any reader of this text who is preparing a paper on library-oriented matters should turn first to *Library Literature* and related abstracting services, and then to *Resources in Education*. Actually, one might reverse the order of search because it is easier to find materials on microfiche than to go through countless periodicals. Researchers in fields ranging from political science and history to psychology and sociology should carefully examine the resources of ERIC. The amount of material to be found there will be a pleasant shock.

SUGGESTED READING

American Library Association, RASD Bibliography and Indexes Committee, "The State of the Art of Bibliography and Indexing of American History," *RQ,* Spring 1976, pp. 219–221. A discussion and a description of general and specific aids for the historian, with suggestions for needed indexes and bibliographies.

Bakewell, K. G. B., "Indexing Methods Used by Some Abstracting and Indexing Services," *The Indexer,* April 1976, pp. 3–8. A clear analysis of various methods of arrangement for indexes, as well as a discussion of subject headings.

Borko, Harold, and Charles Bernier, *Abstracting Concepts and Methods.* New York: Academic Press, 1975. Both a history of abstracting services and a how-to-do-it discussion of organization and publication. Good section on automation.

Collison, Robert, "Public Affairs Information Service, 1915–1975," *IFLA Journal,* vol. 1 (1975), no. 3, pp. 198–209. An informative, critical history of this service, as well as background on the *Foreign Language Index.* Particularly useful for its section on how the service is edited.

Edwards, Tom, "A Comparative Analysis of the Major Abstracting and Indexing Services for Library and Information Science," *Unesco Bulletin for Libraries,* January–February 1976, pp. 18–25; and Keen, E. Michael, "A Retrieval Comparison of Six Published Indexes in the Field of Library and Information Science," ibid., pp. 26–36. Two surveys which not only show comparative data on services of interest to all librarians, but indicate methodology which might be applicable for analysis of other services.

Hickey, Doralyn, "Subject Analysis: An Interpretive Survey," *Library Trends,* July 1976, pp. 273–292. A history of subject headings and a note on the future. The author discusses various systems and gives useful background on the problems of subject headings.

Jackson, Eugene, et al., "Practical Training for Indexing, a Teaching Methodology," *Special Libraries,* September 1976, pp. 428–432. In describing how to teach indexing, the author gives useful hints on the construction of an index and the problems likely to be met by an indexer. Probably of more value to teachers than students, particularly as it ends with a short bibliography on the subject.

Kanwischer, Dorothy, "Subject Heading Trauma," *Wilson Library Bulletin,* May 1975, pp. 651–654. A lighthearted, yet practical examination of subject headings and the confusion they cause for reference librarians. The author suggests a more realistic approach than now employed.

Kermode, Frank, "Getting in by the Back Door," *The Indexer,* April 1977, pp. 141–142. The famous critic presents a historical summary of indexes and a sarcastic whack at jargon employed.

Thaxton, Lyn, and Mary E. Redus, "Of Migraines and Maddox: The Making of the *Atlanta Constitution* Index," *RQ,* Spring 1975, pp. 225–227. Narrative of how two librarians went about indexing a local newspaper, with helpful hints of what to do (and not to do).

CHAPTER FIVE

Encyclopedias: General and Subject

THE PURPOSE OF the general encyclopedia is to capsulize and organize the world's accumulated knowledge, or at least that part of it that is of interest to readers. A good encyclopedia should be the source of answers to almost all questions other than those regarding a local or an immediate event. Most encyclopedias, however, are not.

Sales agents attempt to push sets which "cover the scope of human knowledge, avoiding omissions and duplications," to quote an *Encyclopaedia Britannica* advertisement. And the sales force is aided by the definition of an encyclopedia: "A literary work containing extensive information on all branches of knowledge, usually arranged in alphabetical order."[1] "Extensive" is not "all," but the concept of total coverage is inherent in the myth of the encyclopedia, a myth best summarized by Denis Diderot in the introduction to his eighteenth-century *Encyclopedia*. Diderot stated his classic set's overall purpose was "to collect all knowledge scattered over the face of the earth . . . so that our children, by becoming more educated, may at the same time become more virtuous and happier."[2]

The admirable belief in the efficacy of encyclopedias is no more. Diderot's noble thoughts have been modified by the door-to-door salesper-

---

[1] *The Oxford English Dictionary* (London: Oxford University Press, 1933, vol. 3), p. 153.

[2] Stephen J. Gendzier (ed.), *Denis Diderot's Encyclopedia* (New York: J & J Harper Editions, 1969), p. xv.

son. Since the beginning of the twentieth century, "aggressive salesman-
ship rather than editorial innovation has always been the driving force"
behind the general encyclopedia.[3] The eighteenth-century optimism has
been swamped by the sales pitch and the massive accumulations of data
which threaten to destroy the general encyclopedia. No one is more aware
of the threat than publishers.[4] Looking back over the years which went
into the planning of the fifteenth edition of the *Encyclopaedia Britannica,* its
editor asks:

> *In [our] age is a general encyclopedia even conceptually possible? If it is conceded
> that the lack of theory . . . of general education has made it impossible for the
> encyclopaedist to establish a base of knowledge that can be assumed to be held in
> common by his readers and his authors and his advisers alike, is it possible to do
> more than surrender? [Should we not produce] a series of specialized encyclopae-
> dias for those versed in each of the specializations important enough and suffi-
> ciently well established to have developed their own sub-circles of knowledge?*[5]

The questions proved rhetorical. The publishers of the *Britannica,* to
no one's real surprise, decided a general set was feasible. Still, the debate
goes on, and it is safe to say that the general encyclopedia form is not
likely to multiply. There will be fewer and fewer sets.[6]

While the loss may not be noticed by the electronically trained children of the parents who supported encyclopedias, it will be a loss in libraries. Collison points out that the sets are invaluable for librarians because

> *of the various types of reference works—who's whos, dictionaries, atlases, gazet-
> teers, directories, and so forth—the encyclopaedia is the only one that can be
> termed self contained. . . . Only the encyclopaedia attempts to give a comprehen-
> sive summary of what is known. . . . To this end it employs many features that*

---

[3] Harvey Einbinder, "Politics and the New Britannica," *The Nation,* March 22, 1975, p. 344.

[4] Sales figures indicate the falling off of encyclopedia sales—down almost 8 percent in 1975
as compared with 1974. The only increase cited in this category since 1970 occurred in 1974.
A newsletter for the industry (*Media Industry Newsletter,* March 8, 1976, pp. 2–3) reported that
the strongest sales for encyclopedias occur on the West Coast, followed by those on the East
Coast and then by those in the South. Later figures show sales have improved from 1976
through 1977, but in volume are short of what they were a decade ago. See: J. K. Noble,
"AAP 1976 Statistics," *Publishers Weekly,* July 4, 1977, 41–43.

[5] Warren E. Preece, "The New Britannica," *Scholarly Publishing,* January 1974, pp. 107–108.

[6] Encyclopedia publishers are seeking methods "of exploiting scholarly material at the popular level." The *Britannica* in late 1976 was exploring means of publishing books "designed for
supermarkets." At the same time, "a discreet distance would be maintained between this
kind of product and the encyclopedia as a separate entity sold door-to-door," from Paul
Nathan, "Rights and Permissions," *Publishers Weekly,* November 1, 1976, p. 46.

can help in its task, including illustrations, maps, diagrams, charts and statistical tables.[7]

To give that "comprehensive summary of what is known" may have been possible 30 or 40 years ago. No more. At best the general encyclopedia can give a summary, but it is not likely to be "comprehensive" except in a few areas selected by the publisher. The specialist, and to a given extent everyone is a specialist these days, seeks the same "comprehensive summary" in a subject encyclopedia. Almost all major disciplines now have their own sets, for example, the *McGraw-Hill Encyclopedia of Science and Technology, The International Encyclopedia of the Social Sciences,* and the *Encyclopedia of Photography.* The punishing waves of new information have swamped the general encyclopedia, yet left in their wake excellent subject sets.

Today's reference librarian must know when to turn to a general or a subject encyclopedia. As the general sets are still more prevalent in libraries, they will be considered first.

Publishers[8]

How good is this encyclopedia? Before considering that vital question, as well as the equally interesting one of cost, one must ask: Just what choice do I have in the purchase of a set? The real, as opposed to the theoretical, choice among various general encyclopedias is radically limited by the number of publishers. Four firms control approximately 95 percent of the general encyclopedias published for all age groups in the United States. They are:

(1) Encyclopaedia Britannica Educational Corporation. The Chicago-based publisher, largest of the four, issues *Encyclopaedia Britannica, Compton's Encyclopedia and Fact Index, Britannica Junior Encyclopaedia, Compton's Precyclopedia, Young Children's Encyclopedia, Great Books of the Western World, The Annals of America,* etc. Among other holdings are G. & C. Merriam Company, publisher of Webster's dictionaries; Frederick A. Praeger, Inc.; and the Phaidon Press, Ltd. They also distribute, but do not publish, the two-volume *Random House Encyclopedia.*

---

[7] R. L. Collison, encyclopedia entry in *The New Encyclopaedia Britannica. Macropaedia* (Chicago: Encyclopaedia Britannica, 1974, vol. 6), p. 782.

[8] Beginning with the June 15, 1975, issue of *The Booklist* (pp. 1089–1091), the "Reference and Subscription Book Review" section published a series of explanatory background articles on encyclopedia publishers. Others follow at infrequent intervals.

(2) Grolier Incorporated. The New York firm publishes *The Encyclopedia Americana, The Encyclopedia International, The New Book of Knowledge, The American Peoples Encyclopedia* (published, also, as *University Society Encyclopedia*—same work, different name) and distributes a number of other sets. It also has controlling interest in Scarecrow Press. Sales are close to the *Britannica* in volume.

(3) Macmillan Educational Corporation. Although a large publishing house, it is only fourth in sales of encyclopedias. The only two major sets are *Collier's* and the *Merit Students Encyclopedia*. However, Macmillan publishes a number of related works ranging from the *Encyclopedia of Philosophy* to the *Harvard Classics*.

(4) Field Enterprises. The Chicago firm sells more than half the encyclopedia units in the United States, and its *World Book* is by and large the most popular among the children's and young people's sets. Like Macmillan, the firm is involved in numerous other business interests varying from department stores to newspapers. The firm also publishes *The World Book Dictionary* and *Childcraft*.

The librarian who comes across an encyclopedia whose publisher is not one of four or five of the most reputable publishers has a built-in warning that more than average care should be taken to double-check its authority and, for that matter, everything else about the set.[9]

As in the automobile industry, competition among the big four is fierce, although at the same time there is a noticeable tendency to copy a success. If one automobile design captures the fancy of the public, the other manufacturers tend to copy and modify. Much the same is true of encyclopedias. Rising costs will check changes such as were made in the fifteenth edition of the *Britannica*. It is questionable whether any publisher will risk a similar $40-million investment. Nevertheless, on a more modest scale, such as attention to fashions, non-Western countries, and outer space, the encyclopedias tend to follow one after the other in editorial changes.

A definite result of the competition is a strong emphasis on what the publishers call continuous revision. Actually, this means revising about 10 percent of the set each year.[10] Primary attention is given to current news

---

[9] A fifth publisher with a creditable set is Funk & Wagnalls and its *Funk & Wagnalls New Encyclopedia*. And just to confuse matters, the otherwise reliable Grolier is not always up to its own standards; its *American Peoples Encyclopedia* was rejected by the American Library Association as a purchase for libraries. (*The Booklist*, July 15, 1974, pp. 1206–08.)

[10] The precise percentage of change varies with each publisher, and few, if any, will release exact figures. Typical is *World Book*, which each year adds from 113 to 158 new articles and completely or partially revises 2078 to 2838 articles. Precisely what percentage of the set is revised is difficult to estimate as there are close to 20,000 entries, but not all of these may be

items, which by their very currency are more apt to be noticed by readers. Aspects of literature, philosophy, the social sciences, and even the sciences which are not likely to change drastically are usually skipped over in revision. The result after a number of years is a certain imbalance between current statistical data and out-of-date attitudes and views on everything from social issues to interpretation of history and scientific discovery.

EVALUATING ENCYCLOPEDIAS

A librarian's choice of general encyclopedias for adults, young people, and children is limited by (1) what is available from four or five publishers, and (2) sets tried, tested, and used over the years. Within a half-dozen or so choices, the average library will have either the *Encyclopaedia Britannica* and the *Americana* for adults, or both; possibly a young people's encyclopedia such as *Compton's* or *Collier's;* and a children's work such as *World Book* or the *Merit Students Encyclopedia.* If budget allows, a revised set is purchased every year, or at the least every five or six years.

Problems arise when one must limit the choice to only one or two of these titles, or when (and this is most frequent) a user asks about a set which is not in the library. How, then, does one evaluate an encyclopedia? The publisher has been mentioned, but beyond that there is a direct and an indirect method. The direct one is to evaluate the set personally. The indirect method, and the most often used, is to rely upon reviews.

The advantage of the direct approach, at least here, is that it gives the librarian some method of analyzing encyclopedias and, at the same time, sets rules for the analysis of similar works, particularly subject encyclopedias. So what does one consider? The answer: the purpose of the set; the scope, authority, and writing style; viewpoint and objectivity; format, arrangement, and entry; index; and cost.

Recency is another major point, covered in the preceding discussion of continuous revision. One quick method of checking timeliness or recency: Pick a subject, place, or individual you know and see if the set has the latest information in the entry. Also, check the illustrations to see if they are up to date. A quick check point: fashions, automobile designs, and major political figures.

---

described as "articles." Still, as 10 percent revision of the 20,000 would mean 2000 revisions a year, one may say that *World Book* probably does revise 10 to 15 percent of the set annually, as do other reputable publishers. (Data used here are from a publicity release from *World Book* dated January 1, 1976: "Facts About the World Book Encyclopedia—22 volumes. 1976 Edition.")

Purpose

The purposes of an encyclopedia vary with the reader and with its scope. For the general encyclopedia, there are two primary purposes:

1. To provide a source of answers to fact questions, usually of a simple nature such as who, what, when, where, and how.

2. To provide a source of background information for both the expert and the layperson. For example, intellectuals may be puzzled over C. P. Snow's insistence that they know the second law of thermodynamics. The law is relatively well explained in most encyclopedias. Conversely, a child may be just as much in the dark over what set off the Civil War as the intellectual is about physics. Again, the child will find a clear answer in an encyclopedia.

A third purpose is directional; that is, the bibliographies at the end of articles may help the reader to find additional material in a given subject area. The importance of adequate bibliographies is particularly well recognized at the juvenile level (augmented by the use of study aids) and at the specialist's level (by highly developed bibliographies in narrow subject areas). Many encyclopedias now offer a variety of study guides which indicate related articles the student might employ to put together, with the help of other books, a truly creative paper rather than a carbon copy of an encyclopedia article.

To clear up a common misunderstanding, no general encyclopedia is a proper source for research. (This does not include specialized works.) It is only a springboard. Furthermore, in presenting material with almost no differentiation, the general encyclopedia is not completely accurate or up to date; important facts must be double-checked in another source, if only in another encyclopedia.

At the child's level, another purpose is often falsely advanced. An encyclopedia, no matter how good, is not a substitute for additional reading or for a collection of supporting reference books. In their natural enthusiasm, some salespeople and advertising copywriters are carried away with the proposition that an encyclopedia-oriented child is an educated child. Perhaps in reaction against this false purpose, too many teachers go to the other extreme and insist that a child find information for a paper or a solution to a problem anywhere but in an encyclopedia.

Although any good encyclopedia offers stimulation and information for the young, there is a built-in danger recognized by many teachers. The teacher who forbids the student to use the encyclopedia for classroom assignments is fearful of what one librarian termed engendering the encyclopedia-oriented, rather than the book-oriented, child. When the word gets around that the whole assignment may be garnered out of one work, few students will care to explore the resources of the library.

Scope

The scope of the specialized encyclopedia is evident in name, and becomes even more obvious with use. The scope of the general encyclopedia is dictated primarily by two considerations.

Age Level The children's encyclopedias, such as the *World Book,* are tied to curriculum. Consequently, they include more in-depth material on subjects of general interest to grade and high schools than, say, an adult encyclopedia such as the *Britannica.* Recognizing that the strongest sales appeal is to the adult with children, most encyclopedia publishers aim their advertising at this vulnerable controller of the family pocketbook. All the standard sets claim that an audience ranging from grades 6 to 12 can understand and use their respective works. This may be true of the exceptionally bright child, but the librarian is advised to check the real age compatibility of the material before purchase, not merely the advertised age level.

A consequence of attempting to be all things to all age levels is twofold: (1) Even in many adult encyclopedias, the material is shortened for easier comprehension by a child; and (2) the effort at clarity frequently results in a downright oversimplified approach to rather complex questions.

Emphasis If age level dictates one approach to scope, the emphasis of the editor accounts for the other. At one time, this varied more than it does today; one set would be especially good for science, another for literature. Today, the emphasis is essentially a matter of deciding what compromise will be made between scholarship and popularity. Why, for example, in most adult encyclopedias, is at least as much space given to the subject of advertising as to communism? This is not to argue the merit of any particular emphasis, but only to point out that examining emphasis is a method of determining scope.

Authority

The first question to ask about any reference book is its authority. If it is authoritative, it normally follows that it will be up to date, accurate, and relatively objective. Contributors and publishers constitute the authority for encyclopedias.

Authority is evident in the names of the scholars and experts who sign the articles or are listed as contributors somewhere in the set. There are three quick tests for authority: (1) recognition by the reader of a prominent name, particularly the author of the best recent book on the subject; (2) focus on a field known to the reader and assurance that contributors are leaders in their fields; and (3) finally, determination of whether the authors' qualifications (as noted by position, degrees, occupation, etc.) are related to the article.

An indication of the encyclopedia's revision policy and age can be ascertained from knowledge about the authors. Some contributors may be literally dead, and while a certain number of deceased authorities is perfectly acceptable, too many in this category indicates either overabundant plagiarism from older sets or lack of any meaningful revision.

There is another fascinating aspect concerning authority. At one period, readers were willing to accept a statement because of the value of the so-called expert's public office. Now, reliance on a contributor's office can be perilous, for publishers are ever sensitive to criticism. It is no accident, for example, that the FBI article in the *Britannica* is no longer signed by J. Edgar Hoover, or that the last word on marijuana is no longer the opinion of the U.S. Commissioner of Narcotics, or that the head of the CIA does not now prepare the article on that organization. Not long ago, authorities such as these brought weight and standing to an encyclopedia. Today?

Writing style

When the writing style of today's encyclopedia is considered, none of the general sets is for the expert. As the editor of the *Britannica* puts it: "Perhaps the most critical editorial policy that was established [was] our absolute certainty that general encyclopaedias are inappropriate source books for specialists in their own areas."[11] Basically, everything should be comprehensible to the person Preece calls "the curious intelligent lay reader." For the *Britannica,* at least, this is an about-face since the time when not only advertising but the articles themselves proclaimed the scholarly and pedantic nature of many of the contributions.

Recognizing that the purchasers are laypersons, who considerably outnumber the scholars, encyclopedia firms tend to operate in a relatively standard fashion. Contributors are given certain topics and outlines of what is needed and expected. The manuscript is then submitted to one or more of the encyclopedia's editors (editorial staffs of the larger encyclopedias range from 100 to 200 full-time persons), who revise, cut, and query— all for the purpose of making the contributor's manuscript understandable to the average reader. The extent of editing varies with each encyclopedia, from the extreme for the children's works (where word difficulty and length of sentence are almost as important as the content) to a limited degree for large-name contributors.

[11] Warren E. Preece, "The New Britannica," *Scholarly Publishing,* April 1974, p. 233.

Serving as a bridge between contributor and reader, the editor strives for readability by reducing complicated vocabulary and jargon to terms understandable to the lay reader or young person. The purpose is to rephrase specialized thought in common language without insulting that thought—or, more likely, that eminent contributor. In the humanities and the social sciences, this often works, but only as long as the contributing scholar is willing to have his or her initials appended to something that will not cause a colleague's criticism. Thanks to necessary concepts and language in science which cannot be reduced even for the so-called "intelligent lay reader," the scientific article often defies editing. The definitions of mathematical terms in the *Britannica*, for example, are uncompromisingly difficult and technical, as is the article titled "Atomic Structure," which has to assume the reader's familiarity with, among other items, the quantum theory. Actually, more latitude is given editors of children's and young people's encyclopedias to clip the excessive scholarship of contributors. For this reason, the children's set is usually a much better source of overall information on science for a layperson than an adult encyclopedia.

Viewpoint and objectivity

How objective and fair are encyclopedia articles? Back in 1964, a Columbia professor, Harvey Einbinder, detailed almost article by article the errors and the lack of objectivity in the fourteenth edition of the *Encyclopaedia Britannica*.[12] The attack was so devastating as to be at least one reason for the publisher to revise the complete set. (Interestingly enough, Einbinder was never given credit for this massive push toward revision. *Britannica* officials publicly refused comment on his book.)

Although the fifteenth edition was almost totally revised, the revision hardly pleased everyone. For example, great pains were taken to be objective about Soviet Russia, but when the fifteenth edition was published, there was severe criticism of the article on the Soviet Republics.

In the previous (14th) edition these articles were written by non-Soviet scholars; in the new edition they are by Soviet citizens. As a result [the material] is a rehash of the current thinking at the moment, which in many cases enjoys only a

---

[12] Harvey Einbinder, *The Myth of the Britannica* (New York: Grove Press, Inc., 1964). The analysis is still worthwhile for students who wish to study detailed criticism of a reference work. In the otherwise good *Britannica* article on "Encyclopaedias," the pertinacious Einbinder is not even mentioned—an understandable oversight for the *Britannica*.

tenuous connection with what we in the West consider objective fact. [For example] . . . *None of the articles say that the Communist party is the only one permitted or that republic officials serve at Moscow's pleasure.*[13]

How is the encyclopedia to be objective when such controversial issues are involved as capitalism and communism, civil rights and segregation, conservatism or liberalism? There are two approaches here. One is to ignore the differences entirely, depending on a chronological, historical approach. The other is an effort to balance an article by presenting two or more sides. The reader should expect at least a projection of different views, either by the contributor or by the editor.

Another aspect of the question of viewpoint is what the editor chooses to include or to exclude, to emphasize or de-emphasize. Nothing dates an encyclopedia faster than antiquated articles about issues and ideas either no longer acceptable or of limited interest. An encyclopedia directed at the Western reader can scarcely be expected to give as much coverage in depth, let us say, to Angola as to New York State. Yet, to exclude more than passing mention of Angola will not be suitable either, particularly in view of the emergence of Africa as a new world force. The proportion of one article to another plagues any conscientious encyclopedia editor, and there probably is no entirely satisfactory solution.

Discussing the case of the *Britannica* articles on the Soviet Republics, *Britannica* editor Warren Preece summarizes a common enough escape hatch from controversy: Simply ignore the problem.

There is no word in the Britannica *pieces concerning difficulties imposed anywhere on those [in the Soviet] professing religion. "We don't deal with political freedom or religious freedom," Mr. Preece said. The 14th edition's article on the Estonian Socialist Soviet Republic speaks of rigged elections and of mass deportations and executions. . . . The new article ignores all this. "Figures about deportations are not genuinely encyclopedic—they're yearbook data, . . . I concede the possibility of prejudice by omission as well as commission," Mr. Preece said.*[14]

The *Britannica* is not alone in this rationale. Similar examples may be found in all other sets. And it may be argued that the reason for exclusion of certain data about issues and ideas is more an editorial oversight than a "plot" to mislead.

---

[13] Israel Shenker, "Britannica Yields to Criticism, Alters Soviet Republic Articles," *The New York Times,* September 17, 1975, pp. 1, 40.

[14] Ibid., p. 49.

The best summary of objectivity is offered by an experienced former editor of *The Atlantic* monthly:

> *Objectivity is an illusion of the mechanical age. We rightly, we believe, confer more value on the profoundly perceived irrelevancy than on the casually recorded Fact. We parade invention as truth, experience as history. But reality, too, plants the weed of fiction in the cultivated fields of Fact. Long live the erroneous encyclopedia.*[15]

Format

A good format considers the size, typeface, illustrations, binding, and total arrangement. If components of the format are well done, the set is not necessarily made acceptable thereby, although at least it is not an insult to the senses. Among the components to consider when evaluating format are the following.

Illustrations (photographs, diagrams, charts, maps, etc.)   Nothing will tip off the evaluator faster as to the currency of the encyclopedia than a cursory glance at the illustrations. For example, in discussing the fourteenth edition of the *Britannica,* one reviewer observed that the illustrations dated it most obtrusively, and then cited a few examples:

> *[See] the series of pencil drawings of the Woolworth tower and the photographs of the New York telephone building—in all their angular, Rockefellerian self confidence—under Architecture; Mary Pickford roguish for Motion Pictures; Jacques Tati-like rooms for Interior Decoration, a shingled lady in a satin sheath descending a stairway made of white blocks into an environment of chromium and white leather. . . . This late Jazz Age artwork takes one back to . . . the 1930s.*[16]

Even illustrations of the 1970s will not be suitable unless they relate directly to the text and to the interests of the reader. The librarian might ask: Do the illustrations consider the age of the user, or do they depend on figures or drawings totally foreign, say, to a twelve-year-old? Do they emphasize important matters, or are they too general? Are they functional, or simply attractive? Are the captions adequate?

The reproduction process is important. Some illustrations have a

[15] Stephen Brook, "An Introduction to Omniscience," *Bookletter,* September 16, 1974, p. 4.
[16] Anthony Quinton, "The New, Improved *Britannica,*" *The Times Literary Supplement,* October 11, 1974, p. 1120.

displeasing physical quality, perhaps because too little or too much ink was employed, or the paper was a poor grade, or an inadequate cut or halftone screen was used.

Illustrations are particularly useful in children's and young people's encyclopedias. The *World Book*, for example, has a well-deserved reputation for the timeliness and excellence of both its black and white and numerous colored illustrations. At the same time, an abundance of illlustrations is by way of being a tip-off that an encyclopedia is (1) primarily for children and young people, or (2) primarily a "popular" set or one-volume work purposefully prepared for a wide appeal. Neither purpose is to be censured, but when the librarian is seeking out an encyclopedia, say, which is superior for ready-reference purposes, he or she is likely to be more interested in the amount of text (and how it is presented) than in the number of illustrations. A case in point: See the discussion of *The New Columbia Encyclopedia* and *The Random House Encyclopedia* beginning on page 166.

Size of type   It should not be too large, even for the children's encyclopedias, or too small. Even more important is the type style, the spacing between lines, and the width of the column. All these factors, used wisely, will make the work more readable. If they are used poorly, the encyclopedia will be difficult to read, especially over any length of time.

Binding   It should be suitable for rough wear, particularly in a library situation. Conversely, buyers should be warned that a frequent method of jacking up the price of an encyclopedia is to charge the user for a so-called deluxe binding which often is no better, and in fact may be worse, than the standard library binding.

Volume size   Finally, consideration should be given to the size of the physical volume. Is it comfortable to use? Equally important, may it be opened readily without strain on the binding?

The sheer weight of a single volume, heretofore the concern chiefly of librarians who had to wrestle with giant folios or the prosaic bound volume of newspapers, is worth considering. More and more publishers seem to favor larger and heavier one-volume encyclopedias. A scholarly summary of the situation is given by Ian Hamilton:

> *Newcomers to the reading of encyclopedias, or specifically to the lifting of ency-clopedias into what is known as "the reading position," do not always realize that more than just brute strength is required; far more important than physique are qualities of concentration, of timing and technique. There are two popular and time-honoured styles, but whether the reader chooses the Two-Hand Snatch or the Two-Hand Clean and Jerk similar demands—for skill rather than just*

"shove"—will operate. My own favourite method—the "split" version of the Snatch—will serve as an example; here, the important moment occurs when, as the reader pushes the encyclopedia upwards, he lunges under it, thrusting one foot forward and simultaneously the other foot back to land in a "split" fore and aft position, while at the same time fixing the encyclopedia directly before his eyes with straight arms. One cannot emphasize too strongly that what matters is the precise timing of the lunge. Disaster can result if this is bungled.[17]

Arrangement and entry

The traditional encyclopedic arrangement is the familiar alphabetical approach to material with numerous cross-references and an index. All major sets follow this tradition. Average users are so accustomed to the alphabetical order of information that they may lose sight of an inherent difficulty in the custom:

The alphabetical presentation put a premium on reducing knowledge to its smallest nameable bits: obviously there would be no value in alphabetical organization in a set consisting, for instance, of only five gigantic all-embracing articles. The alphabetical organization also put a premium on the concrete, on the thing that could be named. In a sense, encyclopaedias have served man as mnemonic devices, and such devices are more at home with "the Wars of the Roses" than they are with "dynastic struggles caused by such and such, raging in such and such, from such and such to such and such." Usually, it has seemed necessary in alphabetical encyclopaedias to have an article dealing with the Wars of the Roses, and separate articles dealing with each of the families involved and, on occasion, separate articles dealing with separate battles. But the danger has always been that, more often than not, fragmentation has resulted in a treatment that worked against understanding, at least to the extent that understanding depended on contextual relationships. If an editor has guessed that someone will want to look up the occupation of the Taku Forts, he may call for an article, "Taku Forts"; if he has guessed that someone may want to look up the Boxer Uprising in which that occupation occurred, he may call for an article on that, too, and for one on the Manchu Dynasty, and another on the History of China, and so forth and so on. But he does so at the expense either of much repetition or of loss of understanding on the part of the reader who is unwilling to read the many articles that may now be required.[18]

[17] Ian Hamilton, "This Browsing Life," *The Times Literary Supplement,* July 4, 1975, p. 724. The critic is discussing the 4-pound *Oxford Companion to Sports and Games* (New York: Oxford University Press, 1975). His review of the 10½ pound *New Columbia Encyclopedia* was lost in a bungled lunge.

[18] Warren E. Preece, "The New Britannica," *Scholarly Publishing,* January 1974, p. 109.

The *Britannica's* "solution" to this problem is questionable, although the problem itself has wider implications than the editorial policy for a single encyclopedia. Beginners, for example, are often confused by any reference work from abstracting services to directories which are constructed on other than alphabetical order. Sometimes this is carelessness; but more often it is a concerted effort to put the fragmented humpty-dumpty of a discipline back together again in a logical, non-A-B-C fashion. Be that as it may, the arrangement may be examined in terms of what is known as "specific" or "broad" entry.

General encyclopedias differ not only in terms of target audience but in the length of their articles. Some use the *specific entry,* such as the *Americana.* Here, the information is broken down into small, specific parts. Other sets employ the *broader entry form,* which means longer, more inclusive articles. For example, under the broad entry "Sun," the reader will find all the information on the sun. Under a specific-entry system, there will be a short article on the sun, plus separate articles on eclipses, seasons, tides, and so on.

Specific- and broad-entry forms are important to reference librarians. When one is searching for a quick fact, the specific-entry form is sometimes easier because the librarian rarely has to use the index volume, but simply reaches for the logical subject. Conversely, for the broad-entry form it is safer first to consult the index. The specific subject one is seeking may be part of another article. (Many encyclopedias based upon the broad-entry principle compensate by using numerous cross-references to related items, outline study guides, and such.)

The shift from the long to the short entry form may be explained in a number of ways, but it is primarily an effort to make the works more suitable for general, popular use. Newspapers, television, radio, and films have made many people quite literally unable to follow long, detailed explanations. And where the articles are long, as in *The Random House Encyclopedia,* they are broken up by numerous illustrations and subheadings to give the illusion of not one but hundreds of separate small articles or bits of information.

Index

All general encyclopedias are alphabetically arranged, and some publishers have concluded that with suitable *see* and *see also* references, the arrangement should serve to eliminate the index.

The argument for an index is simply that a single article may contain dozens of names and events which cannot be located unless there is a detailed index. The *Britannica* dropped the index volume to the fifteenth edition, substituting instead the *Micropaedia.* Lack of an index is the single greatest weakness of the set, and will be discussed later.

Cost

Prices for the same sets vary greatly, depending as much upon the honesty of the salesperson as on the actual prices. Aware of the advantage of having their sets in libraries, the big four encyclopedia publishers usually offer the library a special price. However, the lowest *retail* prices, for purposes of comparison, in 1977 were approximately: $699, *Britannica;* $480, *Americana;* $430, *Collier's;* $199, *Compton's;* $299, *Merit;* and $273, *World Book.* Most of the encyclopedias for children are grouped just below $300, those for adults between $300 and $500 (quite a spread), and those for young adults between $200 and $300. Given these prices, it is understandable why laypersons should seriously consider quality "supermarket" encyclopedias such as *Funk & Wagnalls New Encyclopedia* ($65) or secondhand sets of the "basic" encyclopedias available from many bookstores at $50 to $100.

Reviews: Indirect evaluation

There are two major sources of encyclopedia reviews: (1) periodic criticism by the "Reference and Subscription Book Reviews" in *The Booklist;* and (2) Kenneth Kister's *Encyclopedia Buying Guide . . . , A Consumer Guide to General Encyclopedias in Print* (New York: R. R. Bowker Company, 1976, 288 pp.). The American Library Association group, in *The Booklist,* "reviews major (general) encyclopedic works at regular, approximately five-year intervals, or whenever a significant change of structure of format appears."[19] In a previous discussion of the "Reference and Subscription Book Reviews" it was noted they are objective, lengthy, and usually reliable.

Kister's book will be revised every three years. The second edition is to be published in mid-1978. The evaluative guide features critical remarks about some 40 sets and one-volume works. Each entry is arranged in a similar fashion, beginning with basic bibliographical data and concluding with a bibliography. Depending upon the importance of the set, the detailed analysis may run from a single page to 17 pages on the *Britannica.* There is a useful chart on "encyclopedias at a glance," a number of appendixes, and a title-subject index. An important feature in the revised 1978 edition: a section on "Recency" for each encyclopedia profile. According to Kister, the charts will feature numerous subjects and then show in a comparative way which of the sets is "up to date" when discussing the

---

[19] *The Booklist,* July 1, 1976, p. 1541. However, one can be almost certain that non–big four encyclopedias will receive thumbs-down reviews. Of the works reviewed between 1974 and the end of 1976, only two Funk & Wagnalls titles were deemed acceptable besides those of the major companies. The two recommended were *Funk & Wagnalls New Encyclopedia* and the *Young Students Encyclopedia.*

subject. Kister notes: "The recency chart will be repeated in the profiles for each of the sets compared. About five or six topics will be covered in each chart, with more examples discussed in the text of the profile." Intelligent, well-written, and carefully researched, the Kister volume is a required item in all libraries, and particularly in those where people are apt to ask "Which is the best set?" The question "What is best for whom at what price?" is creditably answered here.

In comparison

Is X set better than Y set? One way to check is to follow a comparative road. Using the same subject, a person may check it in two or three or more encyclopedias. For example, Kister sought information on abortion and on court cases "involving leaders of the American Communist Party during the 1950s" in the *Britannica, Collier's,* and *Americana.*[20] The search told him many things about the purpose, objectivity, accessibility, and other characteristics of the sets. A similar practice is followed by writers of the reviews found in "Reference and Subscription Book Reviews." A student needs no particular skill to check a familiar topic in two, three, or more sets.

Sales practices

The dollar volume of all subscription reference books (of which encyclopedias are a good 96 percent) in 1976 was slightly over $286 million. The figure is more meaningful when one considers that the dollar value of adult trade books was only some $573 million. Translated into hard business, these figures mean that the four major encyclopedia publishers are first and foremost sales organizations that, with a limited number of general sets, must constantly attempt to increase dollar volume and the number of annual units sold.[21]

The pressures to push sales have encouraged certain sales methods. In 1976 the *Britannica's* sales of more than $70 million were made through the door-to-door approach. The practice of selling major encyclopedias primarily door to door and not through bookstores results in some dubious practices.

Since the early 1970s the U.S. Federal Trade Commission has warned encyclopedia door-to-door salespersons against deceptive practices, but only by 1976 was an effort made to put teeth into the warnings. A violator now may be fined up to $10,000 per violation. By mid-1976, the

[20] Kenneth Kister, *Encyclopedia Buying Guide . . .* (New York: R. R. Bowker Company, 1976), pp. 102–105.
[21] "AAP 1976 . . ." *Publishers Weekly,* July 4, 1977, p. 41.

FTC reported that it had found the following acts and practices, which are all illegal, being used by many encyclopedia salespeople:

> *Misrepresentation either of the nature of the seller's employment or purpose in contacting a prospective customer;*
>
> *Representations that a prospective customer has been specially selected to receive merchandise or that he can receive merchandise on special terms if he assists in the advertising or promotion of such merchandise when such is not the case;*
>
> *Representations that merchandise is offered free of charge when, in fact, the purchase cost includes that of the "free" merchandise;*
>
> *Misrepresentations as to the period of time over which a product's cost can be paid or the size of the payments.*[22]

The most common deceptive practice is failure to indicate the basic, popular price for a set. For example, the bottom price for the *Britannica* is $699, but this can be increased to $798 simply by offering only a slightly different binding. Then, too, there is a "Commemorative Edition" for $998 which is similar to the $798 set except it is numbered as one of 9000 sets and includes some extra prints and a replica of the first edition. If one adds additional *Britannica* books, such as the previously mentioned *Great Books of the Western World* or *The Annals of America,* the sales figures can go over $2000.[23] The salesperson whose profits are a percentage of the total sale is naturally eager to sell the most expensive and the greatest number of items possible.

Fortunately for the customer who may have second thoughts after the salesperson leaves, the law gives the purchaser a cooling-off period of three days during which time he or she may void a signed contract. Furthermore, a March 1976 FTC ruling requires a salesperson to present a card which clearly states, "The purpose of this representative's call is to solicit the sale of encyclopedias."[24]

Is an encyclopedia necessary?

In all libraries, probably several general encyclopedias, or at least one, are necessary. The question "Is this set necessary?" is valid if one asks it of individual purchasers.

[22] "FTC Launches New Probe of Encyclopedia Selling," *Publishers Weekly,* March 15, 1976, p. 18. Most of these practices are similar to those found five years before by *The New York Times,* September 26, 1971, pp. 1, 58.

[23] Details on the various priced sets with explanations as to actual differences in bindings will be found in a trade journal of the book industry, *Book Production Industry,* March 1974, a section on "Recency" for each encyclopedia profile. According to Kister, p. 32.

[24] "FTC Rules Britannica Uses Deception in Sales," *The New York Times,* March 27, 1976, p. 23.

A set can be useful in a home:

1. If it is written for and used by the children in the home for either recreational or educational purposes, or for both. The possession of a set does not automatically mean the child will use it; or, if it is employed, there is no guarantee of improved grades.
2. The use and need of a general encyclopedia decrease with the age of the user, that is, junior high school students are more apt to use it than senior high school students, and high school seniors are more apt to use it than first-year college and university students. Few adults really need a general encyclopedia.
3. Adults who do feel the need for reference sources might be considerably better off buying one of the subject encyclopedias and/or a number of up-to-date ready-reference sources ranging from the *World Almanac* to a good unabridged dictionary. Furthermore, for the price of a general encyclopedia, a person can build a major reference collection in paperbacks.

There is the excellent annotated guide, *Reference Books in Paperback* (2d ed.; Littleton, Colorado: Libraries Unlimited, Inc., 1976, 317 pp.). Compiled by Bohdan Wynar, this guide lists 715 titles and refers to an additional 1500 books within the comparative annotations. "Comparative" is important because Wynar provides data on both hardback and paperback related titles. There is an author-title-subject index, subdivided by type of material. Although librarians will not want to replace many reference books with paperbacks, the guide serves the useful purpose of listing titles which are usually lower in cost than hardbound editions and, therefore, can often be duplicated for circulation.

If a general encyclopedia is desired for adults' use in the home, money may be saved by purchasing one which is several years old and then supplementing it with current, less-expensive paperback reference sources. Most bookstores, which otherwise do not sell new encyclopedias, an arrangement worked out by the encyclopedia publishers who prefer the door-to-door approach, offer the major used sets at greatly reduced prices.

It should be emphasized again that this advice is for the individual. The library definitely does need current, up-to-date general encyclopedias, if only for basic ready-reference work and for help with junior high and some high school students.

Consumer advice

The librarian has several ways of meeting the request for information about a given set.

1. Give no advice. Several major public libraries, fearful of repercussions from salespersons and publishers, adamantly refuse to advise on the purchase of this or that set. Such a refusal is unprofessional and highly questionable.

2. Give limited advice. Normally, the procedure here is to give the inquirer several reviews of the set or sets under question, leaving the final decision to the user. Of particular assistance in this respect are the "Reference and Subscription Book Reviews" in *The Booklist* and Kister's *Encyclopedia Buying Guide.*

3. Go all out with an endorsement or a condemnation. Privately, of course, many librarians do just this. Such opinionated statements may have some nasty repercussions, particularly when the question is between sets that are approved by ALA and are more or less even in quality.

Between these relative extremes lies a middle path. If the set is not readily recognized by either publisher or reputation, the librarian should not hesitate to point out that the chances are that it is a poor buy from the standpoint of both cost and quality. The librarian should be prepared to support this statement with reviews; or, lacking reviews (either because the set is too new or such a "dog" as not to have been noticed), there should be no hesitation about standing on one's own professional knowledge of the set. If nothing can be found about it in print (and who is familiar with many of the works which pass for encyclopedias in supermarkets and in questionable advertisements?), the librarian should explain that the opinion may be personal, but the odds are all against the quality of the set.

ADULT ENCYCLOPEDIAS

The New Encyclopaedia Britannica, 15th ed. Chicago: Encyclopaedia Britannica Inc., 1974, 30 vols. $699 (with discount to libraries, $499).

The Encyclopedia Americana. New York: Grolier Incorporated, 30 vols. $480 (with discount to libraries, $366). Note: The publisher on the title page is Americana Corporation, a subsidiary of Grolier.

The *Britannica*

The best-known encyclopedia in the Western world is the *Britannica.* First published in 1768, it underwent many revisions and changes until the triumphant Ninth edition in 1889. This was the "scholar's edition" with lengthy articles from such contributors as Arnold, Swinburne, Huxley, and

other major English minds of the nineteenth century. The Ninth was followed by the equally famous Eleventh.

After several changes caused by economic difficulties, the set came to
the United States and by 1929 appeared as the Fourteenth edition. By that
time, the long essays had been reduced and divided, although the set was
being sold (as it is even today) on the reputation built with the Ninth and
Eleventh editions.

The first total revision of the Fourteenth edition of the *Britannica*
appeared in 1974. Between 1929 and 1974 the Fourteenth edition had
undergone continuous revision, but 45 years of this practice had resulted
in a less than a satisfactory set. The decision was then made to rewrite the
entire *Britannica;* the result was the Fifteenth edition or, as some call it,
"Britannica 3" because of its three major parts.

> *The statistics are impressive: 43 million words . . . 30 volumes, or 33,141*
> *pages; some 22,000 illustrations, maps, etc; 4,277 contributors from 131 coun-*
> *tries. . . . It has two major sequences:* Macropaedia *(or "Knowledge in*
> *Depth"): 19 volumes, 14 million words, 102,000 entries, alphabetically ar-*
> *ranged. These are prefaced by the one-volume* Propaedia *(or "Outline of*
> *Knowledge: Guide to the* Britannica").[25]

Once the editorial and sales jargon is cleared away, we can see that
the librarian has not one encyclopedia, but two encyclopedias.[26]

The 10-volume *Micropaedia* may be used independently of the rest of
the set. It gives specific entry facts in alphabetical order, and is an expanded version of the famous quick-fact encyclopedias and handbooks. The
work has proven to be an excellent, relatively accurate source of answers
for ready-reference queries.

The *Macropaedia* is a second set of volumes and the traditional encyclopedia with a balance of long and short essays on a wide variety of
material, again arranged alphabetically. Of limited value for ready reference, it is suitable for students and laypersons seeking in-depth information.

Presumably the publisher who claims "utility was the first consideration" was more optimistic about use of the third part of the set than the
general user. The one-volume *Propaedia* is primarily a classification of
knowledge by Prof. Mortimer Adler, who directed the architectural
scheme of the set. The volume was designed to help the user discover
articles related to the main topic and to serve as a systematic guide to
various aspects of a particular subject. Even a cursory glance at the vol-

[25] C. D. Needham, "Britannica Revisited," *Library Association Record,* July 1975, p. 153.

[26] The three pseudoclassic neologisms mean great learning (*Macropaedia*); little learning (*Micropaedia*); and before learning (*Propaedia*). The terms are dear to the publisher, but apparently some salespersons find them difficult to master.

ume will reveal its complexity. Its utility as part of an encyclopedia which is to be used as a reference source is questionable.[27]

The one major weakness of all these volumes: There is no separate index to the *Macropaedia*. The Fourteenth edition of the *Britannica* had one of the finest indexes of any encyclopedia. No more. Possibly in an effort to link the two encyclopedias, the publishers chose to make the *Micropaedia* serve a double purpose. Not only is it an independent reference set, but it must be used if the reader is to retrieve other than alphabetically arranged materials in the *Macropaedia*, which literally serves as an index to the *Micropaedia*. The references in the *Micropaedia* to the *Macropaedia* are arranged in two parts: (1) "Text article covers," which summarizes what is found in the main article of the *Macropaedia* by one- or two-line descriptors and the volume and page number; and (2) "References in other text articles," which refers the reader to related articles in the *Macropaedia*. The indexing depends on sometimes puzzling subject headings and phrases, confusing grouping under subheadings, and inadequate cross-references, to name only a few of the problems. An excellent example of the problem of locating material is illustrated by Kister in *Encyclopedia Buying Guide*, where under the entry for the *Brittanica* he compares the difficulty of searching in the *Micropaedia* as compared with several other encyclopedias.

This type of indexing is, to say the least, unsatisfactory and virtually eliminates the fine sifting of materials in the *Macropaedia* which would have been possible had the *Britannica* held to the traditional separate index for that set. In quite practical terms, the average user (and possibly even the librarian who lacks the patience to fathom the "easy to use, systematic, and complete" index in the *Micropaedia*) will rely upon finding major articles in the *Macropaedia* by following the standard alphabetical arrangement for subjects in the set.

Substantially new (about 80 percent or more of the material in both sets was new as of 1974 and continuous revision is in effect), the *Britannica* is useful in most libraries. The *Micropaedia* is an excellent ready-reference source, and the *Macropaedia*—where the material may be readily located via the traditional alphabetical order—contains scholarly articles. These articles are signed, whereas those in the ready-reference set are unsigned. There are good bibliographies, for the most part, in the *Macropaedia*, and good to excellent illustrations in both sets. The lack of proper indexing for the *Macropaedia* may be remedied in future revisions, but as of this writing it is a major drawback.

---

[27] Professor Adler's notion of unity of human knowledge was first tried in the 1952 *Syntopticon*, the index to Britannica's 54-volume *Great Books of the Western World*. He expanded this concept for the *Propaedia*, which includes 42 divisions, 189 sections, and 15,000 subjects, each of which refers to related material in the 19-volume *Macropaedia*.

The *Americana*

The Encyclopedia Americana is based on the seventh edition of the German encyclopedia *Brockhaus Konversations Lexikon*. In fact, the first published set (1829 to 1833) was little more than pirated, translated articles from the German work. It was asserted in 1903 that the *Americana* was a wholly new work, but still many of the articles were carried over from *Brockhaus*. The set was reissued in 1918 with changes and additions, albeit still with material from *Brockhaus*. It claims to be the oldest "all-American" encyclopedia in existence, although the claim is a matter more of chronology than of accuracy.

As the title implies, the strength of this work is the emphasis on American history, geography, and biography. This encyclopedia unquestionably places greater emphasis on this area than any of the other sets, and it is particularly useful for finding out-of-the-way, little-known material about the United States. However, general coverage of the United States is matched in other major encyclopedias.

The writing style is clear, the arrangement admirable, the index good, and the general format (including illustrations and type size) adequate. A helpful feature is the insertion of summaries, resembling a table of contents, at the beginning of multiple-page articles. The set is edited for the adult with a high school education. It is not suitable (despite zealous copywriters) for grade school children.

While there has been no new edition since 1920, the continuous revision policy has kept at least the major items up to date. The encyclopedia falters now and then in its biographical data (which make up over 40 percent of the contents) on people who have for one reason or another not been in the news. In technical and social areas the lack of a total revision is sometimes evident. Still, on balance, the set is reliable for its timeliness.[28]

Thanks as much to its history and ease of use as anything else, the *Americana* is a basic set in almost all libraries. If a choice has to be made between it and the *Britannica,* at least in 1977 the scales would tip in favor of the *Britannica* because it is a totally new edition. And yet, the *Americana* has the distinct advantage of a superior 350,000-entry index which is lacking in the *Britannica*.

---

[28] Between 1969 and 1975, the publishers claim 7500 articles were completely revised, 8500 partially rewritten, and 5000 new articles added. And of the 22,000 illustrations, 6500 have reportedly been added since 1969. Nevertheless, as more than one reviewer found in examining the 1975 edition, the editors forgot to mention opposition to the Vietnam war or the arguments over abortion.

English-language sets outside the United States

Chambers's Encyclopedia. London: International Learning Systems Corporation, 15 vols. (distributed in the United States by New York: Purnell Educational). $325.

Encyclopedia Canadiana. Ottawa: Canadiana Company, Ltd., 10 vols. $109.50.

Chambers's is the standard adult British encyclopedia, long ago having replaced what is essentially the Americanized *Encyclopaedia Britannica.* (However, the *Britannica* maintains sales offices in England, as in Europe, and it is sold there, too.) Unlike their American counterparts, the publishers of *Chambers's* do not believe in continuous revision. A completely new edition is brought out every 10 to 20 years. How "completely new" each edition is depends upon editorial viewpoint; and, in the past decade, the revision has not been noticeably extensive. The so-called 1973 "new revised edition" is little different, for example, from the basic 1950 revision. As a result, the primary fault of the set is lack of recency.

In every respect, from the number of illustrations to the total number of words, the British set lags well behind its two American counterparts. It seems to have undergone a number of editorial shifts in policy, but as of 1977 it remains a less than satisfactory entry for American libraries. Subjectively, and in its favor, I find that the articles are better written and more scholarly than those in most American encyclopedias. Furthermore, it does have an extensive coverage of Europe and Asia.

The *Encyclopedia Canadiana* differs from all others in that it is frankly nationalistic. As of this writing (late 1977), there is strong evidence that the Canadian set is not being kept up to date, and many of the articles are now 10 to 15 years old. Geared to adults and high school students, it is useful for the detailed historical, geographical, and biographical information on Canada. However, it lacks the depth and breadth of a general encyclopedia and, as such, must be used with other standard sets.

POPULAR ADULT AND HIGH SCHOOL SETS[29]

Collier's Encyclopedia. New York: Macmillan Educational Corporation, 24 vols. $429 (with discount to libraries, $359).

Encyclopedia International. New York: Grolier Incorporated, 20 vols. $350 (with discount to libraries).

[29] "Popular" is used here to differentiate writing styles among the various encyclopedias, as well as basic editorial approaches. A "popular" set, in contrast with the *Britannica* and *Americana,* is frankly edited for the student or adult with less interest in knowledge in depth.

These two sets share much in common:

(1) *Audience.* The only one of the three adult encyclopedias which may be classed rightfully as "dual purpose" in that it can adequately serve both adults and junior high school students is *Collier's.* (*Americana* is used by senior high school students, but not often at lower levels.) It is more popularly written than either the *Britannica* or the *Americana,* yet never talks down to its readers. It is equally authoritative and comprehensive. It does require reading skills equivalent to a beginning or second-year high school student.

The *International* is a grade school to high school set, in that it is geared to readers in the primary and secondary grades. At the same time, its modest vocabulary and less than dense prose make it a good set for adults with moderate education.

(2) *Coverage.* Both sets tend to stress topics related to high school curriculum and to popular taste. Both have good to excellent articles on the United States and other major nations of the world. More detailed material is handled in easy-to-understand, almost outline, fashion. Of the two, the *International* intentionally puts more stress on the social sciences, humanities, and the sciences. The biographical material in the *International,* again, tends to stress more popular figures, but both encyclopedias are equally good in the relative amount of coverage in this area.

(3) *Illustrations.* The two have approximately the same number of illustrations and maps, but the *International* stresses color plates which are approximately 7 times more numerous than the plates in *Collier's.* Both have many tables and charts, although again the *International* is particularly outstanding for its tabular presentation of much information.

(4) *Objectivity.* As both sets stress short articles, they tend to emphasize fact rather than argument. Where an issue of opinion asserts itself, a concerted effort is made to balance both sides fairly. This emphasis on data rather than on debate may or may not be an asset, depending upon the views of the reader and the librarian.

(5) *Bibliographies.* The *International* has selected bibliographies at the end of longer articles, but they tend to be too few and are often dated. Conversely, among the strong points of *Collier's* are the bibliographies, arranged in separate subject sections in the index volume. Here the books are carefully chosen, usually fairly up to date, and, according to the editors, in print for purchase. This is intended as a self-study aid and a type of selection tool for libraries and individuals.

A major difference seems to be timeliness, particularly of statistical data. The *International* is weak in this area, while *Collier's* (whose editors claim it is revised and reprinted three times a year) is particularly good on recent information and up-to-date statistics. In terms of library use, this timeliness may or may not be important, particularly as other standard reference aids are more likely to be used for up-to-date statistical data. For private purchase, it may be a factor, and one worth pointing out to those who inquire as to which set is best.

The major difference between the two sets is in volume of coverage. *Collier's* has some 25,000 articles and over 21 million words. *International* has 30,000 articles (5000 more than *Collier's*) but less than one-half the total number of words (9 to 10 million). And although both indexes are excellent, *Collier's* has 400,000 entries, compared with just over 120,000 in its rival. An analysis indicates, though, that both cover the same amount of specific material, the essential difference being that *Collier's* tends to give more information on any given subject.

Thanks to its more specific entries, *International* is probably better for fast ready-reference work. Still, *Collier's* is not far behind, and it can be used almost as well.

Which one of these is best? Opinion differs, but one may say that *Collier's* is a good set for anyone with an average to above-average vocabulary who does not require a sophisticated or a detailed explanation of complex matters. The *International* is a better set for those with less education or with problems in reading. If the range of readability is a factor in evaluation, *Collier's* is best in that it tends to serve both the average and the above-average audience. *Collier's* may serve both adults and advanced high school students, the two groups most likely to use an encyclopedia. For younger readers, the librarian should turn to the children's sets.

CHILDREN'S AND YOUNG ADULTS' ENCYCLOPEDIAS

> *Compton's Encyclopedia and Fact Index.* Chicago: Encyclopedia Britannica, Inc., 26 vols. $199 (discount to libraries).

> *Merit Students Encyclopedia.* New York: Macmillan Educational Corporation, 20 vols. $299 (discount to libraries).

> *World Book Encyclopedia.* Chicago: Field Enterprises Educational Corporation, 22 vols. $273 (discount to libraries).

The three encyclopedias listed here are the basic, accepted ones for children and young adults from about nine to eighteen years of age. All are good to excellent, and each librarian seems to have a definite preference.

Comparatively, the prices are about the same, at least when a library discount is given. Still, in terms of "best buy" for the adult with a budget problem, the new *Compton's* may be preferable.

World has the most words (over 10 million), an impressive number of timely illustrations (nearly 30,000), and a reputation for reliable recency. *Compton's* has 8,608,000 words to *Merit's* 9,000,000.

Compton's takes a broad approach to subject matter with some 4000 articles, while *World Book* takes the specific approach with 19,000 entries, as does *Merit*. All have indexes. *Compton's* indexing differs in that there is no single index volume, but an index and a study guide appear at the end of each of the volumes. The advantage to this is that a single index is not tied up by one user, but the disadvantage is obviously that one must turn to 24 indexes, instead of one, for information. *World* and *Compton's* have elaborate cross-references and can be readily used without the index. The cross-references in *Merit* are less evident, and the index contains no references to illustrations.

With the 1972 revision, *Compton's* size was increased by two volumes, i.e., from 24 to 26. This expansion has meant several new features: (1) There are now cross-references in the text to the various fact entries, many of which were heretofore lost unless the fact index was consulted; (2) there is now a page of questions, with page references to answers which serve to introduce reading matter in each of the volumes; and (3) the illustrations are all updated, with many more in full color.

The three sets have much in common. Differences, except for the specific- or the broad-entry form, are minimal in terms of coverage, illustrations, and, to a degree, format. The essential differences may be summed up briefly:

1. *World Book* is probably better organized than the other two, and information is easier and quicker to find.

2. The style of writing in the three is graded, i.e., the articles begin with relatively easy material and definitions and grow progressively more difficult and sophisticated. Still, the style is better in the *World Book* than in its competitors. Conversely, in terms of depth of coverage, *Compton's* is best, while *Merit* scores heavily in individual articles which are written specifically for given grade levels.

3. The strong point of *Compton's* is its "Fact" index at the end of each volume. Combining as it does an index with brief information on subjects not included in the main work, it serves as an excellent ready-reference source for both children and adults. *World Book's* specific arrangement and massive cross-references make it equally good for ready-reference work. *Merit* lags behind both.

4. All three are constantly being revised, but in this respect *World* has a more active revision policy, which it shows in the more up-to-date statistical data and in the illustrations. *Compton's* is close behind, with *Merit* third.

On balance, then, it is difficult to say that one set is really much better than the others. Thanks to its timeliness, organization, and illustrations, as well as its writing style, *World Book* is usually a first choice. *Compton's* rivals *World* on almost all these counts and is a good second. *Merit* is strong, too, but has a number of weaknesses that put it in third place.

PRESCHOOL AND CHILDREN'S ENCYCLOPEDIAS

Britannica Junior Encyclopaedia. Chicago: Encyclopaedia Britannica, Inc., 15 vols. $119.50 (discount to libraries).

New Book of Knowledge. New York: Grolier Incorporated, 21 vols. $280 (discount to libraries). Note: Another version of this set, with the same name, is sold in supermarkets. It is a 25-volume set which, after all the advertising stunts are cleared, sells for approximately $69. In the field it is by way of being a best buy.

Young Students Encyclopedia. Middletown, Connecticut: Xerox Educational Publications, 15 vols. $75. (Also distributed by Funk & Wagnalls, same name, but in 20 vols. $55.)

Information with entertainment is the key to the success of the preschool and children's encyclopedias for ages five to about twelve. They are constructed around the curriculum with attention to vocabulary level and a style to carry the reader through the material.

By far the best of this group is the *New Book of Knowledge,*[30] which compares favorably with the *World Book, Compton's,* and *Merit.* It exceeds its competitors on all counts: It has close to 7 million words and 9000 articles (*Britannica:* 5 million words and 4100 articles; *Young Students:* 1.5 million words and 2400 articles). The *New Book of Knowledge* has almost twice as many illustrations as the *Britannica,* and close to 5 or 6 times the number in the *Young Students.* Among preschool and children's sets, the *New Book of Knowledge* leads in coverage, authority, recency, objectivity, and other criteria for evaluating encyclopedias.

The plus for the *Britannica* is that it is directed to a lower age group (although the reader is hard pressed to find this fact in the advertisements), and it is easier for a six- or seven-year-old to read. On the minus side is its lack of attention to newer material. Not only are many of the articles and pictures dated, but items of interest to the television-aged young child often are not even covered. It has the advantage of a much

---

[30] The older version of this set was based upon the world-famous English children's encyclopedia of the same name. For a history of that work see Anthony Quinton, "The Happy Wanderer," *The Times Literary Supplement,* July 11, 1975, pp. 761–762.

lower price than the *New Book of Knowledge,* but even this advantage is slight when one considers the *Young Students* set.

By far the least expensive of these sets is the *Young Students Encyclopedia,* edited by the staff of *My Weekly Reader* for students from seven to thirteen years of age. The set has some 4500 illustrations and 2400 articles which are qualitatively commendable, but considerably fewer than those found in the standard, better-known titles. There are two versions of the encyclopedia, although in terms of content they differ only in format. The 20-volume set, with the same title, is distributed by Funk & Wagnalls to libraries for $55. While this set will not replace the better-known works in libraries, it is one of the few inexpensive works recommended in the American Library Association's "Reference and Subscription Book Reviews" for home use, as is the annual yearbook.[31] Considering this recommendation and the low price, it would be a good choice after the *New Book of Knowledge,* and it certainly would be preferable to the much older and dated *Britannica Junior.*

The encyclopedia firms all offer preschool types of encyclopedias. The best-known is *Childcraft—The How and Why Library* (Chicago: Field Enterprises Educational Corporation, 15 vols., $159). The set includes stories and factual material about practically everything of interest to a young child from animals and art to the body. Thanks to excellent illustrations and well thought-out texts, the volumes are useful for preschool and early grades.

Another entry is *Compton's Precyclopedia*[32] (Chicago: Encyclopaedia Britannica, 1973, 16 vols., $104.95); on the order of *Childcraft,* it is designed to introduce the child (ages four through ten) to basic learning experiences. The average reading level is at the second or third grade; the material is presented in a story-telling, light fashion, and the set is more of a collection of readings than a true encyclopedia.

Libraries might want one or two of these sets, but they would be used for casual reading, not for reference work with children. None is a substitute for a good encyclopedia.

OTHER ENCYCLOPEDIAS

> *Funk & Wagnalls New Encyclopedia.* New York: Funk & Wagnalls, 1973, 27 vols. $65.

[31] *The Booklist,* February 1, 1974, and July 1, 1975.

[32] Another title for the same set is *Young Children's Encyclopedia.* The only major difference between the two is that the *Young Children's* is somewhat cheaper in that it has a less expensive binding and is available in supermarkets.

American Educator. Lake Bluff, Illinois: Tangley Oaks Educational Center, 20 vols. $209.

There are encyclopedias other than those mentioned in this text. Most of them are not worth the paper they are printed upon, are usually sold in supermarkets to exploit the unsuspecting, and are deceptively inexpensive in that an individual volume may be only a few dollars, but when that is multiplied by 15 or even 30 (the number of volumes in a set), the cost is often as much as a good standard encyclopedia. They fail on almost every point of evaluation, although anyone in a rush may check them out quickly by simply searching for entries on a few current events or individuals in the news. They are usually not there, or are so superficial as to be worthless.

However, there are three or four sets not published by the four major houses which are acceptable and, in fact, good buys for the family with budget problems. The best is *Funk & Wagnalls New Encyclopedia*,[33] a supermarket set for children through adults. It has some 9 million words, 25,000 articles, and almost 8000 illustrations; and while, quantitatively, it is nowhere in the field of the *Britannica, Americana,* or *World Book,* its cost is far below the price of these standard sets. At the same time, the articles are well written, stress recency, and are nicely illustrated. The material is factual if a trifle succinct, and the set is strong on science and technology. Two good features are the index and the subject bibliographies in the final volume. Although the set would be a poor buy for libraries, it is acceptable for family use.

The *American Educator* for children and young adults lacks the quantitative data found in rivals such as *World Book* and *Collier's.* It has a good, concise writing style and an authoritative group of contributors. On the minus side: It is not so up to date as the less expensive Funk & Wagnalls entry, and its biggest fault is its lack of a comprehensive index. At one time it could have been recommended because of its relatively low price. This is no longer true. Consequently, it is one of those peripheral sets which sell for a few dollars below their competitors, but the saving is not enough to warrant purchase.

A similar set is the *New Standard Encyclopedia* (Chicago: Standard Educational Corp., 1975, 14 vols, $219.50). It is directed to much the same audience as the *American Educator,* boasts about 18,000 specific, short-entry articles, and is particularly strong in its updated and timely pieces on such things as the women's movement, science, architecture, and sports. Most of

---

[33] Recommended by "Reference and Subscription Book Review" for "homes and to libraries with limited budgets," *The Booklist,* January 15, 1975, p. 515.

the material is staff-written and not signed, but quite accurate and easy enough to read. Lacking an index, the set has extensive cross-references. These are not always satisfactory, and as of 1978 the publisher is badly in need of an index volume. There are more than 12,000 illustrations, with a little over one-third in color. While up to date, they are often blurred and difficult to relate to the text. In that this is a well-written, timely encyclopedia, it is of real benefit to young adults and to older people with less than strong reading habits. Between this and the *American Educator,* the *Standard* would be preferable, although the price, once again, puts it out of the running when it is compared with standard young adult sets, as well as with the inexpensive Funk & Wagnalls entry.

Among the less-than-recommended sets, one example should suffice: *The Illustrated World Encyclopedia* (Woodbury, New York: Bobley Publishing Corporation, 15 to 21 vols., $39.95) is sold exclusively by mail and through supermarkets, and is known to many because of a heavy advertising campaign carried on in 1975.[34] The material is well written, but oversimplified because the *Encyclopedia* was first issued as a children's set. (This fact is not obvious from the advertisements.) Much of the information is dated, although it claims to be "updated and revised with every printing," and the illustrations are poor. It has nothing to recommend it except the low price; to suggest buying it would be like urging someone to buy a pair of shoes which are much too small on the basis that the shoes are too good a buy to pass up.

Librarians who have doubts about any of these supermarket/direct-by-mail sets should check the publisher's reputation. A more direct way: The librarian should suggest that the would-be purchaser read the succinct summary of the set in Kister's evaluative *Encyclopedia Buying Guide.*

ENCYCLOPEDIA SUPPLEMENTS: YEARBOOKS

There are two basic purposes to the encyclopedia yearbooks, annuals, or supplements. They are published annually to (1) keep the basic set up to date and (2) present a summary of the year's major events. A third, less obvious purpose is in the field of sales; it is comforting for the buyer to realize that the set will never be outdated (a questionable assumption, but one used by almost every encyclopedia salesperson).

All in all . . . the purchaser will find annuals mainly useful for general reading

---

[34] As an example of the exuberant advertising, see the full-page advertisement for the set in *The New York Times,* October 11, 1975, p. 52.

and browsing and for summaries of newsworthy events rather than for systematic updating of their respective encyclopedia sets. . . . Most encyclopedia annuals . . . are valuable enough for their independent worth to merit serious consideration for purchase.[35]

The yearbooks range in price from $8.50 *(World Book Year Book)* to $12.98 *(Britannica Book of the Year)* and are usually available only to purchasers of the initial sets. They all tend to be attractively printed, and they generally feature numerous illustrations.

The supplements are not related to the parent set except in name. The arrangements are broad, with emphasis on large, current topics. Most of the material is not later incorporated into the revised basic sets—a positive and negative consideration. On the positive side, a run of the yearbooks does afford a fairly comprehensive view of the year's events. On the negative side, the library is wise to keep a run of the yearbooks because the revised parent set cannot be depended upon to contain the same material, or at any rate, not in such depth. Consequently, someone looking for more than basic facts on a given topic really should search not only the main encyclopedia, but a number of the yearbooks also.

Aside from the age of the audience for which each is prepared, significant differences between the various yearbooks are difficult to discover. In this, they resemble the daily newspaper. One reader may prefer the slant or emphasis of one newspaper over another, but both papers are drawing from the same general materials. Nor is the analogy as far-fetched as it may seem. In the annuals particularly, the predominantly newspaper-trained staffs of the larger encyclopedia firms have a holiday. Format, content, and the ever-important emphasis on up-to-date, often exciting events reflect more than a scholar behind the final book; they reveal an emphasis on what makes the daily newspaper sell, at least as seen from the standpoint of the ex-newspaperman.

In libraries, it is sufficient to purchase yearbooks for encyclopedias not replaced that given year. If more than a single adults' and children's yearbook is to be purchased, the nod will go to the work preferred by the librarian and the patrons of the library. As long as the preference is within the standards set for encyclopedias, it is a matter more of taste than of objective judgment, and any one of the accepted publishers will serve as well as another.

[35] "Reference and Subscription Book Reviews—Encyclopedia Supplements," *The Booklist,* December 1, 1971, p. 298.

ONE-VOLUME ENCYCLOPEDIAS

The New Columbia Encyclopedia. 4th ed. New York: Columbia University Press, 1975, 3052 pp. $79.50. (Distributed by J. B. Lippincott.)

The Lincoln Library of Essential Information. Columbus, Ohio: Frontier Press Company, 1924 to date, annual, 2 vols. $67.95 (libraries, $59.95).

The Cadillac Modern Encyclopedia. New York: Cadillac Publishing Company, 1973, 1954 pp. $24.95.

The Random House Encyclopedia. New York: Random House, 1977, 2856 pp. $69.95.

"Making a one-volume encyclopedia is like taking the broth of the universe and condensing it into a bouillon cube."[36] This is to say, the typical one-volume, alphabetically arranged encyclopedia offers information denuded of everything except the facts. Such works are ideal ready-reference aids.

For home use, the one-volume works are economical and, compared with multivolume sets in the same general price range, are a better buy.[37] The information is exact, well presented, and more reliable than that in the equally low-priced "supermarket" sets. Where cost is a factor, the librarian should always inform the prospective purchaser of these one-volume works, encouraging a personal comparison of reviews or of the encyclopedias themselves.

Depending on nuggets of information rather than exposition, the 10½-pound *New Columbia Encyclopedia* has more than 50,000 articles, 66,000 cross-references, some 400 integrated illustrations including maps of all major countries, and approximately 6.5 million words. While the content is hardly up to the 14 million words and 102,000 entries in the Britannica's *Micropaedia,* it compares favorably with the content in almost all young adults' and children's sets. More to the point, *The New Columbia Encyclopedia* surpasses such typical supermarket specials as the *Illustrated World Encyclopedia,* whose 15 volumes contain only 7300 articles and 30,000 cross-references, and which is sold for $54.95.

[36] Israel Shenker, "Columbia Encyclopedia: Instant Universe Again," *The New York Times,* August 3, 1975, p. 40.

[37] Where multiple-volume encyclopedias stress the "circle of knowledge," one-volume works inevitably begin the sales talk with the advantage of price. For example, the advertising copywriter for *The New Columbia Encyclopedia* headed advertisements with "Now you can own the best one-volume encyclopedia in the English language for only $69.50." (*The New York Times Book Review,* October 19, 1975, pp. 24–25.) After January 1, 1976, the price went to $79.50. At the same time, the Book of the Month Club offers it as a "bonus" in 1977 for $15.

Qualitatively, the *Columbia* is a valuable ready-reference aid. The fourth edition gives added attention in the 7000 new articles to third-world countries, science, social sciences, and the humanities. Also, the extensive revision dropped cities of under 10,000 population, a mass of World War II generals, and dated geographical information. The strongest area is biography. Biographical sketches will be found here for individuals not included, or at best only mentioned, in the standard multivolume sets.[38]

The articles are unsigned, and the longer ones (e.g., 10,000 words on Great Britain and 16,000 words on Africa as compared with 75 to 150 words for the average biography) include bibliographies. With the assistance of 91 scholars (many of them from Columbia University), the work has been well written. It is intentionally styled, as was the first edition, "in language as intelligible as that of a newspaper."

First issued in 1924, *The Lincoln Library of Essential Information* has the advantage over the *Columbia* of constant revision. New editions appear annually, and each one makes an effort to update material. It is in two volumes, with information arranged under 12 general subject fields from the English language to biography and miscellany. The index is detailed enough to overcome the basic problem of arrangement, which is not ideal for ready-reference work. Among its many good features are its several hundred charts and tables;[39] updated bibliographies; quality illustrations; a good atlas of the world; and broad coverage of general knowledge. The articles are well written and can be easily understood by a junior high or high school student. As the material is arranged under broad sections with over 25,000 different entries, coverage tends to be brief, factual, and unopinionated.

A newcomer to the one-volume group is *The Cadillac Modern Encyclopedia,* which has less than half the words of the *Columbia,* although it is quite close behind the *Lincoln Library.* This volume differs from the other single-volume works in that it contains (1) fewer specific articles, 18,000 in contrast with 50,000 in the *Columbia* and 25,000 in the *Lincoln;* and (2) 300 concluding pages of special reference sections, devoted to biography, history, economics, law, etc., with most of the data in tabular form. While factual data are good, the work is strongest on science and mathematics. There are numerous, generally good cross-references throughout. It is third in size to the other two and, ironically enough in view of the title, the

---

[38] Shenker, op. cit., points out that the encyclopedia's sacred cows are Nicholas Murray Butler, former president of Columbia, and opera. Butler's biography runs to 52 lines while Gerald Ford has 39 lines. Biography constitutes about 40 percent of the number of entries, as does geographical information. The other 20 percent is devoted to various other subjects.

[39] The some 100 tabulations are excellent ready-reference aids in that they give side-by-side comparisons for a wide variety of topics, e.g., abdications, crop production of leading countries, religions of the world, modern inventions, and pen names.

lowest-priced of the group. Recommended by the ALA's References and Subscription Books Committee (*The Booklist,* February 15, 1975, pp. 623–624), it is a good one-volume encyclopedia, and a first choice in homes with a limited budget.

Another one-volume encyclopedia is *The University Desk Encyclopedia* (New York: E. P. Dutton, 1977, $69.95). It has more articles than the *Cadillac* but fewer than the *Columbia,* i.e., about 25,000 entries in some 1050 pages. Although about one-half the size of the *Columbia,* it costs only $10 less. The advantage, or selling point, is the emphasis on illustrations—over 3000 in full color. These illustrations, coupled with numerous charts and diagrams, make it particularly suitable for younger readers and for adults who would rather look than read. The material is clear and up to date, and it covers a wide range of topics. In view of its price and size, the *University Encyclopedia* would be a luxury item for libraries, although welcome enough once the other one-volume encyclopedias had been purchased.

The best publicized new one-volume encyclopedia in years is *The Random House Encyclopedia.* Approximately $1 million is devoted to newspaper advertisements, television spots, etc. Still, this is small compared with the $7 million the publishers have invested. "Publishers" is used advisedly because the volume has a peculiar history. The work was developed jointly by Random House in the United States and Mitchell Beazely in England. (The English version is called *The Joy of Knowledge;* it consists of eight volumes, plus a two-volume index. The contents are the same as the one-volume American work.) A two-volume edition, by the same name and at the same initial price, is distributed by Encyclopaedia Britannica. Finally, at least 14 publishing houses in Europe, Africa, and Asia will use the basic information to produce their own editions.

Once the publicity is analyzed (and this is done nicely in a lengthy article in *Publishers Weekly,* "The Random House Encyclopedia," May 9, 1977, pp. 33–38), the facts are that here is a good work, particularly strong on color photographs, which are on almost every page of the 1792-page "colorpedia." The first part covers seven major topics from the universe to man and machines in long essays rather than by specific entries like those in the other one-volume works. The second section is the index, which is really a modified version of the Britannica's *Micropaedia.* This time it is called the "alphapedia" and consists of 25,000 short entries covering as many topics. It is an index, as well, to the "colorpedia." Comparatively, the Random House work weighs a pound more than its closest rival, the *Columbia.* However, it has 3 million or so fewer words than the *Columbia* and is directed as much to secondary grade students as adults. Its strengths are the close to 14,000 pictures, over 11,000 in color; and the lengthy essays (almost monographs) by such notable scholars as Bernard Lovell,

Christopher Hill, and Salvador E. Luria. As a relatively inexpensive encyclopedia it is a good addition to a home collection, but does not replace the *Columbia* and other one-volume sets now found in libraries. If one had to rank for library purchase, the *Columbia* would be first, with *The Lincoln Library* and the *Random House Encyclopedia* tied for second.

FOREIGN-LANGUAGE ENCYCLOPEDIAS

Most reference questions can be quickly and best answered by an American encyclopedia, but there are occasions when a foreign-language work is more suitable. Obviously, a foreign encyclopedia will cover its country of origin in considerably more depth than an American work will. The same will also be true for such items as biographies of nationals, statistics, places, and events.

Even for users with the most elementary knowledge of the language, several of the foreign works are useful for their fine illustrations and maps. For example, the *Enciclopedia Italiana* boasts some of the best illustrations of any encyclopedia, particularly in the areas of the fine arts. A foreign encyclopedia is equally useful for viewpoint. Some American readers may be surprised to find how the Civil War, for example, is treated in the French and the German encyclopedias, and the evaluation of American writers and national heroes is sometimes equally revealing of how Europeans judge the United States. In more specific terms, the foreign encyclopedia is helpful for information on lesser-known figures not found in American or British works; for bibliographies which emphasize a foreign-language approach; for some rather detailed maps of both cities and regions; and for other information ranging from plots of lesser-known novels and musicals to identification of place names.

In the case of the most generally used foreign encyclopedias (though these are certainly not the only ones), the student may remember them easily in terms of who publishes what, e.g., France, *Larousse;* Germany, *Brockhaus;* Spain, *Espasa.* The Italian and Russian works do not quite fit into this formula.

French

    La Grande Encyclopédie, rev. ed. Paris: Larousse, 1972–1977, 21 vols. (Distributed in the United States by Maxwell Scientific, Inc. $820.)

The name Larousse is as familiar in France as the *Encyclopaedia Britannica* is in the United States. Pierre Larousse was the founder of a publishing house which continues to flourish and is responsible for the basic French encyclopedias. In fact, "Larousse" in France is often used as a synonym for "encyclopedia."

One problem, as with most European encyclopedias, is the alphabetical arrangement. Any student who has had a brush with a foreign language realizes that while the Latin alphabet is employed, there are variations in letters; Spanish, for example, has two letters not found in English, *ch* and *ll*. There are also marked differences in common names. John turns up as Giovanni, Jan, Juan, Johannes, or Johan. Consequently, before abandoning a foreign encyclopedia for lack of an entry, the user should be certain to look for the entry in terms of the language employed.

Larousse continues with the policy of short specific entries, but it does give some rather extensive treatment of major subjects. For example, the length of articles for countries and leading personalities often equals that found in American works.

Working on the old subscription books principle of issuing a given number of volumes per year, the new edition of *La Grande Encyclopédie* began appearing in 1972 and comprises 21 volumes. There is a 400,000-item reference index. The Larousse titles, which include several subject encyclopedias, are particularly renowned for the excellent illustrations, often in full color. And each page of the *Encyclopedia* includes photographs, charts, maps, diagrams, and the like. Regardless of one's command of French, everyone will enjoy the illustrations—even the smaller ones—which are noteworthy for their sharp register.[40]

German

> *Brockhaus Enzyklopädie,* rev. 17th ed. Wiesbaden: Brockhaus, 1966–1975, 20 vols. $900. *Supplement,* 1975–1976, 2 vols. Inquire. *Der Grosse Brockhaus.* rev. 18th ed. Wiesbaden: Brockhaus. 1977—in progress (to be completed in 1981), 12 vols. Inquire.

First issued as *Frauenzimmer Lexikon* (between 1796 and 1808), an encyclopedia primarily for women, *Brockhaus* got off to a bad start. The original publisher, possibly because of his limited audience, gave up the financial ghost; in 1808, Friedrich Brockhaus purchased the set and issued the last volume. A wise man, Brockhaus continued to offer his volumes not as scholarly works, but as books guaranteed to give the average man (or woman) a solid education. In this respect, he was years ahead of the times—in fact, so far ahead of his American and English counterparts that

[40] For a short history of the Larousse firm, see Anthone D. Clifford, "Le Grand Larousse," *Library Review,* Spring 1974, pp. 207–208.

they freely borrowed his text, if not his sales techniques. As noted earlier, the Brockhaus works were the basis for the early *Americana* and *Chambers.*

Brockhaus extended his popular formula to cutting back articles to little more than dictionary length. In this respect, he followed the European form of specific entry. Consequently, all the Brockhaus encyclopedias—and there is a family of them—are an admixture of dictionary and encyclopedia. (The family, for example, includes the basic 20-volume set, the revised 12-volume set, and a 1-volume work, among others.)

As might be expected, the longer articles, some of them over 100 pages, are on European countries. In many respects, the Brockhaus encyclopedia is considerably more provincial than the *Larousse;* and while it is an excellent source of material on German history and personalities, it can be passed up for other items.

Because of its scope, the *Brockhaus* is useful in large research libraries or where there is a German-speaking populace, but it is probably near the bottom among choices of all the foreign-language encyclopedias.

Italian

Enciclopedia Italiana di Scienze, Lettere ed Arti. Rome: Instituto della Enciclopedia Italiana, 1929 to 1939, 36 vols., appendices I-III, 1938 to 1962, 5 vols.

Lavishly illustrated with black-and-white and superb color plates, the Italian encyclopedia is best known for its artwork. As such, it can be used profitably by anyone; and, somewhat like the *National Geographic* magazine, it will afford hours of browsing time even for the person who does not understand a word of the language in which it is written.

At perhaps a more important level, it has an outstanding reputation for detailed articles in the humanities. All the articles are signed, and there are a number of bibliographies. One good example is the article on Rome, which runs to almost 300 pages and has close to 200 photogravure plates illustrating nearly every aspect of the city, present and past.

The basic set is updated continually by the various appendixes, which are equally well written and illustrated. The index to the complete set is excellent, and there is an index to the appendix.

Russian

Bol'shaia Sovetskaia Entisklopediia, 3d rd. Moscow: Sovetskaia Entisklopediia, 1970–1977, in progress, 30 vols. plus index. (*The Great Soviet Encyclopedia.* New York: The Macmillan Company, Inc. Translation in progress in 1973, 30 vols. plus index. $1800.)

The third edition of the *BSE* replaces the heavily doctrinaire second, issued shortly after the death of Stalin. And while it still reflects the "party line," it is said to be considerably more objective than the previous two editions.

> *In many ways [the encyclopedia] is a view distorted by official unwillingness to be candid about shortcomings, especially in the social sciences, but little if any ideology creeps into the abundant and valuable material on science and technology. . . . By adhering faithfully to the original Russian content, without editorial comment or additions, the American publisher is letting the official Soviet authors and editors speak for themselves, even if the result may border on the absurd by American standards.*[41]

The publication of the English version (to be completed in late 1979 or 1980) is running three to four years behind the original Russian volumes, and by 1977 the Russian language set was completed. As most American readers will use the English translation, several points are worth making: (1) An index is published after each five volumes, with a complete index to the whole set scheduled in about 1980. Each new interim index will cumulate previous entries and integrate additional encyclopedia content. For example, in 1977 the publisher issued the index to Vols. 1 through 10. Still, when the index was issued the publisher was up to Vol. 15. So the index lags. (2) The index is necessary because of the unusual alphabetical arrangement of each volume, caused by differences between the Russian and Latin alphabets. For example, the first translated volume contains entries for "Aalen Stage" and the "Zulu War of 1879." (3) The quality of the translation is good. The American version differs from the Russian in that cost considerations made it necessary to delete the fine maps in the original Russian version.

The *BSE* is the basic encyclopedia for the Soviet schools and for families, being somewhat equivalent in scholarship to the older version of the *Britannica*. When completed, the entire set will have more than 21 million words and over 100,000 articles. Combining both the specific-entry and the broad-entry form, the set is a combination of routine dictionary and gazetteer items, with detailed, many-paged articles covering every aspect of Soviet interest.

[41] Theodore Shabad, "Aalen Stage to Zulu War," *The New York Times,* January 14, 1974, p. 25. However, the *Times* reported (May 7, 1976, p. 4) that "the dissident physicist Andrei D. Sakharov, condemned as a traitor in the Moscow press, today made a surprise appearance, complete with photograph in the latest volume of [the encyclopedia]. . . . The only allusion to his activities as a dissident activist comes in oblique form in the final sentence of the entry. 'In the last few years, he departed from scientific activity,' it says."
  For a general discussion of the translated set, see Patricia Grimstead, "Detente on the Reference Shelf," *Wilson Library Bulletin,* June 1975, pp. 728–740.

Meanwhile, another American publisher, Chilton Company, announced in 1976 that it had signed a contract with Russian publishers to translate and distribute nine encyclopedias on American technology for the Soviets. At this time, no plan has been announced to distribute any of the general American encyclopedias in Russia.

Spanish

Enciclopedia universal ilustrada Europeo-Americana (Espasa). Barcelona: Espasa, 1907 to 1933, 80 vols.; 31 annual supplements, 1934 to date. (Distributed in the United States by Maxwell Scientific, Inc. $1900.)

Usually cited simply as *Espasa,* the *Enciclopedia* is a remarkable work. First, it never seems to end. Forgoing the techniques of continuous revision or of new editions, the publishers continue to augment the 80 volumes (actually 70 basic volumes with 10 appendixes) with annual supplements which are arranged in large subject categories and include an index. (The term "annual" must be taken advisedly, as the supplements generally are not issued until three to five years after the period covered. For example, the 1965-1966 volume came out in 1970.)

Second, the publishers have the largest number of entries—they claim over 1 million. Since they evidently do not count on "authority," none of the articles is signed. Again, as in the German and French encyclopedias, the emphasis is on short entries of the dictionary type. Still, there are a number of rather long articles, particularly those dealing with Spain, Latin America, and prominent writers, scientists, artists, and so on who claim Spanish as a native tongue. The longer articles are often accompanied by extensive bibliographies which can be used profitably to find definitive studies usually not listed in other sources. The illustrations are poor, and even the colored plates of paintings leave much to be desired.

SUBJECT ENCYCLOPEDIAS

The subject encyclopedia differs from the general encyclopedia in that it limits its scope to either a narrow or a broad field of interest. An example of the narrow approach is *The Oxford Companion to World Sports and Games;* of the broad approach, the *International Encyclopedia of the Social Sciences.* In an editorial sense, today's subject encyclopedia holds the position the major encyclopedias held in the nineteenth century; that is, it depends more upon thorough scholarship and depth of coverage than upon popularity and a large sales force. Many subject encyclopedias are examples of what can be done in the synthesis and the presentation of knowledge in a clear, understandable, and intelligent fashion. Admittedly stretching an analogy, the subject encyclopedia is the Rolls Royce of the library reference collection, whereas the general encyclopedia is the Ford or Chevrolet.[42]

Purpose and types

The "Reference and Subscription Book Reviews" offers sound advice on subject encyclopedias:

> *The prospective purchaser should realize that numerous specialized encyclopedias are available which might serve his needs better than a general encyclopedia. Special purpose encyclopedias can be divided into three categories: (1) those which cover special fields of knowledge (e.g.,* the International Encyclopedia of the Social Sciences); *(2) those which cover special subjects (e.g., the* Encyclopedia of the American Revolution); *(3) those which cover special viewpoints (e.g.,* The New Catholic Encyclopedia).[43]

A subject or specialized encyclopedia has much the same primary use in a library as the general set. It will be used both for ready-reference queries and for overviews of a given topic. The essential difference is the amount of emphasis on the second use. The scholarly subject set offers not one or two paragraphs on X matter (as does the more general set), but several pages, along with illustrations, and usually an extensive and more up-to-date bibliography.

The subject encyclopedia may suffer from too much detail for the average user, particularly for the layperson or student. Also, it may have considerably more technicality than the inexperienced user is apt to appreciate. Both these characteristics are plus points when the set is used by someone with experience or knowledge of the field.

What usually happens is that the subject set is used as a support for the more general works. When a user expresses dissatisfaction with, or is obviously far ahead of, the general encyclopedia's efforts, the subject volumes are called into use.

Encyclopedias and handbooks

There is a thin line between the subject or specialized encyclopedia and the traditional handbook. The handbook, as discussed in a later section, is a collection of a miscellaneous group of facts centered on one central theme or subject area, e.g., *Handbook of Physics* and *Handbook of Insurance.* An

---

[42] This is not to say that all subject encyclopedias are good, or even acceptable. Their editorial quality may be no better than equivalent publishing efforts by general encyclopedia firms.

[43] "Purchasing a General Encyclopedia," *The Booklist,* March 15, 1969, p. 761.

encyclopedia tends to be more discursive, although the dictionary, specific-entry type may simply list brief facts. A handbook is usually a means of checking for bits of data to assist the user in work in progress. Also, a handbook presupposes a given degree of knowledge in the field. A subject encyclopedia normally assumes that interest, more than knowledge, is the point of departure. If one must draw distinctions, a handbook is a working tool, whereas a subject encyclopedia is more a source of background information which eventually may help the user to formulate a project or a work.

The differences between the traditional encyclopedia and the handbook are not always so evident. The title is not necessarily a clue. The distinction seems to be that a handbook is usually conceived in the old German *Handbuch* sense of being a compendious book or treatise providing guidance in any art, occupation, or study. The encyclopedia may supply equal guidance, but the information therein tends to be more general, less directly involved with use in an actual working situation. The encyclopedia, then, is primarily for retrospective research. The handbook is primarily for ongoing help or guidance.

Evaluation

The same evaluative techniques are used for subject encyclopedias as for general sets. Even with a limited knowledge of the field covered, librarians may judge the set for themselves, although they are more likely to depend upon reviews or subject experts for evaluation of the expensive works. Subject sets are evaluated in scholarly periodicals, which discuss them at greater length than standard reviews do.

Once it is determined the encyclopedia is good, the librarian must ask who, and how many readers, will use the work. The subject encyclopedias will fill gaps in the collection of art, science, or more esoteric subjects. For this reason, a subject encyclopedia is often a better buy for small and medium-sized libraries than multiple sets of general encyclopedias.

Examples

The following pages discuss representative examples and some "classics" in the subject encyclopedia field. The librarian with a need in a particular field should consult a subject bibliography.

Art

Encyclopedia of World Art. New York: McGraw-Hill Book Company, 1959–1968, 15 vols. $695 ($595, to schools and libraries).

The *Encyclopedia of World Art* is the finest set available among encyclopedias devoted entirely to art. It includes art of all periods and has exhaustive studies of art forms, history, artists, and allied subject interests. Arranged alphabetically, it contains many shorter articles which answer almost every conceivable question in the field.

An outstanding feature exists in the illustrations. At the end of each volume, there are 400 to 600 black-and-white and colored reproductions. They are nicely tied to the articles by suitable cross-references and identification numbers and letters.

The writing is uniformly excellent, and the work can boast that almost every scholar in the field has made at least one if not several contributions to the set. There are detailed bibliographies at the end of the longer articles. The last volume is the index, which lists not only the articles in alphabetical order, but also the close to 9000 illustrations. This feature is useful, since there are very few indexes to paintings. The index includes a number of cross-references which, unfortunately, are not always clear.

The multivolume encyclopedia may be supplemented by numerous one-volume works of other publishers. Some are general in nature (e.g., *Oxford Companion to Art.* New York: Oxford University Press, 1970, 1277 pp.); others are of the subject type (e.g., Dora Ware and Maureen Stafford, *An Illustrated Dictionary of Ornament.* New York: St. Martin's Press, 1975, 246 pp.).

Education

> *The Encyclopedia of Education.* New York: The Macmillan Company, 1971, 10 vols. $199.

This is the basic encyclopedia in education, having more than 1000 articles which examine the history, theory, and philosophy of education. All are written by subject experts and are not only authoritative, but also clear and literate. There are detailed bibliographies and an excellent index.

In view of the broad area covered by the term "education," the set may be helpful to persons in related fields. It nicely supplements, for example, the better-known *International Encyclopedia of the Social Sciences,* as well as the *Dictionary of the History of Ideas.* While most emphasis is on American education, there are comparative articles which consider education and related topics throughout the world.

Beyond *The Encyclopedia of Education,* the most useful work for public and school libraries is the frequently revised *Encyclopedia of Careers and Vocational Guidance* (3d ed.; Chicago: J. G. Ferguson, 1975, 2 vols., sold through Doubleday & Company, $44.50), which gives background information in the first volume and job descriptions in the second volume.

History[44]

Adams, James T. (ed.), *Dictionary of American History*, rev. ed. New York: Charles Scribner's Sons, 1976, 7 vols. and index. $340.

The New Cambridge Modern History. New York: Cambridge University Press, 1957–1976, 13 vols. Set, $295; Vol. 14, Atlas, $37.50.

It is questionable whether separate history encyclopedias are needed for small or medium-sized libraries, especially if the library has complementary reference works, such as the *Dictionary of American Biography* and the *Atlas of American History*. Larger libraries will want the more specialized encyclopedias, many of which are described in the basic bibliographical guide to this area, *Harvard Guide to American History* (rev. ed.; Cambridge, Massachusetts: Belknap Press of Harvard University Press, 1974, 2 vols.)

Among works published beyond these shores, the best modern history is the multivolume *New Cambridge Modern History*, which begins with the Renaissance and closes shortly after World War II.

Most of the series can be read as straight history, although the work is obviously useful as a reference aid. The revised *Modern History* has been criticized for a number of failures ranging from too much emphasis on political history to a lack of bibliographies. The latter fault is remedied in part by a separate bibliographical volume, *A Bibliography of Modern History* (New York: Cambridge University Press, 1968). Of particular value is the *Atlas*, which can be purchased separately. All the historical maps are clear and excellent for detail.

In addition to its *Modern History*, the same press has issued *The Cambridge Ancient History*, *The Cambridge Economic History of Europe*, *The Cambridge History of the Bible*, *The Cambridge Medieval History*, and a number of other multiple-volume sets which are standard reference aids in larger research libraries. All enjoy a scholarly reputation; and although each can be criticized for this or that, they are basic and among the most authoritative in the field.

There is nothing quite like the Cambridge volumes for American history. The closest thing is the standard overview of American history for the layperson and the expert, the *Dictionary of American History*. Revised in 1976, it now includes 6045 entries by over 1400 contributors. The revision carries the history through the early 1970s and has new or revised sections on American Indians, Afro-Americans, women, etc. The title derives from

---

[44] Between the 1974 and 1978 editions of this *Introduction to Reference Work*, the only major new multivolume encyclopedia of history published was Joseph McCarthy (ed.), *Record of America* . . . (New York: Charles Scribner's Sons, 1974, 10 vols., $200). It received unfavorable reviews, some of which might be studied to show how the evaluation process works. See, for example, Richard Gray's review in *American Reference Books Annual 1976*, pp. 187–188, and the shorter review in *RQ*, Winter 1975, pp. 175–176.

the fact that a vast number of the articles are brief, but this is more a matter of editing than depth of scope. Actually, major periods are simply broken down into much smaller parts than are normally found in an encyclopedia, and then treated as separate, specific entries. This approach is ideal for reference work. There are no biographical entries, although names mentioned in articles are in the index volume.

A useful companion to the *Dictionary,* and a reference work that can stand on its own, is *Album of American History,* edited by James T. Adams (rev. ed.; New York: Charles Scribner's Sons, 1969, 6 vols.). Using some 6000 contemporary drawings and cartoons, the editor takes a *Life* magazine approach to American history up through 1968. Fortunately, there is an excellent index which enables the user to find material both by subject and by event or individual.

Often found with the encyclopedias of history are the chronology titles which offer a skeletal outline of principal events and dates throughout the world, a specific area of the world, or a country. A single example is the *Chronology of World History* (Totowa, New Jersey: Rowman and Littlefield, 1975, 753 pp.). This list dates from c. 3000 B.C. to the end of 1973 in a six-column tabular form. The information in five of the six columns is geographical, ranging from Western Europe to the Americas and changing as time periods catch up with the national developments. The sixth column shows cultural activities. There is a detailed index of names and events. This work compares favorably with the much revised and standard work, William L. Langer's *An Encyclopedia of World History* (5th ed.; Boston: Houghton Mifflin Company, 1972).

Literature

The Cambridge History of English Literature. New York: Cambridge University Press, 1907 to 1933, 15 vols. $225.

Cassell's Encyclopaedia of World Literature. New York: William Morrow & Company, 1973, 3 vols. $47.95.

There is an overwhelming amount of material concerned with literature and related areas, such as drama and poetry. As with history, the general encyclopedia usually contains enough material for all but the expert. Special sets are useful for particular or unusual query which is so narrow in scope that it cannot be answered via a general source.

The two encyclopedias listed here are representative of the "classics" in the field, and are available in most medium to large academic and public libraries. And in even small collections, there is usually a place for *Cassell's.* First published in 1953, this standard work, consisting of two volumes of biographical data and an opening volume which is devoted to the histories of different literatures and essays on general literary subjects, touches on almost every facet of the subject. The advantage of this set is that it covers all literature, not just American and English entries, and the two-volume biographical work includes a wide variety of writers from many lands.

The Cambridge History of English Literature is the basic set in its field. While quite properly considered a "history" rather than a typical encyclopedia, its wide coverage means it is often used in a library as a type of encyclopedia. If nothing else, it does illustrate the difficulty of categorization of certain types of reference works. For example, see the previous discussion of encyclopedias and handbooks. The discussion in the first volume opens with the earliest literature and closes with cycles of romances. The twelfth through fourteenth volumes carry the history to the twentieth century, and the fifteenth volume is an extensive index. Each chapter is written by an expert and ends with an extensive bibliography.

For libraries that cannot afford the larger set, the *Concise Cambridge History of English Literature* (New York: Cambridge University Press, 1970, 976 pp.) is helpful. Now in its third edition (it is revised about every 10 years), the volume represents a trustworthy abridgment of the original set and costs only $19.95, with a paper edition available at $9.95.

Some idea of the extent of materials in literature may be gained by considering just one of hundreds of titles published in 1975, the *Princeton Encyclopedia of Poetry and Poetics* (rev. ed.; Princeton, New Jersey: Princeton University Press, 1975, 992 pp.). This massive tome has 1000 entries from 20 to 20,000 words in length, and it covers not only poetry but major aspects of literature from rock lyrics to black poetry and structuralism. An interesting aspect of the 1975 edition is that, to save money, the editors chose to add new material in a 90-page supplement. The first part of the book is a reprint of the 1965 edition.

There are numerous guides to literature which list the basic reference works in the field. Among the best are Richard Altick and Andrew Wright's frequently revised *Selective Bibliography for the Study of English and American Literature* (5th ed.; New York: The Macmillan Company, 1975, 168 pp.). Although there are few annotations, the essays place most of the material in context and the work can be used by both the beginner and the graduate student, as well as the librarian.

Music

> *The New Grove Dictionary of Music and Musicians.* New York: The Macmillan Company (publication announced for 1978), 14 vols.

The standard multivolume encyclopedia of music is unquestionably

Grove's, which is scheduled to be completely revised by 1978—for the first time since the 1878–1889 edition.[45] The new edition will be particularly useful for the 25,000 articles by 2000 contributors on various musical forms and concepts, musicians, and composers. The primary strength is the 12,000 articles on composers, as well as extensive materials about early music and folk music. Beginning with the 1978 edition, the editors will break precedent with the past by introducing articles on popular and light music and jazz.

In a reference situation, *Grove's* is valuable not only for the detailed articles, but for such added features as lists of works, bibliographies, and numerous sources of additional information. With revision, the new *Grove's* will not be so closely tied to its English viewpoint as formerly.

Note: As of 1977, the fifth edition is still in print in an inexpensive paperback version of 10 volumes.

Philosophy

> *Dictionary of the History of Ideas.* New York: Charles Scribner's Sons, 1973–1974, 5 vols. $200.

> *Encyclopedia of Philosophy.* New York: The Macmillan Company, 1973, 4 vols. $99.

Both works have a wider use than may be indicated by the titles. The *Encyclopedia of Philosophy* is truly encyclopedic and covers philosophy in the broadest sense. The *Dictionary of the History of Ideas,* which has a wider scope, considers almost every aspect of the human condition and history. Both may be used profitably to augment the sometimes scanty treatment of philosophy in general sets and to give another dimension to ideas found in subject sets such as the *International Encyclopedia of the Social Sciences.*

With 225 contributors, the *Dictionary of the History of Ideas* has slightly over 300 in-depth articles in the first four volumes. The fifth is a detailed index. Most of the articles are highly specific and surprisingly clear, so that they are well within the grasp of the educated layperson, including, in some cases, the advanced high school student. Coverage includes pivotal ideas in history, religion, philosophy, literature, the social sciences, and science. Articles are arranged in alphabetical order, ending with good bibliographies and *see also* references which link related materials in the set. The *Dictionary* offers an ideal overview for the person seeking an intelligent summary of ideas in almost any field of knowledge.

---

[45] Since the new set will not be published until 1978, this brief note is based upon advance publicity, the advice of a music expert who uses *Grove's,* and Bayan Northcott's "The Enchanted Grove," *New Statesman,* August 6, 1976, pp. 188–189.

Encyclopedia of Philosophy is another basic set in the field, and by now is in most medium-sized to large American libraries. Its four volumes contain over 1450 articles by 500 contributors, and the style and the approach are primarily for the educated layperson rather than the expert. Arrangement is alphabetical, and there is a comprehensive index in the last volume. One useful feature lies in the bibliographies. Many of these are annotated and graded. The editor freely admits that because this is the first major encyclopedia of philosophy in English, it represents many of his own biases. For example, John Dewey and A. N. Whitehead have been downgraded, while St. Augustine and Voltaire have received more space than might be expected.

Religion

> *New Catholic Encyclopedia.* New York: McGraw-Hill Book Company, 1967, 15 vols. $550 ($450 for schools and libraries). *Supplement 1967–1974,* 1975, 527 pp. $49.50 ($39.50 for libraries).
>
> *Encyclopaedia Judaica.* New York: Crowell Collier and Macmillan, Inc., 1972, 16 vols. $500.

For the librarian who is considering religious encyclopedias, it is necessary to emphasize that most of them, and especially the two listed here, are significantly broader in scope and purpose than their titles suggest. They provide a vast amount of accurate, generally unbiased information in related fields from philosophy to political science and the social sciences.

The *New Catholic Encyclopedia* is well enough known to be generally accepted in most libraries, and certainly in most Catholic school libraries from high school through the university. Its 17,000 articles by close to 5000 scholars (many of whom have no affiliation with the church) are models of objectivity. The set is quite obviously strongest in the areas of religion, theology, and philosophy; but in literature and history, it compares favorably with more general encyclopedias. In an average reference collection, its primary value would be for the philosophy and comparative religious articles, as well as for many biographical pieces not often found elsewhere. Moreover, it has excellent illustrations, bibliographies, and a fine index.

Unlike many general encyclopedias, the Catholic work issues a supplement to the basic set infrequently. The last, covering 1967 to 1974, has some 400 articles and a detailed index. Again, religion is important, but hardly the major concern, and a good deal of the quite excellent work is devoted to more general matters.[46] And, carrying on the tradition of the

[46] The review in *The Booklist* (September 1, 1975, pp. 67–68) noted that this objectivity is sometimes too objective for Catholic readers, e.g., "Some matters that were very much part of

main set, biographies are included only for deceased persons, the most recent death date in the *Supplement* being 1966. This set should not be confused with the one-volume *The Catholic Encyclopedia* issued in 1976 by another publisher. For a review of this work, see "Reference and Subscription Book Reviews," *The Booklist*, February 15, 1977, pp. 924–925.

Encyclopaedia Judaica is noteworthy as being the first Jewish encyclopedia of major proportions to be published in the past 100 years. It has one peculiarity: the first, not the last, volume serves as the index. There are over 25,000 articles which cover close to 6000 years of Jewish history. Unlike the Catholic set, it makes no effort to deal in non-Jewish subject areas; its primary value is for the biographical material and the historical scholarship which points up the role Jews have played in world civilization. Nevertheless, the subject matter is diverse enough, ranging from articles on art, science, mysticism, and the Bible to modern Yiddish literature. There are over 8000 illustrations and hundreds of maps and charts.

The most comprehensive one-volume encyclopedia covering the broad spectrum of Christianity is *The Oxford Dictionary of the Christian Church* (2d ed.; New York: Oxford University Press, 1974, 1518 pp., $35). It has over 6000 entries and almost as many brief bibliographies. The alphabetically arranged volume is the work of 250 contributors, including the late editor, Leslie Cross. The entries, which run from a few lines to several pages, are comprehensive, and they move from a history of the crozier to theological controversy, including a little note on "Death of God," to numerous biographies. While all aspects of Christianity are considered, the emphasis is more on European than on American Christianity.[47]

Science

> *McGraw-Hill Encyclopedia of Science and Technology,* 4th ed. New York: McGraw-Hill Book Company, 1977, 15 vols. $497 ($447 to schools and libraries).

> *McGraw-Hill Yearbook of Science and Technology.* New York: McGraw-Hill Book Company, 1962 to date, approximately 500 pp. $29.50 ($22.50 to owners of main set).

> *Van Nostrand's Scientific Encyclopedia,* 5th ed. New York: Van Nostrand Reinhold, 1976, 2370 pp. $67.50.

---

the American Catholic consciousness during the 1967–1974 period are passed over or given very minimal treatment."

[47] For a tribute to the editor and a close analysis of a one-volume subject encyclopedia, see Owen Chadwick's "From the Birth of Christ to the 'Death of God,' " *The Times Literary Supplement,* November 24, 1974, pp. 1319–1320.

In the field of science, the best all-around general encyclopedia is the McGraw-Hill entry. The set is periodically revised and kept updated via the *McGraw-Hill Yearbook*. There are some 7800 articles which move from broad survey types to specific shorter entries for specialized areas. Each volume is nicely illustrated, and there are numerous graphs and charts.

The style of writing is unusually clear, and the set may be used both by young adults (such as high school students) and by experts who may be seeking an overview of a field they know little about. Thanks to the arrangement and the index, the set is particularly useful to the librarian for ready-reference questions, especially those which call for brief definitions of terms which may be foreign to the librarian or the user.

The *McGraw-Hill Yearbook of Science and Technology* reviews the past year's work in science. Other approaches are offered by at least two general encyclopedia publishers. *Science Year* (Chicago: Field Enterprises Educational Corp., 1965 to date, approximately 400 pp.) is issued by the publishers of *World Book* and is directed to children and young adults. There are usually 2 general science essays, 15 to 20 special reports on the year's activities, and 50 to 75 shorter articles under general topics, including biography. The many illustrations and the index make this an ideal purchase for libraries serving young people. An equally good annual is offered by the Britannica, *1971—Britannica Yearbook of Science and the Future* (Chicago: Encyclopaedia Britannica, 1968 to date, approximately 450 pp.). This volume contains an average of 16 feature articles and some 30 topical sections. There is an excellent index—one of the best of the group—and bibliographies. This work is suited for high school students and laypersons, while the *McGraw-Hill Yearbook* is better for the reader with some scientific and technical background.

Long considered a model of its kind for a one-volume scientific encyclopedia, *Van Nostrand's Scientific Encyclopedia* covers almost all the sciences from physics and chemistry to space and information science. Arrangement is alphabetical by subject with a vast number of cross-references and over 2500 photographs. The publisher claims the work contains some 2.2 million words (*The Columbia Encyclopedia* has over 6 million). The 7200 entries vary from short explanations to multipage articles. Most begin with simple definitions and become increasingly complex. The writing style and vocabulary are such that the work is more likely to be appreciated by persons with a scientific background who are seeking to refresh their memories or to get an overview of a topic.

Social sciences

International Encyclopedia of the Social Sciences. New York: The Macmillan Company, 1968, 17 vols. $495.

This is unquestionably the single-subject encyclopedia of most use and greatest interest in libraries. Its coverage includes subjects most often central to reference questions and, more particularly, to those calling for a limited amount of research or requiring an unbiased overview of a given area. Some 1500 scholars from 30 countries have contributed lengthy, comparative, analytical articles on all apsects of the social sciences, including anthropology, economics, geography, history, law, political science, psychology, sociology, and statistics. In addition to articles on various subject matter, the set includes some 600 biographies.

The set is arranged alphabetically, and there are copious cross-references and a detailed index. All these features make it extremely easy to use for reference work. Of particular interest is the arrangement of related articles under a single heading: for example, there are 12 contributions under the heading "Learning"; under "Leadership," related articles on psychological aspects, sociological aspects, and political aspects are included in a group.

While this is an entirely new work, it is based upon the equally famous *Encyclopedia of the Social Sciences* (New York: Crowell Collier and Macmillan, Inc., 1937, 8 vols.), which enjoyed continuous use for some 40 years in American libraries. It is still valuable for retrospective, historical material and, more particularly, for over 4000 biographies. In fact, the *International* is not meant to supplement, only to complement, its predecessor.

SUGGESTED READING

"Encyclopedia Sales Frauds," *Consumer Reports,* March 1971, pp. 172–174. Although dated, the frauds listed here are still being perpetuated and the article is a good one for the average purchaser to read before buying a set.

Freudenthal, Juan R., "Gran Enciclopedia Rialp," *Choice,* May 1977, p. 340. This is a perceptive short review of a new Spanish encyclopedia, mentioned here because there are few such reviews of foreign encyclopedias in English and this one is particularly useful as a model.

"The Making of a General Encyclopedia," *The Booklist,* September 15, 1976, pp. 206–214. A reprint of talks given by five major encyclopedia editors at an American Library Association conference in 1976. The papers range from the informative to the sales pitch, but taking them with proper skepticism, the reader will discover much of value.

Miller, Mark C., "Slim Pickens," *The New York Review of Books,* September 16, 1976, pp. 38–40. In this review of two subject encyclopedias (*The Oxford Companion to Film* and *The Filmgoer's Companion*), the author suggests numerous ways of evaluating subject sets, such as looking out for the "easy value judgment" or "tiny errors" which invalidate a reference book.

Needham, C. D., "Britannica Revisited," *Library Association Record,* July 1975, pp. 153–168. A detailed review of the fifteenth edition of the *Encyclopaedia Britannica* and a model for analysis of any general encyclopedia. Recommended for those who wish to learn how an expert carefully dissects a reference work. See, also, an equally perceptive and lengthy review in the "Reference and Subscription Book Reviews" section in *The Booklist,* June 1, 1975, pp. 1021–1028.

Soergel, Dagobert, "An Automated Encyclopedia . . . ,"*International Classification,* No. 1, May 1977, pp. 4–10. A practical view of what it would mean to automate, i.e., to store in a computer, for recall by a user, the contents of an encyclopedia. Advantages and disadvantages are pointed out. (A more technical second section to this article is in the same journal, No. 2, 1977, but it is recommended only for the expert.)

CHAPTER SIX

Ready-Reference Sources: Almanacs, Yearbooks, Handbooks, Directories

THE READY-REFERENCE source is a special form of reference work edited and designed for the specific purpose of supplying answers to ready-reference, quick-fact questions. In one sense, all reference works might be classified in this category, but there is one group especially suited for such questions. This group is composed of almanacs, yearbooks, handbooks, and directories.

As neat as the categorization may seem here, it is hardly that way in real reference service. The difficulty is one of definition. A manual may be a handbook, an almanac more of an encyclopedia, and a directory a first-class biographical aid. Technically, the form is one or the other, but in daily operations, the librarian rarely uses such a classification scheme except in the broadest sense of matching a likely question with a likely source.

Duplication factor

All these forms tend to duplicate, at least in part, much of the basic information found in other forms. For example, the contents of the four or five general almanacs include much of the same data found in encyclopedias, biographical aids, geographical sources, and even dictionaries and bibliographical aids. It has been said that well over half the ready-reference questions in a library may be answered with an encyclopedia, an almanac,

Subject Guide to Books in Print, and a good biographical source—in fact, a handful of titles. There is some truth to this assumption. Duplication of material is so widespread that the librarian soon learns the futility of searching many titles, when one or two will provide answers not only for questions A and B but also for questions C through Z.

The duplication phenomenon explains the small collection of reference books placed near every reference desk in almost every library. This is a core of perhaps 75 to 100 titles wherein most answers are found. Beyond that core collection may stretch shelves and shelves of other reference titles. Why? Because, just as the librarian is certain all answers are in the basic collection, along comes a query that requires going to the larger group of titles—or even beyond that to the general collection or to another library.

The duplication factor, or the multireference character, of many reference titles is important to grasp. In the rush to learn as much as possible about forms and individual titles, the beginning librarian may sometimes feel a surge of frustration and despair. The truth is that the vast multiplicity of information in various titles has a positive element, particularly for the beginner. Given all these sources and the various choices, the librarian may assume there is an answer to almost any ready-reference question—not in one source, but in several sources. Lacking knowledge of, or access to, X or Y almanac or handbook, one is just as likely to find the answer in P encyclopedia or R biographical aid.

Why the duplication? Primarily because nothing breeds success in publishing like success. First there was one almanac. It sold well. Next there were a second and a third, and so on and on. As specific titles and forms become increasingly popular (and lucrative), they tend to spawn similar titles by other publishers. Works tend to divide and subdivide as long as the market (library and public alike) continues to support such specialization and division. This is not to say each new title is a carbon copy of the last. It is not, but the duplication, multi-information factor is always present. This is the factor, after all, which guaranteed the success of Y title, and it should be included and modified in P title. Sometimes the modification of a new title or a version of a form is a distinct improvement; at other times it is less than a happy compromise with quality.

ALMANACS AND YEARBOOKS

Although almanacs and yearbooks tend to be distinctive types or forms of reference work, they are closely enough related in terms of both use and scope to be treated here as a single class of ready-reference aid. Aside from the general almanac, e.g., *World Almanac*, and the general yearbook, e.g.,

Britannica Book of the Year, the subject almanac and the yearbook tend to be similar and often are used for much the same purpose in a reference situation.

Definitions

Almanac   An almanac is a compendium of useful data and statistics relating to countries, personalities, events, subjects, and the like. It is a type of specific-entry encyclopedia stripped of adjectives and adverbs and limited to the skeleton of information.

As the major proportion of special subject almanacs are published on an annual or biannual schedule, they are sometimes called yearbooks and annuals. Traditionally, the almanac per se tended to be general in nature; the yearbook and the annual were more specific, that is, were limited to a given area or subject. No more. There are now subject almanacs and encyclopedia yearbooks which are as broad in their coverage as the general almanac.

Yearbook/Annual   A yearbook is an annual compendium of data and statistics of a given year. An almanac will inevitably cover material of the previous year, too. The essential difference is that the almanac will also include considerable retrospective material—material which may or may not be in the average yearbook. The yearbook's fundamental purpose is to record the year's activities by country, subject, or specialized area. There are, to be sure, general yearbooks and, most notably, the yearbooks issued by encyclopedia companies. Still, in ready-reference work, the most often used type is usually confined to special areas of interest.

Compendium   A compendium is a brief summary of a larger work or of a field of knowledge. For example, the *Statistical Abstract of the United States* is a compendium in the sense that it is a summary of the massive data in the files of the U.S. Bureau of the Census. As both almanacs and yearbooks have many common qualities, they are sometimes lumped together as "compendiums."

Purpose

Recency   Regardless of form and presentation, the user turns to a yearbook or an almanac for relatively recent information on a subject or personality. The purpose of many of these works is to update standard texts which may be issued or totally revised only infrequently. An encyclopedia yearbook, for example, is a compromise—even an excuse for not rewriting all articles in the encyclopedia each year.

Brief Facts   Where a single figure or a fact is required, normally without benefit of explanation, the almanac serves a useful purpose. A yearbook will be more useful if the reader wishes a limited amount of background information on a recent development or seeks a fact not found in a standard almanac.

Trends   With their concern with recency, almanacs and yearbooks, either directly or by implication, indicate trends in the development or, if you will, the regression of civilization. Scientific advances are chronicled, as are the events, persons, and places of importance over the previous year. One reason for maintaining a run of certain almanacs and yearbooks is to indicate such trends. For example, in the 1908 *World Almanac*, there were 22 pages devoted to railroads. The 1977 issue contained about 3, while television performers rated close to 10 pages. The obvious shift in interest of Americans over the past 50 years is reflected in collections of yearbooks and almanacs. More important for the historian, many of these early works are convenient sources of statistical information otherwise lost.

Informal Index   Most of the reliable yearbooks and almanacs cite sources of information and, as such, can be used as informal indexes. For example, a patron interested in retail sales will find general information in any good almanac or yearbook. These publications in turn will cite sources, such as *Fortune, Business Week,* or *Moody's Industrials,* which will provide additional keys to information. Specific citations to government sources of statistics may quickly guide the reader to primary material otherwise difficult to locate.

Directory and Biographical Information   Many yearbooks and almanacs include material normally found in a directory. For example, a yearbook in a special field may well include the names of the principal leaders in that field, with their addresses and perhaps short biographical sketches. The *World Almanac,* among others, lists associations and societies, with addresses.

Browsing   Crammed into the odd corners of almost any yearbook or almanac are masses of unrelated, frequently fascinating bits of information. The true lover of facts—and the United States is a country of such lovers—delights in merely thumbing through many of these works. From the point of view of the dedicated reference librarian, this purpose may seem inconsequential, but it is totally fascinating for any observer of the passing social scene.

General almanacs

The CBS News Almanac.[1] Maplewood, New Jersey: Hammond Incorporated, 1970 to date, $6.95; paper, $3.95.

Information Please Almanac. New York: Simon & Schuster, Inc., 1947 to date. $6.95; paper, $3.95.

The People's Almanac. Garden City, New York: Doubleday & Company, 1975, 1481 pp. $14.95; paper, $7.95.

Whitaker's Almanack. London: Whitaker, 1869 to date. (Distributed in the United States by British Book Center, New York.) $18.95.

The World Almanac and Book of Facts. New York: Newspaper Enterprise Association, 1868 to date (various publishers). $5.95; paper, $2.75.

In the beginning, the almanac was a book which was arranged by months, weeks, and days with pertinent information concerning the rising and setting of the moon, times of low and high tides, a calendar of holy days, and some bits of miscellaneous information. This type dates back to some 1200 years before Christ and was employed primarily by farmers and in connection with holy days.

During the Middle Ages, the horae, psalters, and missals were derived in part from almanacs. Shifting from religion to astronomy and astrology, then to medicine, and finally to scraps of general information, the almanac underwent many changes from the Middle Ages down through the eighteenth century. In America, by far the most famous work of this type was Benjamin Franklin's *Poor Richard's Almanack*, first published in 1732. *The Old Farmer's Almanac*, based on *Poor Richard*, has been published annually in this country since 1792. Between traditional yellow covers, the almanac includes anecdotes and pleasantries, historical dates, zodiac signs, planting tables, puzzles, recipes, and even poetry. Close behind in age and popularity is the 159-year-old *American Farm and Home Almanac*. Published in Lewiston, Maine, it claims a circulation of over 6 million and is distributed free in banks and other institutions. It is sold on

---

[1] This has undergone three name changes. First published in 1970 as *The New York Times Encyclopedia Almanac*, it was continued from 1971 to 1975 as the *Official Associated Press Almanac*, and from 1976 to the present as *The CBS News Almanac*. Little has changed except the name.

newstands under a slightly different name. Most people read these almanacs not so much for weather and planning information as for nostalgia.

As for the more accepted type of almanac, the pattern was first established by the *American Almanac and Repository of Useful Knowledge*, published in Boston from 1830 to 1861. Subsequent almanacs were issued by newspapers, and they rapidly developed into compendiums of useful data and statistics on international, national, state, and local affairs.

All the titles listed here are basic general almanacs which are to be found in most American libraries. If an order of general use and importance were to be given, they might be ranked as follows: (1) *World Almanac*; (2) *Information Please Almanac*; (3) and *Whitaker's Almanack*. The order of preference is based upon familiarity. Sales of the *World Almanac* now exceed the combined sales of its two principal competitors, *The CBS News Almanac* and *Information Please Almanac*. The 1977 edition consists of 976 pages and, according to the editors, is 30 percent new as compared with the 1976 edition. Its contents include precise factual data on people, places, events, and other information ranging from postal zip codes to 25,000 sports facts. There are even income tax advice and maps of various foreign cities. Putting aside for a moment *The People's Almanac* and *The CBS News Almanac*, some comparisons may be made between the top three general titles.

With the exception of *Whitaker's*, all are primarily concerned with data of interest to American readers. In varying degree, they cover the same basic subject matter; and, while there is an appreciable degree of duplication, their low cost makes it possible to have at least two or three at the reference desk. The best one is the one which answers the specific question of the moment. Today, it may be the *World Almanac*, and tomorrow, *Whitaker's*. In terms of searching, though, it is usually preferable to begin with the *World* and work through the order of preference stated in the previous paragraph.

All almanacs have several points in common: (1) They enjoy rather healthy sales and are to be found in many homes; (2) they depend heavily upon government sources for statistics, and readers frequently will find the same sources (when given) quoted in all the almanacs; and (3) except for updating and revising, much of the same basic material is carried over year after year.

Of the three works, *Whitaker's*, the English entry, is by far the most extensively indexed (25,000 entries), followed by the *World Almanac* (9000 entries). *Whitaker's* is distinctive, as might be expected, in that it places considerable emphasis upon Great Britain and on European governments. For example, the 1976 edition boasts of close to 90 pages of an almost complete directory of British royalty and peerage, with another 150 pages devoted to government and public offices right down to salaries paid to officials. Salaries came to be a feature when Whitaker started the almanac. He asked for salaries; they were not given, so Whitaker printed what he thought the employees were worth. The entire subject of Great Britain is dismissed in the American almanacs in less than a dozen pages. Where *Whitaker's* and the American books meet, however, is on standard information about events of the year, foreign countries, and international statistics. *Whitaker's* places more emphasis on emerging nations.

Whereas there is little real duplication between *Whitaker's* and the American works, the almanacs published on this side of the Atlantic are similar to one another in scope if not arrangement and emphasis. The cousins of the *World Almanac* tend to feature discursive, larger units on such subjects as the lively arts, science, education, and medicine. *Information Please Almanac* expanded its contents to include special sections, and it includes many maps. *Information Please* tends to gravitate more to the methods of encyclopedia yearbooks than to the standard form set by traditional almanacs. It is considerably more attractive in makeup (larger type, spacing, and illustration) than the *World*. As for binding, most almanacs come in both hard and soft covers. Libraries normally buy the hardbound editions.

The essential question about these titles is, Are they all needed? That query may be answered by ascertaining the amount of duplication in each, and the ease of finding facts via an index. One may dismiss *The CBS News Almanac* on the first count because, aside from a rather extensive section on biography of world leaders, it duplicates what is found elsewhere. The index is adequate. A special case is the much publicized *People's Almanac*, which runs to almost 1500 pages and denies all the traditional laws of almanacs in that it is more concerned with, as one critic puts it, "a compilation of odds and ends of weird facts and fancies that could make an Elsie Dinsmore the laughing life of the party." In this respect it follows nineteenth-century compilations such as *Brewer's Dictionary of Phrase & Fable*, which is a massive collection of odd facts about all aspects of human culture.[2]

Thanks to a wide variety of hard-to-find facts and data, the *People's* is virtually a one-volume encyclopedia with 32 sections devoted to history, geography, biography, inventions, finance, sex, language, etc. The index is adequate and there are cross-references, but none of the maps or illustrations is indexed. The overall result is that the almanac as a ready-reference source is better than average; but until the indexing is improved, it is not up to the high standards set by some established almanacs. Used with one

[2] Anyone who enjoys *The People's Almanac* should turn to the Brewer work, first issued in 1870 and reprinted and revised many times over the years. The best current edition was edited by Ivor H. Evans, published by Harper & Row in 1970.

of the standard almanacs, it is unquestionably a valuable reference aid. The librarian should not be put off by the popularity of the work, helped no little by the compiler Irving Wallace and his son David Wallechinsky, who are trained, professional writers. The facts are nicely cushioned by a commendable prose style rarely found in almanacs, or for that matter, in many encyclopedias.

Another bestseller by Wallechinsky and Wallace is *The Book of Lists* (New York: William Morrow & Company, 1977), which is literally 500 "new lists on every subject imaginable involving persons, places, happenings and things." For example, there are lists of the 12 windiest cities in the United States, 236 people born the same day, and estimated IQs of 30 celebrated people. Most emphasis is on lists drawn up by famous people especially for the book. How valuable a reference aid this will be remains to be seen, but it has a fascination for anyone involved with facts, not to mention trivia. It also features a good index.

General yearbooks

Facts on File Yearbook. New York: Facts on File, Inc., 1940 to date, annual. $57.50.

The Annual Register of World Events in. . . . London: publisher varies; published in 1977 by Longmans, Roberts and Green. 600 pp. $37.50 (Distributed in the United States by St. Martin's Press, Inc.)

The best-known general yearbooks are those issued by encyclopedia publishers, and they are discussed in Chapter 5 on encyclopedias. For ready-reference purposes, the two titles listed here are the most often used, mainly to check dates, events, and personalities in the previous year's news. (Equally useful is the cumulated *New York Times Index*.)

Facts on File Yearbook is a complete year's cumulation of the data in the weekly *Facts on File* (page 113), gathered under four broad categories: world affairs, United States affairs, other nations, and general. The American section makes up about 50 percent of the work, while about 10 percent of the whole is given over to general information—facts on economy, labor, education, the arts, sports, crime, etc. The reporting is objective and the writing style clear. For ready reference, the *Facts on File* annual is particularly good because it has an excellent, detailed index with specific entries for every item mentioned.[3]

---

[3] The same publisher issues *News Dictionary*, 1965 to date, annual, which is somewhat similar in coverage, but the arrangement is alphabetical by subject and there is no index. Although there are many cross-references, the lack of an index limits its use for reference work. The plus side: It includes data for the complete year, not just for the nine to ten months usually covered in most yearbooks.

By virtue of its longevity and its broad coverage of the past year's events, the *Annual Register* is a basic work in larger libraries. Published in England, it is divided into 16 sections. It gives more attention to world events than its American counterpart does. The first part is a survey of the highlights of the year's past events and developments in each country. Another part is concerned with international organizations, religion, science, etc. A final section includes the text of important documents of the year. The quality of the writing in the *Register* is excellent, and the work has the added advantage of evaluating the year's events. There is an adequately detailed index.

REPRESENTATIVE SUBJECT ALMANACS AND YEARBOOKS

Almost every area of human interest has its own subject almanac, compendium, or yearbook. In a text of this type it is pointless to enumerate the literally hundreds of titles. What follows, then, is a representative group of subject almanacs and compendiums, and more particularly, those "basic" or "classic" works which tend to cross many disciplines and are used in some libraries as often as the familiar index, encyclopedia, or general almanac.

Government[4]

Statesman's Year-Book. New York: St. Martin's Press, Inc., 1864 to date, annual. $16.95.

International Yearbook and Statesman's Who's Who. Surrey: Neville House, 1953 to date, annual. (£15.) $40.

Europa Yearbook. London: Europa Publications, Ltd. (distributed in the United States by Gale Research Company), 1926 to date, annual, 2 vols. $84.

U.S. National Archives and Record Service. *United States Government Manual.*[5] Washington, D.C.: Government Printing Office, 1935 to date, annual. $6.50.

---

[4] "Government" as a descriptor is used here in its broadest sense to include not only the political structure of countries but background on commerce, banking, education, transportation, media, literature, etc.

[5] With the 1973–1974 edition, the descriptor "Organization" was dropped from the title. From 1948 to 1973, the publication was known as the *United States Government Organization Manual*.

> *Congressional Quarterly Almanac.* Washington, D.C.: Congressional Quarterly Inc., 1945 to date, annual. $62.
>
> *Municipal Yearbook.* Washington, D.C.: International City Management Association, 1922 to date, annual. $25.

It is somewhat arbitrary to separate out most of these yearbooks from the "general" category, particularly as they all relate directly to the type of material found in encyclopedia annuals and, for example, *Facts on File Yearbook.* If there is a major difference, it is one of emphasis. The government titles tend to stress the standard, statistical, and directory types of information which change only in part each year. The aforementioned general yearbooks stress the events of the past year.

Published for over a century, the *Statesman's Year-Book* provides current background information on 166 nations of the world. Along with a general encyclopedia and an almanac, it serves as a cornerstone for reference work in almost any type of library. The *Year-Book*, grouping countries geographically, begins with the British Commonwealth, moves on to the United States, and then considers the rest of the world. The quantity of information varies in proportion not so much according to the size of the country as to the definite Western slant of the reference work. For example, in the 1976–1977 edition, over 190 pages are given over to the United States, some 60 to Canada, and equally full coverage to Commonwealth countries. Many of the so-called third-world nations are limited to less than 10 pages.

The book opens with a helpful section on international organizations, and then, for each country considered, arranges the information in a systematic manner. Typical subheadings for almost every entry are: heads of government, area and population, constitution and government, religion, education, railways, aviation, weights and measures, etc. There are excellent brief bibliographies for locating further statistical and general information. Another useful feature is the numerous maps which show such things as time zones and distributions of natural resources.

Given this basic yearbook, one might ask why others are needed. The answer is that while several yearbooks duplicate information, they have additional data which are often useful. Comparatively speaking, the *International Yearbook and Statesman's Who's Who* provides more directory-type information than is found in the *Statesman's Year-Book*, and, as the title suggests, it offers the added bonus of 10,000-plus entries in a biographical section. At the same time, the latter work has bibliographies not found in the *International Yearbook,* and the index is much better. Possibly more important, the data in the *Statesman's Year-Book* tend to be more up to date than those in the rival volume.

The *Europa Yearbook* again covers much of the same territory found in its rivals. It has several advantages: (1) It is as up to date as the *Statesman's Year-Book*, and in this respect, is ahead of the *International*; (2) it is in two volumes, and in words alone, leads both; (3) the first volume covers international organizations and Europe; (4) the second volume covers the remainder of the world and here resembles the other titles. A basic pattern is followed throughout: essential data with statistical tables, information on the political and judicial systems, press and radio, publishing, finance, trade and industry, tourism, and the diplomatic corps. Its coverage of the media is better than either of the other yearbooks, but it is neither better nor worse than the others when the standard data are concerned.

Given these yearbooks, the average library has more than enough material to answer statistical, directory-type, and specific questions about government. However, these three best-known titles hardly exhaust the possibilities. For example, there is the *South American Handbook* (Bath: Dawson & Goodall, 1921 to date, annual, 1100 pp. Distributed in the United States by Rand McNally). It takes each Latin American country in its turn, gives standard information about government, economics, and cities and towns, and then proceeds to the unusual for a handbook. The "unusual" are chatty remarks about practical things such as what to wear, national habits, and food, and bits of data more likely to be found in a travel guide. It all makes for good reading, a characteristic not often associated with handbooks.

A decided problem with all these titles is recency. Most of the data in the 1977 title will be up to date in terms of 1976 or a good part of it, yet of little use for changes subsequent to publication of the annual. Hence, information about particular officers and government administrations should be double-checked with current fact sources such as *Facts on File*, *Keesing's*, or, where absolute precision is necessary, the nearest consular office of the country in question.

If one considers recency a major factor, the *Yearbook of the United Nations* (New York: United Nations Publications, 1947 to date, irregular) is a decided disappointment. The 1972 edition, for example, came out in mid-1975, and since its inception in 1947 it has always been several years behind. The summary of organizational activities of the United Nations, as well as related organizations, tends to become more of a history than an active, ongoing reference aid. Aware of this problem, the United Nations (like many governmental organizations and not a few private publishers) attempts a solution by publication of a monthly running account of its activities in a magazine, *The UN Monthly Chronicle* (New York: United Nations Publications, 1964 to date). Although this periodical does not provide an overall summary, it at least gives a documented survey of current activities which may be retrieved via an annual index.

Monthly publications are a favored way of keeping slow-to-be published annuals updated. Another of many examples is the *Yearbook of International Organizations* (Brussels: Union of International Associations, 1948 to date, irregular) which keeps tabs on over 4500 organizations ranging from the European Common Market to multinational business groups. *International Associations*, by the same publisher, is a monthly publication which updates the *Yearbook*.

Turning from the international scene to the United States, the American equivalent of the yearbooks mentioned is the *United States Government Manual*. In one sense this is an expansion of what is found in the *Statesman's Year-Book*, and if one looks at reference works in other Western countries, one will find its equivalents in Britain, France, Germany and other countries. The basic purpose of the *Manual* is to give in detail the organization, activities, and chief officers of all government agencies. The information includes the legislative, judicial, and executive branches.

Each of the agencies is discussed separately and the units within each organizational pattern are clearly defined. Now and then, charts and diagrams are employed to make matters a bit clearer. The style is factual, yet discursive enough to hold the interest of anyone remotely involved with such matters.

A useful feature of each year's issue is the list of agencies which have been transferred, terminated, or abolished. Full particulars are given. This, by the way, is justification for holding several years of the *Manual* on the shelves. All too often, someone will want information on a certain agency which can be found only in earlier editions of the work.

Students, particularly those struggling through a civics or history class, find the *Government Manual* an excellent source of factual material for papers. Adults use it for names of officials and proper addresses. *Documents to the People* (Chicago: American Library Association, 1972 to date, quarterly) updates the *Manual* from time to time. For example, "Supplement to the 1976/77 U.S. Government Manual" lists new agencies, reorganizations, new addresses, etc. With a new administration, and therefore many organizational changes in Washington, the updating service is particularly valuable for 1977—until a new edition of the *Manual* is published.

The single best retrospective source of information on congressional, and to a degree executive and judiciary, action is the annual *Congressional Quarterly Almanac*. Covering activities of the previous year, it includes information on all major legislation, how congressmen voted, highlights of the Supreme Court, basic Presidential messages, and the like. There are numerous charts and graphs which speed along the ready-reference process, and the whole is brought together by a complete index.

Current information on candidates for national office is easy enough to come by, and their records can be checked in the *Congressional Quarterly Almanac*. At a local, state, or municipal level, the League of Women Voters (among other groups) publishes a biographical and evaluative material on candidates. This material should be available in every library, as should, of course, opposing views of other organizations.[6]

The *Municipal Yearbook* offers an annual review of developments in United States cities. The annual looks at statistics and trends in a comparative way, and does not always give specific data for specific cities. There are several sections, including those on trends, employment and finance, management issues, public safety, and the environment. The overall view of American cities is visually aided by graphs, charts, and tables and is useful to ascertain trends and to get averages for this or that. However, only the directory section can be used for specific cities. Here, there is a directory of municipal officials for cities over 2500. It is the most valuable part of the book for reference work, particularly as, beginning with 1974, it gives the telephone numbers of city halls.

Data for a state or for a city are usually found in local annual or biennial guides, frequently known as "blue books." These vary in scope and depth of presentation, but are of major importance for all libraries; e.g., even the smallest library will want the manual for its state. If there is any question about the title or frequency of such a manual or annual, the librarian should contact the state library or, for that matter, any official in the governor's office. The local manuals are invaluable for biographical information on state legislators, data on various agencies, and the like.

Statistical data

U.S. Bureau of the Census. *Statistical Abstract of the United States*.[7] Washington, D.C.: Government Printing Office, 1879 to date, annual. $5.75.

United Nations Statistical Office. *Statistical Yearbook*. New York: United Nations Publications, 1949 to date, annual. $38.

Statistics are concerned "with the collection, classification, analysis and interpretation of numerical facts or data." The reference librarian is likely to meet the statistical question when the user opens a query with "How much?" or "How many?" Depending on whether the query is motivated by simple curiosity or by a serious research problem, the sources of

---

[6] An almanac frequently found in libraries is *The Almanac of American Politics* (New York: E. P. Dutton & Co., 1972 to date, biennial). This includes information on a state-by-state basis with emphasis on statistical material (income, employment, median voting age, etc.), with names of state officials and information on members of Congress and how they voted on key issues. However, the breakdown is at the state, not the local, level.

[7] As government publications are not copyrighted, the *Statistical Abstract* is published as *The American Almanac* by Grosset & Dunlap, usually at a lower price than the government title. It contains exactly the same material as found in the *Statistical Abstract*.

possible answers are as numerous as the hundreds of reference works which deal peripherally or exclusively with statistical data.

The reference librarian's most difficult problem remains in isolating the source of the esoteric, specialized statistical query. Almost as hard a problem is the translation of the query into the terminology employed by the statistical source. Given the numerous sources and the specialized terminology, it is no wonder that in larger libraries the expert in statistics is as important a figure as the subject bibliographer. Normally, this librarian will be located in the government documents section or the business section. Granted that statistical reference work is highly specialized, all that can be done here is to indicate the basic general sources with which the beginner should be familiar. Fortunately, the basic works tend to be sufficient for most general questions.

The two best sources of answers to general statistical questions are: (1) any of the almanacs or encyclopedias which, in turn, draw upon the second general source, (2) the *Statistical Abstract of the United States*, for most of their data. A third source may be used when the others fail (usually for lack of currency), and this is the group of indexes from *The New York Times Index*, to *Public Affairs Information Service Bulletin* to the *Business Periodicals Index*.

The *Statistical Abstract of the United States* is divided into approximately 35 major sections. Each is preceded by a summary which explains terminology and clearly states sources and origins of data. Broad topics include education, public lands, vital statistics, population, and almost any conceivable area likely to be of interest to either the expert or the layperson. There is an excellent index which is particularly strong on the subject approach.[8]

While a large proportion of statistics are from government sources, close to 75 private firms and organizations supply material. As these are identified, the *Statistical Abstract* serves another worthwhile purpose as a guide to major statistical services outside the government. Most of the data are presented in tabular form. The text is issued annually and each of the tables is updated by one year. For purposes of comparison, figures are usually retained for several previous years.

The level of unemployment, the number of persons on welfare, crime statistics, the amount of aspirin produced, the distribution of television sets and bathrooms in American homes—these are just a few of the various facts which can be ascertained through the *Statistical Abstract*. Statistics for cities and other small geographical units are used only infrequently, and as

---

[8] Even a cursory glance at general almanacs, encyclopedias, yearbooks, etc., will show that publishers rely heavily upon the *Statistical Abstract* for much data, and that no single work is as often quoted.

a consequence, there are a number of other reference titles for small units. Among the most used, with self-descriptive titles, are: *County and City Data Book* (1952 to date, irregular) and the *Congressional District Data Book* (1961 to date, biennial). Also issued by the Bureau of the Census, they offer a local approach to the same type of data found in the more general *Statistical Abstract*.

Some notion of the general public interest in statistics may be found in the relatively recent publication of a number of popular spin-offs of the *Statistical Abstract*, such as the *Pocket Data Book, USA* (1967 to date, biennial) and *We, The Americans* (1967 to date, irregular), both published by the Bureau of the Census in a popular form with multiple colored charts, diagrams, and the like. At the other extreme, almost every governmental department and bureau publishes its own specialized statistical data in such reports as the U.S. Office of Education's *Digest of Educational Statistics* (1962 to date, annual) and the U.S. Department of Housing and Urban Development's *Statistical Yearbook* (1966 to date, annual).

A lesser-known reference title with potential for considerable use by students is the *Historical Statistics of the United States, Colonial Times to 1970* (Washington, D.C.: Government Printing Office, 1975, 2 vols.). Revised over the years, the present edition includes data for more than 12,500 time series grouped in tabular form. It gives comparative figures on statistics ranging from the average wage over the years to the number of residents in a given state or territory. Most material is on the national level, although there are a few sections covering regions and smaller areas.[9]

The majority of Western nations follow the pattern established by the American and British governments in that they, too, issue equivalents to the *Statistical Abstract* and specialized statistical information. On an international level the best-known equivalent is the United Nations *Statistical Yearbook*, which covers basic data from over 150 areas of the world. The information is broken down under broad subject headings ranging from population to transportation, and no effort is made to single out smaller than national units of government. Consequently, one gets only a broad viewpoint, although in the 1976 edition of 914 pages the librarian can find data ranging from the number of people in the world (estimated at 3.89 billion) to the percentage of dwellings in rural Brazil with flush toilets (0.8 percent).

In her "After the *Statistical Abstract*—What?"[10] Nathalie D. Frank briefly discusses over 50 specialized sources for statistics for "those who are

[9] An equally valuable work is *European Historical Statistics 1750–1970* (New York: Columbia University Press, 1975, 827 pp.).

[10] *RQ*, September 1975, pp. 204–210. This is an excellent overview article of specialized statistical sources.

likely to encounter sophisticated inquiries." At the same time, she admits to suggesting only the possibilities, which range from the familiar *Statistical Abstract* to data bases which may be tapped by a computer. But, if one limits oneself to bibliographies, the answer to "After the *Statistical Abstract*—What?" might be limited for most purposes to the following two titles:

Two sources geared specifically to statistics usually will be found in larger libraries: (1) *American Statistics Index* (Washington, D.C.: Congressional Information Service, 1973 to date, annual, monthly, and quarterly supplements). Backed by a microfiche service which provides most of the documents indexed, this service covers virtually all statistical publications issued by the government, i.e., surveys, reports, monographs, studies, periodical articles, etc. By 1978 the *Index* provided access to over 800 currently issued government periodicals from some 140 federal agencies and offices. (2) *Statistical Sources* (4th ed.; Detroit: Gale Research Company, 1974) lists sources under about 12,000 subject headings. The fourth edition claims 21,000 citations which give data on industrial, business, social, educational, financial, and other statistical topics for the United States.

Women

> *Woman's Almanac.* New York: Lippincott, 1976, 624 pp. $12.50; paper, $6.95.
>
> *The Women's Rights Almanac.* Bethesda, Maryland: Elizabeth Stanton Publishing Company, 1974 to date. Paper, $5.95.

Almanacs, yearbooks, and compendiums will be found in almost every area and subject listed in Sheehy, Walford, and the *American Reference Books Annual.* The two titles listed here are representative of what develops with changes in social thinking. Be that as it may, the two works are important in that they are witness to the necessity of a reference librarian's keeping up with change. It is hardly enough to learn a few titles, master a few areas, and then continually, year in and year out, ignore a new world.

Woman's Almanac is typical of a growing group of titles for and about women. It is really a manual in that it gives not only facts, but advice on many of the matters modern women are concerned with—from health and sex to educational opportunities to hobbies. Technically, it is really an anthology, as most of the material in the 12 chapters is reprinted from books and periodicals. Excerpts are clearly noted with full bibliographical data so the interested reader may turn to the original for additional information. The most valuable part of the *Almanac* is the last section, a directory of services listed in typical yellow-page fashion.

Good Housekeeping and the *World Almanac* issued a 576-page *Woman's Almanac* in late 1977 ($7.95; paperback, $3.95). It is less satisfactory than the Lippincott *Woman's Almanac,* in that it emphasizes more popular material; still, it is useful for most libraries.

The Women's Rights Almanac comes closer to the traditional almanac pattern in that it is a collection of statistical data on women at both the national and international levels. There is a state-by-state listing of demographic statistics, women's organizations, voting records of congressional members on women's issues, etc. There is also an annual chronology of women's events. Still, just as one thinks one has the form in hand, one encounters other parts of the *Almanac* which more closely resemble a handbook or manual in that there are articles and essays on a variety of issues.

Inevitably, too, as interest grows in an area, there develop a number of specialized guides and bibliographies to the subject. For example, there is the *Women's Movement Media* (New York: R. R. Bowker Company, 1975) which lists women's movement publishers, research centers, organizations, governmental groups, etc. Then there is the "basic book collection" for women in *Womanhood Media* (Metuchen, New Jersey: Scarecrow Press, 1972, plus a Supplement, 1975).

HANDBOOKS AND MANUALS

It is difficult to distinguish between the average handbook and the average manual. Therefore, the terms are often used synonymously, or the confused writer solves the definition problem by once again using the term "compendium" for either or both forms.

Definition

Handbook A handbook is a miscellaneous group of facts centered on one central theme or subject area. The term literally comes from the German *Handbuch,* i.e., a book which can be held in the hand comfortably. The form developed in the nineteenth century, particularly with the nouveaux riches and the lesser educated who sought quick, reliable information on an art, occupation, or other forms of study.

Manual A manual normally tends to be equated with how-to-do-it material, whether it be on preparing a dinner or repairing an automobile. As a consequence, many manuals are found in the general collection or, in some libraries where use is constant (as for works on etiquette), the books may be duplicated in the reference collection.

Purpose

The primary purpose of handbooks and manuals is to serve as a ready-reference source for a given field of knowledge. Emphasis normally is on established knowledge rather than recent advances, although in the field of science, handbooks that are more than a few years old may be almost totally useless.

The scientific handbook in particular presupposes a basic knowledge of the subject field. A good part of the information is given in shorthand form, freely employing tables, graphs, symbols, equations, formulas, and downright jargon which only the expert understands. Much the same, to be sure, can be said about the specialized manual.

Scope

With some exceptions, a vast proportion of all handbooks and manuals have one thing in common—a limited scope. They tend to zero in on a specific area of interest or a subject. In fact, their particular value is the depth of information they give in a narrow field.

There are countless manuals and handbooks. New ones appear each year, while some old ones disappear or undergo a name change. It is obviously impossible to remember them all. What happens in practice is that owing to ease of arrangement, lack of another substitute, or use, librarians adopt favorites.

General handbooks and manuals

> *Guinness Book of World Records*. New York: Sterling Publishing Co., 1955 to date, annual. $10; paper, $7.95.

> Kane, Joseph N. *Famous First Facts*, 3d ed. New York: The H. W. Wilson Company, 1964, 165 pp. $29.

> *Awards, Honors and Prizes*, 3d ed. Detroit: Gale Research Company, 1975, 2 vols., $38 and $48.

Of the several truly general handbooks, the three listed here are the best known and the most used in conjunction with a general almanac or encyclopedia. Much of the information they list can be found elsewhere, but the arrangement of the three works is such that they are easy to check for isolated facts which might be buried in an encyclopedia article.

The *Guinness Book of World Records*, with 29 million copies in print, now claims in its own pages to be the best-selling book of all time (the editors disqualify the Bible, the sayings of Chairman Mao, and several almanacs). The title has gained fame and readership by dutifully recording representations of the tallest, fattest, longest, and smallest, and similar record-making data. Divided into sections and well indexed, the *Guinness Book of World Records* gives figures on everything from pipe smoking and pogo-stick jumping to a section called "Plants of Death," which "contains the only vivid—not to say shrill—descriptive writing in the book. Strychnine causes 'an appalling form of death'; the green patches of potatoes are extremely poisonous, and their effects gloatingly listed."[11]

The success of the book has resulted in numerous spin-offs which first began to appear in 1977, e.g., *Guinness Book of Surprising Accomplishments, Guinness Book of Women's Records, Guinness Sports Record Book 1977–1978.* All published by Sterling, the titles themselves indicate the expansion of data found in the original volume. And as they each sell for under $5, they will be of some value for the reference librarian.

Kane's *Famous First Facts* is the joy of the librarian seeking out-of-the-way information on such vital issues as who invented the toothbrush or can opener, when did a man first jump off the Brooklyn Bridge, who was the first woman Senator. Despite its obvious catering to the fact fiend and its limitation to events in the United States, it is of value to the scholar or researcher attempting to establish a given fact. The material is arranged alphabetically by subject, with an excellent index which lists the facts geographically, chronologically, and by personal name.

The success of Kane's efforts has sparked several imitators which have the advantage of updating his firsts, e.g., *The Shell Book of Firsts* (London: Michael Joseph, 1974). Over a period of 20 years, Patrick Robertson gathered information for this work, which includes 600 articles about thousands of "firsts," from the first restaurant (1765) to the earliest package tour for travelers (1861). Unlike Kane, Robertson includes data from the world around, although he is strongest on British facts.[12] The alphabetical listing of facts makes this handbook easy to use as a reference aid.

Approaching trivia from the flank, Tom Burnam's *The Dictionary of Misinformation* (New York: T. Y. Crowell, 1976) is a listing of "misinformation, misbelief, misconstruction and misquotation." More of a grab bag

---

[11] "Mouthing Greenery," *The Times Literary Supplement,* May 28, 1976, p. 644. A witty review of the 1976 edition which claims that "no less than one tenth of the book is taken up with listings of large ancient or otherwise impressive trees in New Zealand." Question: Is this the most reviewed reference book of all time?

[12] For a fascinating story on what motivates a collector of this type, see "First Things First," *The Guardian* (London), October 17, 1974, p. 11. This is a good example of the perennial complaint from acquisition librarians that the same title published in England is sometimes disguised by a slightly different title in the United States. This work is distributed here by Crown Publishers as *The Book of Firsts.*

than a reference work, it does serve the purpose of giving each fact as it is generally known (e.g., ostriches hide their heads in the sand), and then giving the real fact. The author claims this is "for rumination and pure delight," but it has limited reference use, too.

Awards, Honors and Prizes, in its first volume, lists more than 4000 items for the United States and Canada. The second volume is devoted to the rest of the world. Listings are alphabetical by subject, under the name of the awarding organization and under the distinctive name of the award. Although full information is given aboout the award, the title does *not* list winners. When the name of a recipient is required, the best source for the more popular awards is any general almanac. Specific award winners might be checked in the numerous indexes. Failing this, the librarian can always call or write the organization which presents the prize.

REPRESENTATIVE SUBJECT HANDBOOKS AND MANUALS[13]

U.S. Department of Labor. *Occupational Outlook Handbook*. Washington, D.C.: Government Printing Office, 1949 to date, biennial. $6.85.

Magill, Frank N. *Masterplots*. New York: Salem Press, 1949 to date. Various prices. 12-volume set, 1976, $250.

Webster's Secretarial Handbook. Springfield, Massachusetts: G. & C. Merriam Company, 1976, 546 pp. $8.95.

Handbook of Chemistry and Physics. Cleveland, Ohio: Chemical Rubber Company, 1913 to date, annual. $28.95.

Physicians' Desk Reference. Oradell, New Jersey: Medical Economics Company, 1947 to date. $12.50.

Occupations

Although vocational guidance in larger libraries is usually not a part of the reference service, it is very much so in medium-sized and small libraries, and certainly in schools. When occupational and professional advice is given to students by trained counselors, there inevitably is a fallout of young men and women seeking further materials—either for personal reasons or, often, for the purpose of preparing class papers. The rush has

[13] Again, as with the almanacs, yearbooks, and compendiums, there are hundreds of subject handbooks and manuals. What follows are only some of the more representative, widely used titles.

become so general that even the smallest library is likely to include a considerable amount of vocational material in the vertical file.

When working with students or, for that matter, with adults, a given amount of probing and patience normally is required. The user may have only a vague notion of the type of information desired, and may be quite uncertain as to particular interests and the possibility of turning those interests into a channel of work. Here the *Occupational Outlook Handbook* is especially useful. Close to 700 occupations are discussed in terms likely to be understood by anyone. Each of the essays indicates what the job is likely to offer in terms of advancement, employment, location, earnings, and working conditions. Trends and outlook are emphasized to give the reader some notion as to the growth possibilities of a given line of work. Unfortunately, the writers are often no more accurate in their predictions than economists and racehorse followers; for example, in the 1972–1973 edition (page 207), it is noted that the employment potential for historians "is expected to increase rapidly through the 1970s. At the college level, hundreds of new history teachers probably will be needed annually, because of expanding enrollments." With some 500 to 1000 applicants for just about every historian's position in universities, one can gather that the crystal ball averages of the *Handbook* are not its strong point. (A good cross-check is to look up the advice given to prospective librarians. Again, the optimism is not quite justified.) An effort to update the title is made through *Occupational Outlook Quarterly* (Washington, D.C.: Government Printing Office, 1957 to date, quarterly). The periodical contains current information on employment trends and opportunities.

Specific employment opportunities are suggested in the *College Placement Annual* (Bethlehem, Pennsylvania: College Placement Council, 1970 to date, annual), which lists needs of about 1300 corporate and governmental employers who normally employ college graduates. Listings are alphabetical by employer, with directory-type information about the employer and the types of jobs offered, if only in a general way. There is an extensive geographical and occupational index. While primarily a recruiting device, the annual is extremely useful for students who wish to get some idea of the number and types of employers in a given field.

Publishers issue a vast number of occupational and vocational guides of general and specific types. A typical general title is Joyce Mitchell's *I Can Be Anything: Careers and Colleges for Young Women* (New York: College Entrance Examination Board, 1975, 256 pp.). It examines 90 occupations and gives data on colleges which award degrees to women in any given field. The photographs and well-written essays assist the reader. The typical specific title: *How to Pass . . .* (New York: Cowles Regnery, various dates) gives information on how to pass civil service examinations for positions ranging from postal employee to boiler superintendent. There are numerous titles in this and other series, and most libraries have a set which is either in the reference section or in the general circulation collection.

Some public libraries now offer specific information on local or national employment opportunities. They, along with employment offices, receive computerized job information lists from the Department of Labor's Employment Service. The Department offers other publications such as "Occupations in Demand," a monthly service describing what the title implies. The librarian will actively seek information on jobs in the community, keep a file of everything from current want ads to pamphlets and clippings on employment, and serve as a center point of information for the person seeking employment. Just how widespread such service was in 1977 was difficult to determine, but more and more librarians are becoming involved. A good example is the service in this area done by the Albany, New York, Public Library.

Literature

As far back as the Middle Ages, there were so-called "cribs" to assist students studying for an examination or working on a paper. There is nothing new about the medium and, in its place, it is a worthwhile form of publishing. A reference librarian may have mixed views about the desirability of such works for students, but that is a problem that students, teachers, and parents must work out together. It is an error to deny a place on the reference shelf to valuable sources regardless of how they may be used or misused.[14]

Plot summaries and other shortcuts to reading are often requested by students. By far the most famous name in this area is Frank N. Magill's *Masterplots*, a condensation of almost every important classic in the English language. Not only are the main characters well explained, but there is also a critique of the plot which gives good, bad, and other points about it. [This series has been reissued numerous times under different titles. The library may have a set called *Masterpieces of World Literature in Digest Form* (New York: Harper & Row, 1952–1969); or *Masterplots* (New York: Salem Press, 1954–1968).] Because of its popularity, the publisher of *Masterplots* each year issues the *Masterplots Annual Volume*, which analyzes some 100 titles published the previous year in the United States. These analyses include both novels and nonfiction. And once again, the set is frequently issued in combined editions.

A more sophisticated attack on plots is suggested by *The Book Review*

---

[14] Daniel H. Gann, "A Plot Beyond the Masterplots," *Choice*, October 1976, pp. 935–946. This is a detailed bibliographical listing and discussion of the scores of publications which consider plots and collective criticism.

Digest approach. Here the student looks up the title of interest and then turns to contemporary reviews of the book. The same approach may be employed by using *Book Review Index, Current Book Review Citations,* or any of the indexes to reviews discussed earlier in the text. Another useful aid is *Contemporary Literary Criticism* (Detroit: Gale Research Company, 1975 to date, irregular). This is an ongoing series of volumes devoted to current criticism and evaluation of both new and older writers. Under each author's name, there are five or six excerpts from identified sources, such as books, journals, or reviews. As in *The Book Review Digest,* the excerpts may be used by themselves, or the reader may turn to the full text of the work quoted. Cumulated indexes to the authors (novelists, short story writers, poets, and playwrights) and critics quoted are found in each volume.

Secretarial practices

Books on secretarial practice have a multiple purpose in a reference situation. First, they assist the professional secretary who is in need of some background information. In this respect, at least one or two of the handbooks should be duplicated in the general collection so they may be taken home and studied. Second, because of the thorough, relatively simple approach to problems of English, letter writing, style, and so on, they are helpful for the student preparing papers or the layperson wanting to write the proper type of letter.

A typical secretarial guide is the *Webster's Secretarial Handbook.* Written by a dozen specialists, it provides information of essentially the how-to-do-it type on almost every secretarial activity from using a calculator to planning a meeting. The best section is the one devoted to business English. A detailed index makes the book useful for quick reference queries.

Science and medicine

Considered to be the bible of chemists and physicists, the *Handbook of Chemistry and Physics* is, as the subtitle explains, "a ready-reference book of chemical and physical data." The data are readily accessible, as they are organized in a way which groups similar and related materials commonly needed in research. Much of the information is in tabular form and, like the rest of the annual, is constantly updated to include reference material in such developing areas as solar radiation, cryogenics, etc. Although using it requires some basic knowledge of chemistry and physics, it is as familiar to beginning students as to experienced researchers.

If the scientific handbooks and manuals presuppose a reasonable degree of technical understanding, there are some areas, particularly in medicine and pharmacology, where laypersons are going to be asking for basic titles. The best-known and most often found pharmacology work in a library is the *Physicians' Desk Reference*. Frequently referred to as the *PDR*, it provides objective information on over 2500 drug products. Brand and generic and chemical names are given, so, with a little experience, one may easily check the content of this or that drug. (A generic and chemical name index is a major finding device.) For each item the composition is given as well as such data as side effects, dosage, contraindications, etc. There is a section which pictures over 1000 tablets and capsules with product identification. The neatly divided six sections are arranged in an easy-to-use fashion.

Although the *PDR* is a classic, there are numerous guides for laypersons which give equally accurate information, but in a more discursive fashion. For example, Larry Massett and Earl W. Sutherland's *Everyman's Guide to Drugs and Medicines* (Washington, D.C.: Robert B. Luce, Inc., 1975) is directed to the interested consumer, is accurate, and has the advantage of a number of indexes including the usual one to brand and generic names, as well as an index to ailments. Another title of the same type is Joe Graedon's *The People's Pharmacy* (New York: St. Martin's Press, 1976). This is a reliable guide to "prescription drugs, home remedies and over the counter medications." The author, who is a pharmacologist, is particularly good in his description of some 200 over-the-counter drugs. Another often-called-for title is Judith M. Jones, *Good Housekeeping Guide to Medicines and Drugs* (New York: Hearst Books, 1977). This offers sound advice on all types of drugs and is a good title for both the reference and the general reading collection.

Two doctors, Richard Burack and Fred J. Fox, are possibly the best known of the group dedicated to informing consumers about drugs. Their *New Handbook of Prescription Drugs* (New York: Ballantine Books, 1975) is available in paperback for only $1.95. This is a revision of a 1966 title which caused a furor because of the frank discussion of the medical habit of prescribing medications by brand names instead of generic names. The first part of the book is a discursive survey of the drug industry and doctors. The second half consists of a detailed "Prescription Drug List," followed by a price list. Prices, of course, change rapidly, but at least the reader has a method of comparison.

Books on medicine have joined the best-seller lists. Probably the most famous is *Our Bodies, Ourselves*, 2d ed. (New York: Simon and Schuster, 1976), which claims to have sold over a half-million copies and is a reliable manual for women. A more general source, often updated, is *The Medicine Show* (Mount Vernon, New York: Consumers Union, 1961 to date, revised annually). Published by the editors of *Consumer Reports*, this book consists of 32 short chapters and a good index on all aspects of medical care from weight loss to how to buy prescription drugs. On the technical side is the

Merck Manual of Diagnosis and Therapy (Rahway, New Jersey: Merck Sharp & Dohme, 1899 to date), which has been published for many years as a manual for physicians; it is equally clear to laypersons with patience and a medical dictionary at hand. Illness and diseases are described in relatively nontechnical language, symptoms and signs are indicated, and diagnoses and treatment are suggested.

There is an ongoing debate among librarians as to how much and what type of medical reference work should be given laypersons. At one time the answer was a simple one: None. The reason for this is explained by Walker and Hirschfeld:

> *A growing need for health-oriented information among the general public has been shown by the rise in consumer activities and complaints directed toward the health care agencies and health care professionals. A survey of the literature shows that the public library . . . is failing to meet this need. The major reasons appear to be twofold—poor knowledge of sources of information and concern among librarians about the ethics of providing such information.*[15]

The librarian who feels that the need for medical advice should be met is advised to subscribe to *Medical Self-Care* (1976, quarterly, $7; P.O. Box 31549, San Francisco, California 94131), a type of *Whole Earth Catalogue* by a Yale medical student. It lists and annotates numerous popular and semipopular guides as well as traditional medical handbooks which can be used by laypersons and librarians. The editor notes in one issue (Summer 1976, page 20) another reason some librarians are hesitant about helping with medical information:

> *One of the Yale medical librarians . . . was telling me the medical librarians were discouraged from giving laypeople medical information for fear it might be a patient gathering evidence for a malpractice suit.*

Be that as it may, the author of this text believes the reference librarian's first duty is to give out information when requested, not to act as a censor between the user and that information. It is an open argument and one worth pursuing more fully in library literature, which to this point has been generally silent about the question.

An annotated bibliographic aid for the librarian is provided by the Boston Public Library's *Medical Books for the Lay Person*. Compiled in 1976

[15] William D. Walker and Lorraine G. Hirschfeld, "Sources of Health Information for Public Libraries," *Illinois Libraries*, June 1976, p. 459. This complete issue is given over to medical reference service, and includes an invaluable, annotated bibliography of sources, pp. 460–502. The "typical" historical approach to health questions has been statistical, i.e., the librarian considered information from *Vital Statistics of the United States* (and related titles) the extent of help to be given users.

by Marilyn McLean, the work consists of 300 titles on diet, health, medicine, etc., for the layperson. Another useful work, particularly for librarians who are seeking this or that organization for assistance with a health question, is Joan Ash's *Health: A Multimedia Source Guide* (New York: R. R. Bowker Company, 1976). It is geared to answering laypersons' queries and includes an annotated list of organizations which supply print and non-print information. A popular annotated list is Cris Popenoe's *Wellness* (New York: Random House, 1977).

Meanwhile, hospitals, medical schools, and even some libraries are solving the problem of how to present medical facts to the layperson by using such devices as tape recordings which may be tapped via a telephone. For example, in Richmond, Virginia, one may call the local hospitals to find information on cancer and related subjects. There are 86 tapes in the "Health-Line" system which deal with cancer. The tapes, prepared by the Medical College of Virginia, are typical of those now found in many urban centers which offer the caller advice on both major and minor medical problems. It is this author's opinion that similar services should be given by libraries, or, at the very least, that the library should advertise the availability of such tapes from other community institutions. Some libraries have such tapes and they are becoming more and more accepted.

Law

Consumer attention has also turned to the law, and once again the librarian's hesitancy about giving out law books to laypersons seems linked more to lack of knowledge than to any real ethical doubts. Fortunately, there are now numerous and reliable laypersons' guides to the law. None of these is likely to reach the classical proportions of *Black's Law Dictionary* or a set of *The Revised Statutes of the Unites States*, but they do answer most basic questions which do not require formal legal action. One of many examples is Henry Shain's *Legal First Aid* (New York: Funk & Wagnalls, 1975), written as a handy guide for the average reader. It includes six sections dealing with the origins of the law, marriage and divorce, civil lawsuits, and other legal matters. Charts at the end of chapters summarize, state by state, laws governing the topics discussed.

Typical of more limited, yet equally popular, approaches to legal rights is Shana Alexander's *State-by-State Guide to Women's Legal Rights* (Los Angeles: Price, Stern, Sloan, 1975, 224 pp.). This volume includes essays on adoption, marriage, divorce, etc., with state-by-state summaries of the law expressed in lay terms.

The librarian who feels totally inadequate in the field of law should, at a minimum, make contact with the nearest law library or legal aid office. Also, renewed attention to the layperson and the law results in frequent seminars such as the one sponsored in late 1977 by the New York

Metropolitan Reference and Research Library Agency on "legal materials for the reference librarian who is *not* a law librarian."

DIRECTORIES[16]

Of all the forms of ready reference considered, the directory is the easiest to define, and it is also one of the most often used reference forms in any library, as well as in any home. A good example is the common telephone directory.

Definition

The *A.L.A. Glossary of Library Terms* defines a directory as "a list of persons or organizations, systematically arranged, usually in alphabetical or classed order, giving addresses, affiliations, etc., for individuals, and address, officers, functions and similar data for organizations." The definition is clear enough for a directory in its "pure" form; but aside from the directory type of information found in biographical sources, it should be reiterated that many other ready-reference tools have sections devoted to directory information. Yearbooks and almanacs inevitably include abundant amounts of directory-type material.

Purpose

The purpose of directories is self-explanatory in the definition, but among the most frequent uses are those involved with answering questions concerning (1) an individual's or a firm's address or telephone number; (2) the full name of an individual, a firm, or an organization; (3) a description of a particular manufacturer's product or a service; or (4) the ubiquitous question that begins with "Who is . . ." for example, the president of the firm, or the head of the school, or responsible for advertising, or in charge of buying manuscripts.

Less obvious uses of directories include (1) limited, but up-to-date, biographical information on an individual—whether he or she is still president, chairperson, or with this or that company or organization; (2) historical and current data about an institution, a firm, or a political group—when it was founded, how many members it had; (3) commercial use, such as selecting a list of individuals, companies, or organizations for a mailing

---

[16] Few reference forms can boast so many individual titles. The result is that there are a number of bibliographies of directories for individual countries. One here is: *Guide to American Directories* (9th ed.; Detroit: Gale Research Company, 1975, 496 pp.). Frequently revised, it describes in detail more than 5200 directories for industrial, professional, and mercantile categories. Annotations are given, and there is an exhaustive subject-title index.

in a particular area; a directory of doctors and dentists serves as the basic list for a medical supply house or a dealer in medical books; and (4) basic sources of random or selective samplings in a social or commercial survey. Directories are frequently employed by social scientists to isolate certain desired groups for study. And so it goes. Because directories are intimately concerned with human beings and their organizations, they serve almost as many uses as the imagination can bring to bear on the data.

Scope

Directories are easier to use than any other reference tool chiefly because the scope is normally indicated in the title and the type of information is limited and usually presented in an orderly, clear fashion.

There are many ways to categorize directories, but they may be broadly divided as follows:

Local Directories   These are limited primarily to two types: telephone books and city directories. However, in this category may also be included all other types issued only for a limited geographical audience—for example, directories of local schools, garden clubs, department stores, theaters, and social groups. The distinction is more academic than important.

Governmental Directories   This group includes guides to post offices, army and navy posts, and the thousand and one different services offered by federal, state, and city governments. These directories may also include guides to international agencies.

Institutional Directories   These are lists of schools, foundations, libraries, hospitals, museums, and similar organizations.

Investment Services   Closely related to trade and business directories, these services give detailed reports on public and private corporations and companies.

Professional Directories   These are largely lists of professional organizations such as those relating to law, medicine, librarianship, and the like.

Trade and Business Directories   These are mainly lists of manufacturers' information about companies, industries, and personal services.

Additional directory-type sources

The almanac and the yearbook often include directory-type information. There are also numerous other sources of directory information:

1. Encyclopedias frequently identify various organizations, particularly those of a general nature which deal with political or fraternal activities.
2. Gazetteers, guidebooks, and atlases will often give information on principal industries, historical sites, museums, and the like.
3. A wide variety of government publications either are entirely devoted to directory-type information or include such information as part of a given work. Also, while some works are technically directories (*Ulrich's International Periodical Directory* and the *Ayer Directory of Newspapers and Periodicals*, for example), they are so closely associated with other forms (periodicals and newspapers) that they are rarely thought of as directories, but rather as guides.

Local directories

The two most obvious, and probably the most used, local directories are the telephone book and the city directory. The latter is particularly valuable for locating information about an individual when only the street name or the approximate street address is known. Part of the city directory includes an alphabetical list of streets and roads in the area, giving names of residents (unless it is an apartment building, when names may or may not be included). The resident usually is identified by occupation and whether or not she or he owns the home. The information may be used illegally; for example, in 1974 a burglar confessed to Albany, New York, police that he obtained information on likely homes to "hit" by careful study of the local city directory, choosing homes occupied by professional people. Many city directories indicate the marital status of a male; if he is married, his name is followed by "head of household" and the names of his dependents. This is not the case for a woman, unless she is divorced and "head of household," or a single parent with children. Some city directories have a section ("Numerical Telephone Directory") which lists numbers and gives names.

The classified section of the directory is a complete list of businesses and professions, differing from the yellow pages of the telephone book in that the latter is a paid service which may not inlcude all firms. Like the telephone book, city directories are usually issued yearly or bi-yearly.

Questions of accuracy and ethics arise in connection with city directories (see *American Libraries,* October 1977, pp. 476–477). But as a published work, the city directory must be made available by the librarian.

Most city directories are published by one firm, the R. L. Polk Co. of Detroit. Founded in 1870, the company issues over 800 publications. In addition to its city directories, it also publishes a directory for banks and direct-mail concerns.

With enough telephone directories, many of the specialized directories might be short-circuited. A telephone book will give the user the address of a friend, business contact, hotel, etc., in almost any community. The location of potential customers or services is a frequent purpose of using the familiar yellow pages.[17] And, from the point of view of a historian or genealogist, a long run of telephone books is a magic key to locating data on difficult-to-find individuals.

Most libraries have at least the local telephone directory, and usually those for larger cities in the immediate area. As the library becomes bigger, so does the collection. It can run to 40 feet of shelf space for the 360 major current Bell Company telephone directories which blanket urban communities and regions in the United States. At least one microphoto company, Bell & Howell, offers a solution to the space problem via Phonefiche, a collection of microfiche cards for the 360 telephone books. This device reduces the 40 feet to a space 8 by 16 inches.

Under the generic "the people's yellow pages," there is a series of directories published at the local level to assist people to find vital information on food co-ops, collectives, drug information centers, political action groups, health advice, etc. These directories fit into any library reference pattern, although they are of special help in those libraries where an effort is made to give what some call I&R, or information and referral assistance. This kind of assistance is discussed in Chapter 1 of the second volume of this text, but "the people's yellow pages" are representative of the type of aids employed. These aids might be described as the formal or informal files which list community resources ranging from health offices to crisis centers for young people. Actually, they supplement the more traditional directory files found at most reference desks—files which are a combination of often asked queries and answers or sources of answers.[18]

Governmental directories[19]

U.S. Congress Joint Committee on Printing. *Congressional Directory*. Washington, D.C.: Government Printing Office, 1809 to date, annual. $8.50; paper, $6.50.

---

[17] One man's view of the "billion-dollar business" of the yellow pages will be found in Ralph Nader's "Yellow Pages; the Quiet Monopoly," *The Nation*, May 31, 1975, pp. 646–649.

[18] "People's Yellow Pages," *Doing It*, May 1976, pp. 17–21. The article includes a list of the best-known directories.

[19] Although dated, a useful guide to government directories is Sally Wynkoop and David Parish, *Directories of Government Agencies* (Littleton, Colorado: Libraries Unlimited, Inc., 1969, 242 pp.). This is an annotated bibliography of 500-plus directories.

U.S. Postal Service. *Directory of Post Offices*. Washington, D.C.: Government Printing Office, 1955 to date, annual. $5.05.

A basic reference source for questions regarding government is the *United States Government Manual*, discussed earlier in this chapter. Equally important is the *Congressional Directory*. This is a "who's who" for Congress, but includes considerable other information. In some 20 sections there are biographical sketches of the Supreme Court justices, items on members of congressional committees, names of foreign representatives and consular offices in the United States, members of the media who cover Congress, and the chief officers of departments and independent agencies. Used with the *United States Government Manual*, the *Directory* will answer virtually any question concerning individuals involved with the federal government at any major level.

Where does one find information on previous members of Congress no longer listed in the *Congressional Directory*? If relatively well known, they will be listed in such sources as the *Dictionary of American Biography* (if they arc deceased) or a good encyclopedia. But for short, objective sketches of all senators and representatives who served from 1774 to 1971, the best single source is *Biographical Directory of the American Congress, 1774-1971* (Washington, D.C.: Government Printing Office). There is a handy first section which includes officers of the executive branch of the government, e.g., the cabinets from George Washington through to the first administration of Richard Nixon. There is also a chronological listing by state of members of the First through the Ninety-first Congress. Among the most used directories and biographical sources for men and women in government (with self-descriptive content titles) is *Who's Who in American Politics* (New York: R. R. Bowker Company, 1967 to date, biennial).

The *Directory of Post Offices* lists post offices by state, city, and town, with their zip codes. This source can be useful for more than its obvious purpose, i.e., when someone is trying to locate a small community in the United States and does not have an exhaustive gazetteer or an atlas at hand. By now, zip code information can be found in almost any general reference book, including most of the almanacs.

Institutional and professional directories

Encyclopedia of Associations. Detroit: Gale Research Company, 1956 to date, biennial, 3 vols. Vol 1, $70; Vol. 2, $50; Vol. 3, $60.

The Foundation Directory. New York: Columbia University Press, 1960 to date, irregular. $35.

American Universities and Colleges. Washington, D.C.: American Council on Education, 1928 to date, quadrennial. $42.

American Library Directory. New York: R. R. Bowker Company, 1923 to date, biennial. $45.

Reference Guide for Consumers. New York: R. R. Bowker Company, 1975, 292 pp. $14.95.

The basic directory to institutional and professional associations, the *Encyclopedia of Associations*, is a single work in three volumes: (1) The basic volume includes descriptions of over 15,000 national organizations of the United States. These are arranged under 17 broad subject categories, and each entry includes the group's name, address, chief executive, phone number, purpose and activities, membership, publications, etc. (The publications often refer to directories issued by the individual associations.) There is a key word alphabetical index, but (2) the second volume is really an index to the first in that it lists all the executives mentioned in the basic volume, again with complete addresses and phone numbers. A second section rearranges the associations by geographical location. (3) Finally, the third volume is really a periodical publication which is issued between editions and keeps the main set up to date.

Given this set, the librarian may easily retrieve information by subject, by the name of the association, and by the name of executives connected with the association, and generally may keep up with changes in name as well as new organizations.[20] A number of the associations are foundations, but the user seeking information on foundations, and more particularly on grants available from these organizations, should turn to *The Foundation Directory*. The 1977 edition, the sixth, lists 2800 foundations by state. Also included is an annotated bibliography which lists basic titles used in grants. Each entry gives the organization's purpose and activities, names of administrators, and grants available. Beginning with this edition, the work lists only foundations having minimum assets of $1 million and making grants of $100,000 in the last year of record. (Individual grants are usually less than $100,000. This figure represents the *total* grants given.) There is an index by subject as well as by cities, by donors, and by foundation name. The work is updated by the publisher's bimonthly *Foundation News* and the annual cumulation of the *News* as *The Foundation Grants Index*.[21]

[20] There are many guides to associations, e.g., *World Guide to Scientific Associations* (New York: R. R. Bowker Company, 1974) and *Directory of Associations in Canada* (Toronto: University of Toronto Press, 1974). In fact, almost every country has at least one directory of associations, and usually more.

[21] Individual graduate students and faculty seeking smaller grants should be directed to *The Grants Register, 1975–1977* (New York: St. Martin's Press, 1975, 801 pp.). This lists over 2000

Education

The amount of interest in college and university education requires that a library of almost any size have a basic reference collection in this area. As an adjunct, there should be provision for a series of college and university catalogs, or, at least, ready information about where such catalogs may be obtained. Even the best of the directories cannot give the bits of information a potential student seeks and can find only in a particular catalog.

The lack of proper advisory services in some high schools makes it particularly important that at least one member of the reference depart-ment be familiar with helping teenagers (and their parents) find informa-tion on colleges and universities. Such items as cost, entrance require-ments, size of school, and strengths and weaknesses of faculty are covered in part in many other directories.[22]

The most useful and authoritative directory in the academic field is *American Universities and Colleges*, issued by the American Council on Educa-tion. Revised about every four years, it is perfect for the first year following the revision; but after that, the material tends to be dated and must be checked against other sources. This is particularly true for fees, but the basic information on the 1250 accredited colleges and 2600 professional schools is reliable. The information on accredited colleges and universities includes history, organizations, resources, staff analysis, size, degrees grant-ed, and almost any other relevant fact a potential student would want to know. The same organization publishes the companion, *American Junior Colleges*, which is revised every four years.

The Handbook of Private Schools (Boston: Porter Sargent Publisher, 1915 to date, annual) is another work often found in libraries. It lists and describes 2000 schools which are listed by geographical area. Lyon's *Private Independent Schools* (Wallingford, Connecticut: Bunting and Lyon, 1943 to

---

agencies which grants. Also, it includes sources of scholarships and fellowships at all levels of graduate study. The directory is international in scope, but emphasis is on the United States and English-speaking countries. Two other useful titles, particularly for reference librarians giving advice about grants: Howard Hillman's *The Art of Winning Foundation Grants* (New York: Vanguard Press, 1974, 192 pp.) is a how-to-do-it manual on how to apply for a grant. It includes a good bibliography. The author has a similar title, *The Art of Winning Government Grants* (New York: Vanguard Press, 1977). See, also, a series of articles in *Michigan Librarian* (Summer 1975, pp. 6–14) with articles and bibliographies on grantsmanship.

[22] Among directories of this type often found in libraries are C. E. *Lovejoy's College Guide* (New York: Simon & Schuster, Inc., 1952 to date, biennial); *Study Abroad* (20th ed.; UNESCO, distributed by: New York: UNIPUB, 1975, 523 pp.), which covers courses administered by more than 70 international organizations and over 2000 national institutions in some 130 countries; and *The World of Learning* (London: Europa Publications, Ltd., 2 vols., 1947 to date), which provides information on over 24,000 universities, colleges abroad, as well as libraries, museums, etc. The first volume includes data on 400 international educational organizations.

date, annual) gives information about fewer individual schools. These titles only suggest the many available, and each year another one appears to meet particular needs, e.g., *Guide to Alternative Colleges and Universities* (Boston: Beacon Press, 1974, 141 pp.).

Libraries

The *American Library Directory*[23] is included here to indicate that there are directories for virtually every profession. Published since 1923, it provides basic information on 27,000 public, academic, and special libraries in the United States and Canada. Arranged by state and city or town, the listings include names of personnel, book budgets, number of volumes, special collections, salaries, subject interests, etc. It has many uses, from seeking addresses for a survey or for potential book purchasers to providing necessary data for those seeking positions in a given library. (Information, for example, on the size of collections and salaries will tell the job seeker sometimes more than can be found in an advertisement.) Not included are school libraries; for the names of these, the user should turn to the *School Library Supervisors Directory* (New York: R. R. Bowker Company, 1970), which lists counties, districts, and cities large enough to have school library supervisors. Scheduled for revision at this writing, the directory includes much the same type of data found in the *American Library Directory*.

Special libraries receive considerably more detailed treatment in the *Directory of Special Libraries and Information Centers* (4th ed.; Detroit: Gale Research Company, 1977, 3 vols.). This work lists over 13,000 units which either are special libraries or have special collections, including a number of public and university libraries. Arrangement is alphabetical by name with a not too satisfactory subject index. (Subject headings are furnished by the libraries, and as this approach is uncontrolled, it tends to be erratic.)[24] The second volume is the geographic-personnel index, and the third is a periodic supplement covering new material between editions. Another work published by Gale is the frequently revised *Research Centers Directory*, updated by the periodically issued *New Research Centers*. Together, these publications list by major subject fields basic information on university-related and nonprofit research centers throughout the United States and Canada.

---

[23] For libraries of the world, see *World Guide to Libraries* (4th ed.; New York: R. R. Bowker Company, 1974, 2 vols.). Briefer data are given for Europe and America in the first volume, and for Africa, Asia, and the rest of the world in the second volume.

[24] Gale issues a five-volume *Subject Directory of Special Libraries and Information Centers*, which is basically a rearrangement of material found in the *Directory*, under main subjects for those who do not need the whole *Directory*.

Related to the directories of libraries are the various museum guides, such as *Museums of the World* (2d ed.; New York: R. R. Bowker Company, 1975), which lists 17,500 museums in 150 countries. Among other data given are an indication of the existence of a museum library and the approximate number of volumes it contains.

Consumer aids

The reference librarian is usually asked one of three questions about consumers and consumer protection: (1) "What is the best product for my needs?" (2) "To whom can I complain, or to whom can I turn for information, about a product or service?" (3) "How can I protect myself from poor-quality products or services?" No one reference source answers all queries, although several are of particular value in locating possible sources. One of the most valuable, and one which includes much directory-type information, is the *Reference Guide for Consumers*. For the reference librarian who is building a collection, the first section is the best in that it comprises about 190 pages devoted to materials which will help to locate consumer information on major products and services. Each of the over 500 sources is briefly annotated and is arranged by subject. The second part of the work is a directory of United States and Canadian federal, private, state, county, and city agencies involved with consumer protection. The third part is a directory of newspapers which include the "Action Line" type of column for consumers. The whole is well indexed.

Also combining directory and consumer information is the *Consumer Complaint Guide* (New York: Macmillan Information, 1976, 497 pp.). The bulk of this often revised work is a list of firms, with full addresses and names of executives, that produce consumer goods. There are over 8000 product names—often with cross-references from a trade name to the actual name of the manufacturer. The first part includes an essay on consumer practices and law as well as information on how to make a complaint. There is also a briefer list of organizations which is not so complete as the list in the *Reference Guide for Consumers*.

An update on who manufactures what is offered by a valuable mimeographed quarterly service, *The Television Sponsors Directory* (Everglades, Florida: Everglades Publishing Co., 1970 to date, quarterly). Here are over 4000 product names heard on television, both national and local. What makes this work of particular value is that under major manufacturers are listed all the company's products, as well as companies owned by the parent concern. For example, under Pillsbury Company one finds the names of the brands owned by that concern. There are numerous cross-references throughout, and for main entries full addresses are given.

There are other basic sources for answering the question: Who manufactures or produces this product? The standard sources, discussed next, include: *Poor's Register* to find names to complain to; and *Thomas' Register of American Manufacturers*. Perhaps easier to use is the *Trade Names Dictionary* (Detroit: Gale Research Company, 1976, 2 vols.), which lists 100,000 names of products, as well as their manufacturers and distributors with their addresses. This is updated by annual supplements.

When one turns to product evaluation and away from directories, there are two basic periodicals which should be in every library: *Consumer Reports* (Mount Vernon, New York: Consumers Union of United States, 1936 to date, monthly), which is the best-known and most quoted source for objective tests of all types of consumer products; and *Consumer Bulletin* (Washington, New Jersey: Consumers' Research, Inc., 1931 to date, monthly), which offers reports of the same type. Both issue annual summaries in paperback form, and these should be kept at the reference desk.

A related work is the quarterly *Consumers Index to Product Evaluations* (Ann Arbor, Michigan: Pierian Press, 1973 to date), which extracts reviews of consumer products from 75 or so periodicals and arranges citations to the reviews under 14 subject headings. The index is valuable when the user cannot find satisfactory data in *Consumer Reports*, the *Consumer Bulletin*, or other consumer titles found in *Reference Guide for Consumers*.

Trade and business directories

Thomas' Register of American Manufacturers. New York: Thomas Publishing Company, Inc., 1905 to date, annual. $55.

Poor's Register of Corporations, Directors, and Executives. New York: Standard & Poor's Corporation, 1928 to date, annual. $140.

Literary Market Place. New York: R. R. Bowker Company, 1940 to date, annual. Paper, $21.50.

The reference librarian, when moving from consumer directories and related reference books to business information, is entering a wider field described as a $2-billion market. The information sources consist not only of directories but also of trade magazines, newsletters, credit information, research services, and data bases, to name a few possible sources.[25] This side of corporate special libraries and business sections in larger libraries, the average academic or public library usually limits reference service to basic directories, indexes, and investment services. At the same time, the librarian is normally able to refer a user to necessary services in larger or more specialized libraries in the area. (All the guides to refer-

[25] *The Business Information Markets 1976–1981* (White Plains, New York: Knowledge Industry Publications, Inc., 1976). At a whopping $450, this report is written for industry and investors and includes profiles of leading business publishers as well as descriptions of services.

ence books, from Sheehy to *American Reference Book Annual*, include sections on business and manufacturing. A brief guide is Lorna M. Daniells's *Business Reference Sources* (Boston: Baker Library, Harvard University, 1971).

Until the advent of separate consumer directories, the usual place to trace an industrial brand name or run down the manufacturer of this or that consumer product was *Thomas' Register of American Manufacturers*. It is still used for that purpose, particularly when additional information is needed about a company, but today it is more likely to be employed by business people for data on companies. Over 75,000 American firms are listed by product in six of the volumes. Under each product, the user finds the manufacturers listed by state and city. Another volume is an alphabetical list of the companies with addresses and, in many cases, the names of the principal officers. Other books in the set are given over to manufacturers' catalogs. The final volume is a detailed subject index with trade names and major chambers of commerce.

Just as the *Official Congressional Directory* is the "Who's Who" of government, so is *Poor's Register* the "Who's Who" for business. It is a basic work found in all business libraries and in most larger public and academic reference sections. Brief biographical information is given for over 80,000 directors and executives in American and Canadian corporations. In addition, the 34,000-plus corporations are listed with the names of officers and the types of products manufactured, as well as the number of employees. There is a Standard Industrial Classification Index which gives the user a broad subject approach to the companies and, indirectly, to the executives listed.

A wide definition of a "trade or business" directory would include related titles such as the *Literary Market Place*, which provides directory-type information on over 20,000 firms directly or indirectly involved with publishing in the United States. It is more likely to be used by the general public than either *Thomas' Register* or *Poor's*. Why? Because it furnishes an answer to a frequently heard question at the reference desk: "Where can I get my novel [poem, biography, or other work] published?" Also, it is of considerable help to acquisitions librarians, as it gives fuller information on publishers than do bibliographies such as *Books in Print* or *Cumulative Book Index*. Among other things, it has a section, "Names and Numbers," which lists 17,000 executives and firms in publishing, with their addresses and phone numbers.

To return to the would-be writer, the *Literary Market Place* includes names of agents which the writer might wish to contact. However, it presupposes some knowledge of the publisher and fails to answer directly the question: Does this publishing house publish fiction or poetry, or other things? For this, the beginner should turn to several much used allied titles: *Writer's Market* (Cincinnati, Ohio: Writer's Digest, 1929 to date, annual), which has a section on book publishers that includes not only directory-type information but paragraphs on types of materials wanted, royalties paid, and how copy is to be submitted. The remainder of the close to 1000-page directory gives similar information for thousands of periodical publishers to whom free-lance writers may submit material. *The Writer's Handbook* (Boston: The Writer, Inc., 1936 to date, annual) gives some of the same information, but at least one-half of each annual volume is devoted to articles on how to write, and its listings are not so complete as those in *Writer's Market*. Writers who wish information on small presses should consult the *International Directory of Little Magazines and Small Presses* (Paradise, California: Dustbooks, 1965 to date, annual).

Investment services[26]

Moody's Investors Service. New York: Moody's Investors Service, 6 vols, annual, semiweekly, or weekly supplements. $240 to $360 per each service. (Note: *Moody Investors Service* is the general title of the set, but each volume has a separate, distinct title.)

Standard and Poor's Corporation Records. New York: Standard & Poor's Corporation, 6 vols. plus its *Daily News.* Prices vary: $405 to $500 the set, plus charge for *Daily News.*

Value Line Investment Survey. New York: Arnold Bernhard and Company, weekly. $248.

Funk and Scott Index of Corporations and Industries. Cleveland, Ohio: Predicasts, weekly. $275.

There are many reasons why investment services are consulted in a library. The basic one is to trace the profit and loss structure of a company and its performance on the stock market. Aside from that, market researchers, job seekers, economists, historians, and consumer advocates may employ the services for background information on particular public or private organizations.

For those seeking in-depth information about a company, the two basic sources are published by Moody's and Standard & Poor's. The two overlap in that they both give detailed information, usually obtained from

---

[26] The basic guide to these services: Mary Grant and Norma Cote, *Directory of Business and Financial Services* (7th ed.; New York: Special Libraries Association, 1976). More than 1000 publications are listed and briefly annotated, and there is a subject index. Broader in scope but equally useful for reference questions about companies or business is Lorna Daniells' *Business Information Sources* (Berkeley, California: University of California Press, 1976). This is a revision, although actually a completely new work, of the legendary Edwin T. Coman's work of the same title.

the companies themselves and/or the Securities Exchange Commission, on four elements: (1) the history of the company, particularly its profits and losses; Moody's services are usually limited to a 7-year period, while Standard & Poor's often goes back 15 or more years; (2) description of its various operations and products, which are covered in more depth in *Moody's* than in the rival service; (3) marketing and research development, about which, again, *Moody's* tends to give more details; and (4) officers and directors' names.

The six Moody manuals (*Bank and Finance, Industrials, OTC Industrials, Municipals and Governments, Public Utilities,* and *Transportation*) are updated twice a week with a *News Report* for each of the services.

The six volumes of *Standard and Poor's* concentrate on companies listed on the New York and the American Stock Exchanges, and give only sketchy treatment to banks, transportation, etc., covered in *Moody's*. On the other hand, *Standard and Poor's* has the advantage of including numerous small companies not found in *Moody's*. Another advantage is that latest developments are reported daily (via the *Daily News* supplement) rather than biweekly, as in *Moody's*. The daily reports are cumulated every two months and become part of the revised set.

There are other differences in arrangement and treatment of information between the two services, but the library that takes one usually takes the other as well. If a choice had to be made, Moody's would be preferable only because of its more comprehensive coverage of individual firms as well as various forms of corporations.

There are countless investor guides, newsletters, and reports which modify or amplify upon the two basic services. One of the best known is the *Value Line Investment Survey*. This differs from *Standard and Poor's* and *Moody's* in that it concentrates on 1500 companies; and while there is at least an 80 percent overlap in information between the services, *Value Line* lists some corporations not covered in the other sources. More important is the format of the *Value Line Investment Survey*, which is a one- or two-page summary with a full sheet of graphs, including one showing historical growth in earnings and book value per share of stock, as well as estimates for the year.

Although it would require a chapter or two adequately to describe how to use these and related services, none is really complicated, and most are arranged with adequate indexing which makes for relatively simple use once the reference librarian has caught on to their jargon.

The basic index in this field, the *Funk and Scott Index*, is simplicity itself. It covers approximately 1000 business and financial magazines, services, newspapers, and reports. Arrangement is by major product or industry, and in each division, companies are listed alphabetically with citations and a brief descriptive phrase. One useful feature: A small black dot indicates the more substantial articles. An index by product, industry, and company gives ready access to the weekly service, which is cumulated monthly, quarterly, and annually.

The Wall Street Journal Index and *The New York Times Index* are other services widely used in business departments. The two-way-street aspect of *The Wall Street Journal Index* which makes it useful for nonbusiness types of information relating to history, the social sciences, etc., is applicable to the lesser known *Funk and Scott Index*. Equally overlooked outside of business, but of considerable value for wider questions, are The H. W. Wilson Company's *Business Index* and the *Canadian Business Periodicals Index* (Toronto: Information Access, 1975 to date, monthly).

Meanwhile, every library will have a section of books on aspects of economics and investment for the layperson. Some of these will be duplicated in the reference section. A good example is *Sylvia Porter's Money Book* (New York: Doubleday & Company, 1975, 1105 pp.). Based on Ms. Porter's syndicated columns in American newspapers, the well-indexed, comprehensive guide gives down-to-earth information on all areas of personal economic life from the cost of rearing a child to funeral expenses.

SUGGESTED READING

Ellsworth, Susan, "The Public Library as an Information Disseminator," *The Unabashed Librarian*, Winter 1975, pp. 29–30. A short report on a survey made to learn how librarians would answer a query about abortion information. Concludes with a brief explanation of the community "hotline" and the library. The article reflects the various attitudes of librarians toward health and other "sensitive" types of questions.

"Everything You Never Wanted to Know about Almanacs and Were Afraid You'd be Told," *Media Industry Newsletter*, January 30, 1976, pp. 8–10. A light, yet informative, overview of present general and subject almanac publishing in America.

Faber, Harold, "Almanac Editor Sees Chivalry in Cards," *The New York Times*, October 16, 1975, p. 41. A short interview with the publishers of *The Old Farmer's Almanac* and its rival, the *American Farm and Home Almanac*.

Frank, Nathalie D., "After the Statistical Abstract—What?" *RQ*, Spring 1975, pp. 204–210. A useful discussion of federal statistical sources (over 60 are listed in a bibliography) and problems and solutions to statistical research.

"How Health Statistics Are Misused," *Medical Record News*, April 1976, pp. 83–84. A single example of numerous articles on the misuse of statistical data. In nontechnical language, this brief piece points up basic errors in statistical interpretation.

"How Much Should We Tell, Some Implications of Medical-Legal Reference," *Bay State Librarian*, December 1975, pp. 12–13. A short, informative discussion of the difficulties with giving direct answers to medical and legal questions in a nonspecialized library.

Kahn, E. J., Jr., "A Reporter at Large," *The New Yorker*, October 15, 22, 1973. A two-part series on the Bureau of the Census and its findings about the United States, "a real land of make believe." Recommended as an imaginative demonstration of how statistics may be employed by a creative writer.

Otness, Harold M., "On the State of American Almanac Maps," *Information Bulletin Western Association of Map Libraries,* March 1977, pp. 115–119. An unusual approach to evaluating the basic but he is equally critical of numerous features.

"People's Yellow Pages," *Doing It,* May 1976, pp. 17–21. The story of how the Boston version of a directory of nonlibrary information sources was compiled. Useful for tips on how a library might compile its own directory for answering health, consumer, legal, and other types of questions.

Reid Alastair, "Ask for Nicolás Catari," *The New Yorker,* July 25, 1977, pp. 80–82. A lively review of *The South American Handbook* which is guaranteed to make the average reader seek out a copy immediately.

Reinhold, Robert, "The Census, All Year Round," *The New York Times* ("Week in Review"), November 30, 1975, p. 7. An informative piece on how the Bureau of the Census gathers information for its many statistical publications.

Sagendorph, Robb, *America and Her Almanacs.* Dublin, New Hampshire: Yankee, Inc. (distributed by Little, Brown and Company), 1970. An informal history of the genre by the late editor of *The Old Farmer's Almanac.* Numerous illustrations and quotes from various almanacs. Short bibliography.

Truelson, Judith A., "Hot on the Corporate Trail," *RQ,* Spring 1976, pp. 223–228. A concise summary of basic business sources which compares the services.

CHAPTER SEVEN

Biographical Sources

**B**IOGRAPHY, AS *The Oxford English Dictionary* defines it, is "the history of the lives of individual men" and—although it may shock the male who wrote this definition—women. Addressing himself to the full-length book biography, Harold Nicholson gives a further definition which seems applicable for reference work:

> *A biography must be a history, in the sense that it must be accurate and depict a person in relation to his times. It must describe an individual, with all the gradation of human character, and not merely present a type of virtue or vice. And it must be . . . written in grammatical English and with an adequate feeling for style.*[1]

Some readers delight in poring over biographical reference sources, but few of the reference works quite measure up to Nicholson's high standards. They are compilations of data which are satisfactory for locating an address, finding information on achievements, or discovering a birth or death date.

---

[1] Harold Nicholson, *Biography as an Art*, James Clifford (ed.), (New York: Oxford University Press, 1962), p. 197. For a basic history of biography, consult any major encyclopedia or the cited essay.

EVALUATION[2]

How does the librarian know whether a biographical source is reliable? There are a number of tests.

Selection Why is a name selected (or rejected) for the various biographical reference aids? The method for the several who's who entries is discussed later, but the process is relatively easy to establish for biographical aids which are limited to a given subject or profession: the compiler includes all the names that qualify for the scope of the work, as in *American Men and Women of Science* or *World Authors*. In both cases, the widest net is cast to include figures and authors likely to be of interest. There are limitations, but they are so broad as to cause little difficulty for the compiler. As one moves from subject and profession to the famous, eminent, or renowned on a national or international scale—or both—the choices become increasingly difficult.

While admittedly the choice of other than subject and professional biographical aids is relative, all the editors of reputable works do establish some objective guidelines, e.g., *Who's Who in America*, where many are "included arbitrarily on account of official position." This means that if you are a congressperson, a governor, an admiral, a general, a Nobel Prize winner, or a foreign head of government, you are automatically included; and there are numerous other categories, as well, which ensure a place in the volume. The *International Who's Who* is certain to give data on members of all reigning royal families. The *Dictionary of American Biography* takes a more negative approach—you must first be dead to be included; after that requirement is met, the editor begins making selections.

Then, too, there are some automatic exclusions. In the case of subject biographical reference works, the exclusion is usually evident in the title: one does not look for poets in *Who's Who in American Art* or *American Men and Women of Science*, although the poetic skills of an artist or a scientist may be considerable.

Length of Entry Once a name is selected, another question presents itself: How much space does the figure warrant? Should the person be given five or six lines or a page? The purpose and scope of the work may dictate at least a partial answer. The who's who data approach calls for a

[2] Both beginners and experienced librarians will find the guidelines employed by the American Library Association Reference and Subscription Books Review Committee helpful in evaluating biographical sources. These are briefly enumerated in *The Booklist*, May 1, 1974, pp. 946–947. The same issue (pp. 948–962) contains systematic annotations for almost 100 "basic" biographical sources arranged in alphabetical order by title.

relatively brief outline or collection of facts. The biographical dictionary may be more discursive. And the essay type of work will approach the same entry in a way peculiar to its own emphasis. Despite form, the editor still has to make decisions about balance and length.

When considering deceased persons, these decisions may be easier than with the ego-conscious living. Still, there is no satisfactory answer for either. Obviously, George Washington will receive more space than, say, Catherine Dorset, an eighteenth-century English poet. But aside from these extremes, J. O. Thorne sums it up nicely:

> *Fame and public esteem are constantly subject to the vagaries of fashion, and critical assessments are changed by modern research. Thus Monteverdi, whose great importance in the history of music is today more fully recognized, now receives 59 lines in place of 5 (over 1962 ed.), T. S. Eliot has 144 instead of 6, and the meagre allowance formerly given to the great impressionistic painters has been increased to match their current status. Conversely, Lord Lytton has less than half the space previously given to him. . . . Other articles, adequate in length and admirable in their time, have been refashioned because modern criticism and scholarship have modified the traditional image.*[3]

And just to confuse the issue, there are those who argue that space cannot always be given in proportion to the importance of the subject. This is particularly true of historical figures where the amount of biographical information is scant, although they may have been major figures—Shakespeare and Malory, to name two examples.

No compiler is going to satisfy every reader regarding emphasis or lack of emphasis on length. The wary librarian who finds recurrent faults in balance of treatment may conclude: (1) The work contains information received through questionnaires without due attention to editing for importance of the figure profiled. The subject may have replied to a request for personal data with due modesty in a brief manner. The not-so-famous may wish to puff their reputations by stretching their personal data. (2) If the source is a retrospective biography, one may assume that six pages for an Idaho businessman, when contrasted with one page for a Nobel Prize winner, shows amazing lack of perspective by the compiler or writer. Lest these two examples seem preposterous, the student is advised to check a year of reviews of recently published titles. One of the most common complaints, aside from exclusion or inclusion, is lack of proper balance. No work will be dead center, but if it is tipped too precariously, the librarian is often well-advised to take warning.

---

[3] J. O. Thorne, "Preface," *Chambers's* Biographical Dictionary (London: Chambers, Ltd., 1969), p. 1. This is one of the few prefaces which may be read as much for entertainment as for information, and it is highly recommended for both the beginner and the expert.

Authority   Biographical sources have several facets not considered in checking the authority for other reference books. First and foremost: Who wrote the biographical entry—an editor, the subject of the biography, an authority in the field, a secretary? In preparing almost any material except statistical information, the person who penned the entry will have had either conscious or subconscious biases. Even in a straightforward presentation of data, if the biographical subject supplied the information (normally the case with most current biographies), there may be slight understatements or exaggerations concerning age (men as often as women lie about this), education, or experience.[4] Apparently the individuals listed in *Who's Who in America*, for example, are causing the publisher some concern, particularly the vast majority who are given the privilege of writing their own biographies. According to one report in late 1975: "Underway now by a well-known author is investigation of one thousand Who's Whoers who presumably gave themselves titles, degrees, directorships and lists of accomplishments that cannot be documented."[5] However, publishers of the who's who type of work are not alone, and almost all biographical sources which rely almost entirely on individual honesty may not be completely trusted. Which leads to the next query: Have sources of information, other than the biographees' own questionnaires, been cited? The preface should make these two points clear.

When the source is questionable, it should be verified in one or more other works. If there remains a serious conflict which cannot be resolved, what should be done? Depending upon how important the conflict is to the patron, the only solution is to attempt to trace the information through primary source material: newspapers, contemporary biographies, or articles about the individual or his or her family or friends. This undertaking involves historical research. An excellent example, mentioned earlier, may be found in the ever recurrent arguments concerning details of Shakespeare's life and times, or the famous attempt to straighten out the facts in the life of Thomas Malory, author of the stories concerning King Arthur and his knights. In many cases, even of well-known individuals, the

[4] Birth dates are a common headache for biographers. Nicolas Slonimsky, in the preface to the fifth edition of Theodore Baker's *Biographical Dictionary of Musicians* (New York: G. Schirmer, Inc., 1958), notes: "Musicians through the centuries have altered their birthdates, invariably in the direction of the juvenation." Beethoven, for example, was eager to prove he was born in 1772 rather than 1770. Furthermore, death dates are often listed a day later, owing to delay in announcement or different time zones. Schoenberg's death is given as July 14, 1951, in most European sources, although he died on July 13, in Los Angeles.

[5] *Media Industry Newsletter*, December 12, 1975, p. 11. The short piece also points out that in the *Who's Who in America* for 1938–1939, there was a sketch of one F. Donald Coster who claimed to be, among other things, a doctor. He proved to be a smuggler of gigantic proportions. He was not listed in the next edition.

records are uncertain or in question, and possibly the correct answers will never be known.

The date of publication of a source is important when attempting to ascertain the relative truth of a given biographical sketch. Viewpoints frequently change radically with time. For example, an entry about President Lincoln in a contemporary source may be quite different from one found in the average encyclopedia, or, for that matter, in the *Dictionary of American Biography*.

A common question asked by laypersons is whether a request by a publisher to include their names in this or that publication is indeed an honor, or a come-on to take part in an ego trip. And there are at least a few biographical publications of this type:

> *Unscrupulous publishers will sometimes include padded or unduly eulogistic articles on comparatively unknown persons, with the expectation, or on condition, that these persons will pay for inclusion or will subscribe for the book. . . . Such books are not necessarily to be rejected if they happen to be the only ones in their field, but they must always be used with caution.*[6]

How, then, does the librarian know whether the work is truly legitimate, i.e., authoritative and based upon an accurate, relatively objective selection policy? A rule of thumb will do in most cases: If the title is not listed (or minimally praised) in any of the basic bibliographies, such as Sheehy, Walford, *American Reference Books Annual*, or the current reviewing services, the flag of warning is out. Another test, based upon the librarian's knowledge of publishers, is whether or not the publisher is reputable. Even the best, to be sure, make errors in judgment about what constitutes a good biographical source, but they cannot be accused of trying to build a book on the gullibility of the biographees.

Other Points   Are there photographs? Are there bibliographies containing material both by and about the subject? Is the work adequately indexed or furnished with sufficient cross-references? (This is important when one is seeking individuals who are connected with a major figure, but who may be mentioned only as part of a larger biographical sketch.) Is the work arranged in a logical fashion? The alphabetical approach is usual, although some works may be arranged chronologically by events, birth dates, or periods, or by areas of subject interest.

In practice, questions concerning biography are of such a nature that few of these evaluative tests are actually employed. If a person is well known, the problem normally is not one of locating a source but of screen-

[6] Eugene Sheehy, *Guide to Reference Books* (Chicago: American Library Association, 1976), p. 209.

ing out the many sources for the pertinent details. If the individual is obscure, usually any source is welcome.

SEARCHING BIOGRAPHICAL SOURCES

There are various methods of dividing and subdividing biographical sources, although in a general way the divisions follow those of any reference form. First come bibliographies of biography, which are quite limited. Second come indexes to biographical material in periodicals and books. Third appear biographical dictionaries, often grouped together with indexes. And all these forms may be arranged again by country and/or by subject.

Another often used approach to division is to separate biographies into current and retrospective groups, the latter being limited, for the most part, to listings or sketches of dead personalities. The problem here is that several sources, such as *Webster's Biographical Dictionary*, list both the living and the dead. Nevertheless, there are many well-known "classics" in both current and retrospective biography which fit neatly into such a categorization, e.g., *Who's Who in America* (current) and the *Dictionary of American Biography* (retrospective).

Still, for most practical reference purposes the biographical sources may be divided into three major types: (1) indexes which help the librarian to locate biographies in various sources; (2) data-type biographies, such as *Who's Who*, which give the directory type of information about an individual, usually a living person; and (3) essay-type biographies which are sometimes extensive and discursive profiles of both living and dead persons.

What to search

In determining what biographical source to search, the librarian will work from two basic beginning queries: How much of the history of an individual life does the user require, and/or what type of data is required? (This query is usually appropriate for a ready-reference question about address, profession, etc.) At what level of depth and sophistication should the answer be geared to the essay type of question? The answer to the second question can be determined by the age, education, and needs of the individual user. The answer to the first quantitative question will require either (1) a silhouette or simple data type of reply or (2) an answer which will require an essay form.

This data type of question is by far the most common in the ready-reference situation. Typical queries: "What is the address and phone number of X?" "How does one spell Y's name?" "What is the age of R?" "When did Beethoven die?" Answers will be found in the familiar who's who directory–biographical dictionary sources. Approach varies in each title, but there is a given consistency in listing names alphabetically and, at a minimum, giving the profession and position (with or without claim-to-fame attributes) of the individual. At a maximum, these sources will give full background on the entry from birth and death dates to publications, names of children, and so on. The information is usually, although not necessarily, in outline form. It is rarely discursive or critical. The data are all.

The second major type of biographical question comes from the person who wants partial or relatively complete information on an individual. The questioner may be writing a paper, preparing a speech, or seeking critical background material. Typical queries: "How can I write a paper on Herman Melville?" "What do you have on X, a prominent American scientist?" "Is there a book about George Washington and the cherry tree?"

Answers will be found in reference sources quite different from those used for the data, who's who approach. Here the emphasis is on essays (300 words to several volumes in length). A biographical directory will be of little value. The reference librarian will turn to essay approaches in sources ranging from *Current Biography* to the *Dictionary of National Biography*.

National biography

Many reference librarians correctly refer to both the essay-type and the data-type biographical source as a "biographical dictionary." The reference is correct because most of the biographical sources employed in reference work are arranged in dictionary order and include sketches, but certainly *not* complete biographical information about an individual. The biographical dictionary may include a few lines or many pages about a person. The entry may be in data or in essay form. Still, for purposes of clarity and purpose, one may distinguish between the biographical directory (i.e., the data, who's who approach) and the biographical dictionary (i.e., the few words or an extended narrative approach).

Once the major categorization is determined, the librarian further divides the query in terms of time: (1) Is the person living or dead? (2) Did he or she recently come into the news? (3) If still living, was the individual important a few years ago, but rarely heard about now? (4) If dead, was the person of enough historical importance to be included in a major retrospective biographical source? When in doubt, the best general method of clearing for further action is to ask the user. If no answers are forthcoming, look up the name in a biographical dictionary or index.

Secondary approaches to biographical searching

The whole library is a source for answering biographical queries. The number of possible approaches for information is almost unlimited. A cursory glance at Slocum's *Biographical Dictionaries and Related Works* will indicate the overwhelming avenues and byways to a current or historical figure.[7] Few libraries have Slocum's 8000 possible entries to biography, yet there are other sources which may be used as well. Most of these have been discussed in previous chapters; they include encyclopedias, periodical or newspaper indexes, almanacs, directories, literary handbooks and manuals, and even dictionaries, which often have a special section on biography. All are secondary or tertiary sources, and on occasion the librarian will be asked for information on primary material, usually manuscripts. Guides to manuscripts are beyond this text, although, once again, a check of Sheehy will show the basic guides.

Anonyms and pseudonyms

An aspect of biography concerns anonyms and pseudonyms. At one time, they were a major consideration in libraries that conscientiously attempted to catalog by the real, not the assumed, name. Catalog streamlining and exhaustion of the subject by literary scholars have greatly decreased the general reference interest in the area. Still, from time to time a question may be asked about the name of this or that author who employs various pen names, abbreviations, and so on.

If a figure is relatively well known, such as mystery writer John Creasey (who also writes under the names of Gordon Ashe and J. J. Marric) or A. E., the Irish poet (whose real name was George Russell), the information is easy to find in most literary handbooks, encyclopedias, and other biographical sources. They usually handle the matter with appropriate cross-references from the pseudonyms or initials to the given name.

---

[7] Robert Slocum (ed.), *Biographical Dictionaries and Related Works* (Detroit: Gale Research Company, 1967, 1056 pp. Supplement, 1972, 852 pp.). This is the basic bibliography of biographical sources, listing over 8000 who's whos, dictionaries, directories, indexes, portrait catalogs, etc. Material is gathered under three main sections: "Universal Biography," "National or Area Biography," and "Biography by Vocation." There is an excellent author, title, and subject index. Slocum lists sources of biographical information, but not the millions of names covered in each title he annotates. All periods of time and most countries are covered, but the work is especially valuable for early to middle twentieth-century titles.

And from 1950 on, the information may be readily found in either *The National Union Catalog* or the *British National Bibliography*, provided the person in question has been published.

Lesser-known figures—who may range from authors to politicians and scientists, not to mention actors—may be more difficult to trace. In these cases, a good dictionary of anonyms and pseudonyms is useful. Dictionaries which cover this type of material are of two types: (1) those listing anonyms, where the usual procedure is to list those citing pseudonyms, which are followed by the real name of the person. Many works, such as the classic Samuel Halkett and John Laing *Dictionary of Anonymous and Pseudonymous English Literature* (Edinburg: Oliver and Boyd, 1926–1962, 9 vols.), combine voth approaches. In most libraries there is more call for the second type of information, and here the single most useful current work is Harold S. Sharp's *Handbook of Pseudonyms and Personal Nicknames* (Metuchen, New Jersey: Scarecrow Press, 1972, Supplement, 1975). The two volumes list about 33,000 real and 55,000 nicknames or pseudonyms in one alphabet with cross-references. Individuals are included from all walks of life, not just literature, and from all parts of the world and historical periods. Given its wide scope, the *Handbook* is of value in all types of libraries, and will be frequently employed at the reference desk to trace an elusive name.

BIOGRAPHICAL DICTIONARIES

Webster's Biographical Dictionary, rev. ed. Springfield, Massachusetts: G. & C. Merriam Company, 1974, 1697 pp. $12.95.

Chambers's Biographical Dictionary, rev. ed., ed. by J. O. Thorne. Edinburgh and London: Chambers, Ltd., 1969, 1432 pp. (distributed in the United States by St. Martin's Press). $20. Also available in a two-volume paperback edition (1974, $7.95 each), which is slightly updated to the end of 1973.

The librarian turns to a biographical dictionary when it can be assumed that the person in question is probably dead. A biographical index (discussed in the next section) is a better first choice when the person is likely to be living.

The best-known dictionary is *Webster's Biographical Dictionary*. Although it includes 40,000 names, approximately 80 percent of the people listed are deceased. The entries are short sketches which give most of the data found in a who's who approach. American and British subjects receive most space, with appropriate attention given to major international and historical figures. The basic problem with this work is that it has undergone only slight revisions since 1943. While useful for retrospective listings, it is less than trustworthy for current personages.[8]

Chambers's claims only 15,000 names (in contrast with *Webster's* 40,000 entries), but this work is proof that quality will outdo quantity. It gives the same vital information found in *Webster's*, although much of it is updated in a considerably better fashion and puts particular emphasis on British and European biography. The major difference between the two is neither number nor scope, but style. *Chambers's* enjoys a unique position because its editors make a conscious effort to add some human interest and critical observations. The difference between reading *Webster's* and the British work is the difference between reading a telephone book and a book of short, clever essays. As style here is embellished with relative currency and accuracy, there simply is no comparison between the two.[9]

Who Was When (3d ed.; New York: The H. W. Wilson Company, 1976, 184 pp.) is a biographical dictionary limited to deceased personalities. Here are listed 10,000 famous persons from 500 B.C. through 1974, under numerous subject categories from government and law to music. The work is different in that, between the birth and death dates of any individual, can be found names and dates of those in the same field. Hence, it is a handy guide to answer questions such as who was writing when Shakespeare was alive and what rulers might Marco Polo have met.

INDEXES TO BIOGRAPHY

Indexes to biographical data in directories and dictionaries

Biographical Dictionaries Master Index. Detroit: Gale Research Company, 1976 to date, biennial, 3 vols. $65.

Marquis Who's Who Publications/Index to All Books. Chicago: Marquis Who's Who, Inc., 1974, annual to date. $24.95.

---

[8] A more satisfactory title, which should not be confused with the dictionary, is *Webster's American Biographies* (Springfield, Massachusetts: G. & C. Merriam Company, 1974, 1233 pp.). Edited by Charles Van Doren, it contains about 3000 short (350-word) essays on both living and deceased Americans.

[9] The librarian will turn to *Chambers's* first, and, failing to find the entry, will then go to *Webster's*. If both fail—which is rather unlikely for average situations—there are other biographical dictionaries. Two of the more popular variety in larger reference collections are: *The New Century Cyclopedia of Names*, edited by C. L. Barnhart (New York: Appleton, Century-Crofts, Inc., 1954, 3 vols.) and the *Universal Pronouncing Dictionary of Biography and Mythology* (5th ed.; Philadelphia: J. B. Lippincott Company, 1930, 2550 pp.). *The New Century* has over 100,000 entries for topics ranging from mythology to place names.

Index to the Wilson Author Series. New York: The H. W. Wilson Company, 1976, 72 pp. $4.

There are two types of indexes to biography. The first, represented by *Biographical Dictionaries Master Index*, is a key to entries found in biographical dictionaries and directories such as *Who's Who in America*. The purpose is to reduce tedious searching of basic, generally current guides to living individuals.

The second type of index, as represented by *Biography Index* (discussed in the next section), includes citations to biographies appearing in books and periodicals. The purpose is to offer the user a key to biographical information about persons both living and dead in a wide variety of general sources.

The first type would be employed for ready-reference work where one wanted the data type of information. The second form of index would more likely be used for someone seeking detailed information for purposes of a paper, research project, speech, or other presentation.

For example, a user who wished to find the address of John Doe or Mary Doe would turn to the *Master Index*, which would indicate the various sources of short data entries in the various biographical dictionaries indexed. The user who wished to write a paper on the achievements of either Doe would need a fuller entry and would turn to biographical information in books and periodicals as indicated in *Biography Index*.

The scope of the three data-type biographical indexes listed here may be described briefly:

(1) *Biographical Dictionaries Master Index*, first published in 1976, is to be updated every two years. It indexes entries found in 53 biographical dictionaries, and claims to list over 800,000 names. Most of the directories indexed list living American personalities from all walks of life. Some of the 53 are *Who's Who in America, American Men and Women of Science, Directory of American Scholars*, and *Black American Authors*. The catch is that the *Index* assumes that the library has most of the directories and dictionaries.

Entries, arranged alphabetically, are taken as they appear in the works indexed. The result is the repetition of some names, i.e., names with prefixes and suffixes, compound surnames, names which have been transliterated into the roman alphabet, etc. For example, Muhammad Ali is listed also as Ali, Muhammad; Cassius Clay; and Clay, Cassius.

(2) At the other extreme, with 7500 listings for only 7 titles, is the *Index to the Wilson Author Series*. This work includes names of both living and dead writers from not only the United States but the world around. The titles indexed are discussed on pages 259–260.

(3) The *Marquis Who's Who Publications Index* duplicates almost ev-

erything listed in the *Master Index*. It is an index of the 11 *Who's Who* titles
discussed later in this chapter. Gale indexes 9 of the 11 major Marquis
publications. The need for both indexes is questionable for other than
libraries which treat the Marquis titles as a unit and which want the index
on the shelf next to the 11 titles.

Thanks to automated editing and publishing, it will be possible to
issue more and more of these indexes to biographical directories and dictionaries. For example, the Marquis and the Gale indexes are computer-
assisted. Historically, this type of indexing had to be done laboriously by
an individual. This fact accounts for the lack of many indexes before the
1970s. An outstanding exception is Albert Hyamson's *A Dictionary of Universal Biography of All Ages and of All Peoples* (2d ed., New York: E. P. Dutton
& Co., 1951, 679 pp.). He analyzed 23 biographical titles, and his book
lists 110,000 names with reference to fuller entries in the 23 titles. It is
particularly useful as an index to *The Dictionary of National Biography* and
the *Dictionary of American Biography*.

Hyamson should be used in conjunction with the *Master Index* because his work is good for hunting down names in retrospective biographical works. The *Master Index* is for current titles.

Indexes to biographical data in books and serials

*Biography Index: A Cumulative Index to Biographical Material in Books
and Magazines*. New York: The H. W. Wilson Company, 1947 to
date, quarterly, annual and three-year cumulations. $32.

Chicorel Index to Biographies. New York: Chicorel Library Publishing Corporation, 1974, 2 vols. $60 each.

Havlice, Patricia. *Index to Literary Biography*. Metuchen, New
Jersey: Scarecrow Press, 1975, 2 vols. $39.50.

The New York Times Obituaries Index, 1858–1968. New York: The
New York Times, 1970, 1136 pp. $75.

The second type of biography index does not analyze short entries in
directories and dictionaries, but considers fuller information found in
books, periodicals, and specialized sources. In this sense it is the familiar
index to material in collections or in magazines.

The best-known and most often used is the *Biography Index*, which is
a key to some 2000 periodicals and numerous books. The indexed biographical information may run to a paragraph or to hundreds of pages.

There are some secondary uses of the *Biography Index*: (1) Illustrations
and portraits are indicated, and it can be used to find a picture of the

subject. (2) An appended index lists the subjects by profession and occupation. The subject classification approach can be of real benefit to the reference librarian. The librarian who is looking for something on a banker or deep-sea diver, but does not have the faintest idea as to who might qualify, will be grateful for the subject breakdown. (3) There is a checklist of the composite books—primarily collective biographies—which are analyzed, and it does have some value for the acquisitions librarian. (4) The juvenile biographies are marked in the main index and are listed under a separate heading in the appended index. (5) Obituary notices from *The New York Times* are included, but this coverage is of less importance now that the *Times* has its own obituaries and biographical indexes.

The *New York Times Obituaries Index* lists in alphabetical order names of persons who rated an obituary in the newspaper between 1858 and 1968 inclusive. There are a total of over 350,000 names, with reference to the notices, often of essay length, in *The New York Times*. Thanks to the worldwide coverage of the *Times*, the list is not limited to Americans and includes almost every prominent world figure who died during the period covered by the *Index*. Its secondary advantages, although they may be primary to many, are: (1) It does include lesser-known personalities not often found in standard biographical works; (2) the obituary often presents a summation of the reputation of the figure at the time; and (3) as each entry includes not only page and issue number, but death date, it can serve as a ready-reference aid. The cutoff date is 1968, but the *Times Biographical Service* (discussed in the next section) fills the gap from 1968 on.

For those who believe, as Bruce Lockhart does, that "the object of biography is to increase self confidence; the object of obituary notices is to increase caution," much is to be gained from Frank Roberts (comp.), *Obituaries from The Times 1961–1970* (London: Newspaper Archives Developments, c.1975, 952 pp.). These obituaries do not represent the time span of the American work or the number of entries. Only about 1500 obituary notices from *The Times* of London are found here, and they are for only those notables who died between 1961 and 1970. (Further volumes are to follow.) Bell offers the justification for such a work:

> *Lord Attlee, his obituarist tells us, was an adept solver of* The Times *crossword puzzle and "delighted to pore over works of personal reference like* Who's Who.*" The notice continues with one of those casual juxtapositions suggesting cause and effect which are a minor glory of obituary style: "His sturdiness of character, his unwavering resolution, his staunch but inarticulate love of British things were qualities of the highest worth. . . . " Those who share Attlee's high regard for the peculiarly analgesic qualities of browsing in* Who's Who . . . *or even those who (like Logan Pearsall Smith) read through the* Dictionary of

National Biography *to indicate or to stave off periodic madness will welcome* The Times's [*work*].[10]

The advantage of the title is that obituaries are printed in total and one does not have to turn to another source, as when using *The New York Times Obituaries Index*. Also, in spite of its English origin, the sketches are international in scope, and only 61 percent of the entrants are British.

The *Chicorel Index to Biographies* is representative of many indexes which take a group of books, analyze their contents, and prepare an index to biographical entries. About 2500 individual biographies, published from approximately 1900 to 1947, are analyzed. Periodicals and collective biographies are not included. The list of some 21,000 entries is arranged alphabetically with subjects interfiled with the names. Occupations, significant activities such as pacifist or feminist, nationality, and historical periods are the subject divisions. Unfortunately, too many of the subject indicators are so broad as to be virtually useless, e.g., the "Englishmen" section spans 32 pages and includes over 600 entries. Despite these reservations, and the fact that the coverage is only to 1947, the *Index* is useful to supplement the *Biography Index* which was first issued in 1947. It in no way is a substitute.

The *Index to Literary Biography* is an example of a specialized biographical index. The compiler analyzes names in 50 literary reference works published between 1931 and 1972 in four languages. Full cross-references are given for pseudonyms. Each entry indicates where the primary information about the writer is to be found and includes the author's name, pseudonym, birth and death dates, nationality, and literary genre.

An often used index to biographies in collections, individual biographical works, and some periodicals is Margaret Nicholsen's *People in Books: A Selective Guide to Biographical Literature Arranged by Vocations and Other Fields of Reader Interest* (New York: The H. W. Wilson Company, 1969, 498 pp., Supplement, 1976, 792 pp.). Grade levels are indicated for the titles analyzed and there are several appended indexes by country and century.

Ideally, the day will come when the two types of biographical indexes are merged and all the information placed in a computer-assisted data bank. The librarian will only have to keypunch in the required name, and reference to sources will be printed out or flashed on a screen. To a limited extent and for other purposes, these types of data banks are now employed by various government agencies and credit bureaus. The technology is available to do the same for listings in the 8000-plus biographical dictionaries and directories and the various indexes to materials in collections and periodicals.

---

[10] Alan Bell, "Summary Justice," *The Times Literary Supplement*, March 5, 1976, p. 260. This is a delightful, lengthy essay on biography in general, obituary notices in particular—and with some hints for evaluating both.

CURRENT BIOGRAPHICAL SOURCES

Essay form: General

Current Biography. New York: The H. W. Wilson Company, 1940 to date, monthly except August, $17; yearbook, $17.

The New York Times Biographical Service: A Compilation of Current Biographical Information of General Interest. New York: Arno Press, 1970 to date, monthly, loose-leaf. $85.

Current Biography is the single most popular current essay-length biographical aid in almost any type of library. Issued monthly, it is cumulated, often with revised sketches, into annual volumes with excellent cumulative indexing.[11] Annual emphasis is on some 170 international personalities, primarily those who arc in some way influencing the American scene. Articles are long enough to include all vital information about the person and usually are relatively objective. The sketches are prepared by a special staff which draws information from other biographical sources and from the person being covered in the article. Subjects are given the opportunity to check copy before it is published and, presumably, to approve the photograph which accompanies each sketch. Source references are cited. Obituary notices, with due reference to *The New York Times Obituaries Index*, are listed for those who at one time have appeared in the work. There is an index by profession, which is helpful for the student who has to write something about "a plumber, a scientist, an artist . . ." but is not particular as to who the individual may be. Another feature in the annual is a list of current "biographical references." This serves as a convenient up-to-date checklist for purchase.

The New York Times Biographical Service serves the same purpose, and usually the same audience, as *Current Biography*.[12] Published each month in loose-leaf form, it is a first choice for any medium-sized to large library. It includes obituaries, the "man in the news," and feature stories from the drama, book, sports, and Sunday magazine section. Each sheet is a reprint of biographical material which has appeared in the *Times*. Each individual section has its own index, which is cumulated every six months and annually. The sketches are often reports on controversial, less than leader, types. Most of the reporting is objective, and where a point of view is

---

[11] It should be noted that, thanks to a new format and rather "catchy" photographs on the cover, *Current Biography* now resembles a magazine which, literally, may be read cover to cover.

[12] The essential difference is that *Current Biography* is staff-written with source references. *The New York Times* biographies are usually written by individuals who do not cite sources.

expressed, the reader is given the reporter's by-line. Profiles may be brief or many pages long, and there is no effort to revise before reprinting. There are a monthly, six-month, and annual cumulative index. The profiles are consecutively numbered, and carry the date of appearance in the *Times*. And usually there is a picture of the subject. The monthly set is about three months behind the time the biographies are published in *The New York Times*.

As these services are monthly and sometimes do not appear in the library for two to four weeks after publication, how does the librarian cope with a request for information on current news figures not found in any of them? Check the various services such as *Facts on File*, newspaper indexes, and, of course, periodical indexes. Still, the answer is too pat. All too often, none of these standard aids helps. It usually comes down to the "automated" memory of the librarian who reads at least one or two newspapers a day and keeps up with current events well enough to recall a profile appearing here or there. Not neat, not systematic, not always an answer, but it often works.

Directory: Who's who form[13]

> *Who's Who in America*. Chicago: Marquis Who's Who, Inc., 1899 to date, biennial, $72.50.
>
> *Who's Who*. London: Black, 1849 to date, annual (distributed in the United States by St. Martin's Press, Inc.). £15.
>
> *International Who's Who*. London: Europa Publications Ltd., 1935 to date, annual (distributed in the United States by Gale Research Company). $70.
>
> *Directory of American Scholars*, 6th ed. New York: R. R. Bowker Company, 1974, 4 vols. $148.50.
>
> *American Men and Women of Science*, 13th ed. New York: R. R. Bowker Company, 1976, 7 vols. $300.

Other than essay-length material for student papers, the most sought-after type of current biographical information is of a ready-reference type, or simple data. The questions are familiar enough: How does X spell his name? What degrees does Y hold? What has Z published? Is she married?

Replies to these and similar queries are found in the familiar directo-

---

[13] The titles listed here are only representative. For an amusing, yet accurate, survey of the hundreds of titles in this area, see Israel Shenker's "What's What in Who's Who," *The New York Times*, June 7, 1977, p. 33.

ry who's who format. They vary in title, publisher, scope, and often accuracy and timeliness; but their essential purpose is the same: to present objective, usually noncontroversial facts about an individual. The approach and style are monotonously the same; most are arranged alphabetically by the name of the person, with a following paragraph of vital statistics which normally concludes with the person's address and phone number.

The who's who aids may be classified by scope as international, national, local, professional or business, religious or racial, etc. This classification presents no problem, as the scope of the work is usually indicated by the title.

Information is usually compiled by sending the candidate a questionnaire. The person is then free to provide as much or as little of the requested information as he or she wishes. The better publishers check the returns for flaws or downright lies. Other publishers may be content to rely on the honesty of the individual, who normally has little reason not to tell the truth, although—and this is a large "although"—some candidates for entry may construct life patterns foreign in both detail and general facts to their real life-styles.

The American *Who's Who in America* has a long history of reliability and is a source for about 75,000 names of prominent American men and women, as well as a few foreigners who have some influence in the United States. As the nation's current population is about 214 million, how do the editors determine who is, or who is not, to be included? The answer is complex, usually based upon some type of outstanding achievement or excellence. But who is eminent?

> *Standards of eminence are by no means easy to establish. Eminence, like many other human qualities, is essentially relative. Eminence is more than celebrity; the state of being publicly known is often ephemeral and, far too frequently, a synthetic marketable commodity. . . . Rarely indeed do two individuals agree as to what constitutes success, let alone eminence. . . . To be eminent is to be prominent rather than conspicuous. . . . Eminence—or at least notability— appears historically to stabilize at a proportion somewhere around 3 in every 10,000 of the population.*[14]

The inclusion-exclusion process is of more interest when the reputation and fame of a work, such as *Who's Who in America*, is purposefully built upon selectivity of a high order. The natural question is one of legitimacy. Is the selection of Y based upon a desire to be included (supported by a

[14] Cedric A. Larson, *Who; Sixty Years of American Eminence* (New York: McDowell, Oblensky, 1958), pp. 2 and 17.

willingness to buy the volume in question, or, in a few cases, literally to pay for a place in the volume), or is it based upon the editor's notion of eminence where no amount of persuasion or cash will ensure selection? In the case of all works listed here, the answer is that they are indeed ligitimate. In these works, one's way to fame cannot be bought. This is not to say there is no room for argument. No one will entirely agree on all names selected or rejected, say, in *Who's Who in America*. As Larson notes: "The Marquis editors are perennially criticized for admission or exclusion of eminent Americans over the years, [and] are quick to admit . . . sins of both omission and admission."[15]

One work which would be unnecessary if women were not treated as the second sex is *Who's Who of American Women* (Chicago: Marquis Who's Who, Inc., 1959 to date). A biennial dictionary of notable living American females, it follows the same general pattern as all the Marquis works. The ninth edition includes 24,000 women's names. The editor's breakdown of 1000 sketches indicates that, according to occupation, a woman's chances to earn an entry were best if she was a club, civic, or religious leader (9.6 percent of all listings) and least if she was a composer (0.4 percent of the entries). Librarians make up a healthy 5.2 percent of the biographies.[16]

Who's Who was first published in Britain on January 15, 1849, some 50 years before there were enough prominent Americans to make a volume possible here. During its first 47 years, *Who's Who* was a slim book of some 250 pages which listed members of the titled and official classes. In 1897, it became a biographical dictionary, and the 1972–1973 edition is close to 4000 pages. Selection is no longer based on nobility but on "personal achievement or prominence." Most entries are English, but it does include some notables from other countries. And in the past decade, it has put more and more emphasis on prominent scholars and professional people as well as political and industrial leaders.

Depending upon size and type of audience served, most American

---

[15] Ibid., p. 9.

[16] Marquis issues a number of regional who's who works which follow the same arrangement and principles of *Who's Who in America*, differing only in that the coverage is limited to a region and includes many names not found in the basic work. Each biennial volume averages some 20,000 entries which clearly indicate whether or not they are duplicated in *Who's Who in America*. These supplementary titles include *Who's Who in the Midwest*, 1949 to date; *Who's Who in the South and Southwest*, 1950 to date; *Who's Who in the West*, 1949 to date; and *Who's Who in the East*, 1943 to date. All these are indexed in Marquis's own aforementioned index and the *Biographical Dictionaries Master Index*.

When entrants of the main *Who's Who in America* die, they are included in *Who Was Who in America* (Chicago: Marquis Who's Who, Inc., 1942 to date, irregular). Entries in the volumes (which numbered seven in 1977) go back to 1897.

public university and college libraries will have *Who's Who in America* and possibly *Who's Who* "possibly" because the better-known figures who are apt to be objects of inquiry in *Who's Who* are covered in the *International Who's Who*. This work opens with a section of names of "reigning royal families," and then moves to the alphabetic listing of some 12,000 to 15,000 brief biographies of the outstanding men and women of our time. The range is wide and takes in those who are prominent in international affairs, government, administration, diplomacy, science, medicine, law, finance, business, education, religion, literature, music, art, and entertainment. Also, Marquis issues *Who's Who in the World* (3d ed.; Chicago: Marquis Who's Who, 1976), which lists 20,000 names often duplicated in the *International Who's Who*.

One of the most frequently consulted professional biographical directories is *American Men and Women of Science*. Over the years this has gone through a number of changes, but beginning with the thirteenth edition of 1976, it consists of seven volumes which list alphabetically some 110,000 United States and Canadian persons in the physical and biological sciences, and also a select number of people in the social sciences. Entry information is typical of this type of biographical aid, i.e., name, discipline, education, professional experience, specialization, address, etc. A seventh (index) volume lists the names by city and state or province and country as well as by discipline. About 30 percent of the people listed are active in more than one discipline.[17]

The *Directory of American Scholars,* with 38,000 names, has the same type of entry form used in *American Men and Women of Science* for teachers and others related to history, English, foreign languages, philosophy, religion, and law. And, again, there is an index, this time included at the end of each volume, which lists the names by subject and geographical location. The fourth volume also includes an alphabetical index to all names in the directory.[18] Between them, the two directories list about 150,000 names, almost double the number found in *Who's Who in America*. Technically, they are professional biographical directories, but thanks to their wide coverage, they are often used in a library as general biographical directories.

---

[17] A previous set, but not this one, is indexed in the *Biographical Dictionaries Master Index*. And this points up a problem with the index. As it is issued only every two years, it often is not up to date in terms of what it is supposedly indexing, i.e., volumes indexed may have been superceded by later publications.

[18] A quick reference source for faculty is the *National Faculty Directory* (Detroit: Gale Research Company, 1970 to date, annual, 2 vols.), which lists 449,000 teachers in junior colleges, colleges, and universities in the United States and in some Canadian institutions. The brief entry gives the teacher's name, department, institution, and address.

RETROSPECTIVE BIOGRAPHICAL SOURCES

Essay form

> *Dictionary of American Biography*. New York: Charles Scribner's Sons, 1974, 11 vols. $515. Supplements 5 and 6, 1977–1978. $45 each.

> *Dictionary of National Biography*. Edited by Leslie Stephen and Sidney Lee, 1885 to 1901; reissue, London: Oxford University Press, 1938, 21 vols. and supplement; 2d to 7th supplements, 1912–1971. Base set, $475; 2d supplement, $51.25; supplements 3–7, $38.50 each.

> *National Cyclopaedia of American Biography*. New York: James T. White Company, 1892–(in progress).

> *Notable American Women 1607–1950. A Biographical Dictionary*. Edited by Edward T. James. Cambridge, Massachusetts: Harvard University Press, 1971, 3 vols. $75.

> *Encyclopedia of World Biography*. New York: McGraw-Hill Book Company, 1973, 12 vols. $300.

> *Dictionary of Scientific Biography*. New York: Charles Scribner's Sons, 1970–1978, 16 vols. $640.

The proper use of these national, retrospective biographical aids depends upon the librarian's or user's recognizing the nationality of the figure in question and the fact that all entrants are deceased.[19] When the nationality is not known, it will save time first to check (1) one of the retrospective biographical dictionaries, such as Hyamson; then (2) an encyclopedia; and finally (3) *Biography Index*.

The titles are particularly useful for information on lesser-known figures, rarely found, or at best only mentioned, in general sources. The famous and near famous are often written up in equal or somewhat equal length in standard encyclopedias.

The *Dictionary of American Biography* (or the *DAB*, as it is usually called), with its supplements, covers some 16,000 figures who have made a major contribution to American life. Almost all are Americans, but there are a few foreigners who significantly contributed to our history. (In this case, they have had to live in the United States for some considerable length of time.) Furthermore, no British officers "serving in America after

---

[19] Only McGraw-Hill's *Encyclopedia of World Biography* and the *Dictionary of Scientific Biography* are international in scope. The other titles limit entry to nationals.

the colonies declared their independence" are included. A separate index gives a subject, contributor, birthplace, topic, and occupation entry to the set and its supplements. The distinctive elements of this basic work are best summed up in the words of the American Council of Learned Societies, which sponsored the set:

> The articles should be based as largely as possible on original sources; should be the product of fresh work; should eschew rhetoric, sentiment, and coloring matter generally, yet include careful characterization . . . and should be written as largely as possible by the persons most specifically qualified.

This last stipulation results in some 3000 scholarly contributors, all of whom add their distinctive styles and viewpoints to the compilation. As a consequence, most of the entries—which vary from several paragraphs to several pages—can be read as essays, rather than as a list of connected, dry facts.[20]

The *Dictionary of National Biography* (or *DNB*) is the model for the *DAB*; and having learned one set, the librarian can handle the other without difficulty. The *DNB*, approximately twice the size of the *DAB*, includes entries on over 32,000 deceased "men and women of British or Irish race who have achieved any reasonable measure of distinction in any walk of life." It also includes early settlers in America and "persons of foreign birth who have gained eminence in this country." The original set, edited by Leslie Stephen, Virginia Woolf's father, includes short to long signed articles with bibliographies. Aside from the scope, it can be used in much the same way and for many of the same reasons as the *DAB*.

Supplements are infrequently issued for both sets. The policy is best explained by the publisher of the *DAB*:

> It is the editorial policy of the Dictionary to allow a sufficient lapse of time between the death of the subject and any attempt to write a just and considered appraisal of his life and contribution to our national history. Therefore, supplements are issued when deemed appropriate.

The *DAB* supplements contain entries on persons who died in 1950 or earlier.[21] The *DNB* supplements incorporate entries on persons who died

---

[20] Smaller libraries will find the *Concise Dictionary of American Biography* (2d ed.; New York: Charles Scribner's Sons, 1977) a substitute for the large set. However, it reduces the primary essays to little more than sketches of highlights of a person's life and is more properly suited to ready-reference work than to research. There are some medium to long essay entries which are almost the same as in the master set, but the choice is limited to better-known figures who usually can be found in numerous other sources.

[21] The 1977 fifth supplement was not available at this writing, nor was the 1978 sixth supplement, but each will update the work by about 10 years, i.e., it is expected the 1978 supple-

through 1960. Librarians seeking essay-length information on prominent Americans or British men or women who have died since these cutoff supplement dates should check other sources, ranging from encyclopedias to *Biography Index.*

Prior to the highly scholarly approach of the *DNB, DAB,* and other national works of the twentieth century, there was no dearth of essay-type biographical works. The other biographical essay-type reference titles are now much dated and are used chiefly for hard-to-find retrospective biographies. In the United States, the most famous is *Appleton's Cyclopedia of American Biography* (New York: Appleton-Century-Crofts, Inc., 1887 to 1900, 7 vols., reprinted in 1968 by Gale Research Company). Before the *DAB,* this was favored in many American libraries, and it still has value for biographies not included in the *DAB* and other standard sources. There are some 20,000 short to quite long signed articles dealing with Americans and foreign-born persons close to the American scene. Except for the bias of the writer, the work is generally quite high in its accuracy. However, "generally" is used advisedly because *Appleton's* is by way of being a literary curiosity, and is not always that scholarly. There are, for example, some 47 sketches of people invented by the contributors. Authors were paid by space and made the most of it. The nonexistent Bernhard Huhne is credited with the discovery of the California coast; another fictitious character is a French epidemiologist who was supposed to have combated cholera in South America some 50 years before the disease reached that continent.

Still another variety of the *DNB* and the *DAB* is the *National Cyclopaedia of American Biography.* The work contains sketches of over 50,000 Americans and is particularly strong on American businesspersons and industrialists. (Most, although not all, of the entrants are deceased.) This work was and continues to be more involved with the subject's ego than with the person's true place in history. The facts are usually correct, but there is a definite bias to make the person look as noteworthy as possible. Hence, except for extremely famous personages, the average entry is closer to the type of oration heard at a funeral service than to the entries read in the *DAB.* The articles, which vary in length from one-half column to several pages, are prepared by the publisher's staff. Information is based on questionnaires, interviews, and data obtained from relatives. The gathering process leaves little latitude for criticism of the subject.

Despite the method of gathering biographical data, the *National Cyclopaedia*—and other members of the genre—is still useful for locating in-

---

ment will carry biographies to about 1970. The supplements are usually included in the basic set, which is republished from time to time in a varying number of volumes.

formation on lesser-known Americans. A short sketch of an Ohio banker's life may prove the key to solving a historical problem; or, at a more mundane level, it serves the curious who are attempting to trace roots of a family tree. Perhaps fitting to the focus, the arrangement of the *National Cyclopaedia* is arbitrary and complicated.

None of the material is in alphabetical order, and the more than 55 volumes include several completed sets and sets in progress. Most of the problems before November 1971 are solved by the *National Cyclopaedia of American Biography Revised Index; Permanent and Current Series* (New York: James T. White Company, 1971). This is an alphabetical index by name, subject, and topic. Apparently, the publisher will update the index from time to time.

Notable American Women includes 1359 biographies of subjects (who died prior to 1950) whose "lives and careers have had significant impact on American life in all fields of thought and action." The long, signed biographies are similar to those in the *DAB*[22] and *DNB*, and the author of each entry has special knowledge of the subject. In explaining who was included or excluded, the editors noted that the usual test of inclusion—being the wife of a famous man—was not considered. (The only exception is the inclusion of the wives of American Presidents.) Once more, the domestic skills of a woman were seldom considered, and no moral judgments as to a female's being a criminal or an adventuress were used to exclude a name. There are an excellent 33-page introduction which gives a historical survey of the role of women in American life and an index of individuals grouped by occupations.

Combining elements of all the biographical sets, the McGraw-Hill *Encyclopedia of World Biography* offers 5000 essays (articles run about 500 to 3000 words) about famous deceased figures. The scope is universal; it considers famous men and women of all periods and countries. And like the *DAB* and *DNB*, it includes famous persons from all fields—history, literature, art, science, music, and so on. Articles are by scholars and stress commentary and evaluation as much as facts. The *Encyclopedia* is primarily directed to students from junior high school through college, but the brief summary sketch of a subject for each entry is of value for reference work with other library users. Furthermore, the set boasts 6000 portraits, maps,

---

[22] The similarity is no accident. One editor, Edward James, is editor of the *DAB*. Incidentally, as his coeditor Janet James points out, in 1955 there were only 750 women among the 15,000 names entered in the *DAB*. Much the same percentage seems true of the *DNB* although in the seventh supplement, the editor notes in the preface that the supplement differs in three regards from past volumes: "Nobody was killed in battle; there are more scientists and engineers to be discovered here; and there are more women." How many of the 750 additional names are women he does not say.

and illustrations which should prove as useful as the classified index (persons, places, treaties, ideas, pictures, styles, and the like) in the final volume. Also, a study guide in this same last volume offers related biographies and related book titles.

As with current biographical sources, there are numerous subject approaches to retrospective biography. A much used set, for example, is the *Dictionary of Scientific Biography*, which consists of 14 basic volumes issued between 1970 and 1976. A supplement is being published in 1977 and an index volume in 1978. The *Dictionary* is the ideal work for critical, thoughtful essays on outstanding scientists. It is patterned after the *DAB* and, when completed, will include short to long pieces on some 5000 deceased scientists from more than 60 countries. The worldwide scope makes it particularly useful for even ready-reference work when dealing with scientists from non-Western countries who are not easily found in the standard sources. The index volume will tie the whole together in terms not only of individual biographies but also of scientific concepts which will help the reader trace the history of science.

RELATED BIOGRAPHICAL AREAS

Genealogy[23]

American Genealogical Research Institute Staff. *How to Trace Your Family Tree: A Complete and Easy to Understand Guide for the Beginner.* Garden City, New York: Doubleday & Company, 1975, 191 pp. Paper, $1.95.

Filby, P. William. *American and British Genealogy and Heraldry*, 2d ed. Chicago: American Library Association, 1976, 467 pp. $25.

Genealogy, the study of family history and the tracing of ancestors, is a specialized subdivision of biography. Its importance as a source of biographical data sometimes escapes the general librarian, who is more inclined to dismiss the whole business as somewhat snobbish, smacking of the D.A.R., European nobility, and cranks in search of their elusive family roots. Nevertheless, many large libraries have special genealogical depart-

---

[23] There has been a growing interest in genealogy by librarians and historians; e.g., see Robert E. Wagenknecht, "Genealogy Reconsidered," *Illinois Libraries*, June 1976, pp. 456–458; Richard S. Lackey, "Genealogical Research: An Assessment of Potential Value," *Prologue*, Winter 1975, pp. 221–225; and Samuel P. Hays, "History and Genealogy . . ." *Prologue*, Spring 1975, pp. 39–43; Summer 1975, pp. 81–84.

ments and there are a number of private and special libraries devoted to the work. Numerous state and historical libraries have a genealogical department specializing in pioneer histories.

Genealogy has importance for the average reference librarian on three counts: (1) to answer direct genealogical questions, if only to tell where a person can turn to find such information; (2) to be at least familiar with the common books that explore heraldry, orders, and decorations, a recurring theme of fascination for those who have no particular interest in genealogy per se; and (3) as a clue to solve more difficult biographical and historical questions which may be only incidentally related to genealogy.

Since genealogy is a highly specialized field, as much so in its way as patent law or keeping up with research reports from various scientific areas, the untrained librarian is advised to "field" direct questions. He or she should ascertain whether such service is offered in a nearby library (it usually can be found in one form or another in almost every state and large community), and be prepared to send the patron to that library. Here interlibrary loan procedure is rarely a good idea. Either the person does not know precisely what he or she wants; or if the book or document is known, usually it will not be loaned, primarily because of its value.

As all genealogy is concerned with history and biography, these specialized works will frequently serve to answer a difficult related question. This is particularly true when one is working in local history. Much of the writing at this level has been in the hands of dedicated amateurs, and while all such materials suffer from various degrees of clumsiness, they are usually excellent sources of factual detail.

Among the many guidebooks for both the librarian and the layperson, *How to Trace Your Family Tree* is typical in that it gives basic steps in research, lists basic printed sources, and considers major libraries with genealogical collections. Other works of this type are considered by Filby in his basic bibliography. More than 5000 of the best-known titles in genealogy are fully annotated.[24]

Portraits

> Hayward and Blanche Cirker (eds.). *Dictionary of American Portraits*. New York: Dover Publications, 1967, 756 pp. $30.

A photograph, drawing, painting, or sketch of a biographical subject is often required. Such portraits are usually featured in the longer essay-

---

[24] A quick look at procedures and titles in the field for smaller libraries is provided in "Genealogy Collection Offers Special Services," *Texas Libraries*, Fall 1975, pp. 104–111.

type works listed in this chapter—*Current Biography* and the McGraw-Hill *Encyclopedia of World Biography*, to name two. Also, many of the indexes from *Biography Index* to *The Readers' Guide to Periodical Literature* indicate whether the article includes a picture of the subject. And, of course, encyclopedias are another excellent source. Still, there are some reference works which specialize in portraits. The now dated American Library Association *Portrait Index* (Washington, D.C.: Government Printing Office, 1910) is still useful as an index to portraits of some 40,000 persons in 6000 books and periodicals; but it is frustrating too, if the library does not have a retrospective collection of books and magazines covered by the *Index*.[25]

The *Dictionary of American Portraits* requires no second step. It in itself is a collection of over 4000 engravings, drawings, and photographs of prominent men and women from financial and government leaders to notorious characters such as Billy the Kid. A more limited, although sumptuous, collection of 2420 entries and 1000 illustrations will be found in the much-applauded New York Historical Society's *Catalogue of American Portraits* (New Haven: Yale University Press, 1974, 2 vols.). This work includes portraits in various media and both of famous persons and of those remembered now only because artists painted their portraits.

PROFESSIONAL AND SUBJECT BIOGRAPHIES

The importance of biography to almost everyone from the researcher to the layperson has not escaped publishers. Consequently, almost every publisher's list will include works of a biographical nature from individual biographies to collective works to special listings for individuals engaged in a profession. The increase in the number of professions (almost every American claims to be a professional of sorts), coupled with the growth in education, has resulted in a proliferation of specialized biographical sources.

The reliability of some works is a trifle questionable, primarily because almost all (and sometimes all) the information is supplied directly to the editor or published by the subject. Little or no checking is involved, except in cases where there is a definite question or the biographical sketch is evaluative. Entries tend to be brief, normally giving the name, birth date, place of birth, education, particular "claim to fame," and address.

---

[25] Librarians often keep vertical files of portraits and other types of graphics to avoid the problem of searching them out in periodicals and books. A useful service here is *International Portrait Gallery* (Detroit: Gale Research Company, various dates and series. Complete set as of 1976, $425). This is a set of over 2300 portraits, $8\frac{1}{2} \times 11$ inches, on heavy stock with a caption giving the person's name, nationality, occupation, and birth and death dates.

There are exceptions to this brief form. The H. W. Wilson Company series on authors features rather long, discursive essays. Still, this approach is rare. Most biographical works devoted to a subject or profession have mercifully short entries.

The primary value of the specialized biographical work is:

1. Source of addresses
2. Source of correct spelling of names and titles
3. Source of miscellaneous information for those considering the person for employment or as an employer, as a guest speaker, or for a number of other reasons
4. If maintained for a number of years, as an invaluable aid to the historian or genealogist seeking retrospective information

Following are examples of professional and subject sources. The examples touch only the periphery of a truly large field. Again, Slocum's *Biographical Dictionaries* should be consulted for the range of this type of biographical aid.

Art

Who's Who in American Art. New York: R. R. Bowker Company, 1935 to date, biennial. $37. (Publication period varies.)

Limited to living artists of both the United States and Canada, this is the standard *Who's Who* guide in the field. Among the 9000 entries are not only artists, but persons in related areas from executives of museums and foundations to craftpeople and even collectors. Standard biographical information is given for each entry, but with the twelfth edition (1976) there is an added bonus. Many of the artists have included short statements about their own work. Useful bibliographies after many of the entries include works by and about the subjects. There are two indexes: a geographical index and an index of specialty.

When the librarian is looking for a biography of a famous living or dead artist, the best general place is the general encyclopedia or such current essay sources as *Current Biography*. The *Dictionary of American Biography* has numerous long essays on dead American artists. And, once again, a reminder that a standard index to periodicals, such as *Art Index*, is a likely place to find all the information needed for anyone but the most demanding expert.

The two "classics" in the field are Daniel Mallet's *Index of Artists . . .* (New York: R. R. Bowker Company, 1935, 493 pp.; supplement, 1940, 319 pp.) and Ulrich Thieme's *Allgemeines Lexikon der Bildenden Kunstler . . .* (Leipzig: Seemann, 1907–1950, 37 vols). The former title is an index by artist to material in 22 basic reference works as well as in 1000 more specialized titles. Coverage is international. The problem is that the index is dated and most of the sources are by now relatively rare and difficult to find except in the largest libraries. Thieme, on the other hand, is complete in itself in that it gives both brief and long articles on thousands of the world's artists from early times through the nineteenth century.

There are numerous individual biographies as well as sets; a representative one is John Canaday's *Lives of the Painters* (New York: Norton, 1969, 4 vols). Modeled after Vasari's famous *Lives of the Great Italian Painters*, Canaday's volumes cover four centuries of painting from the Middle Ages through the nineteenth century. As each of the chapters groups the artists around a theme, the 29 chapters on 450 painters can be read as much as essays as for reference purposes. The final volume consists of 500 reproductions of the works discussed. As with others of this genre, the set should be duplicated (where budget allows) for both the general collection and the reference room. Finally, the best general art encyclopedia, the McGraw-Hill *Encyclopedia of World Art*, is filled with biographical information.

Black Americans

Who's Who Among Black Americans. Northbrook, Illinois: Who's Who Among Black Americans, Inc., 1976, 772 pp. $40.

Although blacks represent something like 10 percent of the American population, there are only 2000 to 3000 blacks among the 75,000 names in *Who's Who in America*, and about the same ratio will be found in other standard biographical reference works, both current and retrospective. The lack of representation is usually explained by the equal lack of national prominence among blacks. The obvious catch is that "prominence" is defined by whites. Be that as it may, there are some encouraging signs that a fairer balance is at least being struck by newer works and new editions in biography. Meanwhile, there is a need for a separate work such as discussed here, if only to list those blacks of achievement who may not necessarily have reached national prominence.

Who's Who Among Black Americans follows the same data type of approach as other *Who's Who* titles. There are about 10,000 entries here, "the largest total of biographical entries of high achieving Blacks ever published in one volume," according to the editor. The volume concludes with a geographical and a professional index, neither of which is complete or entirely accurate. In reviewing this title, ALA's Reference and Subscription Books Committee made an important point about some reference works which are flawed but, because they are unique, are a necessary addition for most libraries. The committee points out that the book is needed but "it is not comprehensive, because too many writers, educators, city officials and state legislators are missing. . . . However, there is no comparable directory and the work is useful because it contains facts about a wide diversity of persons not represented in any other single biographical source."[26]

A footnote to all these comments: About 1970 the publishers of *Who's Who in America* admitted that fewer than 10 percent of the entries represented blacks. They suggested this imbalance might be remedied, as it was for the same lack of attention to women, by bringing out a *Who's Who* of blacks just as they had brought out *Who's Who of American Women*. Following considerable controversy, the publishers dropped the plan because it was felt such a volume would polarize or separate the blacks from the rest of our society.[27] Needless to say, some blacks took strong exception to the decision. The result was that in 1976 a smaller company did bring out the title discussed here, and if it lacks all the sophistication of a Marquis *Who's Who*, at least it is published.

There are an increasing number of related biographical works for black Americans, e.g., *Black American Writers, 1773–1949* (Boston: G. K. Hall, 1975, 221 pp.). This lists works of about 1500 black authors by subject, but is not complete in that many titles by a given author are not listed. No biographical information is given. A much better work, although not complete, is *Black American Writers*, discussed later in the subsection on literature.

Of some help in tracing biographies is the annual *Index to Periodical Articles By and About Blacks* (Boston: G. K. Hall, 1950 to date, annual). This work has gone through a number of changes, but today indexes about 25 periodicals, many of which carry biographical information. Cumulative indexes are available for 1950–1959 and 1960–1970. *The Negro Almanac* (3d ed.; New York: Bellwether Co., 1976, 1206 pp.), which is issued at irregular intervals (the first edition appeared in 1967), contains some biographical information on musicians, entertainers, women, etc. There are, to be sure, other articles and shorter pieces on various aspects of life in the United States, as well as a whole section on the African countries.

Business

> *Who's Who in Finance and Industry.* Chicago: Marquis Who's Who, Inc., 1936 to date, biennial. $47.50.

The two basic biographical business reference sources are this and the aforementioned *Poor's Register*. The *Who's Who* entry is not so extensive,

---

[26] *The Booklist*, November 1, 1976, pp. 421–422.

[27] *The New York Times*, November 15, 1970, p. 47. This is a brief report on the controversy.

having about 25,000 sketches as compared with 80,000 listings in *Poor's*. However, more information is given about individuals in the Marquis publication, and it has the added advantage of including not only Americans and Canadians, but businesspeople from around the world. (Also, it costs $47.50, compared with $140 for the other title.) There is a handy index to principal businesses which lists the executives cited in the volume.

Aside from biographical works relating to literature, there are more biographical directories and dictionaries for business than for almost any other profession. At least two dozen or more who's who forms are available for insurance, railroads, chemistry, the automobile industry, etc. For current information on individual executives, the best single source is the *Wall Street Journal Index*, followed by the index to *The New York Times*. And, to be sure, there is always The H. W. Wilson Company *Business Index*. If the individual is notable only in the locality, the best source of information for the librarian is the local newspaper, if it has a library; or, failing that, contact can be made with the local chamber of commerce.

Librarianship

> *Biographical Directory of Librarians in the United States and Canada.* 5th ed. Chicago: American Library Association, 1970, 1268 pp. $45.
>
> *Dictionary of American Library Biography.* Littleton, Colorado: Libraries Unlimited, Inc., 1977. $65.

The basic directory for librarians is the American Library Association publication, which lists some 20,000 names. Brief biographical data are given for each individual—data which were gathered by questionnaires completed by the various entrants. The results are generally accurate, although here and there one finds a friend or two whose age is possibly a bit more than indicated. The problem: the *Directory* is now much dated. A revision is in progress at this writing. Meanwhile, the *American Library Directory*, mentioned in Chapter 6, is at least a good way of checking who works where, although it does not give specific biographical information.

Thoroughly researched biographies of over 300 outstanding American librarians and other figures in United States library history are the scope of the *Dictionary of American Library Biography*. The major difference between this and the *American Library Directory* is this: Entrants must be quite dead to be included. Also, it contains essays rather than short directory-type data. The signed biographical sketches vary from 1000 to 6000 words and conclude with a selected bibliography of source material about the individual.

Literature

> *World Authors, 1950–1970.* New York: The H. W. Wilson Company, 1975, 1594 pp. $60.
>
> *Contemporary Authors.* Detroit: Gale Research Company, 1962 to date, quarterly. $38. (Note: Frequency varies.)
>
> Rush, Theressa, and Carol F. Myers. *Black American Writers Past and Present: A Biographical and Bibliographical Dictionary.* Metuchen, New Jersey: Scarecrow Press, 1975, 2 vols. $30.
>
> *The Junior Book of Authors*, 2d ed. New York: The H. W. Wilson Company, 1951, 309 pp. $12. *More Junior Authors*, 1963, 253 pp. $12. *Third Book of Junior Authors*, 1972, 320 pp. $14.
>
> Commire, Anne. *Something About the Author. Facts and Figures About Contemporary Authors and Illustrators of Books for Young People.* Detroit: Gale Research Company, 1972 to date, annual. $25.

There are biographical essay collections for many subject areas. One of the most often consulted concerns writers and writing. Primarily because of having to write class reports, students use the library often for information on specific authors. When the author is well known, there is little difficulty. A good encyclopedia will give information, supplemented by literature handbooks and periodical articles.

Where information is desired about lesser-known, deceased writers or modern writers, the normal ready-reference sources rarely suffice. Here, a particular series is especially useful.

The best-known series on authors is edited by Stanley J. Kunitz. All the works are issued by the Wilson Company. They are useful because they not only give the essential biographical information but also include bibligraphies of works by and about the author. The source of much of the material is the author, if living, or careful research, if the author is deceased. Some of the entries are printed almost verbatim as written by the author and are entertaining reading in their own right.

An example of the series is *World Authors 1950–1970*, edited by John Wakeman, with Stanley Kunitz as a consultant. International in scope, the alphabetically arranged volume includes material on 959 authors, most of whom came to prominence between 1950 and 1970, or for one reason or another were not included in previous volumes. Entries run from 800 to 1600 words, with a picture of the writer and a listing of published works as well as major bio-bibliographies. The style is informative, and about one-half the biographies include autobiographical essays.[28]

---

[28] Related titles in the H. W. Wilson series, *Twentieth Century Authors*, 1942; and the *Supplement*, 1955. Until publication of *World Authors*, the two titles were the basic sources of "current"

The Wilson series leave a serious gap in that the volumes are revised infrequently and do not offer access to newer writers. Also, the Wilson works disregard authors of more ephemeral titles. Here *Contemporary Authors* is of assistance.

Almost any published American writer is included in the *Contemporary Authors* volumes; the qualifications according to a publicity release by the publisher are:

> *The author must have had at least one book published by a commercial, risk publisher or a university press within the last three or four years. . . . Novelists, poets, dramatists, juvenile writers, writers of nonfiction in the social sciences or the humanities are all covered.*

In fact, just about anyone who has published anything (this side of a vanity or a technical book) is listed. And in late 1977 the publisher went a step further, expanding coverage to include newspaper and television reporters, columnists, editors, syndicated cartoonists, screenwriters, and just about anyone in the media.

The information is gathered from questionnaires sent to the authors and arranged in data form—personal facts, career data, writings, and "sidelights." The last feature is relatively new and includes discursive remarks about the author and his or her work. As the "sidelights" are written by the author, they are somewhat less than objective. On an average, an entry consists of about 300 words per author, in contrast with much longer entries in the Wilson series.

As of late 1977, the various volumes included about 46,000 contemporary writers.[29] This makes *Contemporary Authors* the most comprehensive biographical source of its type, and it is a blessing when one looks for little-known writers. There is an index at the end of each volume, as well as a cumulative index to the first 40 issues. Major world authors are included, but only about 40 percent of the names found in *World Authors* are listed. The work is primarily of value for finding data on American writers who are included nowhere else.

Unfortunately, most of the biographical works still continue to skim the surface, adopting and perpetuating the conventional notion that the blacks and other minorities (often including women) have been less than

---

information on writers. They now may be used to supplement *World Authors*. For deceased writers, Wilson has four author titles: *American Authors, 1600–1900*, 1938; *European Authors: 1000–1900*, 1967; *British Authors before 1800*, 1952; *British Authors of the Nineteenth Century*, 1936. All these follow the style of *World Authors* and are indexed in the aforementioned *Index to the Wilson Author Series*.

[29] Since it began, the series has undergone numerous publishing changes. Now issued quarterly, the cumulated volumes are numbered as 1–4, 57–60, 61–64, etc.

important in history. This practice seems particularly true in studies of writers, and *Black American Writers . . .* is an effort to begin to balance the biographical sources. The two volumes include bio-bibliographical sketches of some 2000 black American writers from the early eighteenth century through the close of 1973. Its numerous other features include a 60-page general bibliography and a section of statements by living authors which reflect their ideas. Although far from perfect—some entries are only a line or two and there is no discrimination regarding the quality of a writer's work—nonetheless, this is the most exhaustive source of its type.

Children's writers also are often overlooked, although here the matter is somewhat better handled by the Wilson series, *Junior Book of Authors.* The series is the most reliable in-depth material on writers for young people compiled in a single place. Somewhat less satisfactory, although more up to date, is the Gale work, *Something About the Author*, which follows the same general style as *Contemporary Authors* with the added visual advantage of large pictures of the authors and, often, illustrations from the works of artists who are covered. The volumes, which appear approximately on an annual basis, include about 200 writers and illustrators per volume, and there is a good system of cumulative indexing.

The ever-present problem of currency—i.e., of locating an author who has just appeared on the scene and is not recorded in any of the standard titles—can be met to a degree by consulting various indexes and the current sources mentioned in this chapter. Particularly useful is *The New York Times* service; but, in addition, there are two other excellent sources. The first is the announcement issue of the *Library Journal* three times a year. Normally, each announcement number includes 30 to 60 articles, usually prepared by the author in reply to specific questions by the *Journal* staff. The second is *Publishers Weekly*, another R. R. Bowker publication, which begins each issue with a "PW Interview," usually of an author, an illustrator, or even a publisher. Additional information on contemporary figures may be found in reviews of their works via *The Book Review Digest, Book Review Index*, and *Current Book Review Citations*.

Music

The first three of the following, edited by David Ewen, are published by The H. W. Wilson Company.

Great Composers: 1300–1900. 1966, 429 pp., $15.

Composers since 1900. 1969, 639 pp., $20.

Popular American Composers. 1962, 217 pp., $8; first supplement, 1972, 121 pp., $6.

Baker, Theodore. *Biographical Dictionary of Musicians.* 5th ed.

New York: G. Schirmer. Completely revised by Nicolas Slonimsky, with 1971 supplement. 1855 pp. plus supplement, 262 pp. $40.

As when searching for a literary biography, the librarian will have little difficulty in finding an adequate biographical sketch or essay on a prominent composer or musician. Almost all encyclopedias devote considerable space to such biographical material, and the truly "greats" are to be found in both the current and the retrospective general sources discussed earlier. The works listed here are only a few of dozens which are useful not so much for the well-known musicians as for additional information on lesser-known figures. For example, the three Wilson entries, with their essays written by David Ewen, cover both well-known and almost forgotten composers. They generally consist of rather long biographical pieces with bibliographies and portraits. The series is not intellectually taxing and is particularly suited for the nonspecialist in the public or the high school library. One note: The supplement to *Popular American Composers* includes numerous biographical sketches of rock and roll composers of the 1960s, as well as a few motion picture and Broadway theatre musicians. An added reference feature in the main work and the supplement is the index to over 4000 songs and other compositions mentioned in the text. The work is dated, but still extremely useful for running down this or that elusive bit of music or composer.

Baker's *Biographical Dictionary of Musicians*, a classic in the field, includes a number of popular musicians in the 1971 supplement, but the strength of the work is primarily in its provision of biographical sketches of older figures in the field. These figures include not only composers, but singers, pianists, conductors, etc. There are now some 16,000 entries which vary from a few lines to several pages. Despite the work's long life span—going back to 1900—the various editors have managed to update the information with each new edition. This is evident in the useful bibliographies, which include periodical articles. The problem, as of this writing, is that it is almost 20 years since a new edition was issued, and one is badly needed.

A good example of another long-lived biographical source is Oscar Thompson's *International Cyclopedia of Music and Musicians* (New York: Dodd, Mead & Company, 1975, 2511 pp.). Actually, however, it is a bad example in that Baker's strong point of including older figures is a weak point here. Oscar Thompson died in 1945 and the work was taken over by Bruce Bohle, who issued a tenth edition in 1974. This was a landmark of sorts in that it offered Americans an American viewpoint of serious music and musicians. (Baker, an Englishman, is long dead, but the English influence continues.) Almost all aspects of classical music are discussed, from composers to opera titles to popular names of orchestral works. So far, fine.

The trouble is that the tenth edition really is little more than a reprint of the ninth edition. There are some additions and some corrections, but on the whole the editor failed to learn the lesson so well mastered by Baker's editor, i.e., a new edition should be just that, and not merely a copy of the previous work.

The standard work in this field, noted in Chapter 5, on encyclopedias, is *The New Grove Dictionary of Music and Musicians*. There are some 12,000 articles on composers, and many more on other musicians. And, of course, the librarian should never forget the existence of a number of specialized indexes to music, e.g., *Music Index* (Detroit, Michigan: Information Coordinators, 1949 to date, monthly), which include references to biographies in the indexing of over 300 periodicals. *Popular Periodical Index* and *Access* are two general indexes which are particularly useful for tracking down the elusive modern singer, composer, musician, and other performers.

SUGGESTED READING

"Biography for the Young Reader," *Children's Literature in Education*, no. 22, Autumn 1976. Most of the issue is devoted to articles on what constitutes good or bad biography for children, and includes information of value to a reference librarian seeking data on the subject.

Goldman, Eric F., "Dictionary of American Biography," *The New York Times Book Review*, September 30, 1973, pp. 14–16. A short history and analysis of the DAB and its supplement by a leading history professor.

Halpenny, Frances G., "The Advancement of Biography: Reference Needs and the Dictionary of Canadian Biography," *Ontario Library Review*, September 1977, pp. 171–175. A discussion of how names are selected for a national biography. While the discussion is limited to Canada, the general rules are applicable to other sets of this type.

Hoffberg, Judith, "The Taming of Who's Who," *The Unabashed Librarian*, Spring 1976, pp. 19–20. An amusing, yet accurate story of what it means to fill out a type of who's who questionnaire for one service. They all began to write asking for your name.

Rosenfeld, Patti, "Playing the Fame Game," *Medical Dimensions*, January 1974, pp. 22–23. The author asks, "How much does it actually help to have a listing in *Who's Who*?" In answering the query, the writer gives a history of the work.

Safire, William, "In the Name of the Plume," *The New York Times*, December 2, 1976, p. 45. A short, amusing article on "the flight from pseudonymity," the current trend away from using pseudonyms in writing. The result, Safire says, is that writers "now oppress us with the reality of their true names."

CHAPTER EIGHT

Dictionaries

T HE GENERAL DICTIONARY has a main mission and a secondary mission. Regardless of price, number of entries, or any other considerations, a dictionary must indicate spelling, meaning, pronunciation, and syllabication (word division). Surprisingly enough, there are some that fail on one or several of these counts.

As a secondary mission, a dictionary, preferably in a single alphabet, should indicate etymology; major place names (with a clear indication of whether the entry represents a river, a mountain, or other item); major personal names from history, mythology, and the Bible; foreign terms; phrases; synonyms and antonyms; abbreviations; and general slang terms, clearly marked. Some dictionaries include other types of information almost encyclopedic in nature, and most have illustrations of varying number and quality.

The main mission is self-evident, but there are other, less apparent, uses tied in with the secondary mission. As many dictionaries include quotes to trace either the meaning or the history of a word, one may use the key word of a quote to trace its source (when a book of quotations is not available or all such sources have been exhausted). For example, under "prudence" in *Webster's Dictionary of Synonyms,* a searcher recently found the source of the quote "That type of person who is conservative from prudence but revolutionary in his dreams." It is by T. S. Eliot. A good historical dictionary will also indicate the first time a word was employed, hence the source of so-called first facts. Using *The Oxford English Dictionary*, it may be established that flypaper first came into use in 1848. (*The Dictionary of American English* gives the date as 1847, but this is another matter.)

A dictionary is to be used to define not only words we do not know but also words we think we know. Usually words of this latter type are known imperfectly, and the chances are good that any student paper will reveal such words. For example, every cub reporter soon learns that it is dangerous to use the word "consummate" in a wedding story, and that the "past ten days" is considerably better form than the "last ten days."

Language, which relies on emotive symbols, is a slippery beast and is insusceptible to being exactly fixed. Logicians and philosophers attempt to do so, of course, and with varying success, but no single dictionary is totally satisfactory. Any so-called emotive word (for example, "happiness," "democracy," "freedom," "love," etc.) requires interpretation, and this is the best one can expect a dictionary to do, normally by astute quotations from spoken and written speech.

There is, also, the differences in word use and pronunciation not only between England and America, but from region to region—differences not often noted in general dictionaries. For example, the average dictionary gives one pronunciation for the nation's capital, but in New England it is called *Wash*ington while in parts of the South it is pronunced *Wush*ington, and it becomes *Wursh*ington in the Southwest. And even the most brash Englishman would not call a "wireless" by the Americanism "radio," or manage to change a "barber" into a "tonsorial artist." In other words (pun intended), not all words are to be found in dictionaries as they are used person to person.[1]

Scope

The public is apt to think of dictionaries in only one category, but they cover almost every interest. Categorization usually is reduced to (1) general English-language dictionaries which include unabridged titles (i.e., those with over 265,000 entries) and desk or collegiate dictionaries (those having from 130,000 to 180,000 entries); these are for both adults and children; (2) historical or etymological dictionaries which show the history of a word from date of introduction to the present; (3) foreign-language dictionaries which are bilingual in that they give the meanings of the

---

[1] Dialect geography is one answer to this problem, and there are numerous experts in this field both here and in England, as well as in other countries. For an explanation of these cousins to Prof. Henry Higgins, see William Safire, "Secrets of American English May Yield to Dialect Geography," *The New York Times* ("The Week in Review"), September 28, 1975, p. 8.

words of one language in another language; (4) subject dictionaries which concentrate on the definition of words in a given area such as science and technology; and (5) "other" dictionaries including almost everything from abbreviations to slang and proper usage. For example, a library not only will have on its shelves the standard *Webster's Third New International* and the usual desk, foreign-language, and subject dictionaries, but also may include such titles as *The Misspeller's Dictionary, Funk & Wagnalls Crossword Puzzle Word Finder,* and *The Poet's Manual and Rhyming Dictionary.* These are only isolated examples of "other" or specialized dictionaries for particular groups and interests.

Compilation

As the written and spoken words are the source for the dictionary entry, how is a dictionary compiled?

In the beginning, it was basically an individual effort. Dr. Johnson, for example, worked alone, although he did have six assistants for clerical duties. He wrote all the definitions himself, and Boswell explains:

> The words, partly taken from other dictionaries and partly supplied by himself, having been first written down with spaces left between them, he delivered in writing their etymologies, definitions, and various significations. The authorities were copied from the books themselves.[2]

Today, the smaller publishers freely copy other dictionaries. They begin by an out-and-out borrowing of words from a dictionary that is no longer copyrighted. More conscientious publishers then hire free-lance lexicographers to make a minimum number of corrections and additions. Others, some of whose handiwork are the dictionaries on display in some supermarkets or low-priced pocket dictionaries, merely borrow without benefit of any editing.

A curious feature of the second edition of *Webster's Unabridged* was the inclusion of a "ghost word." The word "dord" was simply an error, on the part of an overzealous clerk, which resulted in its inclusion as a loose synonym for density. After the error was discovered, the publishers decided to keep it in the dictionary for a few years in the hope that one of the aforementioned publishers might pick it up and be caught as a plagiarist. The word later was eliminated, and there is no record of whether or not it served its purpose.

Plagiarism is not unknown, then, in the dictionary business; but a

---

[2] *Boswell's Life of Johnson,* ed. by G. B. Hill (New York: Bigelow, Brown & Co., n.d.), vol. 1, pp. 217–218.

certain amount of guidance from other dictionaries is legitimate. Dr. Johnson checked previous works to ascertain what might or might not be included in his dictionary, and much the same procedure is used by all compilers today. Smaller verions of "unabridged" works, such as *Webster's New Collegiate Dictionary,* are common.

EVALUATION

For those who seek to evaluate any dictionary, the golden rule was laid down first by Dr. Johnson, who said, "Dictionaries are like watches: the worst is better than none, and the best cannot be expected to go quite true." There is no perfect dictionary and there never will be until such time as the language of a country has become completely static—an event as unlikely as the discovery of a perpetual-motion mechanism. Language is always evolving, if only because of the addition of new words and the change in meaning of older words. Nor is any single dictionary sufficient. Each has its good points, each its defects.

The second rule should be self-evident, but rarely is it followed: Consult the preface and explanatory notes at the beginning of a dictionary. The art of successfully using a dictionary, or any other reference book, requires an understanding of how it is put together. This is important because of the dictionary's constant use of shortcuts in form of abbreviations, various methods of indicating pronunciation, and grammatical approaches.

The best single source of evaluation of dictionaries is Kenneth Kister's *Dictionary Buying Guide* (New York: R. R. Bowker Company, 1977. 500 pp.). This follows the same general style as his *Encyclopedia Buying Guide,* gives data on some 350 English-language dictionaries and complementary wordbooks on slang, usage and so on. Comparison is often made between dictionaries, and the librarian-author is quick to point out both strong and weak points in each publisher's offering.

For ongoing reviews, the source is "Reference and Subscription Books Reviews" in *The Booklist.* Dictionaries are frequently considered, and from time to time there is a "roundup" of titles in which comparisons are made between the different dictionaries.

Authority In order to discuss with any meaning how to evaluate a general English-language dictionary, it should be first understood that, as in the case of encyclopedias, there are only a limited number of publishers whose works have been accepted as satisfactory by any reliable authority.

In the unabridged field, there are three major publishers:

1. G. & C. Merriam Company (Encyclopaedia Britannica, Inc.), which publishes *Webster's Third New International Dictionary.*
2. Funk & Wagnalls, which publishes *Funk & Wagnalls New Standard Dictionary.*
3. Random House, Inc., which publishes *The Random House Dictionary of the English Language.*

The same publishers issue abridged, college, or desk dictionaries, but a number of other reputable firms are also in this more limited field. More particularly, Houghton Mifflin, the World Publishing Company, and Doubleday are longtime publishers of quite acceptable abridged dictionaries.

In specialized fields and other areas where dictionaries are employed, there are almost as many reputable publishers as there are works. No particular monopoly of either quality or quantity exists outside the standard unabridged and desk dictionary fields.

Often, the name "Webster" is the golden sign of reassurance, and it frequently is found as the principal name of a number of dictionaries. The original claim to use the name is held by G. & C. Merriam Company, which bought out the unsold copies of Noah Webster's dictionary at the time of his death. For years, the use of Webster's name was the subject of litigation. G. & C. Merriam finally lost its case when the copyright on the name lapsed. It is now common property and may be used by any publisher. Hence, the name "Webster's" in the title may or may not have something to do with the original work which bore the name. Unless the publisher's name is recognized, "Webster" per se means nothing.

For example, in 1976 full-page ads in many newspapers offered an "authentic" *Webster's Dictionary* for the "incredible" and "unprecedented" price of $19.95. The implication was that the publisher (Ralph Ginzburg of *Moneysworth,* a magazine to save consumers money and protect them from fraudulent advertising) offered the G. & C. Merriam dictionary, which retails for over $50, at only $19.95. There was absolutely no connection between the two dictionaries except the name "Webster's." Incidentally, the $19.95 version could be had in many bookstores for $14.98.

Vocabulary Vocabulary may be considered in terms of the period of the language covered and the number of words or entries. These terms may be extended to include special features such as slang, dialect, obsolete forms, and scientific or technical terms. Still, the primary consideration comes down to the question of how many words or definitions will be found.

In the United States, this problem is divided nicely between the "unabridged" and the "abridged" types of dictionary. Most dictionaries are abridged or limited to given areas. The three unabridged works vary from some 450,000 entries each for *Webster's* and *Funk & Wagnalls* to 260,000 for *Random House*. The abridged dictionaries normally run from 130,000 to 150,000 entries.

How important is it to have a dictionary of more than, say, 100,000 words? Potentially, the number of words in the English vocabulary is infinite, but several experts have surmised that only 340,000 different graphic forms or types exist in our language at any one time. Which is to say, some 100,000 of the words found in *Webster's Third* are (1) obsolete; or (2) unusual items extant only in isolated contexts; or more likely, (3) in large part, not really different types, but simply different definitions of the same word.

What, then, constitutes a legitimate entry which may be counted as one word? Most dictionaries—at least for the advertising copywriter—count each of the definitions, not the separate entries. For example, *The Random House Dictionary of the English Language, College Edition,* claims 155,000 entries. A careful critic estimated the real number of entries, i.e., separate words, at under 100,000.

How many words are really required for most users? D. R. Tallentire, who has done an extensive study of the subject, reports:

> *Even our most prolific and admired writers seldom exhibit more than 30,000 different types in a lifetime of writing. Of course, their latent vocabularies (the words known though not necessarily used) far exceed this number. . . . For example, Shakespeare's prodigious output comprises only 29,066 different words. . . . Shakespeare's vocabulary is less than three times larger than the 10,666 types of W. B. Yeats or the 10,097 of Matthew Arnold, though Shakespeare's total works comprise more than six times the output of either poet. . . . Though Shakespeare's revealed vocabulary represents less than 10 percent of the extant 340,000 words of English, it still accounts for more than 90 percent of the words appearing on any page of literature we care to examine . . . 10 percent of the vocabulary of English cover 90 percent of the text of all the volumes of literature in all our libraries.*[3]

Furthermore, Tallentire found that "about 135 words recur with sufficient frequency to constitute 50 percent of most texts." In another study, researchers excerpted 10,000 samples of 500 words each from 1000 of the most frequently used titles in grades 3 through 9. Overall, the survey found some 87,000 different words; but of these, 35,000 appeared only

[3] D. R. Tallentire, "The Mathematics of Style," *The Times Literary Supplement,* August 13, 1971, p. 973.

once in the sample. They were typically such unusual items as "goody-goody," "Hippiesque," and "hightail."[4]

Continuous Revision   A very large number of dictionaries (unabridged and abridged) tend to be 5 to 10 years old. Each year, a new work, or a new edition, comes along; but, on the whole, the original copyright date signifies the time when most of the words in the dictionary were entered. (Possibly, although not necessarily, revision is indicated, as in encyclopedias, by the new copyright date; on the verso of most title pages will be found, for example, "Copyright 1966, 1970, 1977," and so on. The first date indicates the initial work.)

Somewhat like encyclopedia publishers, the major dictionary firms employ a type of continuous revision. With each new printing, they may add or delete a given number of words. This is particularly true of the desk dictionaries which are most used by young people and must reflect current usage and new words introduced into the language via radio, television, music, technology, and the like. On the whole, the system works rather well. No library, then, should necessarily scuttle a standard title merely because a new one comes along which claims to be entirely revised. Where a completely new approach is offered, the library may then want to add the work to its general dictionary collection. Otherwise, by purchasing a revised edition of a standard desk dictionary each year, the library will be able to keep up with most problems of current vocabulary.

Special Features   In addition to being concerned with authority and the number of words, the average layperson is most interested in the added features. Many dictionaries are encyclopedic in that they include items such as illustrations, special lists, historical data, and biographical information. For example, *Funk & Wagnalls Comprehensive Standard International Dictionary* contains some 2000 pages, of which about one-fifth carry supplementary material such as quotations, almanac-type information, and a section on writing business letters. Almost all this material is readily available elsewhere in libraries, and although the dictionary may be acceptable for home use, it is a poor choice for the average library. A dictionary of the same size with double the number of words will be much more useful.

---

[4] Andrew H. Malcolm, "Most Common Verb in Schools . . ." *The New York Times,* September 4, 1971, p. 22. The study was conducted by the editors of *The American Heritage Dictionary.* A more current published study is Edgar Dale and Joseph O'Rourke, *The Living World Vocabulary, The Words We Know: A National Vocabulary Inventory* (Chicago: Field Enterprises, 1976). The study is used by the *World Book* editors.

Format In evaluating the format of a dictionary, the most noticeable item is the print size and how its readability is affected by spacing between words, the use of boldface type, and the differences in type families. Individual tastes will play an important part in evaluating this factor, but from the viewpoint of many users, *The American Heritage Dictionary* is the best for its typography. Here it is instructive simply to compare the typography of this single dictionary with that in other works.

With the exception of some colored plates, most dictionary illustrations are black-and-white line drawings. Where appropriate, the actual size of the object illustrated should be indicated, as, for example, in the case of an animal or a plant. As to number: The average desk dictionary has from 600 to 1500 illustrations, the unabridged from 7000 to 12,000.

None of the dictionaries by major publishers can be severely criticized on grounds of format, but it is interesting to note that many questionable works frequently give themselves away by the very lack of a pleasing format. A distasteful appearance is more often the result of using old, worn plates from another dictionary than of a design of the publisher. When the paper is of poor quality, the typography runs toward gray, and the illustrations are obviously dated or inconsequential, these facts constitute a good warning signal that the dictionary is possibly inferior.

Usage Although traditional titles have regularly prescribed rules for correct usage by most Americans, the ultimate authority is the dictionary. But which dictionary? Up until the publication of *Webster's Third*, it was *Webster's Second*. With the advent of the latter title, the editors broke with tradition. The third made little or no effort to prescribe correct usage. Critics contend that it opened the floodgate of permissiveness, providing no rule other than popularity. This laxity, it is argued, not only removes *Webster's* as a source of proper usage, but in so doing, clears the road for progressive deterioration of the language.

The editors abolished such labels as "colloquial" and "slang" and replaced them with general prescriptive terms such as "standard" and "substandard." Furthermore, many words labeled as slang in the earlier edition are now left unlabeled. Today it is safe to generalize that almost all modern dictionaries are descriptive rather than prescriptive. However, and this is a major "however," while most dictionaries are descriptive in giving current usage, they may become prescriptive when they use labels to reflect what is poor, best, or better usage. For example, *The American Heritage Dictionary* gives the same definition of a word, at least in essence, as *Webster's Third*, but makes a point of advertising the extensive use of proper usage labels. Conversely, the *American College Dictionary* is less rigorous in labeling because the editors do not believe it is the function of a dictionary to be a guide to usage.

Arguments for the descriptive and prescriptive schools may be summarized briefly. The *descriptive* advocates who now govern the compilation of almost every major dictionary claim:

1. The people dictate the proper usage of the language. Consequently, when illustrating the definition of a word in a modern dictionary, it is important to use quotes not only from good literature, but also from newspapers, television programs, and speeches.
2. One does not go to the dictionary to find language standards or rules for proper usage. Spelling, pronunciation, and definitions are important, but standards and usage are not.
3. A particular word used frequently enough by many people becomes acceptable.

The *prescriptive* group asserts that the major role of a dictionary is to set standards:

1. Word definitions and approved usage should adhere to tradition and authority based upon correct historic usage.
2. Support of this philosophy is essential in order to prevent the contamination of the pure language by jargon, lingo, and fashionable jargon.
3. Failure to maintain these principles is virtually an agreement to debase the language.

The descriptive-prescriptive debate goes far beyond the attitudes of a dictionary's editorial board. One example of the continuing controversy (which is considerably more complex than the above outline might indicate) will be found in the writings of Noam Chomsky, a partisan of the descriptive or generative grammar school as opposed to the prescriptive or structuralist school.[5]

Webster's Third is essentially descriptive, whereas the only other unabridged dictionary, *Funk & Wagnalls,* is prescriptive but dated. The best usage source is *The American Heritage Dictionary,* supported by a good handbook of usage. The argument as to what is and what should be, though, will continue to rage as long as there are dictionaries.

The librarian, faced with a question about usage, is advised to consider three possible steps: (1) Consult *The American Heritage Dictionary,* which is the best desk dictionary with extensive proper-usage notes. (2) Consult a second desk dictionary, *Webster's New World Dictionary* (published

[5] A clear summary of both viewpoints is given by George Watson in "Chomsky: What Has It to Do with Literature?" *The Times Literary Supplement,* February 14, 1975, pp. 164–165. A brief bibliography is included.

by Collins-World, *not* G. & C. Merriam Company). As of 1977, this was the choice of *The New York Times* as its primary guide.[6] (3) For a difficult query, consult one of several guides to usage, such as the *Harper Dictionary of Contemporary Usage,* which concentrates on usage rules exclusively.

Even when indication of proper usage is the most debated aspect of word treatment in a dictionary, there are other elements that are of equal concern.

Spelling Where there are several forms of spelling, these should be clearly indicated. *Webster's* identifies the English spelling by the label *"Brit.";* other dictionaries normally indicate this variant by simply giving the American spelling first, e.g., "analyze, analyse" or "theater, theatre." Frequently, because of usage, two different spellings may be given, either of which is acceptable. The user must determine the form to use. For example, "addable" or "addible" and "lollipop" or "lollypop."

Etymologies All dictionaries indicate the etymology of a word by a shorthand system in brackets. The normal procedure is to show the root word in Latin, Greek, French, German, Old English, or some other language. Useful as this feature is, the student of etymology will be satisfied only with historical dictionaries, such as Mencken's *The American Language,* to trace properly the history of a word and how it developed.

Definitions Modern general dictionaries usually give the most common meaning of the word first. *Webster's* is the only one which gives definitions in historical order. Where there are several meanings, the difference is clearly indicated by numbering each of the definitions. Parts of speech (noun, adjective, verb, and so on) are separate entries.

The wording of the definition is of primary importance, and the modern trend is to be short and to employ commonly understood terms. Here, for example, are two definitions for "anthropomorphic" from two dictionaries: (1) "ascribing human form or attributes to a being or thing not human, esp. to a deity"; (2) "described or conceived in a human form or with human attributes: represented with human characteristics or under a human form: ascribing human characteristics to nonhuman things: crudely human or man-centered in character." For most purposes, not only is the first definition quite long enough, but in many ways it is clearer than the second.

---

[6] William Safire, "Newswordy Events," *The New York Times,* December 25, 1975, p. 21. The conservative columnist reports on the adoption of the dictionary by the *Times,* but admits to favoring *The American Heritage Dictionary* for usage.

Pronunciation There are different methods of indicating pronunciation, but the most common is the diacritical one. Usually, a handy key to the system is given at the bottom of every other page. Acceptable pronunciation is usually indicated, not only in general, but for specific regions.

Synonyms The average user does not turn to a general dictionary for synonyms, but their inclusion helps to differentiate between similar words. Some desk dictionaries indicate the differentiation and shades of meaning by short essays at the conclusion of many definitions.

Syllabication All dictionaries indicate how a word is to be divided into syllables. The method is usually a centered period or hyphen. The information is mainly for helping writers and editors, not to mention secretaries, in the division of a word at the end of a line. There are special short desk dictionaries which simply indicate syllabication of more common words without benefit of definition or pronunciation.

Grammatical Information The most generally useful grammatical help a dictionary renders is to indicate parts of speech. All single entries are classified as nouns, adjectives, verbs, and so on. Aside from this major division, dictionaries vary in method of showing adverbs, adjectives, plurals, and principal parts of a verb, particularly the past tenses of irregular verbs. Usually the method is clearly ascertainable; but, again, the prefatory remarks should be studied in order to understand any particular presentation.

Bias One aspect of dictionaries generally overlooked until the early 1970s was their bias against women and minority groups. Cultural prejudice against women was particularly evident. For example, many English-language dictionaries failed to distinguish any difference, other than a chronological one, between the terms "girl" and "woman." Sexist attitudes toward women in a patriarchal society are often reflected in words which reinforce what many women believe to be their second-class status.

> *Thus while* Webster's Third *describes "grandmotherly" as "having the characteristics conventionally attributed to a grandmother, specif: (a) kindly, indulgent; (b) fussy, interfering," the* [same dictionary] *defines "grandfatherly" as "benignant, old, and venerable."*[7]

With revisions, most reputable dictionaries have made a concerted

---

[7] William E. Farrell, "Feminists Find that Words Fail Them," *The New York Times,* January 28, 1974, p. 33.

effort to eliminate such definitions—helped along, one imagines, by alert reviewers, such as those for the American Library Association's Reference and Subscription Books Committee, who are quick to evaluate dictionaries for elements of racial or sexist tendencies in definitions. In considering *The Macmillan School Dictionary* (New York: Macmillan Publishing Company, 1974) and *The American Heritage School Dictionary* (Boston: Houghton Mifflin, 1972), the committee observed:

> *Both dictionaries have, apparently, made some attempt in illustrations to reflect changes of concept regarding male and female roles. Both eliminate, in most instances, the use of either gender in descriptive phrases, explaining a word by "a person who."*[8]

UNABRIDGED DICTIONARIES

Webster's New International Dictionary of the English Language. Springfield, Massachusetts: G. & C. Merriam Company, 2d ed., 1934, 3195 pp. (600,000 entries), o.p.

Webster's Third New International Dictionary. Springfield, Massachusetts: G. & C. Merriam Company, 1961, 2736 pp. (450,000 entries). $59.95. *6,000 Words, A Supplement to Webster's Third New International Dictionary*, 1976, 220 pp. $8.50.

Funk & Wagnalls New Standard Dictionary. New York: Funk & Wagnalls (Thomas Y. Crowell), 1964 (last totally revised in 1913), 2816 pp. (458,000 entries). $62.50.

Webster's

The single unabridged dictionary found in the majority of libraries and government agencies, *Webster's* was published first in 1909. A second edition came out in 1934 and a third in 1961. A 1977 dictionary has two copyright dates: 1961, the date of the original revision, and 1971, which implies some revisions since 1961. However, the work is primarily representative of the original 1961 edition. While the 1909 edition is rarely found in any library, both the second and third editions are quite commonly stocked. The two vary so radically from one another that many consider them to be almost two different works.

The differences may be summarized as follows.

[8] *The Booklist*, June 15, 1975, p. 1087.

Vocabulary The 1934 edition contains 600,000 entries; the 1961 edition, 450,000 entries. The Third was cut by eliminating some 250,000 words from the earlier work and then adding 100,000 words which have come into the language between 1934 and 1961. Because many obsolete and rare words have been deleted, the older work is absolutely necessary for historical purposes.

Special Features The 1934 edition had an appendix with abbreviations, arbitrary signs and symbols, forms of address, pronouncing gazetteer, and biographical dictionary. A reference-history edition included a supplement, "Reference History of the World," which was a basic handbook on world history. The 1961 edition deleted all these features, but major abbreviations are included in the main alphabet. However, there are few proper names or geographical entries. This means that a library must either retain the earlier edition or purchase separate volumes for biographical and gazetteer information.

Format The format is basically the same in the 1934 and 1961 works. An important typographical exception is that in the third edition, all proper names and adjectives are in lower case. For example, "Christmas," "French," and "English" are noted in lowercase, but marked, where appropriate, "usu cap" or "often cap." The only words capitalized in the dictionary are "God" and tradenames such as Kodak, Kleenex, Frisbee, and others. The rigid noncapitalization is not followed in the other versions of *Webster's*. See, for example, the explanatory notes in any *Webster's* desk dictionary.

Word Treatment The treatment of words was the single most controversial point regarding the 1961 edition. Following the descriptive school, the third edition included many words not qualified by certain terms found in the earlier editions. The label "colloquial" was completely dropped, being replaced by "substandard" or "nonstandard." Labeling with these terms, and others such as "slang," is used cautiously. Many items were left unlabeled, e.g., "ain't" ("though disapproved by many . . . used orally by many cultivated speakers"). The new concept of acceptability is reason enough for all libraries to have the second edition on hand to double-check the proper use of a given word. The earlier work definitely was under the control of the prescriptive advocates.

Quotations The Second tended to use classical and standard quotations; the Third's 100,000 or so quotes are largely drawn from contemporary sources, i.e., newspapers, magazines, speeches of politicians, and writers such as P. G. Wodehouse and Mickey Spillane.

Other Elements In both works, the historical meaning is given first; pronunciations are indicated by methods unique to *Webster's,* and the third edition represents a radical change in procedure from the Second; quotations in the 1934 edition are chiefly from literary classics, but in the Third, they are from many popular sources as well as the classics.

There are other differences, many of them controversial, but suffice it to say that both editions will be essential in any library. The Second may be difficult to obtain. Booksellers report a constant demand for the earlier work.

In 1976 G. & C. Merriam published a supplement to the main work, with the title *6,000 Words . . . ,* which adds that number of terms to the 1961 edition. Most of the new entries come from science and technology, but the supplement is equally good for popular music and slang.

Funk & Wagnalls

While a completely new revision of this work has not been made since 1913, it has been kept relatively up to date by inserting new words, compressing definitions of older words, and adding supplements with newer printings. It includes some 450,000 entries; but of these, over 65,000 are proper names not found in *Webster's Third.*

The essential differences between this work and *Webster's* are that in the *Funk & Wagnalls*:

1. Common, modern definitions precede the historical.
2. The pronunciation key is considerably easier to use and understand.
3. The format is more pleasing, particularly the judicious use of boldface and good spacing.
4. There are a number of illustrative phrases and quotations which differ from *Webster's* in terms of both sources and emphasis.
5. Usage is clearly indicated by standard labels, and in this respect, the *Funk & Wagnalls* is better than *Webster's Third,* but not up to the Second.
6. More encyclopedic information is included than in *Webster's.*

There are other differences, such as the *Funk & Wagnalls* preference for simplified spelling and the emphasis on illustrations; but one major drawback to the work is that it is spotty. Although the continuous revision program is well done, it must be kept within the pagination of the 1913 edition. Consequently, for everything added, something must be deleted or compressed and supplements added. Were it not for this one significant fault, it would be a real competitor in a library to *Webster's*. As it now stands, it is only a second choice.

With the exception of the aforementioned dictionaries, there are no unabridged dictionaries entirely suitable for either library or personal use. The abridged *Oxford English Dictionary* in one volume, distributed widely by a national book club, is an excellent dictionary, but in no way replaces the American works.

ENCYCLOPEDIC-TYPE DICTIONARIES

The Random House Dictionary of the English Language. New York: Random House, 1966, 2059 pp. (260,000 entries). $35.

Funk & Wagnalls Comprehensive Standard International Dictionary: Bicentennial Edition. New York: Funk & Wagnalls (Thomas Y. Crowell), 1973, 1929 pp. (175,000 entries). $49.95.

Chiefly because of bulk size and added material, the "encyclopedic" dictionary stands between the unabridged and the standard desk dictionary. With the exception of the Random House entry, most encyclopedic dictionaries have no more words than a desk dictionary, but add to their price by including extraneous materials (usually at the end of the dictionary proper) which are encyclopedic in nature. Many "supermarket" dictionaries are of this variety, particularly the ubiquitous *"Webster's,"* which may be made to look as large as the unabridged versions simply by padding with usually dated, unorganized information.

Random House

Many libraries are likely to bypass the usual rule against encyclopedic dictionaries in the case of *The Random House Dictionary*. The reason is that this title includes 260,000 words, or about 100,000 more than contained in the usual desk or encyclopedic dictionary. While still not up to the 450,000 words in *Webster's Third*, the *Random House* is impressive in the number of words included, and it more than meets the needs of smaller libraries where an unabridged dictionary may not be necessary.

Aside from the rather pointless (at least from a library point of view) added material at the end of the volume, many critics were disenchanted with *The Random House Dictionary* because it is divided between the descriptive and prescriptive philosophy. It tends to be more liberal (giving "nonstandard," "informal," "slang," and similar usages) than *Webster's*; but at the same time, it accepts many questionable words. Definitions are fairly concise (some users claim, too brief) but usually quite clear. Quotations support the definitions, albeit the majority are composed by the editors. The results are sometimes ludicrous. For example, quotations used to support "begin," "contain," and "naked," are "Where shall I begin?" "This glass contains water." "The children swam naked in the lake." More difficult words often slip by without quotations.

Although not mentioned in the following section on desk and college dictionaries, *The Random House College Dictionary* (rev. ed.; New York: Random House, 1975) is based upon the larger work. It has some 170,000 entries, and because of its relatively recent revision, is one of the most up-to-date dictionaries of its type. It is rightfully found in many libraries.

Funk & Wagnalls

Although a good dictionary, this is an example of the dictionary not needed in libraries. It is suitable for home use because of the 420 pages of encyclopedic supplemental material which includes quotations, ready-reference types of materials, grammar and usage, geographical and historical data, etc. For the same reason it is a poor choice for libraries, if only because the price is a few dollars less than either of the unabridged dictionaries, and considerably higher than that of the best standard desk dictionaries which have an equal number of words—about 170,000—as the Funk & Wagnalls entry. And, like so many desk dictionaries, the work is descriptive rather than prescriptive.

DESK (COLLEGIATE) DICTIONARIES

The American Heritage Dictionary of the English Language, New College Edition. Boston: Houghton Mifflin Company, 1969, 1550 pp. (155,000 entries). $9.95.

Webster's New World Dictionary of the American Language. New York: Collins-World, 2d ed., 1972, 1728 pp. (157,374 entries). $10.95.

Webster's New Collegiate Dictionary, 8th ed. Springfield, Massachusetts: G. & C. Merriam Company, 1973, 1568 pp. (152,000 entries). $9.95.

Note: All prices are for thumb-indexed versions. Prices are usually about $1 less for the non–thumb-indexed work.

The standard publishers' dictionaries are periodically revised and all are authoritative. Differences are essentially of format, arrangement, systems of indicating pronunciation, and length of definitions. All feature synonyms, antonyms, etymologies, and limited biographical and gazetteer information. Price variations are minimal, the normal range being under $10. There are enough variations in binding, thumb indexing, and other such things that publishers' catalogs should be consulted for versions of the basic editions.

Houghton Mifflin

In terms of price, format, scholarship, and ease of use, *The American Heritage Dictionary* is the "best buy" in dictionaries of the desk and college type. It has two major claims for attention. (1) Illustrations: The publisher claims there are 3500 illustrations and more than 200 maps. These are placed at irregular intervals down the broad and otherwise blank outer margins of the pages. Most are halftones based upon great paintings and drawings. They are far better than those in any other dictionary, regardless of size. Furthermore, the typography, spacing, and so on, are excellent. These features all add up to ease of reading and explanation through illustrations. (2) Prescriptive entries: One of the major selling points of this dictionary is that it provides definite guidance on acceptable usage. The *Random House* does the same, but it tends to be more temperate; the *Heritage* is more forthright.

Another valuable feature is the appendix, which includes a lengthy list of the Indo-European roots and the English words that embody them. This etymology feature complements rather extensive etymologies in the body of the dictionary.

Many dictionary publishers have just as many versions of the standard desk dictionary. A good example is Houghton Mifflin and its American Heritage series, which not only includes *The American Heritage Dictionary* listed here, but also a "larger format" edition, *The American Heritage Dictionary of the English Language* ($12.95); *The American Heritage School Dictionary* ($8.95) for schools; *The Concise Heritage Dictionary* ($5.95) with 55,000 entries for middle schools; and *The Word Book* ($2.95), which cuts back the number of entries to the 40,000 most often used words. Furthermore, there is an encyclopedic version, *The Illustrated Heritage Dictionary and Information Book* ($29.95), which is the basic dictionary plus added sections on American history, quotations, a five-language dictionary of French, Italian, etc. Each of these publications fulfills some need, but not for the library. In the library, the best bet is the "new college edition" which has the basic vocabulary, less all the frills, or, as the case may be, more words than are provided in the cut-down versions. Other publishers tend to follow the same approach, and in every case this side of the unabridged dictionaries, the library is better off with the standard "college" editions, no matter what they may be called. Another possible exception might be the special dictionaries, such as *The Concise Heritage Dictionary*, which can be used in junior high schools and even high schools as a bridge between the children's dictionary and the college dictionary.

World

Webster's New World Dictionary of the American Language is not a G. & C. Merriam *"Webster's"*; but unlike any supermarket dictionaries that boast the same name, it is a quite legitimate desk dictionary. Published by World, it represents, like the *The American Heritage,* a new work not based upon a larger dictionary. It includes some 157,000 entries in a single alphabet but definitions are given in chronological order rather than by frequency of modern usage.

It is particularly strong on contemporary American vocabulary and the latest technological terms. Another feature is the inclusion of a considerable number of colloquialisms, slang expressions, and idiomatic expressions, all clearly labeled. In fact, a point for the World entry, and one that recommended it for use by *The New York Times* editorial staff, is this emphasis on identifying and showing the roots of Americanisms. It follows the descriptive school although it has a liberal number of usage labels.

As previously noted, some publishers have several versions of the same title. Here, for example, World takes the basic *New World Dictionary,* cuts it back to 108,000 entries, reduces the price to $8.95, and simply calls it: *New World Dictionary of the American Language, Students Edition.*

Webster's

Now in its eighth edition, *Webster's New Collegiate Dictionary* is based upon the unabridged Third. It reflects the philosophy of the larger work, and it places considerable emphasis on contemporary pronunciation, definitions, and, more important, usage. Labels for illiterate or slang terminology are kept to a minimum. The type size is quite small, at least in comparison with competitors such as the *American Heritage* work.

The pronunciation system is a bit difficult to follow; and, as in all Webster's dictionaries, the definitions are in chronological order with the modern meaning coming last. Added features include appendixes which cover biographical data, a gazetteer, forms of address, colleges and universities in the United States, vocabulary rhymes, and the like.

There are other acceptable desk dictionaries, including such basic titles as Random House's *American College Dictionary* and the Funk & Wagnalls *Standard College Dictionary.* Each of them has something to recommend it, and most larger libraries make a point of including the basic desk dictionaries in a collection.[9] Timeliness being the major problem with the

[9] A new contender, too late for examination at this writing, is *The Scribner Bantam English Dictionary* (New York: Charles Scribner's Sons, 1977, 1136 pp.), which is distinctive because it is limited to 80,000 entries, including only those words "in current use in American English."

best dictionary, a rule of thumb for purchase is this: (1) Annually, acquire the new editions of standard publishers' desk dictionaries. There are not many, particularly if the librarian is quick to notice whether the entry is a new edition or merely an annual revision. (2) Have on hand the three basics listed here, namely, the *American Heritage,* the *New World Dictionary,* and *Webster's New Collegiate.*

CHILDREN'S DICTIONARIES

World Book Dictionary. Chicago: Field Enterprises Educational Corporation, 1976, 2 vols. (revised annually). $59.

Thorndike Barnhart Beginning Dictionary, 7th ed. Garden City, New York: Doubleday & Company, 1972, 704 pp. $8.50.

Children's dictionaries are composed of words based on frequency of occurrence in speech and reading encountered in school. Definitions are written in simplified language, the type is usually large, there are many illustrations, and the format is generally pleasing.

The most ambitious is the two-volume *World Book Dictionary,* edited by the expert in the field, Clarence L. Barnhart. (His name in connection with a children's dictionary, by the way, is as good a guarantee of quality as G. & C. Merriam is for adult dictionaries. For a short biographical sketch of Barnhart, see Israel Shenker's "Publishing: Words Never Fail Him," *The New York Times,* July 15, 1977, p. 42.) The dictionary contains 190,000 words. All entries are in a single alphabet, pronunciation is simple to follow, and there are more than 2000 pictures. The work, which may be used by adults, is considered by experts to be excellent, and it is recommended for all school libraries.

The Thorndike Barnhart dictionary is one of a series which includes beginning to high school dictionaries. The beginners' version is for grades 3 to 4, and it includes 15,000 entries and 1300 black-and-white illustrations. The high school dictionary triples the number of entries but includes the same number of illustrations. Among other reputable publishers of children's dictionaries are Macmillan, Doubleday, Collins-World, and G. & C. Merriam.

The problem with children's dictionaries is: (1) Should the format and general editorial policy stress material for the beginning reader, or (2) should the editors balance beginning material with enough adult matter to offer the reader the best of two worlds? Larger firms solve the problem by offering a family of dictionaries for every level; for example, G. & C. Merriam starts the child off with the *New Elementary Dictionary,* moves to the *Intermediate Dictionary,* and from there goes to the *New Students' Dictionary* and the *New Collegiate Dictionary*. Other publishers follow the same procedure, although they may not be so successful.[10] The need for all these staged dictionaries in a library is questionable. For most purposes, a dictionary for a child, along with a standard collegiate or desk edition, is enough—with, to be sure, an unabridged version.

HISTORICAL DICTIONARIES

Murray, James, et al. *New English Dictionary on Historical Principles*. Oxford: Clarendon Press, 1888 to 1933, 10 vols. and supplement; reissued in 1933 as 13 vols., under the title *The Oxford English Dictionary*. $395.

———. *The Compact Edition of The Oxford English Dictionary*. New York: Oxford University Press, 1971, 2 vols. $90.

———. *A Supplement to The Oxford English Dictionary*. Edited by R. W. Burchfield. New York: Oxford University Press, 1972, 1977, 2 vols. $60 each.

H. L. Mencken called it "the emperor of dictionaries," and *New English Dictionary on Historical Principles* (usually cited as the *OED*) is truly the English-language dictionary. It took longer to prepare than almost any other book in the English language. In 1857 Dr. Richard Trench (1807–1886) launched the project, which was to take 70 years to complete. The first of the 10 basic volumes was issued in 1884, the last supplementary volume in 1933. The work was first under the charge of Sir James Murray, then Dr. Henry Bradley, then Dr. William A. Craigie, and finally C. T. Onions. All these men made other major contributions to historical dictionaries, and thousands of other scholars took part in the giant undertaking.

Each of the 10 basic volumes weighs approximately 10 pounds, and together they define about 500,000 words. The whole is supported by 2 million quotations.

The *Compact Edition* includes the entire contents of the 13 volumes, a feat made possible by photographically reducing the size of the type. The result is two volumes, weighing a total of some 17 pounds and measuring almost 14 by 10 inches. The miniaturization of the typeface is compensated for by the inclusion of a magnifier. Use is troublesome, particularly to locate desired words, but the decrease in price and size of the set probably

---

[10] The special problems in the evaluation of a children's dictionary are discussed at length in the review of *The Charlie Brown Dictionary* (New York: World Publishing Company, 1973), in "Reference and Subscription Books Reviews," *The Booklist*, November 1, 1974, pp. 297–298.

compensates for the reduction in ease of use. Most libraries, it is hoped, can afford the printed set, but purchasers with limited budgets (such as individuals) will find the compact work satisfactory.

As the outstanding historical dictionary in the English language, the OED has the purpose of tracing the history of English words. Volunteers and the staff ransacked printed books, public records, manuscripts, and even private papers to come up with words and quotations. The contributions were arranged alphabetically, and each section was prepared by competent scholars. The discovery of antedating citations to establish the earliest use of a word is an extremely trying and skilled task as well as a time-consuming one. Speaking of the original *OED,* a critic observes: "One person alone, indeed, had submitted over a hundred thousand citations of all kinds—he was a doctor with unlimited time in jail."[11]

The OED is not a dictionary for ready reference. But it is encyclopedic in its treatment of individual words. Under every word, anything that could be found about the historical development of the word is traced in chronological order. Meaning, origin, relations to similar words, various dialects, fashions in speaking, pronunciation, compounds, derivatives, and even more are treated in full. Every change is illustrated by an example, and each quotation is dated and the source clearly indicated.

The result is both forbidding and fascinating. For example, the word "set" is explored in 20 full pages. It has 150 main divisions. The word "so" receives 15 columns showing 50 different uses, each one illustrated with an example. Obviously, this is a work for scholars and not the gentle reader seeking a simple definition or spelling.

As a source of information about words, the *OED* is miraculously accurate and complete. It is weak only in one area, that of American words. However, these are treated in some fullness by Craigie and Mathews in two other works to be discussed in the following subsection. The library will find many uses for it; and, as indicated, it is an oblique source for quotations or for "first" facts when other, more conventional books of quotations and ready-reference tools fail to produce results.

The *OED* abstains from any critical judgments, and there are no usage labels. The validity of some of the forms is open to question, but the editors purposefully saw their duty as recorders. Consequently, the *OED* is beloved by prescribers and describers alike.

Nor is there any question that it is the most famous and most quoted dictionary in the English language. It has served everyone from sports writer A. J. Liebling to poet Robert Graves. The librarian who does not

---

[11] David Shulman, "Antedate Dictionary Citations," *Verbatim,* February 1976, p. 7. The author of this short article tells how he collects citations for the supplements for the *OED.*

know the *OED* can be rightfully accused of plain ignorance. There are not many reference books which deserve a lasting place in a collection, but the *OED* is one of the numbered few.[12]

The planned four-volume supplement to the *OED* is to be completed in 1982 or 1983. Two volumes are now available. The set will include approximately 50,000 words that have "entered the language" since the *OED* was completed a half-century ago. Among the new words are colloquial expressions and modern slang that were expressly not included in the basic work.[13]

A more familiar version of the *OED* for many Americans is *The Shorter Oxford English Dictionary on Historical Principles* (New York: Oxford University Press, 1973, 2672 pp., $47.50).[14] Since the first publication of this third edition in 1944 (there were two other editions, 1933 and 1936), it has undergone three revisions, the most complete in 1973 when most of the etymologies were updated. Also, there is a 74-page addendum which includes a number of words from the *OED Supplements*. As with earlier versions, the emphasis is almost entirely on definitions, with names of people and places eliminated. The emphasis on quotations is cut back. The net result is that the abridgement includes about two-thirds the number of words.

The same publisher issues *The Concise Oxford Dictionary* (6th ed.; New York: Oxford University Press, 1976), a 74,000-word desk dictionary as common in English libraries and homes as the G. & C. Merriam *Webster's New Collegiate,* the *American Heritage,* and other desk versions are in the United States. It is a standard nonhistorical dictionary, not another version of the *OED*. According to a reviewer in the *London Sunday Times* (July 25, 1976, p. 12): "It sells 300,000 copies a year, come hell or high water, and is an essential tool of every self respecting library and classroom in the English speaking world." Also, crossword puzzle fans claim it is one of the best for their preoccupation.[15]

---

[12] There are, to be sure, some faults of omission and definition in the *OED,* and they are pointed out by Robert Graves in his essay, "Best Man, Bore, Bamboozle, etc.," in *Crowning Privilege* (London: Cassell & Co., Ltd., 1955). Graves also observes that one of the few people who were disappointed with the work was Thomas Hardy. Seeking to find a word in an early volume, Hardy discovered that the authority for the word was one of his own quotations.

[13] For a view of what goes on in the work of updating the *OED,* see: "In the Lexicographer's Lair," *The Observer Review (London),* June 13, 1976, p. 32.

[14] "More familiar" because versions of the shorter *OED* are often featured at cut-rate come-on prices by the Book-of-the-Month Club. Unfortunately, it may not always be clear that this is a historical dictionary.

[15] Israel Shenker, "A British Concise Dictionary Editor . . . ," *The New York Times,* September 7, 1976, p. 31. However, there are a number of specific dictionaries for crossword puzzle fans, e.g., *The New York Times Crossword Puzzle Dictionary* (New York: Quadrangel, 1975, 685 pp.) and *Webster's New World Crossword Puzzle Dictionary* (New York: Collins-World, 1975, 656

American regional dictionaries

> Craigie, William, and James R. Hulbert. *A Dictionary of American English on Historical Principles*. Chicago: The University of Chicago Press, 1936 to 1944, 4 vols. $100.

> Mathews, Mitford. *A Dictionary of Americanisms on Historical Principles*. Chicago: The University of Chicago Press, 1951, 2 vols., 1946 pp. $19.50 per volume.

As broad a survey of the English language as it is, the *OED* could not account for every detail in the history of English in other countries and regions. Partly for this reason, W. A. Craigie (who was one of the editors of the *OED*) developed *A Dictionary of American English on Historical Principles*.

Craigie supplements the *OED* by demonstrating changes in English words (many included in the *OED*) which took place in the American colonies and the United States. In order to trace a word used in both the United States and the British Isles, it is necessary to use both Craigie and the *OED*.

Craigie includes words which originated on the American continent, giving a complete history and showing the development, as in the *OED*, by use of quotations. This feature makes it valuable as an aid to tracing quotations and early facts about American folklore, habits, and customs.

Mathews's work is confined to words that are peculiar to America and augments Craigie nicely. He also includes over 400 useful pen-and-ink drawings. There are approximately 50,000 words, many adopted from other languages. Place names and names of plants and animals were drawn from American Indian words, whereas the Dutch and Germans furnished us with many domestic words.

In any discussion of the history of the American language, there is one outstanding work which many have enjoyed reading, literally from cover to cover. This is Henry Mencken's *The American Language* (New York: Alfred A. Knopf, Inc., 1936 to 1948). In three volumes, the sage of Baltimore examines a very large proportion of all American words in a style and manner that are extremely pleasing, always entertaining, and informative. The initial one-volume work of 1936 was supplemented with two volumes. All are easy to use as each volume has a detailed index.[16]

---

pp.), which are frequently revised. Words are in alphabetical order with synonyms. Arrangement within each entry is by number of letters. Libraries should have several of these, although (1) they are more suitable for home use; and (2) true crossword fans consider such aids less than honorable methods of solving puzzles. A standard dictionary, however, is acceptable.

[16] For a discussion of recent (1974 and 1975) printings of the Mencken classic, with notes on his contribution, see James E. Redden's review of the book and supplements in *Verbatim*, February 1976, pp. 4–5.

SLANG

> Wentworth, Harold, and Stuart Flexner. *Dictionary of American Slang,* 2d supplemented ed. New York: Thomas Y. Crowell Company, 1975, 766 pp. $12.95.

A culture accustomed to a dictionary providing authority on correct English usage, even to the point of overlooking and not recording substandard slang, requires some corrective measures. Corrections have been provided. (1) The change in the times has influenced *The American Heritage Dictionary* (for one) clearly to define our more common slang and obscene terms.[17] This trend against the Victorian stance is gaining ground and, as already noted, is accepted by even the editors of the *Supplement* to *The Oxford English Dictionary.* (2) There are specific dictionaries which record and define characteristic slang and special terms from various vocations, regions, and groups. A good slang dictionary gives exhaustive definitions, provides additional quotations, and tends to be more up to date on current jargon.

General in scope, Wentworth and Flexner's *Dictionary of American Slang* gives definitions for more than 22,000 words, each supplemented by a source and one or more illustrative quotations. First published in 1960, this work caused some furor regarding the clear definitions of vulgar words and terms. It is now accepted in libraries, and certainly by all scholars. The particular merit of the work is its broad general approach to all aspects of the culture from the slang of space scientists and FBI men to the jargon of strip-teasers and Madison Avenue advertising tycoons. Where possible, the history of the term is given with the approximate date when the slang entered the written, not the oral, language. And there is an excellent preface which anyone who questions the merit of such dictionaries would do well to read. Unfortunately, the arrangement is wanting in that the additional words in the 1967 first supplement and the 1975 second supplement are incorporated into appendixes in the revised edition.

The basic general title in the field of slang, however, remains Eric Partridge's *A Dictionary of Slang and Unconventional English* (7th ed.; New York: The Macmillan Company, 1970, 1528 pp.). The work includes 50,000 entries, more than double the number found in Wentworth and Flexner. One of the first scholars to approach the subject in our time, Partridge has a fine sense of balance and gives appropriate quotations to

---

[17] In 1976 the Anchorage, Alaska, school board voted to remove the *American Heritage* from schools. A member of the board explained that the recommendation was to prevent a child's looking up "dirty words." For details, see *Newsletter on Intellectual Freedom,* September 1976, pp. 15–16.

illustrate his meaning.[18] He is particularly devoted to tracing the history of phrases and words. As useful as this work is, the emphasis is on English terms; for American libraries, the Wentworth and Flexner title would be preferable. Larger libraries will want them both.

On occasion, slang enjoys a real vogue. For example, the introduction of citizen band radios has resulted in sales of close to a half-million copies of *The Official CB Slanguage Language Dictionary* (New York: Louis J. Martin Associates, 1976). Then there is Cyra McFadden's *The Serial—A Year in the Life of Marin County* (New York: Alfred A. Knopf, 1977), which documents "psychobabble" talk or slang among the upper middle classes.

Few of the thesauruses, discussed in the next section, include slang words, and the writer who is looking for a slang expression as a substitute for an established English word will be at a loss. (Dictionaries of slang assume, of course, the user knows the word.) The best thesaurus of slang is now much dated, although still useful. This is Lester Berry and Melvin Van den Bark's *American Thesaurus of Slang* (2d ed.; New York: Thomas Y. Crowell Company, 1953, 1272 pp.). It is particularly good for writers because, in addition to the regular thesaurus section, it includes slang by classes and occupations ranging from the underworld to sports. There are more than 100,000 words listed under subjects, classes, and occupations. The entry itself is in standard English with the slang equivalents.

SYNONYMS AND ANTONYMS

Webster's New Dictionary of Synonyms. Springfield, Massachusetts: G. & C. Merriam Company, rev. ed., 1973, 909 pp. $8.95.

Roget's International Thesaurus, 3d ed. New York: Thomas Y. Crowell Company, 1962, 1258 pp. $8.95.

Webster's Collegiate Thesaurus. Springfield, Massachusetts: G. & C. Merriam Company, 1976, 944 pp. $8.95.

A book of synonyms often is among the most popular books in the private or public library. It offers a key to crossword puzzles and an instant vocabulary, and it serves almost everyone who wishes to increase or disguise his or her command of English. There are several dictionaries giving both synonyms and antonyms in English, but the titles listed above appear more often in libraries. Certainly, the most popular and best known is the work by Peter Mark Roget (1779–1869), inventor of the slide

---

[18] Partridge by 1977 was 83 and was working on his next dictionary in the British Library. For an appreciation of this remarkable man, see Israel Shenker, "The Definition of Partridge," *New York Times Magazine,* October 2, 1977.

rule and a doctor in an English lunatic asylum. He began the work at age seventy-one and by his ninetieth birthday had seen it through 20 editions. (The term "thesaurus" means a treasury, a store, a hoard; and *Roget's* is precisely that.) His optimistic aim was to classify all human thought under a series of verbal categories, and his book is so arranged. There are approximately 1000 classifications; and within each section, headed by a key word, there are listed by parts of speech the words and phrases from which the reader may select the proper synonym. Antonyms are usually placed immediately after the main listing. Thus: "possibility/impossibility"; "pride/humility."

Modern editions vary slightly from the first edition (1852). The Crowell work retains the idea of grouping words according to their ideas. Editor C. O. Mawson, however, has added new categories from science and technology. An index is absolutely necessary to locate a word, and the Crowell edition has an excellent one. (Like "Webster," the term "Roget" is not copyrighted, and a number of works with this name appear which are indifferent to good.)

The advantage of grouping is that like ideas are placed together. The distinct disadvantage is that *Roget* offers no guidance or annotations; and an overzealous user may select a synonym or an antonym which looks and sounds better but is far from expressing what is meant. Sean O'Faolain, the Irish short story writer, recalls giving a copy of *Roget's* to a Dutch-born journalist to improve his English, but the effect was appalling. For example, the journalist might wish to know the synonym for "sad." He would consult the index and find four or five alternatives, such as "painful," "gray," "bad," "dejected," and, surprisingly, "great." When he turned to the proper section, he would find two or three hundred synonyms. Unless the user has a clear understanding of the language, *Roget's* can be a difficult work.

Publicized as the "first totally new thesaurus in over 120 years" (a slight exaggeration), the *Webster's Collegiate Thesaurus* offers more than 100,000 synonyms and antonyms. The editors have managed to avoid the pitfall described in the previous paragraph. After each main entry, there is a definition which takes the guesswork and error out of the thesaurus reference tool. There are brief verbal illustrations of the main entry word to make the meaning even more precise. These are followed by a list of exact synonyms, after which come words that are closely related, but not quite the same in meaning. The entry concludes with antonyms and contrasting words. Thanks to these features and a simple alphabetical arrangement of ideas, it is much easier to use than the standard *Roget*.

The *Webster's Thesaurus* lists related words, but *Webster's New Dictionary of Synonyms* offers short essays on words, often making their usage much clearer than is done in a thesaurus. One looks up a word and finds several synonyms. Shades of meaning are carefully explained and then illustrated with appropriate quotations. Antonyms and contrasted words follow the main entries. The difficulty with this approach is that, despite cross-references, not all words can be found.

Early in 1977, *The Doubleday Roget's Thesaurus in Dictionary Form* (New York: Doubleday & Company, 1976) appeared. Published at only $4.95, it is a good home-desk book of synonyms because the publisher purposefully limits the number of entries to an average of about 20 synonyms for each word, and pays special attention to new words. Israel Shenker gleefully compares various publishers' editions of the original *Roget* in "And Now, Another 'Completely New' (Unique) Thesaurus," *The New York Times,* March 19, 1977, pp. 21, 32.

USAGE AND MANUSCRIPT STYLE

Fowler, Henry Watson. *Dictionary of Modern English Usage,* 2d ed., rev. by Sir Ernest Gowers. New York: Oxford University Press, 1965, 725 pp. $10.

Morris, William, and Mary Morris. *Harper Dictionary of Contemporary Usage.* New York: Harper & Row, 1975, 648 pp. $15.

Turabian, Kate L. *A Manual for Writers of Term Papers, Theses, and Dissertations,* 4th ed. Chicago: The University of Chicago Press, 1973. $6.95.

Mark Twain is supposed to have said that "the difference between the right word and the almost right word is the difference between lightning and the lightning bug." Now that almost all general dictionaries have moved from the prescriptive to the descriptive editorial policy, they are no longer reliable for answering reference questions regarding lightning or lightning bugs. It is essential that libraries augment the general dictionary with one or two prescriptive works on usage.

Author and critic Dwight Macdonald once observed that Fowler's *Dictionary of Modern English Usage* is more than a book; it is an attitude toward life. Fowler and the other works are listed here for the aid and comfort of those who wish a dictionary to be prescriptive. There must be rules and regulations governing good usage, and Fowler and company lay down these rules, usually without doubt or question.

The works are invaluable for the layperson who is attempting to distinguish what is or is not good usage. Fowler, for example, deals extensively with grammar and syntax, analyzes how words should be used, distinguishes clichés and common errors, and settles almost any question that might arise concerning the English language. The dictionary, and the revision by Sir Ernest Gowers, has a special flavor treasured by all readers. Fowler commented on practically anything that interested him, and the hundreds of general articles can be savored for their own literary quality, aside from their instructional value.

Prepared by the editor of *The American Heritage Dictionary*, with the aid of his wife, the *Harper Dictionary of Contemporary Usage* offers short usage notes for words. Unlike Fowler and editors of Fowler, the Harper editors place emphasis on quick answers to queries about vogue words, regionalisms, slang, idioms, and pronunciation. A unique feature: Where there is any difference between the editors and the public regarding the use of a word or phrase, there is a brief discussion in which various experts give other opinions. The problem is that often little is really resolved and the reader is still in doubt, particularly as the experts' statements too often are tentative, even humorous where humor is not needed. In other words, the editors and experts tend to have it both ways when there is any serious question, and the librarian is forced to turn back to the much more reliable versions of Fowler. Still, as a handy reference aid, the Harper entry is at least relatively up to date.[19]

A more specific work, even more used by students, is the Turabian title. The *Manual for Writers* gives hints on style, but it is primarily a guide to the mechanics (from footnotes to bibliographies) of preparing term papers. Turabian gives precise rules which are of considerable help to anyone working in this area. The book is based on the larger *Manual of Style* (12th ed.; Chicago: The University of Chicago Press, 1969).

ABBREVIATIONS AND ACRONYMS

DeSola, Ralph. *Abbreviations Dictionary*, 5th ed. New York: American Elsevier Publishing Company, 1977, 640 pp. $27.

Acronyms, Initialisms, and Abbreviations Dictionary, 5th ed. Detroit: Gale Research Company, 1976, 757 pp. $38.50. *New Acronyms, Initialisms, and Abbreviations*, 1971 to date, annual. Paper, $35.

Most general dictionaries include basic abbreviations as part of the main work or as an appendix. Many acronyms (i.e., a word formed from the initial letters of words of the successive parts of a compound term such as CARE, WAVE, NATO) are included, too. Also, encyclopedias, almanacs, and numerous handbooks include sections for general or specific

---

[19] For a lengthy, critical discussion of this and other works of usage, see Joseph Epstein, "Idioms of Our Time," *The Times Literary Supplement*, February 13, 1976, pp. 161–162. The reviewer does not care for the Harper title.

abbreviations and acronyms. Still, for ready reference, it is desirable to have at least one good, up-to-date source at hand.

One of the best is Gale's *Acronyms,. . . .* Terms are in alphabetical order, by abbreviation, acronym, or initial, and various meanings are given. There are over 130,000 entries, and each of the supplements adds some 12,000 more from all fields. (Precisely what this may be doing to the language, not to mention the sanity of the average reader, is not considered by the compilers.) If one considers that there are at least 12,000 new acronyms, abbreviations, and initials added each year, the need for a current source is obvious. A companion volume to *Acronyms, . . . , Reverse Acronyms, Initialisms, and Abbreviations Dictionary* (Detroit: Gale Research Company, 1976, 757 pp.), gives the term first and then the acronym.

The basic guide to abbreviations, DeSola's *Abbreviations Dictionary* is often revised—usually every four or five years. Entries are arranged alphabetically, letter by letter. Some notion as to possibilities can be gained by looking at the first entry for the lower case "a," which has over 25 possible meanings. The capital "A" lists over 30 meanings. DeSola differs from the Gale work in that the Gale entry is longer and extremely strong on those words which are composed of initialisms. But DeSola includes items not found in Gale, e.g., slang, nicknames, contractions, signs and symbols, and anonyms. There is just enough difference between the two that both should be found in larger collections.

SUBJECT DICTIONARIES[20]

Dictionaries devoted to specialized subject fields, occupations, or professions make up an important part of any reference collection. This is especially true in the sciences. General dictionaries tend to be stronger in the humanities, weaker in the fast-changing scientific fields. Consequently, there are a vast number of scientific dictionaries, but relatively few in the humanities.

The major question to ask when determining selection is: Does this dictionary offer anything that cannot be found in a standard work now in the library? A careful answer may result in bypassing a special dictionary. It is surprising, particularly in the humanities and social sciences, how much of the information is readily available in a general English dictionary.

[20] Reproducing Library of Congress cards under a large number of subject headings, the editor of *Dictionaries, Encyclopedias and Other Word-Related Books* (Detroit: Gale Research Company, 1975, 591 pp.) offers the widest selection of subject dictionaries. While limited to Library of Congress cataloged titles between 1966 and 1974, the listing is impressive.

While all evaluative checks to other dictionaries apply, there are also some special points to watch:

1. Are the illustrations pertinent and helpful to either the specialist or the layperson? Where a technical work is directed to a lay audience, there should be a number of diagrams, photographs, or other forms of graphic art which frequently make it easier for the uninitiated to understand the terms.

2. Are the definitions simply brief word equivalents, or is some effort made to give a real explanation of the word in context with the subject?

3. Is the dictionary international in scope, or limited chiefly to an American audience? This is a particularly valuable question when the sciences are being considered. Several publishers have met the need by offering bilingual scientific dictionaries.

4. Are the terms up to date? Again, this is a necessity in a scientific work, somewhat less so in a social science dictionary, and perhaps of little relative importance in a humanistic study.

Many of the subject dictionaries are virtually encyclopedic in terms of information and presentation. They use the specific-entry form, but the entry may run to considerably more than a simple definition.

FOREIGN-LANGUAGE DICTIONARIES (BILINGUAL)

The New Cassell's series, all published by Funk & Wagnalls, different editions and dates, various pagination, e.g., *New Cassell's French Dictionary; New Cassell's German Dictionary; Cassell's Italian-English, English-Italian Dictionary;* etc. Price Range: $4.50 to $12.50.

Mawson, C. O. Sylvester. *Dictionary of Foreign Terms.* 2d ed. rev. and updated by Charles Berlitz. New York: Thomas Y. Crowell, 1975, 368 pp., $9.95.

Sheehy's *Guide to Reference Books* dutifully lists and annotates 641 various types of foreign-language dictionaries under headings from Afrikaans to Zulu. There are only 129 English-language titles. The compiler rightfully notes that "foreign language dictionaries are important in any library."

Most readers are familiar with the typical bilingual dictionary which offers the foreign word and the equivalent English word. The process is then reversed with the English word first, followed by the equivalent foreign word. For other than large public, academic, and special libraries, the bilingual dictionary is usually quite enough, particularly as the number is limited to European languages, with possibly a nod to Latin and Chinese. For that purpose the Cassell's entries are standard, familiar desk dictionaries. Most have gone through numerous editions and revisions by just as many editors. Pronunciation is given clearly enough for even the amateur to follow, and the equivalent words are accurate. Definitions, of course, are not given. All the dictionaries usually include slang words, colloquialisms, idioms, and more common terms from various subject areas. The number of main entries differs from 120,000 to 130,000.

Scribner's Sons publishes a similar variety of bilingual dictionaries, equally good. The library wishing the most up-to-date version should simply check *Publishers Trade List Annual* under the two publishers and find the most current dictionaries required. In other words, over the years Funk & Wagnalls and Scribner's have established themselves as reliable sources of standard college-type bilingual dictionaries, and the library can rarely go wrong ordering from either one. Among other standard publishers are Harrap, Springer, Random House, Cambridge University Press, and several other well-established large houses which may be located via the listings in Sheehy.

When the librarian moves toward less or more specialization, there are two avenues open. The Mawson title is a good example of the less-specialized aid for ready-reference work. It contains about 15,000 words and phrases from some 50 languages, listed in alphabetical order by the word or phrase with an English equivalent. Words from both classical and modern technical literature are included. Actually, it is a good dictionary for the avid reader to have when reading over authors likely to employ foreign terms. It is true that many of the standard English-language dictionaries include at least major foreign words and expressions, but they hardly touch the surface. For both ready-reference and home purposes, a dictionary with a wide variety of foreign terms is of considerable help.

The Mawson work is one of too few in this field. The few others are equally good, or excel in one particular area. For example, Mario Pei's *Dictionary of Foreign Terms* (New York: Delacorte Press, 1974) is quite suitable for European languages, but falters with other, non-Western tongues. However, thanks to the limited number of titles, the library would probably want both the Mawson and the Pei because, at this writing, they are the most up to date and the most reliable.

At the other extreme is the standard monolingual dictionary which may range in size from the equivalent English-language desk dictionary to the unabridged version. The flaw for reference work is that the dictionary is completely in the language of origin and presupposes a fairly solid command of the language. This is particularly true of the historical and the unabridged current dictionaries, such as the classic Littre *Dictionnaire de la*

Langue Francaise, issued in the late nineteenth century, which contains numerous supporting quotations and thus is on the order of *The Oxford English Dictionary.*

One is inclined to agree that monolingual dictionaries are important for large libraries, certainly for those serving a foreign population of any size, but of only passing interest for reference work. This is not entirely true, especially if the reference librarian is thorough and possibly frustrated in seeking a bit of information about a quote (which can be checked in the larger, historical type of foreign dictionaries) or a point of local history (again, often traced down through the dictionary). Even facts on folklore, technical developments in industry, etc., are possible to find in a large dictionary.

Finally, the librarian may deplore the lack of interest in most foreign languages—although all seem to enjoy a vogue from time to time—while still keeping at least a minimum collection of dictionaries. They are an important part of the reference collection, if only to reassure the user that some things never change. In a more pragmatic way, the librarian should not forget that almost all the disciplines, and particularly those in science, have their special foreign-language dictionaries.

SUGGESTED READING

Burchfield, R. W., "The Treatment of Controversial Vocabulary in the Oxford English Dictionary," *Transactions of the Philological Society,* 1973 (c. 1974). The *Transactions* are published by the compilers of the *OED,* and this article explains the problems of making decisions about slang and obscene words—particularly as related to the 1972 *Supplement* to the *OED.*

———, "The Art of the Lexicographer," *Book News,* April 1975, pp. 230–232. A further discussion of the problems associated with editing the *OED Supplement.*

Emblen, D. L. "Dr. Roget: His Book," *The Bookseller,* February 13, 1971, pp. 412–416. The author of a life of Roget traces the history of the various editions of the most famous thesaurus.

Douglas, George H. "What's Happened to the Thesaurus?" *RQ,* Winter 1976, pp. 149–155. Comparing and analyzing *Roget* and *Webster's Collegiate Thesaurus,* the English professor points out some common misunderstandings about the thesaurus and relates the history of the form. He gives some fascinating examples.

Morgan, John S., *Noah Webster.* New York: Mason-Charter, 1975. A biography and analysis of Webster and his spelling books and dictionaries. Scholarly, but hardly exciting. A contemporary wrote of the twenty-three-year-old Webster: "In conversation he is even duller than in writing, if that is possible."

Murray, B. K. M., *Caught in the Web of Words: James A. H. Murray and the Oxford English Dictionary.* New Haven: Yale University Press, 1977. A thoroughly beguiling biography of her grandfather, the editor of the *OED.* Murray died in 1915, 13 years before the last part of the dictionary appeared. For a review of the book and a tribute to

Murray, see George Steiner's "Give the Word," *The New Yorker,* November 21, 1977, pp. 221–230.

Shenker, Israel, "Middle English Dictionary Gets a Deadline After 50 Years: 1982," *The New York Times,* August 27, 1975, p. 28. A detailed story on the problems and joys of editing a specialized dictionary, with hints applicable to the compilation of any historical dictionary.

Verbatim. Essex, Connecticut, 06426. This is not an article or a book, but a 16- to 20-page newsletter which offers running commentaries on language and new dictionaries. Issued since 1974, it offers both entertaining and informative reading.

Wells, Ronald, *Dictionaries and the Authoritarian Tradition.* The Hague: Mouton, 1973. Both a history and a scholarly discussion of the prescriptive and descriptive debate in the compilation of dictionaries.

CHAPTER NINE

Geographical Sources

 **I**T IS SOMETIMES difficult to manifest excitement over reference works. Geographical sources are the happy exception. On the purely imaginative level, they have the ability to transport the viewer to any part of the world and, in this day, to the universe. The difference between geographical sources and other works is that they are primarily graphic representations which allow the imagination full reign. Indeed, many of them are works of art, and they provide a type of satisfaction rarely found in the purely textual approach to knowledge.

Useful as they may be to the romantic, in the hard world of reference work, geographical sources are an invaluable part of any basic collection. There are as many reasons for consulting these sources as there are patrons, and most are self-evident—the location of a small town in some country, the nearest railroad or airline serving a village, the condition of roads in a state, the number of hotels in a city, and so on. More specialized or thematic sources will serve to answer almost every geographical question from the location of a specific archaeological site to the name and size of a canyon on the moon.

The variety of the sources requires a basic understanding of general features shared by all. Beyond that, the reference librarian must become familiar with the specific qualities of the individual works. Answers to geographical questions are not necessarily limited to specialized books. Geography is a component part of many other reference tools. Encyclopedias usually have individual maps or separate atlas volumes. Information about cities, towns, states, and countries frequently will be found in greater detail in an encyclopedia, a yearbook, or an almanac than in many of the geographical sources cited here. The distinct advantage of geographical works over more generalized reference books is that (1) they give information for smaller units not found in general works; (2) the information given often will be more precise; and (3) since they are limited to one area, they are usually easier to use.

Definition and scope[1]

Geographical sources used in reference work may be subdivided into three large categories: maps and atlases, gazetteers, and guidebooks.

Maps and Atlases   Geographical sources have terms peculiar to this category. Everyone understands that a map is, among other things, a representation of certain boundaries of the earth on a flat surface. (These days, it may include the representation of the moon and planets as well.) An atlas is a volume containing a collection of these maps, and the nature of a globe is too self-evident to need definition. There are a great variety of maps designed for every purpose from indicating soil content to traffic flow. A map showing such specific conditions is normally referred to as a thematic map.

A physical map traces the various features of the land from the rivers and valleys to the mountains and hills. A route map shows roads, railroads, bridges, and the like. A political map normally limits itself to political boundaries (e.g., towns, cities, counties, states) but may include topographical and route features. Either separately or as one, these three types make up a large number of maps found in general atlases.

Cartography is the art of mapmaking, and a major headache of cartographers has been the accurate representation of the features of the earth on maps. This task has resulted in various projections, i.e., the effort to display the surface of a sphere upon a plane without undue distortion. Mercator or his forerunners devised a system, still the best known today, which is based upon parallel lines, that is, latitude (angular distance north or south from the prime meridian) and longitude (angular distance east and west from the prime meridian). This system works well enough except at the polar regions, where it tends to distort the facts. Hence, on any

---

[1] For a historic overview of cartography, the best source is *Five Centuries of Mapmaking* (Chicago: The University of Chicago Press, 1976). The series of luxuriously illustrated essays by various experts considers the several means of publishing maps, including present-day procedures.

Mercator projection, Greenland is completely out of proportion to the United States. Since Mercator, hundreds of projections have been designed; but distortional qualities are always evident, if not in one section, in another. For example, the much praised azimuthal equidistant projection, with the North Pole at the center of the map, indicates directions and distances more accurately, but in other respects it gives a peculiar stretched and pulled appearance to much of the globe.

The only relatively accurate representation of the earth is a globe. The necessity for a globe in a reference situation is probably questionable, although it is certainly desirable to have one. Reference questions per se rarely require its use. This, to be sure, is not to discount the importance of a globe, which is both a work of art and an important aid in specialized situations. However, the reference librarian who has had occasion to use a globe instead of a map to answer particular reference questions is rare indeed.

Gazetteers In addition to general and thematic maps, the reference librarian is most likely to use a gazetteer in answering questions regarding geographical sources. A gazetteer may be defined as a geographical dictionary, differing from the index to an atlas in that it usually is more comprehensive. A good gazetteer includes names of towns, villages, rivers, mountains, lakes, and other geographical features, population, longitude and latitude, and, in some cases, brief to rather long entries tracing the history and economic and political features of particular places.

Travel Guides Supplementing the gazetteer is the guidebook, usually limited to a single area (town, city, county, state, nation) and serving, as the title implies, to point up the highlights of travel. Generally, these books give a minimum of historical background and emphasize routes and itineraries. They usually present information on hotels, motels, museums, public buildings, restaurants, and anything else of general interest to the traveler. They are distinct from encyclopedic presentation in that they are highly pragmatic, stressing "how much," "how good," and "how long." Also, the better guidebooks are issued or revised annually.

History

An atlas is a volume of maps, so called because Gerhard Mercator (1512–1594) employed the term in the title he gave to a collection of 107 maps. This was issued after his death in 1595. The fact that the publisher employed on the title page an engraving of Atlas, the Greek god holding up the world, helped to establish the term.

Although Mercator is frequently called the "father of modern geography," there were a number of mapmakers before the Flemish geographer gained fame. Individual maps date back to the Egyptians and Babylonians. Even before people took to the seas, there were land maps; the earliest recorded maps are clay tablets of about 600 or 500 B.C. (The Chinese have extant examples from as early as 1125 B.C.)

Sea charts probably go back to the early Greeks, and certainly were known prior to the most famous mapmaker of them all, Ptolemy of Alexandria (A.D. 87 to 150). His treatise on geography was the first to give a graphic representation of the known world; that is, he was the first cartographer. His principles were lost, only to be found again at the end of the Middle Ages. Meanwhile, the Arabs and the church carried on with improving cartographic tools until the close of the fifteenth century, when printing became widespread.

The early printer and the early mapmaker grew up together. Because maps need to be precise, printing solved the problem by ensuring that once the engraving (usually a woodcut or a copper engraving) was made, the map could be repeated indefinitely. It was subject to error only at the early stage when the design was transferred to the block or plate. Prior to that, a drawn chart suffered all the possibilities of error, sometimes fatal in navigation, associated with repeated and labored hand copying.

There are five editions of *Ptolemy's Cosmographia* printed before 1500, and the 17 maps supplemented with text were the first true printed atlases. Even at this early date the publishers were aware of changes in geography and added "modern" maps to the collection. Additions were made with relative ease because maps were issued unbound (a normal enough procedure for most books of the period). The general practice continued through the seventeenth century. The advantage of enabling the publisher to correct one or more maps without reworking the whole edition has resulted in several modern publishers' resorting to the earlier loose-leaf approach for modern atlases.

In addition to Mercator, the Netherlands gave the world another famous mapmaker, Abraham Orteluis (1527–1598). By the seventeenth century Spain, France, and England were busy exploring and mapping Europe, America, and the East. The atlas was now firmly established as a cartographic form. However, at best it was a limited form with little attraction for the average person. It would take the industrial revolution, the mass migration of peoples, and the exploration of land on an unheard-of scale, to make the demand for maps a major one. Today the demand is great and is increasing. Maps not only are used in the conventional method, but have become a form of expression that is increasingly important to most areas of life from science to the humanities.

Despite the obvious need for maps, the world as a whole is poorly mapped, particularly in terms of accuracy and completeness. The older nations are better represented, but when one attempts to find a detailed map of parts of Africa, for example, it is nonexistent. Various cartographic conferences are held annually to discuss the problem, and the United Nations is actively engaged in a program of attempting to solve worldwide mapping problems.

Modern technology has accounted for rapid progress in both methods of cartography and the production of maps. The normal procedure is to conduct a survey, now done as much by air as by foot. With the survey data the cartographer prepares the map for the lithographer and the printer. Today developments include the use of air photographs as actual maps, computers for storing continuous data which may be employed for updating and for large- or small-scale maps, and forms of printing that are considerably faster and cheaper than the lithographic process.

What these developments eventually will mean for the average atlas is problematical. However, they serve to stress the highly specialized nature of cartography, a specialization which can be too easily overlooked by the casual user of a map or atlas. The history of mapmaking is considerably more complex and varied than the average layperson suspects.

Scope

Maps and atlases may be divided into two general classes. The first is the so-called general map which is either political or physical, or a combination of both; the second, the thematic map which serves some special purpose.

In the average library the collection will consist of the major atlases, possibly some single maps in a vertical file, and selected thematic atlases. That there is considerably more scope to maps than such a collection indicates may be ascertained simply by examining the basic bibliographies cited in Sheehy and Walford, the number of periodicals devoted to geographical subjects including maps, and the fact that the Special Libraries Association has a separate division, with its own publication, devoted to problems of maps and map collecting.

Larger, research, and special libraries may have either separate map collections or collections integrated with particular subject areas. For, unlike many other reference sources, the map is a form which crosses all disciplines, all subject areas. It is a highly specialized topic with its own variations in cataloging, acquisitions, and maintenance. The Library of Congress, for example, has its own map division, as do a number of other large libraries.

EVALUATION

Maps and atlases are a mysterious area for the average librarian or patron.[2] They depend primarily upon the graphic arts and mathematics for presentation and compilation. Skill in determining the best map or atlas draws upon a type of knowledge normally not employed in evaluating a book.

Map printing is a specialized department of the graphic arts; and while simple maps can be prepared by any artist or draftsperson, more complicated works require a high degree of skill. More important, their proper reproduction necessitates expensive processes which the average printer of reference works is not equipped to handle. As with dictionaries and encyclopedias, the inherent expenses and skills of the field narrow the competent cartographic firms down to a half-dozen or so. In the United States, the leading publishers are Rand McNally & Company, C. S. Hammond & Company, and the National Geographic Society.[3] In England, the leaders are John G. Bartholomew (Edinburgh) and the cartographic department of the Oxford University Press.

When the cartographic firm is not known, it is advisable to check on its reputation and integrity through other works it may have issued. The mapmaker may differ from the publisher and, in the case of an atlas, both should be checked.

Few geographical sources can hope to keep up with changes in Africa and Asia. Place names change as frequently as countries and their boundaries. For example, in October 1976, every geographical aid in every library became dated when the first of the South African black homelands was created as Transkei. And just to add to the difficulty, as the transitional state is highly controversial, there is some question whether or not it will retain either its present name or its independence. Mapmakers cannot wait on political trends, and in 1977 the revised maps showed Transkei. Next year is another problem.

Reputable mapmakers follow a policy similar to that of encyclopedia firms: continuous revision and reprinting. This practice normally is clearly

[2] Mai Treude, "Reference Service with Maps," *Bulletin. Special Libraries Association, Geography and Map Division,* December 1975, pp. 24–29. The author explains how map reference work differs from general reference procedures, and in so doing, gives numerous hints on necessary attributes for the successful reference interview dealing with geographical sources.

[3] "The Phenomenal Success of the National Geographic's Book Operation," *Publishers Weekly,* January 8, 1973, pp. 40–44. A discussion of one company's operations, with references to other atlases and map publishers.

indicated by two methods: (1) copyright date on the verso of the title page; and (2) revision date, with some indication in the preface, introduction, or jacket blurb as to the extent of the revision.

Sometimes the date of publication (usually the copyright date) and the date the maps were actually produced are different. The publisher that does not clearly indicate this is aware of the discrepancy. The librarian foolish enough not to recognize that there may be a difference between publication date and the currency of the maps had better turn in his or her geography merit badge. The largest, most complete revision usually takes place the year after the census; for example, Hammond and Rand McNally completely revised their standard atlases in 1971, and the copyright date for all their basic titles is rightfully 1971. A similar policy will be followed in 1980 and every five years thereafter.

There are at least four ways for the library to avoid the problem of currency. First, one or more new acceptable atlases should be purchased annually, always, to be sure, with a clear knowledge that the purchase is really current and not merely a new printing without revision. Second, at least two publishers have methods of keeping maps current. Bartholomew of Edinburgh updates *The Times Atlas of the World* by bimonthly supplements in the *Geographical Magazine.* Rand McNally issues its *Commercial Atlas and Marketing Guide* annually with changes as needed. Third, the library may keep individual maps issued during the year by the National Geographic Society and various government agencies. Finally, current sources, such as encyclopedia yearbooks, almanacs, yearbooks, and periodical indexes, will sometimes serve when standard geographical sources fail.

The desirable atlas concentrates on an integrated collection of maps and includes other material only if it contributes directly to the use of those maps. Many critics of American atlases are quick to point out that publishers attempt too much and end by doing too little. In order to make their atlases competitive in price, they will (1) cover the United States well, but not the remainder of the world; and (2) add encyclopedic information which fattens the volume but is of little real worth.

The encyclopedic approach in an atlas, as in a dictionary, may suit the private buyer. In a library it tends to duplicate, and usually not too well, other materials. By crowding incomplete information into the back or the front of the volume, the editor must sacrifice the number of maps or run the price up beyond the reach of the average purchaser. Normally, the former choice is made.

A good atlas should include a map that shows all parts of the world equally. There should be a table of contents, a glossary of geographical terms and abbreviations, an introduction or a preface explaining essentials of use, and a detailed index. Other minor additions might include such items as geographical equivalents and population comparisons. This is the ideal, rarely achieved. However, when an atlas attempts to go completely beyond the ideal into something more representative of a packaged product than a workable atlas, the librarian has every reason to exercise caution.

Within the normal atlas, regardless of content, arrangement usually follows a standard pattern. There are general maps showing the whole of the world; then come thematic maps indicating various data ranging from population, rainfall, and wind and ocean currents to crop and industrial production. If the atlas is an American publication, the next series is usually of the United States, then the other countries of North America, and finally, the other continents. A good atlas will indicate the order clearly by a table of contents and, more important, by world maps showing how the world is divided in the atlas, together with key page numbers.

The ultimate aim of a good map, whether it be a single sheet or part of an atlas, is to be accurate, easy to read, and esthetically pleasing. To achieve this goal, a mapmaker must consider several factors: scale, color, symbols, projections, grid systems, typography, and marginal information.

Scale   The scale is the size of the map in relation to the actual area it represents. The larger the scale—that is, the less reduction—the more accurate the map will tend to be, particularly for details. The smaller the scale, the more difficult it is for the mapmaker to produce a truly accurate and reliable map.

The page size, or the size of an individual sheet map, will be a rapid indicator of the probable scale. Normally, the larger the page, the larger the scale. Hence, the *Rand McNally Commercial Atlas,* which concentrates on large-scale reproductions of states and cities, has a map-page size of 21 by 15 inches. Other large atlases will vary from 16 by 13 to 19 by 12 inches. Smaller works range from 10 by 7 inches to 12 by 9 inches.

Page size is not always indicative of scale. For example, an atlas may concentrate on showing only major countries and not divisions of those countries. It will have a large format, but small-scale maps. Another atlas may emphasize thematic maps of a small area and have a relatively large scale for its maps, yet may have a small to medium-sized format. Also, the page may include other material besides the map. This will increase the page size while not visibly increasing the scale of the map. Conversely, another publisher will use the full page for the map.

The format, then, is a poor guide; in every case, the librarian needs to check the scale employed. There are two basic methods of indicating scale; and one or both should be clearly visible on each map. A bar scale is a bar divided in a standard way to indicate distances. It is the only accurate method of ascertaining distances when a map has been enlarged or reduced. A natural scale, usually indicated by numerals or fractions, is a worldwide specification established in 1913 by mapmakers. As a map represents a *linear* proportion, the scale 1:1,000,000 (usually noted as 1:1M) means 1 inch represents $1,000,000^2$ sq. in. This may be divided by inches or meters to arrive at approximate distances. Hence, the aforesaid natural scale divided by 63,360—the number of inches in a statute mile—works out to approximately 16 miles per inch.

The natural scale is an excellent method of comparing the scales on various maps. In discussing maps, a base of 1:50,000 is used as the average scale of European maps. Consequently, if one wishes to ascertain how finely the nations of the world have mapped their countries, one may use the average as a comparative base. Russia, for example, is mapped at a scale of 1:100,000, whereas the program of topographic mapping of the whole of the United States is at the scale of 1:24,000. England, one of the best-mapped nations in the world, is at a scale of 1:2500.

Within an atlas, the scale from map to map may vary considerably. This variation has the advantage of allowing larger scales where more detail is needed, and the disadvantage of giving a rather peculiar notion of relative sizes. China may appear no larger than Chile or New York State, particularly if the same page size is used to show all three. American atlases are often faulted for failure to maintain the same relative scales throughout their works. This is true when the American and the Canadian provinces are given emphasis and the remainder of the world is pushed into a small section of the atlas. It may be argued, and justifiably in some cases, that the atlas is primarily for nationals who are more interested in particulars of North America than the remainder of the world. And European atlases frequently are guilty of the same fault, with emphasis on Europe at the sacrifice of the remainder of the world.

One solution is to give each major area of the world equal space and to employ approximately the same scale. This is the great advantage of *The Times Atlas* over other atlases. Another solution is to concentrate almost wholly on one part of the world, as does the *Rand McNally Commercial Atlas,* or to abandon atlases in favor of individual maps employing the same or approximately the same scale.

Color Color's chief value is to enable different classes of data to be related to one another and to show distinctions among details. On physical maps, color clarifies approximate height by hatch lines, hill shading, and special cross sections.

At one time most maps were printed in black and four fundamental colors: brown for relief, blue for water, green for vegetation, and red for structures built by humans. A major problem with using basic colors is that the dominant ones tend to emphasize an area or item as being more important than the portion of the map in lighter tones. Consequently, various hues and shades are now often employed to give reasonably equal weight and emphasis. For example, on a thematic map, population density may be shown by using progressive shades of the same basic color to represent different densities.

A factor often overlooked by the librarian and the map producer alike is that about 10 percent of the population is color-blind, particularly in the ability to distinguish between red and green. Hence, some mapmakers overcome this by the use of varying patterns to identify the features the colors are supposed to delineate.

Printing requirements, especially for less-expensive maps and atlases, may restrict the choice of colors, so that one or two basic colors are employed for many tasks. Where there is no emphasis on detail or the map is limited to a single theme, this approach may suffice. A general rule is that an atlas or map lacking meaningful tints or tones is probably a poor one. On the other hand, a map in which one color (or more) dominates all the others is equally poor.

The success or failure of color depends upon careful consideration in printing. Most multicolor maps are printed on two- or three-color lithographic offset presses, the latter allowing six-color reproduction. This is delicate work, and where it is not successful, there is a lack of perfect registration. In a word, where colors slop over, where the color for a town is removed from the outline of the town, the librarian can be sure that the map was poorly printed. And a poorly printed work is indicative of the publisher's whole attitude toward the map.

Symbols   Equally important as the choice of colors is the selection of symbols. A standard set of symbols for roads, streams, villages, cities, airports, historical sites, parks, and the like is shown on most maps. While these legends are fairly well standardized in American maps, they vary in European maps. Consequently, the symbols should be clearly explained on individual maps, or in an atlas at some convenient place in the preface or introductory remarks.

Thematic mapmakers have a considerable problem with symbols, and here the variation from map to map and country to country will be significant. The problem becomes complicated when a number of different subjects are to be displayed on a single map. Frequently, the task is so complicated that the map becomes illegible. Hence, in the case of thematic maps, it is best to have different maps indicating different items, such as population, rainfall, or industry, rather than a single map.

Projections   All maps are distorted, and it has been estimated that despite any single method employed to indicate surface, well over 200 distortions are possible. Normally, an atlas will use a number of projections to overcome distortions and to indicate the degree of distortion in a map. These may range from global views of continents as seen from space to the world as seen from an airplane crossing the North Pole. The projections should be clearly indicated, although the technique may be of more interest to the professional cartographer than to the casual reader.

Grid Systems   Latitude and longitude are the essentials of any map, and are particularly helpful for locating a special place on the map. These are further subdivided by degrees, minutes, and seconds—$45°12'18''$N, $1°15'$E, for example, is the location of a certain French town. The advantage of this sytem is its ultimate accuracy, but it has the distinct disadvantage of being a number of such length as to be difficult to remember from index to map. Consequently, most maps also are divided into grids, or key reference squares. Index references are then made to these squares, usually by letter and number—E5, D6, etc., with the page number of the map.

The usefulness of a map may be evaluated by the size of the grid system. Obviously, the larger the squares, the more difficult it is to pinpoint a place.

Type   There is clearly scope for considerable improvement in the design of lettering on most maps. Even the best of them often use typefaces developed for display or book texts, and not specifically for maps. Sans serif is used as the basic face for many maps, variation being shown more in the size of the type than in the different kinds of faces. The normal procedure is to use a scale whereby large places are indicated by large type, medium ones by medium-sized type, and so on.

The defects of sans serif type are obvious when parts of the letters are obscured by other lines, too heavy colors, or physical features. Recognizing this, some mapmakers are returning to serif faces and hand lettering.

Regardless of the kind of type used, the major question is its legibility, not only in the maps themselves, but in the text, index, and other features often found in an atlas. Where a large scale is employed in a map, the type legibility rarely is a problem. The test comes in a small-scaled map, and can easily be applied by the librarian attempting to make out the smallest towns and communities, particularly around a densely populated area. Placement should be accurate and done in such a manner that the user can tell the relative location of a place.

Publishers of small-scale maps and atlases frequently circumvent the problem of type legibility by simply deleting place names. A given amount of deletion is necessary, but an adequate number should be shown. What constitutes an adequate number may be ascertained by comparing maps and atlases in the same price category and of the same scale.

Binding   The need for a sturdy binding is self-evident, but in addition to strength it must be of such a nature that the atlas can be opened easily. When the book is lying flat, the entire map should be visible and not hidden in part of the binding. Oddly enough, this latter fault is more frequent than the relatively high prices of some atlases would indicate.

Marginal Information   Each map should give certain basic information, usually in the margin. A quick way of ascertaining the worth of a map is to check for this type of information. It should include, at minimum, the scale (inclusion of both a bar and natural scale is desirable), the type of projection, and where thematic maps are employed, the symbols and significance of the colors. In an atlas, the meaning of the general symbols may be given in the preface or introduction, as well as the date of printing, the dates of revision, and other such data. Normally the directions are not given in an atlas, it being understood that north is at the top of the map. On single sheets, there should be a compass rose indicating direction.

The index

A comprehensive index is as important in reference work as the maps, and the emphasis on content. A good index is in alphabetical sequence and clearly lists all place names which appear on the map. In addition, there should be reference to the exact page and the exact map, and (above all) latitude, longitude, and grid information. A page number alone is never enough, as anyone will testify who has sought to find an elusive town or city on a map lacking such information.

The index in many atlases is really an excellent gazetteer; that is, in addition to basic information, each entry will include data on population and country. When an index becomes a gazetteer, it should include not only place names shown on the map, but places so small or inconsequential as not to be located on the maps. The difference may be indicated by some type of marking or special column. But the difference must be apparent or the user may be searching in vain for something not in the atlas proper.

Other useful index information will include pronunciation, standard transliteration of non-Romanized place names, and sufficient cross-references from spellings used in a foreign country to those employed by the country issuing the atlas or map, e.g., Wien, Austria, should be cross-referenced to Vienna, as well as an entry from Vienna to "*see* Wien."

A useful check: Try to find four or five names listed in the index on the maps. How long did it take, and how difficult was the task? Reverse this test by finding names on the maps and trying to locate them in the index. Failure of either test spells trouble.

Bibliographies[4]

Winch, Kenneth L. *International Maps and Atlases in Print,* 2d ed., New York: R. R. Bowker Company, 1976, 900 pp. $60.

For the average library, the listing of maps and atlases in *Subject Guide to Books in Print* is sufficient. Librarians seeking a type of *Books in Print* for geography will turn to Winch. Based upon an earlier British work, it lists maps and atlases published throughout the world. There are approximately 8000 entries by 700 publishers. Arrangement is by country, with subdivisions for general maps of roads; political, physical, and historical subdivisions; official surveys; earth resources; etc. For each entry title, scale, series reference, number of sheets, edition, author, place of publication, and other vital bibliographical data are supplied.

Librarians seeking evaluations of geographical publications other than those in standard reviews should consult the *Bulletin, Special Libraries Association, Geography and Map Division,* by far the best single American source of evaluative reviews. Equally excellent reviews are found in the *Information Bulletin, Western Association of Map Libraries.* Also reliable are the reviews in *Geographical Review* and "Reference and Subscription Book Reviews" in *The Booklist.*

WORLD ATLASES

The Times Atlas of the World: Comprehensive 5th Edition. London: Times Newspapers Limited, 1975, 125 map plates, 232 pp. $75 (distributed in the United States by Quadrangle/The New York Times Book Company).

[4] Two excellent bibliographies to maps and map collecting are Mary Galneder, "Acquisition Tools and Sources of Maps," and Tim Jones, "Maps in Libraries," *Illinois Libraries,* May 1974, pp. 342–348 and 385–386.

Hammond Medallion World Atlas. Maplewood, New Jersey: Hammond Incorporated, 1975, 655 pp. $29.95.

Rand McNally Cosmopolitan World Atlas. Chicago: Rand McNally & Company, 1975, 360 pp. $24.95.

National Geographic Atlas of the World, 4th ed. Washington, D.C.: National Geographic Society, 1975, 330 pp. $23.90.

At least one, and probably all, of these American-published atlases will be found in libraries. They are compiled by the leaders in the field and are frequently updated and totally revised.

By any judgment, *The Times Atlas* is the best world atlas in the English language, or for that matter in any language. That it happens to be the most expensive is chiefly because such loving care has been taken, with emphasis on large-scale, multiple maps for several countries and an attention to detail and color rarely rivaled by other American atlases. At one time (1955 to 1959), this was a five-volume work, but since 1967, the publisher has chosen to issue the *Atlas* as a large (12 by 18 inches) single volume.

The volume consists of three basic parts. The first 51-page section is a conspectus of world minerals, sources of energy and food, and a variety of diagrams and star charts. The atlas proper comprises 128 double-page maps, the work of the Edinburgh house of Bartholomew. This is the vital part, and it is perfect in both typography and color. The clear typeface enables the reader to make out each of the enormous number of names. A variety of colors are used with skill and taste to show physical features, railways, rivers, political boundaries, and so on. A remarkable thing about this atlas is that it shows almost every noteworthy geographical feature from lighthouses and tunnels to mangrove swamps—all by symbols which are carefully explained.

The Times Atlas is suited for American libraries because, unlike many other atlases, it gives a large amount of space to non-European Countries. No other atlas matches it for the detailed coverage of the Soviet Union, China, Africa, and Southeast Asia—lands hardly overlooked in other atlases, but usually covered in considerably less detail.No uniform scale is now used for most maps, as it was in earlier editions. The United Kingdom and Europe maps are 1:1,000,000 or larger scale, e.g. 1:550,000. Maps of the larger land masses are supplemented with smaller, detailed maps which range from maps of urban centers to maps of the environs of Mt. Everest.

The final section is a 200,000-name index, which, for most purposes, serves as an excellent gazetteer. After each name, the country name is given with an exact reference to a map.

The Times Atlas is frequently updated. The 1975 edition includes new countries and name changes, particularly those in Africa; plans of more cities than previously; and completely revised prefatory material on physiography, oceanography, and detailed up-to-date thematic maps.

The *Hammond Medallion World Atlas* has some 600 maps, including one for each of the 50 states. Among other basic features: a world index of over 100,000 place names (some 100,000 less, let it be noted, than *The Times Atlas*); numerous subindexes interleaved with the maps; zip codes; sections on ecology and the Bible, as well as history; numerous diagrams and photographs; and so on. The maps are passable and the index is excellent. One way to avoid the frills and save money is to purchase Hammond's *Ambassador* edition, which sells for $16.95 and is the same as the *Medallion* except for its omission of the extra materials.

Rand McNally's entry follows much the same pattern of offering something in a price range for just about everyone. Still, the basic set of maps is found in its often revised *Cosmopolitan World Atlas*. This work offers 400 maps with numerous map inserts in a format similar to the Hammond title. Scales range from 1:2,000,000 to 1:16,000,000, compared with up to 1:15,000,000 for some Hammond maps. There is a 100-page index which lists some 82,000 places and features. The "Planet Earth edition" means illustrations, diagrams, and brief articles on weather, geology, oceans, and the like. The less-expensive *Premier World Atlas* and the *World Atlas, Family Edition,* are only two of several versions of the same work.

A larger, higher-priced Rand McNally title is *The International Atlas.*[5] First published in 1969 and revised in 1974, it includes 278 regional maps and a 222-page index of over 180,000 names. It also has numerous charts and diagrams, and information on world populations, resources, etc. One good feature is a separate section of city maps.

The *National Geographic Atlas* proper has 190 pages, including 151 pages of maps drawn to no single scale. They run from 201 miles to the inch for political maps of South America to 109 miles to the inch for southern South America. Sections usually open with small physical and political maps followed by large-scale political maps (usually covering two pages) of individual countries with numerous insets for cities. There is the imbalance of coverage which is almost expected in such atlases, i.e., about one-fifth of the volume is devoted to maps of the United States, while 40 percent of the work consists of maps of the rest of North America and of Europe. The index provides over 140,000 entries and is one of the largest for an atlas of this price range. In itself, this is an advantage, made even more valuable by the fact that the maps are crowded with names but nevertheless are extremely legible. In overall quality, the maps are equal

---

[5] Except for revisions and minor differences, this is the same as the *Britannica Atlas* (Chicago: Encyclopaedia Britannica Inc., 1972), which was produced for Britannica by Rand McNally. No library needs both.

to, if not better than, those found in the Rand McNally and Hammond atlases. Some rather inane introductory material appears before each of the sections but, on the whole, the padding is minimal. Important features are shown, including both roads and railroads. All in all, the National Geographic entry equals, if it does not surpass, most other atlases; and as it is continually appearing in new editions, it would be among the basic choices in libraries.

The atlases listed here, as indicated, are only a few of literally dozens available in almost every price range for almost every audience from children to sophisticated students of geography. For example, in its 1977–1978 catalog, Hammond Incorporated lists at least a dozen world atlases priced from $1.80 to $29.95. The other large publisher, Rand McNally, has an equal, if not a greater, number of atlases. And both issue an equally overwhelming number of thematic atlases. The librarian may find one or all of these useful, although for most purposes the atlases listed here are probably a good first choice—always, though, taking heed to keep them current by a careful watch for reviews, particularly those of world atlases appearing in the "Reference and Subscription Book Reviews" section of *The Booklist.*

World atlases: Foreign-language

When one speaks of "foreign" world atlases, there seems to be an agreement that the term does not include atlases produced in England, e.g., *The Times Atlas of the World* or *The New Oxford Atlas* (London: Oxford University Press, 1975). The key is "foreign language," meaning not only that the descriptive matter is in another language, but that often the spellings are particular to a country, like the previously cited Wien, which we know as Vienna. The result is that fewer and fewer of the really foreign atlases are now used in American libraries other than special or large academic libraries; even here, one wonders how much they are truly employed for anything but admiration of the maps. This conclusion is a sad commentary on our command of other languages, but it is borne out by Sheehy's *Guide to Reference Books,* which lists over 600 foreign-language dictionaries, but no more than 50 world atlases and national and regional maps from other countries. And even these are only briefly annotated.

Still, two of the most highly regarded foreign-language world atlases which should be found in larger libraries are the Soviets' *Atlas Mira,* and the Italian *Atlante Internazionale.* The *Atlas Mira,* 2d ed. (Moscow: 1967, 250 pp.), actually is in English, a translated version. Another edition, issued in 1968, includes the 190,000 names found in the index, but it is not in English. Be that as it may, the atlas is a joy to look at in that the maps are some of the best drawn in the world. Interestingly enough, only about 20 percent of the total is devoted to the U.S.S.R., the remainder being given over to the rest of the world. An added feature is the numerous city maps, which tend to be extremely detailed. Equal care, according to experienced cartographers, is given to slightly misrepresenting the location of certain vital industrial areas and cities in the Soviet Union.

Certainly the winner for appearance and for general excellence is the frequently revised Italian world atlas: Touring Club Italiano, *Atlante Internazionale* (Milan: Touring Club, 1968). Most of the maps are double-page and have the added advantage of lying flat when the atlas is opened. Also, there are quite excellent thematic maps which include a vast amount of detail. Major metropolitan areas are equally well represented. Although most emphasis is on Europe, the atlas is held as a model of its kind. It has another advantage: The index lists more than 250,000 names in the spelling of the country in which they are located, not in Italian.

NATIONAL MAPS

U.S. Geological Survey. *The National Atlas of the United States of America.* Washington, D.C.: Government Printing Office, 1970, 417 pp. $100.

The Times Atlas of China. London: Times Newspapers Limited, 1976, c. 170 pp. $75 (distributed in the United States by Quadrangle/The New York Times Book Company).

After 18 years of work and some 100 years of dreaming, the United States has its own national atlas—considerably behind some 40 other nations which have had such maps for years. The purpose of the atlas and its long history are explained in a lucid introduction.

The $3 million project is a 14-pound oversized volume with 335 pages of maps and a 41,000-entry index. It is the most expensive single volume ever produced by the United States government; and although $100 may seem comparatively high, it is well worth the price.

The volume is in two sections: "General Reference Maps" and "Special Subject Maps." The short, first part consists of a general United States atlas. Most of the maps are at the scale of 1:200,000,000, with urban areas at 1:500,000 and certain other areas at 1:1,000,000. These are the basic maps familiar to the general atlas user. They show every geographical feature from national parks and wildlife refuges to 13 different varieties of water features. There are only a limited number of physical maps.

The second section consists of some 750 thematic maps in 281 pages. They cover myriad topics from history, culture, climate, crime, marriages, and divorces to zip codes. In many ways, this section is the answer to almost any question likely to be asked at a reference desk about major features of the United States and its peoples. The maps are prepared at three different scales: 1:7,500,000 on two pages; 1:17,000,000; and 1:34,000,000.

Edited by a professor of Chinese at Cambridge, *The Times Atlas of China* has three basic parts. The first is a history with suitable maps. The second part consists of 12 double-page maps, accompanied by text and diagrams covering various items ranging from railroads and population to climate and agriculture. But the bulk of the atlas consists of detailed maps and a comprehensive gazetteer. Some four pages are devoted to each province and there are city maps, including several pages of street maps for Peking. This is one example of a combination atlas, encyclopedia, and thematic approach to a country. Similar treatment, although rarely with such distinguished maps, is available for other countries and regions.

Sources of government maps

In compiling *The National Atlas,* some 80 government bureaus and offices supplied information and material. Many of these agencies publish separate maps of a much more modest type, all of which are available either from the departments themselves or from the Government Printing Office. They may be located via the *Monthly Catalog of United States Government Publications.*

A basic bibliography for American maps is John L. Andriot's *Guide to U.S. Government Maps* (McLean, Virginia: Documents Index, 1975, 2 vols.). This is a "preliminary" edition of a still-to-be-expanded work which lists 4800-plus U.S. Geological Survey maps issued from 1879 through 1974. The second volume has a reprint of the index section of *The National Atlas.*

A useful overview, for both beginners and experienced map librarians, will be found in Jane Low's "The Acquisition of Maps and Charts Published by the United States Government," *Occasional Papers No. 125* (Urbana: University of Illinois Graduate School of Library Science, November, 1976). This includes about 30 pages of text and 6 pages of references.

Local maps

Every library will have a suitable map of its own state and city or town—preferably in clear view—plus maps of the county and surrounding states. As noted, these maps are easily obtained. A problem arises when someone wants to locate a particular street in a distant city. Lacking a specific map such as those in the Rand McNally *International Atlas,* the next best thing is one of the larger atlases, an encyclopedia, or a guidebook. Guidebooks frequently include maps of many smaller cities not found in the standard works.

Local maps may be obtained from a number of sources. Usually the chamber of commerce in a specific city has local maps available for the asking. Frequently, companies issue detailed block maps, particularly if they have interests in real estate. Also, the telephone company will often give the library a copy of its local map which shows areas where tolls are not charged. Usually this map is quite large and extremely detailed, and it often shows considerably more than is found on most standard local maps.

Among the countless road atlases available, the best is the *Rand Mc-Nally Road Atlas: United States—Canada—Mexico* (Chicago: Rand McNally & Company, 1926 to date, annual). At about $14, it consists of large, easy-to-read maps that include details of larger cities and regions. There is a 27,000-plus name index as well as bits of information on various aspects of travel from toll roads and selected AM stations to traffic sign language.

THEMATIC MAPS AND ATLASES

Rand McNally Commercial Atlas and Marketing Guide. Chicago: Rand McNally & Company, 1876 to date, annual. $90.

Shepherd, William. *Historical Atlas,* 9th ed. New York: Barnes & Noble, Inc., 1964, 226 maps. $22.50.

These are two examples of many thematic maps and atlases which graphically show the tides of economic or historical events. Other examples suffer from one major fault: Since most are not revised on a regular basis, they are soon out of date. The value of the *Rand McNally Commercial Atlas* is that it is revised every year, and for the library which can afford to rent it (it is rented, not purchased), the *Atlas* not only solves the problem of adequate United States coverage, but solves it in the best form possible.

The *Commercial Atlas* accurately records changes on a year-by-year basis. All information is the most up to date of any single atlas, or, for that matter, any reference work of this type. It is an excellent source for current statistical data, and the first 25 or so pages offer general information on business facts ranging from United States agriculture and communications to retail trade and transportation. The maps give basic, demographic, and business data for some 116,000 places in the United States.

Technically, the *Commercial Atlas* is not devoted entirely to the United States; but aside from a small number of world and foreign maps, the concentration is on the individual states. Each of the state maps, usually a double-page spread, places emphasis on the political-commercial aspects of the state. The maps are especially useful for indicating city and county boundaries. There is a wealth of statistical information (retail sales maps and analyses of businesses, manufacturers, and principal business centers) in each of the state sections. By far the finest atlas for detailed treatment of the individual states, the whole is tied together with a superb index.

The index serves as a fine ready-reference source for (1) location of cities and towns by state and county; (2) the number and names of railroads and airlines serving the community; (3) estimated current population, including a separate figure for college and university students; and (4) zip codes. (In fact, the publisher claims there are more than 60,000 zips not listed in the official post office *Zip Code Directory*.)

As both an atlas and a handy compilation of up-to-date statistics, the *Rand McNally Commercial Atlas* is unrivaled. Limited for the most part to the United States as it largely is, the encyclopedic information not only seems legitimate, but also is a blessing.

Another good thematic atlas is the *Oxford Regional Economic Atlas: The United States and Canada* (2d ed.: London: Oxford University Press, 1975). After introductory material, the *Atlas* consists of 128 maps in numerous sections such as urban maps of cities, topographic maps, physical maps which show relief, geological maps, and maps showing climate, agriculture, and air and surface communications. These are followed by a detailed gazetteer.

Historical maps are quite literally that; for this reason, it is hardly necessary to have a totally up-to-date collection. If useful at all, some of the older, standard titles in this area can, and will, be used for many years to come. The average user is more interested in the past than in the immediate future; hence, a title with a copyright date in the 1960s, 1950s, or even earlier is not in any real reference sense out of date.

Shepherd's *Historical Atlas* has been standard for years. The last edition covers world history from about 2000 B.C. down to A.D. 1955. Outline maps prepared by Hammond indicate developments of commerce, war campaigns, adjustments of boundaries after various wars, and countless other useful approaches to history. There is a full index of names. Despite its usefulness, the volume is relatively poor typographically and the colored maps tend to be somewhat out of register.

At the other extreme of format and cost ($125) is the *Atlas of Early American History* (Princeton, New Jersey: Princeton University Press, 1976, 157 pp.), a magnificently designed and produced volume 14 by 18 inches in size. It contains 286 data-filled maps, 271 of them reproduced in as many as six colors. Dramatic as the *Atlas* is, it covers only the Revolutionary era 1760–1790.[6]

---

[6] A review of this work which points up some of the problems of thematic atlases: George F. Scheer, "Atlas of Early American History," *The New York Times Book Review*, September 19, 1976, p. 31.

The standard American thematic atlas is Kenneth T. Jackson (ed.), *Atlas of American History*, rev. ed. (New York: Charles Scribner's Sons, 1977). This includes 197 maps covering American history from the beginning through to the Vietnam war. Its black and white maps represent the work of some 65 scholars. There is a detailed index. It is an excellent work for tracing the country's political, social, and economic changes over the years.

GAZETTEERS

Columbia Lippincott Gazetteer of the World. New York: Columbia University Press, 1952 (supplements, 1962), 2148 pp. + 22 pp. $100.

Webster's New Geographical Dictionary, rev. ed. Springfield, Massachusetts: G. & C. Merriam Company, 1972, 1370 pp. $14.95.

In one sense, the index in any atlas is a gazetteer—that is, it is a geographical dictionary or finding list of cities, mountains, rivers, population, and the features in the atlas. A separate gazetteer is precisely the same, usually without maps. Why, then, bother with a separate volume? There are three reasons: (1) The gazetteers tend to list more names; (2) the information is usually detailed; and (3) the advantage of a single, easily managed volume is often welcomed. Having made these points, one can argue, and with some justification, that many atlas indexes have more entries, are more up to date, and contain a larger amount of information than one finds in a gazetteer. The wise librarian will first consider what is to be found in atlases before purchasing any gazetteer.

The number of gazetteers and the indexes found in good atlases, the expense of preparation, and the limited sales probably account for the lack of interest by many publishers in gazeteers as a separate group. The fact that most information sought by the layperson can be found in even greater detail in a general or geographical encyclopedia does not increase the use of gazetteers. Their primary value is as a source for locating places possibly overlooked by a standard atlas and as informal indexes.

The two American gazetteers, found in almost every reference department, differ in two important respects. The *Columbia* work has some 130,000 entries as compared with about 48,000 in *Webster's,* although its price is about 7 times that of the *Webster's.* A minor difference which makes the *Webster's* more attractive for casual use is its comparatively compact size. Also, it has the advantage of being more up-to-date than the *Columbia.*

Aside from sheer volume, the *Columbia Gazetteer* tends to give considerably more information about each place. For example, it devotes one and one-half long columns to Berlin, while *Webster's* dismisses the former German capital in a few short paragraphs. Entries in both include pronunciation, location, area, population, geographical and physical description, and economic and historical data.

TRAVEL GUIDES

American Automobile Association. *Tour Book*. Washington, D.C.: American Automobile Association, various dates, titles. Free to members.

American Guide Series. Prepared by Works Progress Administration, Federal Writers' Project. Various publishers, 1937 to 1950; frequently reprinted and reissued by numerous publishers.

Hotel and Motel Red Book. New York: American Hotel and Motel Association Directory Corp., 1886 to date, annual. $16.50.

The purpose of the general guidebook is to inform the traveler about what to see, where to stay, where to dine, and the best way of getting there. It is the type of book best carried in the car or in one's pocket. Librarians frequently find these works useful for the vast amount of details about specific places. Atlases and gazetteers are specific enough about pinpointing location, yet rarely deal with the down-to-earth facts travelers require.

The travel agency or automobile club usually furnishes the traveler with much of what is needed in the way of immediate information. The American Automobile Association, for example, has a series of tour books covering the United States and the rest of North America; they are "produced as an exclusive service for members" but do find their way into some library collections. They offer a wealth of ready-reference material from average monthly temperatures in states and cities to historical data. Particularly useful are detailed, up-to-date maps of downtown areas of larger cities and even many small towns. The set runs from 15 to 16 volumes for the United States, with separate titles for Canada, Mexico, and Central America. The association also issues trip maps with up-to-the-minute information on the best roads, detours, and the like—again, only for members.

Of all the guides, the single most useful work for reference is unquestionably the *American Guide Series*. Originally produced during the Depression by writers for the Federal Writers' Project of the Works Progress Administration, the series includes over 150 volumes.[7] Either private publishers or historical groups working within the various states have man-

---

[7] Those in print are listed in *Subject Guide to Books in Print* under the state name. The whole series is in E. A. Baer's *Titles in Series* (Metuchen, New Jersey: Scarecrow Press, 1954, vol. 1, nos. 492 to 660, 2 vols., 1964).

aged to update many of these works and to keep them in print. The guides include basic, usually accurate, historical, social, and economic information for almost every place in the state from the smallest unmarked hamlet to the largest cities. Maps, illustrations, and highway distances add to their usefulness, and most also have excellent indexes. For the reference desk, they are particularly helpful for locating information on communities, either entirely overlooked or only mentioned in standard reference books.

Putting more emphasis on comfort than on courage, the *Mobil Travel Guides* (Chicago: Rand McNally & Company, 1958 to date, annual) are a typical example of annual guides organized to inform the traveler about the best motels, hotels, restaurants, and resorts. The work is divided into seven regional volumes, and each is divided by state and town. There are a number of city maps and the usual data on each place are covered. Some 21,000 different spots are graded with the star system—one for good, five for the best.

If the more adventuresome American traveler wants a simple listing of hotels and motels without ratings but including prices, the old standby is the *Hotel and Motel Red Book*. Revised annually, it is arranged by state and city and gives basic information about each accommodation. Since it lists only association members, facilities in small towns are often not included. There are advertisements that further indicate features.

Beyond these basic guides, the library will have a number of series. Among the standards are *Fielding's Travel Guide to Europe* (New York: Sloane, 1948 to date, annual) and the *Fodor's* modern guides (New York: McKay, 1953 to date, annual) which cover much the same material as found in *Fielding's*, although in a different fashion. Guides to guides include *Selected Guide to Travel Books* (New York: Fleet Press, 1974 to date, biennial), containing brief, uncritical annotations of some 700 titles; and *Suit Your Spirit: Travel Guidebooks in Review* (2d ed.; Ann Arbor: University of Michigan, International Center, 1975, 157 pp.), an objective listing which mildly evaluates travel guides. Frequently revised and costing under $5, it is a "best buy" for any library with an interest in the field. A useful source of information on new titles is the special section "Travel Guides" in each annual edition of *American Reference Books Annual*.

SUGGESTED READING

Baker, John F., "Temple Fielding," *Publishers Weekly*, December 8, 1975, pp. 6–7. A short interview with the "dean of travel guides." Insights into how the *Fielding* guides are planned and researched.

Brewer, J. Gordon, *The Literature of Geography: A Guide to Its Organization and Use.* Hamden, Connecticut: Shoe String, 1973. The most practical guide to reference materials in geography now available. Although written with a British audience in mind, its value to American users is equally important. A more up-to-date guide, again for a British audience, is: Nichols, Harold, *Map Librarianship*. London: Clive Bingley, 1976. Particularly useful for its extensive section on cataloging.

Chernofsky, Jacob L. "Exploring the World of Maps & Atlases," *AB Bookman's Weekly*, August 23–30, 1976, pp. 987–1004. A report on the American Library Association rare books meeting which is valuable for indicating the scope of interest in maps and atlases among librarians.

Drazniowsky, Roman, *Map Librarianship: Readings*. Metuchen, New Jersey: Scarecrow Press, 1975. A compilation by the map curator for the American Geographical Society that covers a wide range of topics, as well as bibliographies—including additonal ones compiled by the editor.

"Map Collections," *Illinois Libraries*, May 1974. The whole issue of approximately 100 pages is devoted to aspects of maps, including a good section on reference titles and bibliographies on maps in libraries.

Schorr, Alan, "Map Librarianship, Map Libraries and Maps, A Bibliography," *Bulletin Geography and Map Division Special Libraries*, March 1977, pp. 2–18. A supplement to an earlier bibliography in the same publication (*Bulletin* 95, 1974, described here). Between the supplement and the original listing, the librarian has over 800 entries which cover all aspects of the subject. The basic bibliography is updated from time to time.

Wise, Donald, "Treasure Maps," *Bulletin. Special Libraries Association, Geography and Map Division*, September 1975, pp. 15–22. A history and bibliography with useful references for further reading. This is only one example of the wealth of materials found in the *Bulletin*, and imaginative librarians might well build special displays and collections around such an article. See, also, his: "Cartographic Sources and Procurement Problems," *Special Libraries*, May/June 1977, pp. 198–205, which is a practical guide on where to buy what.

Woodward, David (ed.), *Five Centuries of Map Printing*. Chicago: The University of Chicago Press, 1975. A beautifully illustrated collection of essays on the technical aspects of cartography through the ages, with particular reference to various printing and reproduction processes.

CHAPTER TEN

Government Documents[1]

THE BASIC MYSTERY for many beginning reference librarians is the government document. For some peculiar reason, the very term seems to frighten and confuse. Most of the cause may be attributed to a simple fact: Too many libraries tend to forget that the purpose of a government publication is to inform, to answer questions, and not to be an ignoble excuse for setting off hot discussion on organizational cataloging and administration.

Definition

A government document is any publication that is printed at government expense or published by authority of a governmental body. Documents may be considered in terms of issuing agencies: the congressional, judiciary, and executive branches, which include many departments, and agen-

---

[1] In view of the nature of government publications, most accredited library schools offer one or more special documents courses. It is as complicated and as rewarding a study as any of the specialized subject areas. Throughout this text, various government publications are noted as parts of units. This approach stems from a conviction that they should be an integral part of a reference collection and should not be treated as separate items.

cies. In terms of use, the documents may be classified as (1) records of government administration; (2) research documents for specialists, including a considerable number of statistics and data of value to science and business; and (3) popular sources of information. The physical form may be a book, pamphlet, magazine, report, monograph, or microform.

While this discussion mainly concerns federal documents, state, county, and municipal publications are also a major concern of any library.

Some of the mystery surrounding government documents will be dispelled if one likens the government to the average private publisher. The latter may well issue a record of government action, although normally the commercial publication will be in somewhat more felicitous prose and with editorial comments. The transcendent purpose is to publish documents that may be considered useful for research, while the substantial returns are realized by popular works.

What, then, is the difference between using the government document and the average work issued by one of the publishers whose items appear in *Books in Print?* The source, the retrieval, and the organization puzzle most people.

One may freely admit that the bibliographical control and daily use of documents in reference work often are difficult and require expertise beyond the average experience of the reference librarian. Nevertheless, there are certain basic guides and approaches to government documents which should be familiar to all librarians.

In describing the problems with government documents, Joe Morehead observes:

> No one can gain mastery of federal documents by perusing a text; skills that the documents librarian must possess require the day-to-day practice that comes only with professional service.[2]

Too many librarians read into this perfectly sensible statement that as they will not be working on a "day-to-day" basis with government documents, they need not bother learning anything about them. Fine, except that cutting out government documents, or at least the basic guides, is similar to eliminating equally vital reference works such as *The Readers' Guide to Periodical Literature,* or, for that matter, the card catalog.

---

[2] Joe Morehead, *Introduction to United States Public Documents* (Littleton, Colorado: Libraries Unlimited, Inc., 1975), p. xxvi. The author goes on to state another truism: "The rewards of working with public documents far outweigh the frustrations."

GUIDES

Morehead, Joe. *Introduction to United States Public Documents.* Littleton, Colorado: Libraries Unlimited, Inc., 1975, 289 pp. $10. (A second edition is scheduled for 1978.)

Schmeckebier, Laurence F., and Roy B. Eastin. *Government Publications and Their Use,* 2d ed. Washington, D.C.: The Brookings Institute, 1969, 502 pp. $12.50.

Working his way through the maze of government documents, Morehead manages to leave the reader with a detailed map of the intricate territory. His textbook is by far the best available for (1) a clear explanation of how government documents are organized in a library, and (2) the basic structure (and superstructure) of the three branches of government which produce the documents. Thanks to a careful plan of attack along with an excellent index, the text serves the beginner or the expert who seeks to solve problems with federal publications.

Published shortly after Schmeckebier's death, the standard *Government Publications and Their Use* describes all aspects of documents from how they are produced to how they are used. The text is sometimes difficult to follow, but on the whole the book is useful for historical material and for broad, unchanging outlines of how laws are made and how bills are passed.

The basic bibliography in the field is *Government Publications: A Guide to Bibliographic Tools* (4th ed.; Washington, D.C.: Government Printing Office, 1975). First issued in 1927, this work lists about 3000 catalogs, indexes, abstracts, guides, etc., used for work not only with federal documents, but with those of individual states, the United Nations, and other countries. Most of the entries, arranged by geographical area, have brief annotations. In addition, there are a short history of each of the United States agencies and an excellent index.

CATALOGS AND INDEXES

The majority of federal documents are printed by the Government Printing Office (GPO) in Washington, D.C. The distribution and sales of the documents are handled largely by the Superintendent of Documents' office.[3]

[3] In the early 1970s, separate processing facilities were opened in Colorado and in Philadelphia. (The latter facility closed in 1976, but may reopen in the Carter administration.) Laypersons who often order documents listed in *Selected U.S. Government Publications* are now

There are two basic listings or bibliographies of ongoing government documents:

U.S. Superintendent of Documents. *Monthly Catalog of United States Government Publications,* Washington, D.C.: 1895 to date, monthly. $45.

U.S. Superintendent of Documents. *Selected U.S. Government Publications,* Washington, D.C.: 1928 to date, monthly. Free.

The *Monthly Catalog* is the record of, and an index to, published government documents.[4] It is used to locate specific documents by either subject, author, or title. It has numerous secondary uses, but it is primarily the current bibliography of publications issued by the government. A long run of the *Catalog* is virtually a catalog of government publications issued since 1895.

Beginning in July 1976 the *Catalog* format was changed radically. However, arrangement is much the same as before, i.e., by Superintendent of Documents classification number assigned to each publication. The number is generally, but not always, the same as the issuing agency's number. Therefore, in most cases documents issued, say, by the Library of Congress are dutifully listed under the Library of Congress.

The real change since July 1976 is in the amount of information for each publication, and the assignment of subject headings and indexing. Full cataloging information is now given so that entry data are much the same as in a Library of Congress card. Subject headings are derived from the *Library of Congress Subject Headings* and fit in nicely with subject headings found in most card catalogs. The catch: The subject headings rarely match the subject headings employed from 1895 to 1976 in the *Catalog.* The implications for searching are obvious. One set of subject headings must be used after July 1976, another set for the previous years.

Another major change is in the indexing. There are now four separate indexes. The first is author, the second title, the third subject, and the last an index to series and reports. More important, instead of only an annual index, there are now a six-month cumulative index and an annual cumulation. Thanks to the additional indexing and added subjects, the July–December 1976 cumulation (issued in mid-1977) consists of 1755

---

directed to the Pueblo, Colorado, center. However, the majority of documents from the *Monthly Catalog* are ordered directly from Washington, D.C.

[4] Jaia Heymann, "The 'New' Monthly Catalog, a Review," *The Unabashed Librarian,* no. 22, 1977, pp. 5–6. A succinct, clear review that details the basic changes in the *Catalog,* and the problems caused, as well as the debates which the changes have generated. Also, see almost any current issue of *Government Publications Review* for more on this controversial subject.

three-column pages. This compares with only 999 two-column pages for the whole year of 1975 in the old catalog.

It is worth repeating that for the average user and the average librarian, the *Catalog* is not difficult to use. Despite the changes for better or for worse, it does fulfill its primary mission of listing most of the 15,000 to 20,000 government documents issued each year and likely to be of interest to most users. The *Catalog* does not include all government documents, although the addition of at least some printed and processed reports has increased the coverage since July 1976.

A private publisher has published the *Cumulative Subject Index to the Monthly Catalog . . . 1900–1971* (Washington, D.C.: Carrollton Press, 1973–1976, 15 vols. plus annual supplements) which eliminates the necessity of searching each and every annual index. The set provides a subject approach to over 800,000 documents issued over a 72-year period. The citation is to the appropriate year of the *Monthly Catalog* and the page number. This is a two-step index. The user must look up the subject, locate the year and page in the *Monthly Catalog,* and then turn to the *Catalog* to find the Superintendent of Documents classification number to locate the document on the shelves.[5]

As one moves from the annual indexes in the *Monthly Catalog* to the massive Carrollton Press work, the tendency is to move from "basics" to research materials.[6] The other movement is back to the basic of basics, the monthly *Selected U.S. Government Publications,* often called by librarians simply the *Selected List.* This is a free buying guide for small to medium-sized libraries of all types. It has gone through several formats, and is now a 15- to 20- or 25-page booklet which lists by broad popular subject headings some 200-plus government publications each month. There are usually illustrations and annotations of several titles that the compiler believes will be of greatest interest to the general public.

It should be clear that while the *Monthly Catalog* is primarily a bibliography and index to publications, the *Selected List* is not cumulated or indexed. It is only a method of indicating to librarians and laypersons

---

[5] The *Decennial Cumulative Index* (Washington, D.C.: Government Printing Office, various dates) covers a much shorter period of time; that is, it is a cumulative index to the *Monthly Catalog* for 1941–1950 and 1951–1960 but is suitable for smaller libraries without extensive collections.

[6] Just as there are retrospective bibliographies for books, e.g., Evans, Sabin, etc., so are there for government documents which are explained in Morehead's text (op. cit., pp. 75–81) and in various articles, e.g., Mary Larsgaard, "Beginner's Guide to Indexes to the Nineteenth Century U.S. Serial Set," *Government Publications Review,* no. 4, 1975, pp. 303–312, which, as the title indicates, is useful for the beginning researcher in nineteenth-century documents.

what is available among both new and older government publications. Therefore, many libraries with small government documents collections may take the *Monthly Catalog,* as they would extra indexes, to assist as a finding device for documents to be borrowed on interlibrary loan.[7]

Retrieval

In most library situations where government documents are either a major or a minor consideration, the basic method of retrieval is to use the *Monthly Catalog* as a type of index to what is needed. There are more sophisticated, necessary approaches, but recourse to the *Catalog* is usually the beginning step. If documents are kept in a separate collection, the tendency is to follow the Superintendent of Documents classification system. This consists of a combination of letters and numbers assigned to documents. Unlike the more common systems known to librarians, the classification has no visible relationship to subject matter. It is related to the issuing agency.

The Superintendent of Documents classification system is used as a method of identification in all current Superintendent of Documents bibliographies and lists—of which the *Monthly Catalog* is basic—as well as lists issued by various departments and agencies. Consequently, the lists serve most libraries as a catalog, and the documents are organized and arranged on the shelves according to this system.

In smaller libraries, the documents and periodicals are integrated into the general collection and/or are variously classified as other ephemera in the vertical file. Little or no effort is made to consider them as unique.

Just as the separate collection tends to isolate the documents, so does the separate classification scheme. Since entries in the indexes and bibliographies are not normally repeated in the card catalog, the user may never know that a document concerning labor management exists and may be just what is needed. Some link has to be provided to get the user from the catalog to the necessary index, but even *see* and *see also* references are frequently insufficient.

A distinct advantage of the new *Monthly Catalog* is that it allows entries to be put into a data base which may be tapped via a computer terminal. This, coupled with the adoption of *Library of Congress* subject headings, will eventually tie the main collection and the government documents closer together. Until then, most government documents are listed under a corporate entry in the card catalog, rarely by title or by subject. A corporate entry is a listing under the name of the author, that is, the

[7] Almost every community has within its region a depository library where the user might go to find the needed document. The libraries are listed, alphabetically by state and city, in the September number of the *Monthly Catalog.*

government body responsible for its issue. For example, a corporate government entry will be under the country (United States), state (New York), city (St. Paul), or other official unit that sponsored publication. Thus, someone requesting a publication about foreign affairs would probably first look under the U.S. Department of State. Since there are a vast number of governmental agencies, it is frequently difficult to remember the proper point of entry. For example, in the January–June 1976 cumulative index, over 300 pages of the 460-page author index consist of entries which begin with "U.S." The reference librarian should consult the December cumulated index of the *Monthly Catalog* for the likely author heading.

Still another problem is that someone may ask for a document by its popular, rather than its official, name. Historical examples range from the "Warren Report," officially titled *Report of President's Commission on the Assassination of President John F. Kennedy,* to the "Shafer Report," officially entitled *Marihuana, Signal of Misunderstanding.* The *Monthly Catalog* may or may not index these popular reports by subject. The solution, at least if the report has been published prior to the last edition, is the often revised *Popular Names of U.S. Government Reports: A Catalog* (Washington, D.C.: Government Printing Office, 1966 to date, irregular). Revised about every four years (the latest edition at this writing is dated 1974), it provides reproduction of catalog cards, alphabetically by popular name, of close to 800 reports. The listing is selective, ranging over both the nineteenth and the twentieth century. It is not inclusive, thus raising one more barrier to the easy use of documents. (The apparent solution for ongoing publications is for the *Monthly Catalog* to list popular titles in the index. This has yet to be done.)

Another aspect of retrieval, and for that matter selection, is the failure of most trade and national bibliographies to list government documents. *Books in Print* and *Subject Guide to Books in Print* rarely concede there is such a thing as a government document unless it has been reissued by a private publisher. Periodical indexes list some documents, but these are highly selective. Encyclopedias, biographical dictionaries, handbooks, yearbooks, and other forms of reference works rarely cite government documents in their bibliographies, even though they may draw heavily upon them for statistical and research materials.

Beyond the *Monthly Catalog,* there are numerous specialized methods of retrieving government documents. Among those most frequently used for ongoing materials are:

1. *Congressional Information Service. Index to Publications of the United States Congress.* Washington, D.C.: Congressional Information Service, 1970 to date, monthly. Service basis.

The *Monthly Catalog* analyzes only complete congressional documents, but the *CIS/Index* analyzes what is in those documents, covering nearly 600,000 pages of special studies, bills, hearings, etc., each year. Published by a private concern in loose-leaf form, the *Index* averages between 100 and 200 pages a month. It is in two parts: *(a)* The index section, which will run to over 60,000 entries in a year, offers access by subject, author, and title to almost every document issued by the U.S. Congress during the previous month. This section is cumulated quarterly and there is an annual. *(b)* The summary section gives the full title of the document and includes an abstract of most, although not all, of the items indexed. An easy-to-follow coding system relates the index to the summary section.

There is a complete system for the library that can afford to purchase all the indexed materials. These are made available by Congressional Information Service (CIS) on microfiche. The user locates the desired item in the index and through a simple key system finds the microfiche copy.

As one of the most comprehensive of document indexes, although limited to the activities of Congress, the *CIS/Index* is a blessing for the reference librarian who is seeking information on the progress of a bill through Congress. Popular names of bills, laws, and reports are given as well as the subject matter of those materials. In addition, there is an index which covers the same material by bill number, report number, etc. Furthermore, as hearings are covered as well as the names of witnesses, committees, and the like, the librarian may easily keep up with the development of legislation.

The comprehensive quality of this *Index* is such that, with a little practice, the reference librarian will feel fully capable of tracking down even the most elusive material. It is an exemplary index and abstracting service for current materials. (In time, of course, it will be an equally useful work for retrospective searching.)

2. *American Statistics Index.* Washington, D.C.: Congressional Information Service, 1973 to date, annual, monthly, and quarterly supplements. Service, $310 to $790.

Discussed briefly in the subsection "Statistical Data," in Chapter 6, the *Index* is worth listing again because it is as comprehensive for government statistics as the *CIS/Index* is for congressional documents. Again, this work is in two parts, with a separate exhaustive index section and a separate abstract section with the same detailed data as found in abstracts for the *CIS/Index*. The user begins with the first annual volume—the index. An accession number refers the reader to the second volume, i.e., the abstracts where details about the publication are given. The same procedure is followed with the monthly supplements, which are issued in two parts.

Virtually the complete statistical output of the federal government, from periodical articles to detailed reports, is included here. Also, like the *CIS/Index*, it offers subscribers the entire collection, or part of the indexed material, on microfiche.

3. *CQ Weekly Report.* Washington, D.C.: Congressional Quarterly, 1945 to date, weekly. Service, $139 to $195+.

Both the *CIS/Index* and the *American Statistics Index* present the problem of abundance, especially for users not requiring detailed analysis. At the same time, the two works are only relatively recent. Issued weekly and with less detail, the *CQ Weekly Report* is, nevertheless, a much used reference aid which is similar in some ways to a congressional version of *Facts on File,* and as such, was mentioned earlier in the text.

The *Weekly Report* is *not* an index. It is a summary of the week's past events—a summary which is often sufficient either to identify a government document to be later found in a specialized work, or to answer in one step a reference query.

Each issue analyzes in detail both congressional and general political activity of the week. The major bills are followed from the time they are introduced until they are passed and enacted into law (or killed along the way). A handy table of legislation shows at a glance where bills are in the Congress. Cross-references to previous weekly reports allow easy access to material until the quarterly index is issued and cumulated throughout the year. The service is also indexed in the *Public Affairs Information Service* PAIS *Bulletin.*

A somewhat similar service is the *National Journal* (Washington, D.C.: Government Research Corp., 1969 to date, weekly). Weekly reports are supported by charts and statistical data and there are good indexes which cumulate regularly. While some duplication is found between this and *CQ,* there's enough difference to warrant purchase by large research libraries of both.

4. General Subject Indexes

There are a number of subject indexes which make at least some effort to index government periodicals and documents selectively. The best known, most often used in the *Public Affairs Information Service Bulletin,* followed by *Resources in Education* published by the U.S. Educational Resources Information Center (ERIC). Beyond that, librarians will approach documents in terms of subjects as focused in more specialized indexes as *Science Research Abstracts, Nuclear Science Abstracts,* and other technical and scientific services which usually include government documents and reports. With the exception of ERIC and *PAIS* (both discussed in Chapter 4), few of the more general subject indexes in the humanities and the social sciences include government titles. A good single source is the previously discussed *Index to U.S. Government Periodicals,* which is exclusively concerned with what the title implies. However, it must be stressed that the service does limit itself to no more than 120 or so periodicals, so that it hardly begins to touch the really specialized government titles.

A guide (not an index) to periodicals issued by the federal government is John Andriot's frequently updated *Guide to U.S. Government Publications* (McLean, Virginia: Documents Index, 1959 to date, annual). This work gives basic data on over 2000 government agencies and what they publish. The multivolume set lists a vast number of periodicals. A somewhat more limited approach, although even more useful for smaller libraries, is Philip A. Yannarella and Rao Aluri's *U.S. Government Scientific & Technical Periodicals* (Metuchen, New Jersey: Scarecrow Press, 1976). It includes 266 titles, fully annotated, as well as additional information on agencies and bibliographies and lists. The authors note, "Federal publications are in constant flux. Titles, prices, corporate authors and almost everything else seems to change at whim and it is impossible to keep abreast of them." True; and this is all the more reason why the Andriot work is of tremendous value for larger collections that must keep abreast of changes.

The Andriot *Guide* can be a valuable retrieval tool. As it lists and annotates the publications of almost all government agencies, the work will lead the librarian to materials suited for a given field of interest or study. Andriot, as Morehead so aptly puts it in his text, is a "one-man cottage industry" who produces numerous guides and checklists of government documents.

Beginning in 1977 there is a separate mid-year publication, *Serials Supplement.* Included in the subscription price to the *Monthly Catalog,* the *Supplement* lists major serials (including periodicals) by agency with an author, title, subject, and serial/report index. This is not as complete as the Andriot *Guide,* nor are there annotations, but it still is a useful addition.

Many of the aforementioned indexes and services offer at least limited access to government-sponsored reports. Literally thousands of reports on every aspect of human life are issued each year. Those in education are controlled via ERIC, but when a larger net is cast to include science and technology, as well as much of the social sciences, the single best service is *Government Reports Announcements* [Springfield, Virginia: National Technical Information Service (NTIS), 1946 to date] and the accompanying index to the abstracts, *Government Reports Index.* Both are discussed in detail in *Reference Services and Reference Processes,* the second volume of this text. However, the reader should know that the *Announcements* arranges and abstracts reports under several broad subject headings. The index service offers access to the abstracts via subject, author, contract number, etc. The reports may be from the government, corporations, or private individuals, and are obtainable from NTIS, the publisher. The report material is prepared by persons who have participated in government sponsored or -financed research and development. It usually is detailed, technical, and fairly timely. About 60,000 reports are covered each year.

ORGANIZATION AND SELECTION

The organization and selection of government documents in all but the largest of libraries are relatively simple matters. Librarians purchase a limited number of documents, usually in terms of subjects of interest to users and/or standard titles, such as the *Statistical Abstract of the United States*. If pamphlets, they are usually deposited by subject in a vertical file. If books, they are cataloged and shelved as such.

The reference librarian normally will be responsible for the acquisition of documents, although in many libraries the *Selected List*, like the book and nonbook reviews, is regularly routed to all in the library. At any rate, confusion is minimal at this level because government documents are rightfully treated as any other information source and are shelved, filed, or clipped like other media.

When one moves to the large or specialized libraries, the organizational pattern is either a separate government documents collection or an integration of the documents into the general collection. Other libraries combine the two systems. Libraries are about evenly divided in the use of these three approaches.

The justification for separate collections is that the volume of publications swamps the library and necessitates special considerations of organization and classification. There are other reasons; but on the whole, it is a matter of the librarian's seeking to find the simplest and best method of making the documents available. Some argue that separation tends to limit use, and they try to compromise by separating the administrative and official works while integrating the more popular and highly specialized subject documents into the general collection.

A distinct disadvantage of a separate documents collection is that it isolates the materials from the main reference collection. The reference librarians are inclined to think of it as a thing apart and may answer questions with materials at hand rather than attempt to fathom the holdings of the documents department. If patrons are referred to the documents section, the librarian there may attempt to answer questions that might be better handled by the reference librarian.

For most librarians, the matter of organization is not a problem, chiefly because they are coming to rely more and more upon the large research and depository libraries for help in answering questions which call for specialized documents. This is to say that the two major factors which determine the selection and use of government documents are similar to those governing the selection and use of all forms of communication: the size of the library and its purpose. In regard to government documents, the majority of large libraries are depository libraries. Since the Printing Act of 1895, modified by the Depository Act of 1962, approximately 1210 libraries have been designated as depositories for government documents. They are entitled to receive publications free of charge from the Superintendent of Documents. The purpose is to have centers with relatively complete runs of government documents located throughout the country. These are likely to be state, regional, and large city public libraries, and the major college and university libraries.[8]

Selection

For depository libraries, the selection of government documents is effectively accomplished by the government's automatically sending almost everything published to those libraries. Freed of the flood, the nondepository library's "selection of U.S. public documents becomes an autonomous pleasure," as Morehead so aptly puts it. "In addition, participation in the selection of individual publications engenders familiarity, which in turn broadens one's reference capabilities."[9]

The basic buying guide for most libraries is the *Selected List*, with a boost from the *Monthly Catalog*. However, as neither makes any value judgments, librarians tend to rely on critical reviews, many of which appear in the general reviewing journals. On either a regular or a recurring basis, reviews will be found in *Library Journal* and *Choice* (normally in the reference book sections); *The Booklist* (under "U.S. government publications," a highly selective list which is useful for school and small to medium-sized public and college libraries); *RQ*; Frederick O'Hara's column in *Reference Service Review*; etc. Morehead, who was among the first to introduce a column on government documents in any journal, moved from *RQ* and is now writing regularly for *Serials Librarian*.

Two journals deserve attention. The first is *Government Publications Review* (New York: Pergamon Press, 1973 to date, quarterly), which devotes about 100 pages and a dozen or so articles exclusively to government publications at all levels from federal to local. Harry Welsh has a column,

---

[8] The depository system is more complex than indicated here, and is the topic of a complete chapter in Morehead's *Introduction to United States Public Documents,* op. cit., pp. 29–46.

[9] Morehead, op. cit., p. 70. This comes near the end of a solid chapter on "administering documents collections," which gives considerable detail about how depository libraries acquire and organize documents.

"What's New in Documents," and there are a number of other features of use to both experts and occasional government documents users. The second journal is *Dttp, Documents to the People* (Chicago: American Library Association, 1972 to date, bimonthly), which is the official 25- to 50-page newsletter of the ALA Government Documents Round Table (better known by the unlikely acronym GODORT). Not only does this periodical include the normal run of articles, but, as the title indicates, it has a special mission of keeping a watchful eye on any bureaucratic action which threatens the free flow of information.

There are several subject guides which both aid in selection and assist the user in finding specific documents for a given subject area. The best known is Philip Leidy's *A Popular Guide to Government Publications* (4th ed.; New York: Columbia University Press, 1976, 440 pp.). This is by now a classic in the field, and is especially valuable for the wide scope of the entries. About 3000 different items are listed under broad subject headings. Many of the entries are annotated. Prepared for the layperson, the list covers multiple subjects from aging to wildlife and is often a source of unexpected, useful materials. A detailed subject index adds to its reference value. Thanks to its popular scope, the *Guide* is an ideal buying guide for small to medium-sized public and school libraries.

A more specialized, although equally useful, list is offered in Alan Schorr's *Subject Guide to Government Reference Books* (Littleton, Colorado: Libraries Unlimited, Inc., 1976). This work includes about 1300 essential and usually substantial titles issued by the government over a number of years. Most are in print and most are necessary for any detailed work with government documents. The annotations are excellent. Arrangement is by broad subject headings with detailed indexes.

The same author keeps a watchful eye on documents, and since 1970 has been offering librarians a selected list of the better, more useful items in her *Government Reference Books* (Littleton, Colorado: Libraries Unlimited, Inc., 1970 to date, biennial). The number of titles varies, but usually hovers around 1300. The scope is limited to titles issued during the previous two years and those which are of possibly lasting reference value. Again, a detailed subject, author, and title index is helpful.

Acquisition[10]

Once a document has been selected for purchase, its acquisition is no more difficult—indeed, often somewhat easier—than acquiring a book or pe-

[10] Practical procedures for acquisition of government documents in smaller libraries will be found in Anthos Hungerford, "U.S. Government Publications Acquisition Procedures for the

riodical. Depository libraries do have a peculiar set of problems, but for the average library, the process may be as follows:

1. Full information is given in the *Monthly Catalog* on methods of purchase from the Superintendent of Documents. Payment may be made in advance by purchase of coupons from the Superintendent of Documents. In case of extensive purchases, deposit accounts may be established.

2. Some documents may be obtained free from members of Congress. However, as the supply of some documents is limited, the specific member should be warned in advance. It is particularly advisable to get on the regular mailing list of one's representative or senator to receive such publications as the *Yearbook of Agriculture.*

3. Issuing agencies often have a stock of publications which must be ordered directly from the agency. These are noted by a plus sign in the *Monthly Catalog* and frequently include valuable specialized materials from ERIC documents to scientific reports.

4. A growing number of private firms now publish government documents; for example, the *CIS/Index* offers a complete collection of the working papers of Congress on microfiche. Most of the publications are highly specialized, expensive, and dutifully reviewed in a number of the aforementioned reviewing services.

For a variety of reasons, not all government documents may be acquired by libraries or by individuals.[11] The controversy over the "Pentagon Papers" focused on this problem. And in 1976 former CBS television newsman Daniel Schorr released for publication a copy of the House committee report on intelligence activities—a report which the House had voted to keep secret. The drama of the case was played out on national radio and television, ending in a draw and in controversy expressed in scores of articles.[12] The intriguing question of just what should be kept secret by the government will never be resolved in a democracy. A cursory

Small Special Library," *Special Libraries,* January 1974, pp. 22–25. (The price-list information in the article is no longer applicable.) Also, Carol Kaczmarek, "Government Publications for Elementary Libraries," *Hoosier School Library,* October 1975, pp. 18–23.

[11] A discussion of availability of federal, state, and city records is reported by a journalist in Elsie S. Hebert's "How Accessible Are the Records in Government Records Centers?" *Journalism Quarterly,* Spring 1975, pp. 23–29, 60. Useful references to material not found in most library sciences indexes.

[12] Coverage of the Schorr case was extensive in the national press. A good summary: Anthony Lewis, "The Press and Its Right to Silence: Not Yet Clarified," *The New York Times* ("The Week in Review"), September 19, 1976, p. 1. Those seeking a more conservative interpretation need look only at copies of the *National Review* for the same period.

glance at almost any issue of the newsletter *Documents to the People* (mentioned in the previous subsection), as well as at numerous library periodicals, will indicate the continuing debate over this issue among librarians.

The best notion of the dimensions of secrecy regarding documents can be found by looking at the *Declassified Documents Quarterly Catalog* (Washington, D.C.: Carrollton Press, 1975 to date, quarterly).[13] The Freedom of Information Act of 1973 resulted in declassification of more than 10,000 former top secret, secret, and confidential federal documents (which, needless to add, never made the *Monthly Catalog*). And while the implications of this act and the declassification of documents are still being debated, more than 10,000 items are now available via the *Quarterly Catalog*—and more will be added as items are continually being declassified.

Evaluation

When speaking of evaluating government materials, sources cite qualities rather than actual methods of evaluation.

Government publications, for the most part, can be considered from the following standpoints:

Authority   Authority applies particularly to the official source material which records a law, a hearing, a debate, or the like.

Cost   In the second edition of *Introduction to Reference Work,* it was noted that one advantage to documents was that "the cost is usually minimal." No more. The traditional benefit of nominally priced, sometimes free documents is past. The 48-page best-seller "Pocket Guide to Babysitting," which sold for 70 cents in 1975, by mid-1976 cost $1.20. And "Your Child from One to Six," once priced at 20 cents, is now $1.10.[14] By law, the prices of government publications must cover the rising costs for paper, postage, and printing. There is a consumer-conscious group that argues popular, informational documents should now be subsidized, but this is not likely to happen soon.

Timeliness   Timeliness is another valuable feature, particularly in the statistical reports and with the present methods of keeping up with scientific and technological advancement. Many publications are issued

[13] A review and explanation of this valuable reference work will be found in *The Booklist,* February 15, 1976, pp. 875–876.

[14] Reflections on the price rises and the drop in government document sales will be found in a short article by Frances Cerra, "U.S. Is Doing Well as Publisher but Charges More," *The New York Times,* February 25, 1976, p. 38.

on a daily or weekly basis. Still, the problem remains of frequency of indexing or abstracting; e.g., the *Monthly Catalog* has been almost five months behind the material published.

Range of Interest   The range of interest is all-encompassing. No publisher except the government has such a varied list.

Indexes and Bibliographies   Indexes and bibliographies are improving, not only in the documents themselves, but in works intended as finding devices for those documents.

Other aspects, such as arrangement, treatment, and format, may not be perfect, but the reference librarian hardly has any choice. There is, after all, only one *Congressional Record*; it is judged not for its intrinsic value but in terms of whether it can be used in a particular library.

TYPES OF PUBLICATIONS

Too much emphasis can be placed upon categorizing the various forms or types of government publications. The user, after all, is interested only in information, not in whether this or that source happens to be an executive document or a congressional work. The categorization is useful primarily as a mnemonic device for the librarian or an organizational device for teachers of document courses. For example, a question about current legislation will require one type of document; a statistical question, quite another. Recognizing the likely branch of the government dealing with the subject of the request helps to narrow the search.

Executive Publications   This category does not mean simply papers of the President; all papers issued by the ten departments and the various agencies of the government are likewise called executive documents. Agencies, related to the main departments, also publish a variety of documents.

From a reference viewpoint, these documents are of interest mainly for the information given on subject material. Anyone doing research in such fields as economics, labor, industry, or education will inevitably need a number of executive publications.

They may be located through the various catalogs and indexes, particularly the *Monthly Catalog*. If the document is known to be the publication of a particular department or agency, a number of department lists and indexes will give fuller information than any of the general catalogs and indexes. Most of the departments issue current lists, and they are discussed in Morehead's text. A number of the documents of more general interest may be located through standard periodical indexes.

Congressional (Legislative) Publications   Congressional publications are basically a record of congressional activities from debates in Congress to committee hearings and reports. There are a number of aids, discussed in the section "Catalogs and Indexes" (pages 325–333), to help the librarian locate ongoing activities and publications of Congress. The legislative history, though, may be traced through a number of publications:

1. *The Congressional Record*   This serial is the daily record of the proceedings of Congress. There are an index every two weeks and a cumulative index at the end of the session. Although the *Record* is supposed to be a verbatim report of activities, it is not. Members of Congress reserve the right to add and to delete.[15] Nor does the *Record* usually contain the texts of bills and resolutions.

2. *Laws*   The process of passing a law is an involved, although not necessarily complicated, matter. It is fully explained in the often revised *How Our Laws Are Made* (Washington, D.C.: Government Printing Office, 1976). Briefly, the process is this: *(a)* A "bill" either introduces new legislation or amends a previous legislative act. The bill may originate in either the House or the Senate. Various forms of "resolutions" are similar to bills. About 25,000 bills and resolutions are introduced during a congressional session. *(b)* A bill passed by either house goes to the other as a printed "act." If the act is accepted by both houses and passed, it is signed or vetoed by the President. *(c)* Once the bill is signed into law, it becomes a "slip law." These are simply the unbound, first printing of laws passed by Congress, and they may run anywhere from one to several hundred pages. The slip laws are gathered and bound in the *Statutes at Large.* Every six years the *Statutes* is consolidated into the *United States Code,* which affords a subject approach to the laws, as well as various tables which indicate the acts' popular names.

---

[15] The wonders of the *Congressional Record* never cease, as, for example, this story from *The New York Times* of May 11, 1976: "The Congressional Record, citing a rule against publishing obscenities, refused today to publish excerpts from the works of Kurt Vonnegut, Jr., Bernard Malamud, Langston Hughes and four other books banned last March by the Board of the Island Trees School District on Long Island. . . . The general purpose of the rule is to keep the *Congressional Record* from becoming a 'pornographic document' (according to Representative Wayne L. Hayes)."

How does the librarian locate this material? The *Statutes at Large* is issued in printed volumes, as is the *United States Code,* and they are usually readily available via the card catalog. The catch is trying to locate the bills, acts, and slip laws. There are numerous, sometimes complicated, approaches, but the various stages of the bill to the act to the slip law may be traced via the *Congressional Record,* the *CIS/Index,* or *CQ Weekly Report.*

3. *Hearings*   The transcripts (as well as the presentation) of testimony before a congressional committee or subcommittee are known as "hearings." Where made public, the printed hearings may be indexed in the *CIS/Index* and similar publications. Occasionally they are printed as parts of larger reports; where published as separates, they are usually offered for sale by the Superintendent of Documents.

4. *Committee Prints*   Publications issued by the various committees, in addition to transcriptions of the hearings themselves, are called committee prints. These are of major importance as they often are independent studies requested by the various committees, e.g., a two-volume study of American foreign policy ordered to the Senate Committee on Foreign Relations. These are indexed in the *CIS/Index* and are usually, though not always, sent to depository libraries, but they may not be listed in the *Monthly Catalog.*

5. *The Serial Set*   The reports and documents of the Senate and the House are accumulated after each session into bound volumes. The set offers a way of finding needed material which is listed usually as an individual report or document in the *Monthly Catalog.* While the *Monthly Catalog* is better known, often used reports and documents are issued both as part of the serial set and as separates. There are some reports and documents which are never issued in unbound form and appear as only part of the serial set. The set is legendary in its difficulty of use, and here one can only refer the reader to the section in Morehead's text. Suffice it to say, for the beginner many reports and documents are found in two forms: *(a)* as separates and *(b)* as part of the bound serial set.

Judicial Publications   Judicial publications consist primarily of the publications of the courts; the most important consist of the decisions of the Supreme Court. Of all the areas of government documents, the area of judicial publications is the most highly specialized. Work with these materials requires a considerable knowledge of governmental organization and, except for general questions, is probably best left to the special law library or legislative reference service. This is not to say that the reference librarian should not be aware of judicial publications or how to use them, but any use in depth is beyond the scope of the present text. (Of considerable help, even to the less than law-educated librarian, are the basic *Judicial Opinion Reporters* issued by the West Publishing Company. The publisher offers an informative booklet on their use, and they are described in many of the government document guides.)

In terms of subjects, perhaps 15 to 20 percent of all types of documents issued may be of enough general interest to warrant consideration as "popular" sources of information. By far the greatest number of them are for the expert in government or in a given subject area; as such, they are for reference work chiefly in large libraries. The number of state and local documents which can be termed "popular" are even fewer.

STATE AND LOCAL DOCUMENTS

U.S. Library of Congress. *Monthly Checklist of State Publications,* 1910 to date. $21.90.

Index to Current Urban Documents. Westport, Connecticut: Greenwood Press, 1972 to date, quarterly, $125; annual, $145.

If federal documents are little understood in many libraries, the state and local documents are even more in limbo. The reason is twofold: (1) Proper bibliographical control is lacking, although it is improving; (2) even with such control, the average librarian rarely thinks of state documents as a vital source of information. The reason for this latter assumption is that most states issue "blue books" which, as manuals, give answers to recurrent questions: "Who is my representative?" "What is the address of X agency?" "Who is the head of Y agency?" With the "blue books" or legislative manuals at hand, most questions involving the state are readily answered. Furthermore, at a local level, the library tends to rely more on its own clipping file and possibly its own local newspaper index.

Where there is no concerted effort to collect state and local documents, the library should be aware of other libraries in the immediate area that have such collections. Usually the best single source of information about these collections, as well as of the documents themselves, is the state library. By law, most state agencies must file copies of their various reports with the state library. The state library, in turn, will maintain its own collection and have some arrangement for distributing the excess documents to other libraries in the state, either on a systematic basis to state depository libraries (the system varies, but is somewhat the same as federal depositories) or on an informal basis to the smaller units.

At the state level, there is no entirely satisfactory bibliographical tool that lists the majority of publications. Of considerable help is the *Monthly*

Checklist of State Publications. Prepared by the *Library of Congress,* it represents only those state publications received by the Library. Arrangement is alphabetical by state and then, as in the *Monthly Catalog,* by issuing agency. Entries are usually complete enough for ordering purposes, although prices are not always given. There is an annual, but not a monthly, subject and author index. The indexes are not cumulative. Since 1963, periodicals have been listed in the June and December issues.

The *Index to Current Urban Documents* is an effort to exert bibliographical control over state, regional, and city documents. Including documents issued by the 200 largest cities and 26 counties of 1 million or more population in both the United States and Canada, the *Index* is in two parts. The geographical section is alphabetical by city or county and then by issuing department. Full bibliographical information is given for each document, as well as descriptive notes. There is an exhaustive subject and author index. The whole is tied to a plan whereby the listed documents are made available to the library on microfiche.

SUGGESTED READING

Bell, John, "CIS," *Illinois Libraries,* March 1976, pp. 194–199. A spokesperson for Congressional Information Service explains how the service is edited and published. While the scope is limited to a single operation, the article is worthwhile in that it gives an accurate picture of the problems involved with bibliographic control of government documents.

Daniel, W. Ellen, and William C. Robinson, "Time Lag in the 1972 Monthly Catalog of United States Government Publications," *Government Publications Review,* no. 2, 1976, pp. 113–122. Although dated, the study is a model of how to evaluate the timeliness of this or that reference source. The authors found that "the mean time lag was 4.7 months" between the period of publication and appearance in the *Catalog.* The lag appears to be about the same in 1977.

Hernon, Peter, "The Academic Reference Librarian as Documents Specialist and Promoter," *PLA Bulletin,* March 1975, pp. 27–28. A practical look at organization and how the reference and the documents librarians can help in the use of government documents, both federal and local.

Illinois Libraries, April 1974. Another full-issue approach to documents similar in scope to the *Drexel Library Quarterly* effort, January–April 1974. Some overlap, but are different enough, particularly in viewpoint, to warrant including both these special numbers on any reading list.

Kaczmarek, Carol, "U.S. Government Publications for Secondary School Libraries and Classrooms," *Hoosier School Libraries,* April 1977, pp. 25–34. This is typical of bibliographies which appear from time to time in various regional library journals. It is a reminder that government documents can be used in all types of libraries. The annotated list, by the way, is quite good and useful for other types of libraries.

Klempner, I. M., "The Concept of 'National Security' and Its Effect on Information Transfer," *Special Libraries,* July 1973, pp. 263–269. A timely discussion on various methods used to check the free flow of government documents and information. Professor Klempner has lectured and written widely on this subject, and for current materials, his name should be checked out in library literature indexes.

"Micropublishing and the Government Printing Office/Three Viewpoints," *Microform Review*, April 1974, pp. 85–95. A good discussion of various attitudes toward the micropublishing of government documents.

"Policies and Practices in the Bibliographic Control of United States Government Publications," *Drexel Library Quarterly*, January–April 1974. The whole of this double issue is devoted to eight articles on government documents and includes articles on the GPO, the *Monthly Catalog*, and a number of government information services.

Schwartz, Shula, "GPO—Are You Listening," *Special Libraries*, February, 1977, pp. 62–68. Report of a survey which pinpointed the problems librarians have in dealing with the Government Printing Office. Some practical recommendations are offered to improve matters.

Texas Libraries, Summer 1976. The 50-plus pages are devoted almost exclusively to government documents. The eight articles are particularly suitable for librarians with smaller collections, and give still another view of various publishers and the Government Printing Office.

INDEX

"Aalen Stage to Zulu War," 172n.
"AAP 1976 Statistics," 136n.
Abbreviated Citation, The, 124n.
Abbreviation dictionaries, 292–293
Abbreviations Dictionary, 292, 293
ABC-Clio, 127n.
Abridged Readers' Guide, 105
Abstracts and abstracting services, 97–103,
    106, 111, 125–132
  as bibliographic aids, 16
  computer scanning for, 126–128
  evaluation of, 99–103
  "indicative" and "informative," 125n.
  physical format of, 98–99
Abstracts and Abstracting Services, 62n.
Abstracts and Indexes in Science and Technology:
    A Descriptive Guide, 110
Abstracts of Popular Culture, 106
Access, 105–106, 263
Acquisition(s), 9
  of government documents, 335–337
"Acquisition of Maps and Charts Published
    by the United States Government,
    The," 316
"Acquisition Tools and Sources of Maps,"
    311n.
Acronym dictionaries, 292–293
*Acronyms, Initialisms, and Abbreviations Diction-
    ary,* 292, 293
Adams, James T., 177, 178
Adler, Mortimer, 154, 155n.
Administrative work in the library, 8
"After the *Statistical Abstract*—What?" 201–
    202
ALA Bulletin, 104

A.L.A. Glossary of Library Terms, 213
ALA Government Documents Round Ta-
    ble (GODORT), 335
Album of American History, 178
Alexander, Shana, 212
Allgemeines Lexikon der Bildenden Kunstler . . . ,
    255–256
Almanac(s), 17, 188–203, 300
  definition of, 189
  general, 191–194
  guidelines for discarding, 51
  purpose of, 189–191
  subject, 195–203
Almanac of American Politics, The, 199n.
*Alternative Press Index: An Index to Alternative
    and Underground Publications,* 111
Altick, Richard, 179
Aluri, Ray, 332
*America: History and Life; A Guide to Periodical
    Literature,* 99, 127
*America: History and Life; Part A, Article Ab-
    stracts and Citations,* 126, 127
American Almanac, The, 199n.
*American Almanac and Repository of Useful
    Knowledge,* 192
American and British Genealogy and Heraldry,
    252, 253
American Automobile Association,
    320
*American Bibliography: A Chronological Diction-
    ary of All Books, Pamphlets and Periodical
    Publications Printed in the United States of
    America From the Genesis of Printing in
    1639 Down to and Including the Year 1800,*
    72, 74, 75

American Bibliography: A Preliminary Checklist, 73–75

American Book Prices Current, 75, 76

American Book Publishing Record, 64, 67–69, 71

American Book Trade Directory, 66*n.*

American Catalogue of Books, 1876–1910, 73, 75

  (See also *Books in Print*)

American Catalogue of Books, Published in the United States from January 1861 to January 1871, with Date of Publication, Size, Price, and Publisher's Name, 73–75

American Chemical Society, 125

American College Dictionary, 272, 282

American Council on Education, 218, 219

American Council of Learned Societies, 249

American Educator, 163, 164

American Farm and Home Almanac, 191–192

American Genealogical Research Institute Staff, 252, 253

American Guide Series, 320–321

American Heritage Dictionary, The, 271*n.*–274*n.*, 288

American Heritage Dictionary of the English Language, The, 281, 283

American Heritage Dictionary of the English Language, New College Edition, 280, 281

American Heritage School Dictionary, The, 276, 281

American Junior Colleges, 209

American Language, The, 274, 287

American Library Association (ALA), 86*n.*, 138*n.*, 149, 153, 162, 254, 258

  Reference and Subscription Books Reviews Committee, 20, 41, 168, 230*n.*, 256, 276

  Standards Committee of the Reference and Adult Services Division of, 6

American Library Directory, 218, 220

American Library Resources: A Bibliographical Guide, Supplement, 1961–1970, 93*n.*

American Men and Women of Science, 21, 230, 239, 244, 247

American Newspapers, 1821–1936 . . . , 82

American Peoples Encyclopedia, The, 138

American Reference Books Annual (ARBA), 37–38, 40–42, 78, 83*n.*, 110, 177*n.*, 202, 223, 233, 321

American Statistics Index, 110, 202, 330–331

American Thesaurus of Slang, 289

American Universities and Colleges, 218, 219

Analytical bibliography, 35–36

"And Now, Another 'Completely New' (Unique) Thesaurus," 291

Anderson, Dorothy, 55*n.*

Andrew, Christine, 13*n.*

Andriot, John L., 316, 332

Annals of America, The, 137, 151

Annual Register of World Events . . . , 194, 195

"Antedate Dictionary Citation, " 285

Anthologies, indexes to material in, 98, 117–124

Antonyms, dictionaries of, 289–291

APLA Bulletin, 39

Appleton's Cyclopedia of American Biography, 250

Applied Science & Technology Index, 98, 107, 109

Arnold, Darlene, 80

Arrangement and entry in encyclopedias, 147–148

Art:

  biographical works, 255–256

  encyclopedias, 175–176

ARTbibliographies, 127*n.*

Art Index, 99, 107

Art of Winning Foundation Grants, The, 219*n.*

Art of Winning Government Grants, The, 219*n.*

Ash, Joan, 212

Ash, Lee, 61–62

Atlanta Constitution, index to, 117

Atlante Internazionale, 314, 315

Atlantic, The, 145

Atlas(es), 215, 300

  definition of, 300–301

  evaluation of (*see* Geographical sources, evaluation of maps and atlases)

  index to, 310–311

  national, 315–320

    local, 316–317

    sources of government, 316

  sources of, 303

  thematic, 317–319

  world, 311–315

    foreign-language, 314–315

  (See also Gazetteers)

Atlas Mira, 314–315

Atlas of American History, 177, 319

Atlas of Early American History, 318

"Atlas of Early American History," 318*n.*

Audiorecord, definition of, 85
Audiovisual Market Place, 87, 89
Author-Title Index to Joseph Sabin's Dictionary of Books Relating to America, 72, 74
Authority (*see specific types of reference sources, evaluation of*)
Awards, Honors and Prizes, 204, 206
Ayer Directory of Publications, 82–83, 215

Baer, E. A., 320*n.*
Baker, Theodore, 232*n.,* 261–262
Balay, Robert, 13*n.*
Barnhart, Clarence L., 238*n.,* 283
Bartholomew, John G. (Edinburgh), 304, 305
Bartlett, John, 122–123
"Basic Bibliographic Control: Plans for a World System," 55*n.*
Beazely, Mitchell, 168
"Beginner's Guide to Indexes to the Nineteenth Century U.S. Serial Set," 327*n.*
Bell, Alan, 241–242
Bell & Howell, 216
Benn's Guide to Newspapers and Periodicals of the World, 83*n.*
Berkeley Serials Union List, 78
Berlitz, Charles, 294
Berry, Lester, 289
"Best Man, Bore, Bamboozle, etc.," 286*n.*
Best Reference Books: Titles of Listing Value Selected from "American Reference Books Annual," 1970–1976, 41
Besterman, Theodore, 92
Bible concordances, 121
Bibliographic control, 55*n.*
Bibliographic Index: A Cumulative Bibliography of Bibliographies, 91–92
Bibliographic inquiry, 12
"Bibliographical Scholarship in the United States, 1949–1974: A Review, 36*n.*
Bibliograhische Berichte, 92*n.*
Bibliography(ies), 31–93
  analytical, 35–36
  of bibliographies, 16, 35, 91–93
  of biography, 234
  as control-access-directional type of source, 16, 18
  defined, 31–32
  of geographical sources, 311
  to government documents, 338
  guides to reference materials, 35–41
  index to, 16

national library catalogs, 55–63
national or trade, 34, 64–93
of reference sources, 16
subject, 34–35
systematic enumerative, 16, 32–36
  characteristics of adequate, 32–33
textual, 35–36
union lists of card catalogs, 16, 55–56
universal, 33, 55–56
"Bibliography Bargains," 93
Bibliography of Modern History, A, 177
Biblioteca Americana, 73–75
Biblioteca Americana. Dictionary of Books Relating to America from Its Discovery to the Present Time, 72–74
Binding:
  of atlases, 310
  of encyclopedias, 146
Biographical Dictionaries Master Index, 238–240, 246*n.,* 247*n.*
Biographical Dictionary of Musicians, 232*n.,* 261–262
Biographical Directory of Librarians in the United States and Canada, 258
Biographical Directory of the American Congress, 1774–1971, 217
Biographical sources, 17, 21, 229–263
  almanacs and yearbooks as, 190, 196, 199
  anonyms and, 236–237
  definition of biography, 229
  dictionaries, 234, 235, 237–238
  directories as, 213, 235, 244–247
  evaluation of, 230–234
    authority, 232–233
    length of entry, 230–231
    other points, 233–234
    selection, 230
  genealogy, 252–253
  guidelines for discarding, 51
  indexes to, 234, 238–242
  national biography, 235–236
  portraits, 253–254
  professional and subject, 254–263
  pseudonyms and, 236–237
  retrospective, 248–252
  searching, 234–237
  secondary approaches, 236
Biography as an Art, 229*n.*
Biography Index: A Cumulative Index to Biographical Material in Books and Magazines, 239–241, 248, 250, 254

Black American Authors, 239

Black American Writers, 1773–1949, 257, 261

Black American Writers Past and Present: A Biographical and Bibliographical Dictionary, 257, 259, 261

Black Americans, biographical works on, 256–257

Black's Law Dictionary, 212

"Bless You Samuel Green," 6*n.*

Bohle, Bruce, 262

Bol'shaia Sovetskaia Entisklopediia, 171–173

Boodson, K., 103*n.*

Book Auction Records, 76

Book of Firsts, The, 205*n.*

Book of Lists, The, 194

Book Production Industry, 151*n.*

Book Review Digest and *Author/Title Index,* 46–48, 208–209, 261

Book Review Index (BRI), 46–48, 209, 261

"Book Selection Tools for Subject Specialists in a Large Research Library: An Analysis," 45

Booklist, The, 43, 45, 47, 137*n.,* 149, 153, 162*n.,* 181*n.,* 182, 230*n.,* 257*n.,* 268, 284*n.,* 311, 314, 334, 337*n.*

Bookman's Price Index, 76–77

Books in Print, 33, 46, 64–71, 73, 80, 91, 118, 311, 329

Books in Print Supplement, 64, 66

Books on Demand, 90

Booth, Barbara, 130*n.*

Boston Public Library, 211–212

Boswell's Life of Johnson, 267*n.*

Bottorff, Robert, 105

Bowker, R. R., 64–65, 70, 261

Bowker's Medical Books in Print, 70*n.*

Boyer, Calvin, 20*n.*

Boyle, Deidre, 88

Bradley, Henry, 284

Brewer's Dictionary of Phrase & Fable, 193

Brewton, John, 121

Brigham, Clarence S., 82

Britannica (see *Encyclopaedia Britannica: New Encyclopaedia Britannica, The*)

Britannica Atlas, 313*n.*

Britannica Book of the Year, 165

Britannica Junior Encyclopaedia, 137, 161–162

"Britannica Revisited," 154*n.*

"Britannica Yields to Criticism, Alters Soviet Republic Articles," 144*n.*

British Books in Print, 71

"British Concise Dictionary Editor, A," 286*n.*

British Educational Index, 106

British Humanities Index, 104, 106

British Museum, 56
   national library catalogs, 62–63

British National Bibliography, 71, 237

British Technology Index, 106

Brockhaus, Friedrich, 170

Brockhaus, 169

Brockhaus Enzyklöpadie, 170–171

Brockhaus Konversations Lexikon, 156

Brook, Stephen, 145*n.*

Browsing in almanacs and yearbooks, 190–191

Bruntjen, Grace, 74

Bruntjen, Scott, 74

Bulletin. Special Libraries Association, Geography and Map Division, 311

Bunge, Charles, 44

Burack, Richard, 210

Burchfield, R. W., 284

Burke, John, 41

Burnam, Tom, 205–206

Business Books in Print, 70*n.*

Business Index, 226, 258

Business Information Markets 1976–1981, The, 222*n.*

Business Information Sources, 224*n.*

Business Periodicals Index, 81, 107, 200

Business Reference Sources, 223

Business reference sources, biographical, 257–258

Cadillac Modern Encyclopedia, The, 166–168

Cambridge Ancient History, The, 177

Cambridge Economic History of Europe, The, 177

Cambridge History of English Literature, The, 178, 179

Cambridge History of the Bible, The, 177

Cambridge Medieval History, The, 177

Cambridge University Press, 295

Canada:
   guide to reference sources of, 37, 38
   reference sources of, 38–39

Canaday, John, 256

Canadian Book Review Annual, 48

"Canadian Books and American Libraries," 39

Canadian Books in Print, 39

Canadian Business Periodical Index, 226

Canadian Essay and Literature Index, 119

Canadian News Facts, 113, 114

Canadian Periodical Index, 39, 104, 106

Canadian Reference Sources: A Selective Guide and Supplement, 37, 38

Card catalog(s), 12, 16, 118
  union lists of, 16, 55–56

Carrollton Press, 112, 327

Carter, Edward, 92*n.*

Cassell's Encyclopaedia of World Literature, 178–179

Cassell's Italian-English, English-Italian Dictionary, 294

"Catalog, Bibliography or Index," 16*n.*

Catalog of Books Represented by Library of Congress Printed Cards Issued to July 31, 1942, A, 60

Catalog of Books Represented by Library of Congress Printed Cards: Supplement: Cards Issued August 1, 1942–December 31, 1947, 60–61

Cataloging, 9

Catalogue of American Portraits, 254

Catholic Encyclopedia, The, 182

Catholic Periodical and Literature Index, The, 108

CB dictionaries, 289

CBS News Almanac, The, 191–193

CBS News Index, 117

Cerra, Frances, 337*n.*

Chadwick, Owen, 182*n.*

Chambers's Biographical Dictionary, 231*n.,* 237, 238

Chambers's Encyclopedia, 157

Chaplin, A. H., 55*n.*

Chapman, Dorothy, 121

Charlie Brown Dictionary, The, 284*n.*

Chart, definition of, 85

Checklist of American Imprints, A, 1820 +, 73, 74

Chemical Abstracts, 125

Chicago Tribune, 116

Chicorel Index to Biographies, 240, 242

Chicorel Index to Poetry in Anthologies in Print, 120

Chicorel Index to Short Stories in Anthologies and Collections, 120*n.*

Chicorel Theater Index to Plays in Anthologies and Periodicals, 120

Chicorel's Index Abstracting and Indexing Services, 81

Childcraft—The How and Why Library, 162

Children:
  dictionaries for, 283–284
  encyclopedias for, 159–162

Children's Book Review Index, 48

Children's Books in Print, 65, 70

Children's Literature Review, 48

Chilton Company, 173

Choice, 38, 43–45, 47, 334

Chomsky, Noam, 273

"Chomsky: What Has It to Do With Literature?" 273*n.*

Christian Science Monitor Index, 115, 116

Chronology of World History, 178

Cirker, Blanche, 253

Cirker, Howard, 253

City directories, 275

City documents, 341–342

City maps, 316–317

Clifford, Anthone D., 170*n.*

Clifford, James, 229*n.*

Colburn, Edwin R., 104

Collections, material in, indexes to, 98, 117–124

College and Research Libraries, 38*n.*

College Placement Annual, 207

Collier's Encyclopedia, 138, 139, 149, 157–159

Collins-World publishers, 274, 283

Collison, Robert, 62, 136–137

Columbia Encyclopedia (see *New Columbia Encyclopedia, The*)

"Columbia Encyclopedia: Instant Universe Again," 166*n.,* 167*n.*

Columbia Lippincott Gazetteer of the World, 319–320

Coman, Edwin T., 224*n.*

Combined Retrospective Index to Journals in History, 1838–1974, 112

Combined Retrospective Index to Journals in Political Science, 1886–1974, 112

Combined Retrospective Index to Journals in Sociology, 1895–1974, 112

Commercial Atlas and Marketing Guide, 305

Commire, Anne, 259

"Commitment to Information Services, A," 6

Compact Edition of the Oxford English Dictionary, The, 284–285

"Comparison of the Readability of Abstracts with their Source Documents, A," 103

Compendium, definition of, 189

Complete Corcordance to the Old and New Testament . . ., 121
Composers since 1900, 261, 262
Comprehensive Dissertation Index, 1861–1972, 128–129
Compton's Encyclopedia and Fact Index, 137, 149, 159–161
Compton's Precyclopedia, 137, 162
Computer(s), data base information retrieval with, 14, 18–19
Computer Output Microfilm, 19
Computer record, definition of, 85
Concise Cambridge History of English Literature, 179
Concise Dictionary of American Biography, 249n.
Concise Heritage Dictionary, The, 281
Concise Oxford Dictionary, 286
Concise Treasury of Bible Quotations, A, 123
Concordances, 121
Congressional Directory, 216, 217
Congressional District Data Book, 201
Congressional Information Service, 329–330
Congressional Information Service. Index to Publications of the United States Congress (CIS/Index), 329–331, 336, 340
Congressional (legislative) publications, 339–340
Congressional Quarterly Almanac, 196, 198–199
Congressional Quarterly Service Weekly Report, 113, 114
Congressional Record, 338–340
Consumer advice on encyclopedias, 152–153
Consumer aids, directories of, 221–222
Consumer Bulletin, 222
Consumer Complaint Guide, 221
Consumer Reports, 210, 222
Consumers Index to Product Evaluations, 222
Contemporary Authors, 24, 259, 260
Contemporary Literary Criticism, 209
Copyright date, 23–24
Cote, Norma, 224n.
County and City Data Book, 201
Covey, Alma C., 45
CQ Weekly Report, 331, 340
Craigie, William, 284, 285, 287
Crane, Stephen, 121
Cross, Leslie, 182
Crowell Company, Thomas Y., 289, 290
Cruden, Alexander, 121
Cumulative Author Index for Poole's Index . . . , 111

Cumulative Book Index, 64, 67–69, 71, 73, 118
Cumulative Subject Index to the Annual Bulletin 1915–1974, 109–110
Cumulative Subject Index to the Monthly Catalog . . . 1900–1971, 327
Current Biography, 17, 243, 254, 255
Current Book Review Citations (CBRC), 46–48, 209, 261
Current events, indexes to, 112–117
Current Index to Journals in Education, 101, 129–132

Dale, Edgar, 271n.
Daniells, Lorna M., 223, 224n.
Data bases, 14, 18–19
    abstracts and indexes on machine-readable, 98–99, 109–110, 112, 127–128
    evaluating, 26
Decennial Cumulative Index, The, 327n.
Declassified Documents Quarterly Catalog, 337
Denis Diderot's Encyclopedia, 135n.
Depository Act of 1962, 334
Depository libraries for U. S. government documents, 333–334, 336, 340
DeSola, Ralph, 292, 293
"Detente on the Reference Shelf," 172n.
Development of Reference Service Through Academic Traditions, Public Library Practice and Special Librarianship, The, 6n.
"Development of a Vertical File, The," 84n.
Dickinson, Fidelia, 41
Dictionaries, 17, 265–296
    abbreviation, 292–293
    acronym, 292–293
    antonym, 289–291
    biographical, 234, 235, 237–238
    children's, 283–284
    compilation of, 267–268
    desk (collegiate), 280–283
    evaluation of, 268–276, 294
        authority, 268–269
        bias, 275–276
        continuous revision, 271, 294
        definitions, 274, 294
        etymologies, 274
        format, 272, 294
        grammatical information, 275
        pronunciation, 275
        scope, 294

special features, 271
spelling, 274
Dictionaries:
evaluation of:
syllabication, 275
synonyms, 275
usage, 272–274
vocabulary, 269–271
foreign-language (bilingual), 294–296
guidelines for discarding, 51
historical, 284–287
American regional, 287
of place names, 17
purposes of, 265–266
scope of, 266–267
slang, 288–289
subject, 293–294
synonym, 289–291
unabridged, 276–280
usage and manuscript style, 291–292
Dictionaries, Encyclopedias and Other Word–Related Books, 293n.
Dictionary Buying Guide, 268
Dictionary Catalog of the G. Robert Vincent Voice Library at Michigan State University . . . , 1975, 62
Dictionary of American Biography, 177, 217, 230, 233, 234, 240, 248–250, 251n., 255
Dictionary of American English, The, 266
Dictionary of American English on Historical Principles, A, 287
Dictionary of American History, 177–178
Dictionary of American Library Biography, 258
Dictionary of American Portraits, 253, 254
Dictionary of American Slang, 17, 288, 289
Dictionary of Americanisms on Historical Principles, A, 287
Dictionary of Anonymous and Pseudonymous English Literature, 237
Dictionary of Contemporary Quotations, 124
Dictionary of Foreign Terms (Mawson), 294, 295
Dictionary of Foreign Terms (Pei), 295
Dictionary of Misinformation, The, 205–206
Dictionary of Modern English Usage, 291–292
Dictionary of National Biography, 240, 248–250, 251n.
Dictionary of Scientific Biography, 248, 252
Dictionary of Slang and Unconventional English, 288–289
Dictionary of the History of Ideas, 176, 180
Dictionary of Universal Biography of All Ages and All Peoples, A, 240, 248

Dictionnaire de la Langue Francaise, 295–296
Diderot, Denis, 135, 136
Digest of Educational Statistics, 201
Diorama, 85
Directories, 17
almanacs and yearbooks as, 190, 213, 214
as biographical sources, 213, 235
consumer aids, 221–222
definition of, 213
education, 214, 219–220
governmental, 214, 216–217
guidelines for discarding, 52
institutional and professional, 214, 217–218
of investment services, 214, 224–226
library, 220–221
local, 214–216
other directory-type sources, 214–215
purpose of, 213–214
scope of, 214
trade and business, 214, 222–224
Directories of Government Agencies, 216n.
Directory of American Scholars, 239, 244, 247
Directory of Associations in Canada, 218
Directory of Business and Financial Services, 224n.
Directory of Newspaper Libraries in the U.S. and Canada, 83
Directory of Post Offices, 217
Directory of Special Libraries and Information Centers, 220
Dissertation Abstracts, 128
Dissertation Abstracts International, 126, 128
Documents to the People, Dttp., 110n., 198, 335, 337
Doubleday & Co., Inc., 269, 283
Doubleday Roget's Thesaurus in Dictionary Form, The, 291
Downs, Robert, 93n.
Doyle, Kenneth O., 80
Dttp, Documents to the People, 110n., 198, 335, 337
Duplication and gaps in indexes and abstracts, 100–101

Eaames, Wilberforce, 73
Eastin, Roy B., 325
Education directories, 214, 219–220
Education encyclopedias, 176
Education Index, 101, 107, 131n.

"Education Index and *Current Index to Journals in Education:* Do We Really Need Both?,"* 131*n*.

Education/Psychology Journals: A Scholar's Guide, 80

Educational Media Index, 88*n*.

Educational Media Yearbook, 86*n*.

Educational Resources Information Center/(clearinghouse for) Information Resources (ERIC/IR), 99, 128–132, 331, 332, 336

Educator Guides, 89

Einbinder, Harvey, 136*n*., 143

El-Hi Textbooks in Print, 70*n*.

"Enchanted Grove, The," 180

Enciclopedia Italiana di Scienze Lettere ed Arti, 169, 171

Enciclopedia universal ilustrada Europeo-Americana, 173

Encyclopaedia Britannica, 17, 50, 135–137, 139, 142–145, 148–151, 153–156, 183

Encyclopaedia Britannica Educational Corporation, 137

Encyclopaedia Judaica, 181, 182

Encyclopedia(s), 17, 135–184, 215, 254, 299–300, 316
  adult, 153–157
  art, 175–176
  children's and young adults', 159–161
  definitions of, 135
  education, 176
  evaluation of, 139–153, 175, 177*n*.
    arrangement and entry, 147–148
    authority, 141–142
    by comparison, 150
    consumer advice, 152–153
    cost, 149
    is the encyclopedia necessary? 151–152
    format, 145–146
    index, 148
    purpose, 140, 174
    reviews as indirect evaluation, 149–150
    sales practices, 151
    scope, 141
    viewpoint and objectivity, 143–145
    writing style, 142–143, 160
  foreign-language, 169–173
  guidelines for discarding, 51
  history, 177–178
  literature, 178–179
  music, 179–180
  one-volume, 166–169
  other English Language, 162–164
  philosophy, 180–181
  popular adult and high school sets, 157–159
  preschool and children's, 161–162
  publishers of, 137–139
  religion, 181–182
  revisions of, 24, 138–139, 143–144, 156, 160, 167
  science, 182–183
  social science, 183–184
  subject, 137, 173–184
    evaluating, 175
    handbooks and, 174–175
  supplements and yearbooks, 164–165

Encyclopedia Americana, The, 138, 139, 148, 149, 156

Encyclopedia Buying Guide . . . , A Consumer Guide to General Encyclopedia in Print, 149, 153, 155, 164

Encyclopedia Canadiana, 157

Encyclopedia International, The, 138, 157–159

Encyclopedia of Associations, 217, 218

Encyclopedia of Careers and Vocational Guidance, 176

Encyclopedia of Education, 176

Encyclopedia of Philosophy, 138, 180, 181

Encyclopedia of Photography, 137

Encyclopedia of the American Revolution, 174

Encyclopedia of the Social Sciences, 51, 184

Encyclopedia of World Art, 175–176, 256

Encyclopedia of World Biography, 248, 251–252, 254

Encyclopedia of World History, An, 178

Epstein, Joseph, 292*n*.

ERIC/IR, 99, 128–132, 331, 332, 336

"ERIC: What It Can Do for You/How to Use It," 129*n*.

Espasa, 169, 173

Essay and General Literature Index, 117–119
  Works Indexed 1900–1969, 119

Europa Yearbook, 195–197

European Historical Statistics 1750–1970, 201*n*.

Evaluating reference sources (*see* Reference sources, evaluating questions to consider)

Evans, Charles, 72, 74, 75

Evans, Ivor H., 193*n*.

Everyman's Guide to Drugs and Medicines, 210

Ewens, David, 261, 262

"Exchange, The," 11*n*.

Executive publications, government, 338–339

Fact sources, 17, 115
  (*See also specific types of reference sources; e.g.,*
    Almanacs; Newspapers; Yearbooks)
"Facts About the World Book Encyclope-
    dia—22 volumes. 1976 Edition," 139*n.*
*Facts on File, a Weekly World News Digest with
    Cumulative Index,* 23, 113–114, 194,
    197, 244
  Five-Year Master News Index, 144
Facts on File Yearbook, 194, 196
Familiar Quotations, 122–123
Famous First Facts, 204, 205
Farrell, William E., 275*n.*
"Feminists Find that Words Fail Them,"
    275*n.*
Field Enterprises, 138
Fielding Travel Guide to Europe, 321
Filby, William, 252, 253
Film Literature Index, 111
Filmstrip, 85
Finnegan's Wake, 121
"First Things First," 205*n.*
Fitzgerald, F. Scott, 121
Five Centuries of Mapmaking, 300*n.*
Flashcard, 85
Flexner, Stuart, 288, 289
Fodor's modern guides, 321
Foreign-language atlases, 314–315
Foreign-language dictionaries, 294–296
Foreign-language encyclopedias,
    169–173
Foreign Language Index, 109
Format of reference sources, 18–19, 25–
    26
  encyclopedias, 145–147
  indexes, 98–99, 102
  national or trade bibiographies, 34
  systematic enumerative bibliography
    and, 32
Forthcoming Books, 64, 69
Foundation Directory, The, 217, 218
Foundation Grants Index, 218
Foundation News, 218
Fowler, Henry Watson, 291–292
Fox, Fred J., 210
France, encyclopedias of, 169–170
Frank, Natalie D., 201–202
Franklin, Benjamin, 191
Frauenzimmer Lexikon, 170
Freedom of Information Act of 1973, 337
Freidel, Frank, 39, 40
"From the Birth of Christ to the 'Death of
    God'," 182*n.*

"FTC Launches New Probe of Encyclope-
    dia Selling," 151*n.*
"FTC Rules Britannica Uses Deception in
    Sales," 151
Functions of Bibliography, The, 32*n.*
*Funk and Scott Index of Corporations and Indus-
    tries,* 224–226
Funk & Wagnalls, 138*n.*, 149*n.*, 162, 164,
    269, 294, 295
*Funk & Wagnalls Comprehensive Standard Inter-
    national Dictionary: Bicentennial Edition,*
    271, 273, 279–280
*Funk & Wagnalls Crossword Puzzle Word Find-
    er,* 267
Funk & Wagnalls New Encyclopedia, 138*n.*,
    149, 162, 163
Funk & Wagnalls New Standard Dictionary,
    269, 278–279

Gale Research Company, 220, 240, 259,
    292, 293
Galneder, Mary, 311*n.*
Games, 85
Gann, Daniel H., 208*n.*
Gargal, Berry, 80
Gazetteers, 17, 125, 310, 319–320
  definition of, 301
Gellatly, Peter, 78*n.*
Gendzier, Stephen J., 135*n.*
"Genealogical Research: An Assessment of
    Potential Value," 252*n.*
"Genealogy Collection Offers Special Ser-
    vices," 253*n.*
"Genealogy Reconsidered," 252*n.*
Genealogy sources, 252–253
General Catalogue of Printed Books, 62–63
Geng, Veronica, 123*n.*
Geographical Magazine, 305
Geographical Review, 311
Geographical sources, 17, 299–321
  bibliographies, 311
  definition of, 300–301
  evaluation of maps and atlases, 304–311
    arrangement, 306
    binding, 310
    color, 307–308
    grid systems, 309
    marginal information, 310
    material included, 305–306
    projections, 309
    scale, 306–307
    symbols, 308–309

Geographical sources:
  evaluation of maps and atlases:
    timeliness, 304–305
    type, 309–310
  gazetteers, 319–320
  guidelines for discarding, 52
  history of, 301–303
  indexes in, 310–311
  national maps, 315–317
    local, 316–317
    sources of government, 316
  scope, 300–301, 303
  thematic maps and atlases, 317–319
  travel guides, 320–321
  world atlases, 311–315
    foreign-language, 314–315
Germany, encyclopedias of, 169–171
Ginzburg, Ralph, 269
Giordano, Frank, 123n.
Globe, 85
GODORT (ALA Government Documents
  Round Table), 335
Good Housekeeping Guide to Medicines and
  Drugs, 210
Government documents, 18, 323–342
  aquisition of, 335–337
  bibliographies to, 338
  catalogs, 325–333
  Congressional (legislative) publications,
    339–340
  definition of, 323–324
  depository libraries, 333–334, 336, 340
  directory-type information in, 215
  evaluation of, 337–338
  executive publications, 338–339
  guidelines for discarding, 52
  guides, 325
  indexes to, 110, 325–333, 338
    general subject, 331–333
  judicial publications, 340–341
  organization and selection of, 333–338
  retrieval of, 328–333
  state and local, 341–342
  types of, 338–341
  (See also United States)
"Government Periodicals: Seven Years
  Later," 110n.
Government Publications: A Guide to Bibliographic Tools, 325
Government Publications and Their Use, 325
"Government Publications for Elementary
  Libraries," 336

Government Publications Review, 326n., 334
Government Reference Books, 335
Government Reports Announcements,
  332–333
Government Reports Index, 332–333
Governmental directories, 214, 216–217
Gowers, Sir Ernest, 292
Graedon, Joe, 210
Grande Encyclopedie, La, 169–170
Granger's Index to Poetry, 98, 117, 120–121
Grant, Mary, 224n.
Grants Register, The, 218n.–219n.
Gray, Richard, 177n.
Great Books of the Western World, 137, 151,
  155n.
Great Britain:
  national library catalogs, 62–63
  national or trade bibliographies, 71
Great Composers: 1300–1900, 261, 262
Great Gatsby, The, 121
Great Soviet Encyclopedia, The, 171–173
Green, Samuel, 5–6
Grimstead, Patricia, 172n.
Grolier Incorporated, 138
Guardian, The, 205n.
Guide(s), 17, 215
  to government documents, 325
  to nonprint media, 86–89
  to reference books, 35–41
  [See also Handbook(s); Travel guides]
Guide to Alternative Colleges and Universities,
  220
Guide to American Directories, 213n.
Guide to Ecology Information and Organization,
  41
"Guide to Indexing of U.S. Government
  Periodicals," 110n.
Guide to Magazine and Serial Agents, 78n.
Guide to Microforms in Print, 90
Guide to Reference Books, 16, 37–42, 72, 78,
  83n., 110, 202, 223, 233, 294, 295, 303,
  314
Guide to Reference Books for School Media Cen-
  ters, 39n., 86, 87
Guide to Reference Materials, 37–41, 72, 78,
  110, 202, 233, 236, 303
Guide to the Study of the United States Imprints,
  75
Guide to Theses and Dissertations, 128n.
Guide to U.S. Government Maps, 316
Guide to U.S. Government Publications, 332
Guidebooks [see Guide(s); Handbooks(s)]

Guides to Educational Media, 86–87
Guiness Book of Surprising Accomplishments,
    205
Guiness Book of Women's Records, 205
Guiness Book of World Records, 204
Guiness Sports Record Book 1977–1978, 205

Halkett, Samuel, 237
Hall, G. K., Company of Boston, 62
Hamilton, Ian, 146–147
Hammond & Company, C. S., 304, 305,
    314, 318
Hammond Medallion World Atlas, 312, 313
Hanchey, Marguerite, 110
Handbook(s), 17, 203–213
    definition of, 174–175, 203
    general, 204–206
    purpose of, 204
    scope of, 204
    subject, 206–213
    subject encyclopedias and, 174–175
    [*See also* Guide(s)]
Handbook of Chemistry and Physics, 206, 209
Handbook of Insurance, 174
Handbook of Physics, 174
Handbook of Private Schools, The, 219
*Handbook of Pseudonyms and Personal Nick-
    names,* 237
Handbuch der Organischen Chemie, 24
Handling Special Materials in Libraries, 86n.
"Happy Wanderer, The," 161n.
Hardy, Thomas, 286n.
Harleston, Rebekah, 110n.
Harper Dictionary of Contemporary Usage, 274n.,
    291, 292
Harrap (publishers), 295
Harvard Classics, 138
Harvard Guide to American History, 39, 40, 177
*Harvard University Dictionary Catalogue of the
    Byzantine Collection . . . , 1975,* 62
Havlice, Patricia, 240
Hays, Samuel P., 252n.
Hearney, Howell J., 36n.
Hebert, Elsie S., 336n.
Heim, Kathleen, 110n.
Heymann, Jaia, 326n.
Hill, G. B., 267n.
Hillman, Howard, 219n.
Hirschfield, Lorraine G., 211n.
Historical Abstracts, 127n.
Historical Atlas, 317

*Historical Statistics of the United States, Colonial
    Times to 1970,* 201
"Historical Studies in Documentation,"
    92n.
History:
    atlases on, 317–319
    dictionaries on, 284–287
    encyclopedias, 177–178
    of maps, 301–303
*History and Bibliography of American Newspa-
    pers, 1690–1820,* 82
"History and Genealogy . . . ," 252n.
Holler, Frederick, 40
Home Book of Quotations, The, 122–123
Hospital Literature Index, 111
Hotel and Motel Red Book, 320, 321
Houghton Mifflin, 269, 280, 281
Houston Post, 116
"How Accessible Are the Records in Gov-
    ernment Records Center," 336n.
"How I Made $17,500 Robbing a Li-
    brary," 49n.
How Our Laws Are Made, 339
How To Find Out in Iron and Steel, 36
How to Pass . . . , 207–208
*How to Trace Your Family Tree: A Complete and
    Easy to Understand Guide for the Beginner,*
    252, 253
Hulbert, James R., 287
*Humanities: A Selective Guide to Information
    Sources, The,* 40–41
Humanities Index, 104, 106–107
Humanities reference books, guidelines for
    discarding, 52
Hungerford, Anthos, 335n.
Hutchins, Margaret, 49
Hyamson, Albert, 240, 248

IBZ, 107
*I Can Be Anything: Careers and Colleges for
    Young Women,* 207
"Idioms of Our Time," 292n.
Illustrated Dictionary of Ornament, An, 176
*Illustrated Heritage Dictionary and Information
    Book, The,* 281
Illustrated World Encyclopedia, The, 164
Illustrations:
    biographical indexes to find, 240–241
    dictionary, 272, 281, 283
    in encyclopedias, 145–146, 158, 161, 162,
        164, 167–171, 176, 182, 183
    evaluating, 26

"In the Lexicographer's Lair," 286n.
Index(es) and indexing services, 97–125
    abbreviations used in, guides to, 124–
        125
    in almanacs, 192–196, 198
    almanacs and yearbooks as informal,
        190
    as bibliographical aid, 16–17
    to bibliographies, 16
    to biographical material, 234, 238–
        242
    to current events, 112–117
        last week's events, 113–114
        newspaper indexes, 115–117, 244
    encyclopedia, 148, 155, 156, 160, 167,
        171–173, 176, 178, 181–183
    evaluation of, 99–103
    to geographical sources, 310–311
    to government documents, 110, 325–333,
        338
        general subject, 331–333
    on machine-readable data bases, 98–99,
        109–110, 112
    to material in collections, 117–124
        concordances, 121
        quotations, 122–124
    periodical, 104–112, 244
        retrospective, 111–112
    physical format of, 98–99
    in reference sources, importance of, 21
    to reviews, 46–49
    types of, 97–98
Index Medicus, 98
Index to American Periodical Verse, The, 121
Index of Artists . . . , 255–256
Index to American Reference Books Annual,
    1970–1974: A Cumulative Index to Authors,
    Titles and Subjects, 38n.
Index to Black Poetry, 121
Index to Book Reviews in the Humanities, 48
Index to Current Urban Documents, 341, 342
Index to Free Periodicals, 111
Index to Instructional Media Catalogs, 89n.
Index to Legal Periodicals, 107
Index to Literary Biography, 240, 242
Index to Periodical Articles By and About Ne-
    groes, 257
Index to Poetry for Children and Young People:
    1964–1969, 121
Index to Scientific Reviews, 48n.
Index to the Times, 115, 117
Index to the Wilson Author Series, 239

Index to U.S. Government Periodicals, 108, 110,
    332
Indexed Periodicals, 81
Indexer, The, 103
Information Bulletin, Western Association of Map
    Libraries, 311
Information Please Almanac, 191–193
Information Science Abstracts, 126–127
Information sources (see Reference sources)
Information Sources of Political Science, The, 16,
    40
Institutional directories, 214, 216–217
Interlibrary loan, 7, 12, 78, 82
Intermediate Dictionary, 283
International Associations, 198
International Atlas, The, 313, 316
International Bibliography of Book Reviews of
    Scholarly Literature, 107n.
International Bibliography of Reprints, 91
International Cyclopedia of Music and Musicians,
    262–263
International Directory of Little Magazines and
    Small Presses, 224
International Encyclopedia of the Social Sciences,
    The, 137, 173, 174, 176, 180, 183–
    184
International Index to Multi-Media Information,
    89–90
International Maps and Atlases in Print, 311
International Portrait Gallery, 254n.
International Standard Book Number
    (ISBN), 33, 65n.
International Standard Serial Numbers
    (ISSN), 79
"International Style for Bibliographic Ref-
    erences, An," 56n.
International Who's Who, 230, 244, 247
International Yearbook and Statesman's Who's
    Who, 195–197
Internationale Bibliographie der Zeitschriften Li-
    teratus; Aus Allen Gebieten des Wissens,
    107
"Introduction to Omniscience, An," 145n.
Introduction to United States Public Documents,
    324n., 325, 327n., 334n., 340
Investment services directories, 214, 224–
    226
Irregular Serials and Annuals, 80n.
Italy:
    atlas of, 314, 315
    encyclopedias of, 169, 171–173

Jackson, Kenneth T., 319
James, Edward T., 248, 251n.
James, Janet, 251n.
Johnson, Samuel, 267, 268
Jones, Judith M., 210
Joy of Knowledge, The, 168
Joyce, James, 121
Judicial Opinion Reporters, 341
Judicial publications, 340–341
Junior Book of Authors, The, 259, 261

Kaczmarek, Carol, 336n.
Kaiser, F. E., 86n.
Kane, Joseph N., 204, 205
Katz, William, 78n., 80
Keesing's Contemporary Archives, 113, 114, 197
Kelly, James, 73–75
Kerler, Dorothea, 41
King, Rosemary, 103n.
Kinney, Mary R., 124n.
Kirkus, 47
Kissinger, Henry, 6
Kister, Kenneth, 149–150, 153, 155, 164,
   268
Kit, definition of, 85
Knight, Nancy H., 57n.
Kosa, Geza A., 45n.
Kunitz, Stanley J., 259

Lackey, Richard S., 252n.
Laing, John, 237
Langer, William L., 178
Larousse, Pierre, 169–170
Larsgaard, Mary, 327n.
Larson, Cedric, 245n., 246
Law, handbooks and manual on, 212–213
   [See also Government documents, Con-
      gressional (legislative) publications]
"Le Grand Larousse," 170n.
"Learning centers," 84
Legal First Aid, 212
Leidy, Philip, 335
Lewis, Anthony, 336n.
Leypoldt, Frederick, 75
Librarians:
   bibliographies by, 92–93
   current events information and, 113
   public and, 6
   unconventional reference work and, 19–
      20

Library(ies):
   biographical sources, 258
   depository, 333–334, 336, 340
   directories, 220–221
   instruction in use of, 7
   reference service and, 8–10
Library and Information Science Abstracts, 102,
   126–127
Library Bibliographies and Indexes, 93
Library Journal, 38, 41, 43–45, 47, 261, 334
Library Literature, 102, 108, 126, 132
Library of Congress, 341, 342
   cards, 293n.
   map division, 303
   national union catalogs, 56–61, 77–78
   newspaper union lists on microform,
      82n.
Library of Congress Author Catalog: A Cumula-
   tive List of Works Represented by Library of
   Congress Printed Cards, 1948–1952, 61
Library of Congress Catalog. Books: Subjects, 57,
   71
Library of Congress Catalogs: Subject Catalog,
   57, 59
Library of Congress Main Reading Room Refer-
   ence Collection Subject Catalog, 39
Library of Congress Subject Headings, 103, 131,
   326, 328
Library of Literary Criticism, A, 49
Library Science Abstracts, 102
Lincoln Library of Essential Information, The,
   166, 167
Line, Maurice, 101n.
Literary Market Place, 66n., 222, 223
Literature:
   biographical sources on, 259–261
   encyclopedias on, 178–179
   handbooks and manuals, 208–209
Literature of Political Science, The, 36
Littre (publishers), 295–296
Lives of Painters, 256
Living World Vocabulary, The Words We Know:
   A National Vocabulary Inventory, The,
   271n.
Lockhart, Bruce, 241
London Sunday Times, 286
"Look at ERIC After Ten Years, A,"
   130n.
Lorca, Federico Garcia, 121
Los Angeles Times, 116
Lovejoy's College Guide, 219n.
Low, Janet, 316

McBride, Elizabeth A., 110n.
McCarthy, Joseph, 177n.
Macdonald, Dwight, 291
McFadden, Cyra, 289
McGraw-Hill, 256
McGraw-Hill Encyclopedia of Science and Technology, 137, 182–183
McGraw-Hill Yearbook of Science and Technology, 182–183
McLean, Marilyn, 212
Macmillan Company, 283
Macmillan Educational Corporation, 138
Macmillan School Dictionary, 276
Magazines [see Periodical(s)]
Magazines for Libraries, 80
Magill, Frank N., 206, 208
Malcolm, Andrew H., 271n.
Mallet, Daniel, 255–256
Mangouni, Norman, 56n.
Manual(s), 17, 203–213
    definition of, 203
    general, 204–206
    guidelines for discarding, 51
    purpose of, 204
    scope of, 240
    subject, 206–213
Manual for Writers of Term Papers, Theses, and Dissertations, A, 291, 292
Manual of Style, 292
Map(s), 85, 86, 300, 311–320
    definition of, 300–301
    evaluation of (see Geographical sources, evaluation of maps and atlases)
    history of, 301–303
    national, 315–317
    scope of, 303
    thematic, 317–319
    world, 311–315
    [(See also Atlas(es)]
Marconi, Joseph, 81
Marquis Who's Who Publications/Index to All Books, 238–240, 246n.
Martin, Irene, 39
Massett, Larry, 210
Masterpieces of World Literature in Digest Form, 208
Masterplots, 206, 208
Masterplots Annual Volume, 208
"Mathematics of Style, The," 270
Matthews, Mitford, 285, 287
Mawson, C. O. Sylvester, 290, 294, 295

Media Industry Newsletter, 136n., 232n.
Media Programs: District and School, 86n.
Media Review Digest (MRD), 89, 90
Medical Books for the Lay Person, 211–212
Medical College of Virginia, 212
Medical handbooks, manuals, and tapes, 210–212
Medical Self-Care, 211
Medicine Show, The, 210
Mencken, H. L., 274, 284, 287
Mercator, Gerhard, 301–302
Merck Manual of Diagnosis and Therapy, 211
Merit Students Encyclopedia, 138, 139, 149, 159–161
Merriam Company, G. & C., 137, 269, 274, 278, 283–284
Michigan Librarian, 219n.
Microform(s), 19
    bibliographies, 90–91
    definition of, 85
"Microform Catalog Data Retrieval Systems: A Survey," 57n.
Microform Review, 90
Microlist, 90
Microscope slide, 86
Model, definition of, 86
Middle East Record, The, 102
Minneapolis Tribune Services, The, index to, 117
Misspeller's Dictionary, The, 267
Mitchell, Joyce, 207
Mobil Travel Guides, 321
Molnar, John, 72, 74
Moneysworth, 269
Monthly Catalog of United States Government Publications, 110, 316, 326–330, 332, 334, 336–338, 340
Monthly Checklist of State Publications, 341–342
Moody's Investors Service, 224–225
More Junior Authors, 259
Morehead, Joe, 324, 325, 327n., 332, 334, 339, 340
Morgan, Mary L., 110n.
Morris, Mary, 291, 292
Morris, William, 291, 292
"Most Common Verb in Schools . . . ," 271
Motion picture, 86
"Mouthing Greenery," 205n.
Multi Media Reviews Index, 89
Municipal Yearbook, 196, 199

Murray, James, 284
Museums of the World, 221
Music:
  biographical sources for, 261–263
  encyclopedia, 179–180
Music Index, 263
Myers, Carol F., 259
Myth of the Britannica, 143n.
My Weekly Reader, 162
Nader, Ralph, 216n.
Nathan, Paul, 136n.
National Aeronautic and Space Administration, 130
National Atlas of the United States of America, 315–316
National bibliographies, 34, 64–93
  bibliographies of, 91–93
  of books, 64–77
  of newspapers, 82–83
  of nonprint materials, 84–91
  of pamphlets, 83–84
  of periodicals, 77–81
National Cyclopaedia of American Biography, 248, 250–251
National Cyclopaedia of American Biography Revised Index; Permanent and Current Series, 251
National Faculty Directory, 247n.
National Geographic Atlas of the World, 312–314
National Geographic Magazine Cumulative Index, 98
National Geographic Society, 304, 305
National Index of American Imprints Through 1800; The Short Title Evans, 72, 74
National Information Centers for Educational Media, 87, 88
National Journal, 331
National library catalogs, 55–63
  subject collections, 61–62
National Library of Medicine, 93
National Observer Index, 115, 116
National Review, 336n.
National Union Catalog, The, A Cumulative Author List, 16, 33, 56–63, 71, 77–78, 237
  history of, 60
  uses of, in reference work, 58–59
National Union Catalog: A Cumulative Author List, 1953–1957, 61
National Union Catalog: A Cumulative Author List, 1956 to date, 57

National Union Catalog: A Cumulative Author List, 1956–1967, 61
National Union Catalog: A Cumulative Author List, 1958–1962, 61
National Union Catalog: A Cumulative Author List, 1965–1967, 61
National Union Catalog: Pre-1956 Imprints, 57, 60, 71, 72
"National Union Catalog Pre-1956 Imprints: A Progress Report, The," 61n.
Needham, C. D., 154n.
Negative selection of reference books, 49–51
Negro Almanac, The, 257
Nemo's Almanac, 123–124
"*Nemo's Almanac,*" 123n.
New Acronyms, Initialisms, and Abbreviations Dictionary, 292, 293
"New Bibliographic Tools Proposed by LC," 61n.
New Book of Knowledge, The, 138, 161–162
"New Britannica, The," 136n., 142n., 147n.
New Cambridge Modern History, The, 177
New Cassell's foreign-language dictionary series, 294, 295
New Cassell's French Dictionary, 294
New Cassell's German Dictionary, 294
New Catholic Encyclopedia, The, 174, 181–182
New Century Cyclopedia of Names, 238n.
New Collegiate Dictionary, 284
New Columbia Encyclopedia, The, 146, 147n., 166–169, 183
New Elementary Dictionary, 283
New Encyclopaedia Britannica, 137n., 143–144, 153–156
  Macropaedia, 154, 155
  Micropaedia, 148, 154, 155
  Propaedia, 154–155
New English Dictionary on Historical Principles (OED), 284–285
New Grove Dictionary of Music and Musicians, 179–180, 263
New Handbook of Prescription Drugs, 210
"New, Improved Britannica, The," 145n.
" 'New' Monthly Catalog, a Review, The," 326n.
New Orleans Times Picayune, The, 116
New Oxford Atlas, The, 314
New Periodicals Index, 106
New Research Centers, 220
New Serial Titles, 57, 58, 77–80

New Serial Titles — Classed Subject Arrangement, 79
New Serial Titles, 1950–1970, 77–79
Subject Guide, 77, 79
New Standard Encyclopedia, 163–164
New Students' Dictionary, 283
New World Dictionary of the American Language, Students Edition, 282
New York Historical Society, 254
New York Metropolitan Reference and Research Library Agency, 212
New York Times, The, 12–13, 47, 115, 151n., 164n., 172n., 257n., 274, 282, 339n.
New York Times Biographical Service: A Compilation of Current Biographical Information of General Interest, 243–244, 261
New York Times Book Review, The, 45, 49
New York Times Book Review Index, 1896–1970, 49
New York Times Crossword Puzzle Dictionary, The, 286n.
New York Times Encyclopedia Almanac, The, 191n.
New York Times Index, The, 17, 98, 99, 101, 113, 115–117, 194, 200, 226, 258
New York Times Obituaries Index, The, 240–243
New Bank, 114
News Dictionary, 194n.
Newsletter on Intellectual Freedom, 288n.
Newspaper(s):
    bibliographies of, 82–83
    indexes to, 98, 113–117, 244
    local, 117, 258
    (*See also* Periodicals)
Newspaper and Gazette Report, 82n.
Newspaper Index, 115, 116
Newspaper Press Directory, 83n.
Newspapers in Microform, 1948–1972, 82n.
"Newswordy Events," 274n.
NICEM Media Indexes, 87–89
Nicholsen, Margaret, 242
Nicholson, Harold, 229
1971—Britannica Yearbook of Science and the Future, 183
Nineteenth Century Readers' Guide to Periodical Literature, 111–112
Noble, J. K., 136n.
Nonbook Materials: A Bibliography of Recent Publications, 87, 88
"Nonconventional Information Sources and Services in the Library: Our Credo," 20n.

Nonprint materials, bibliographies of, 84–91
Nonprint Media in Academic Libraries, 86n.
North American Film and Video Directory, 89
Northcott, Bayan, 180n.
Notable American Women 1607–1950. A Biographical Dictionary, 248, 251
"Novice's Guide to *ERIC,* A," 129n.
Nuclear Science Abstracts, 331

Obituaries from the Times 1961–1970, 241–242
Occupational Outlook Handbook, 206, 207
Occupational Outlook Quarterly, 207
"Occupations in Demand," 208
Official Associated Press Almanac, 191n.
Official CB Slanguage Language Dictionary, The, 289
O'Hara, Frederick, 334
Old Farmer's Almanac, The, 191
Onions, C. T., 284
O'Rourke, Joseph, 271n.
Ortelius, Abraham, 302
Ottemiller's Index to Plays in Collections, 120
Our Bodies, Ourselves, 210
Owen, Dolores B., 110
Oxford Companion to Art, 176
Oxford Companion to Sports and Games, 147n., 173
Oxford Dictionary of the Christian Church, The, 182
Oxford English Dictionary, The (OED), 135n., 166, 284–287
Oxford Regional Economic Atlas: The United States and Canada, 318
Oxford University Press, 304

PAIS, 108–110, 331
Palais, Elliot S., 81n., 101n.
Pamphlets, bibliographies of, 83–84
Paperbound Books in Print, 64, 69–70
Parch, Grace D., 83
Parish, David, 216n.
Partridge, Eric, 288–289
Pearson, J. D., 92
Pei, Mario, 295
People in Books: A Selective Guide to Biographical Literature Arranged by Vocations and Other Fields of Reader Interest, 242
People's Almanac, The, 191–194
People's Pharmacy, The, 210
"People's Yellow Pages," 216n.

Periodical(s):
bibliographies of, 77–81
indexes to, 98, 104–112
current events, 113–114, 244
guides to abbreviations used, 124–125
retrospective, 111–112
where they are indexed, sources for, 81
(*See also* Newspapers)
Periodical Title Abbreviations, 124
Periodicals for School Libraries, 80
Peterson, Carolyn, 39, 87
Phaidon Press, Ltd., 137
"Phenomenal Success of the National Geographic's Book Operations, The," 304*n.*
Philosophy encyclopedias, 180–181
Phonefiche, 216
Physicians' Desk Reference, 206, 210
Picture, definition of, 86
Play Index, 118, 120
"Plot Behind the Masterplots, A," 208*n.*
Plotnik, Art, 38*n.*
Pocket Data Book, USA, 201
Poet's Manual and Rhyming Dictionary, The, 267
"Politics and the New Britannica," 136*n.*
Polk Co., R. L., 215
Poole, William Frederick, 111
Poole's Index to Periodical Literature, 111
Poor Richard's Almanack, 191
Poor's Register of Corporations, Directors, and Executives, 222, 223, 257, 258
Popular American Composers, 261, 262
Popular Guide to Government Publications, A, 335
Popular Names of U.S. Government Reports: A Catalog, 329
Popular Periodical Index, 104–106, 263
Portrait Index, 254
Portraits, sources for, 253–254
"Pounds, Dollars and Deutschmarks," 76
Praeger, Inc., Frederick A., 137
Preece, Warren E., 136*n.*, 142, 144, 147*n.*
"Preface," 231
Premier World Atlas, 313
"Press and Its Right to Silence: Not Yet Clarified, The," 336*n.*.
Prices of books, references for, 75–77
Princeton Encyclopedia of Poetry and Poetics, 179
Printing Act of 1895, 334
Private Independent Schools, 219–220
Problems in Literary Research: A Guide to Selected Reference Works, 41

Professional directories, 214, 216–217
Prostano, Emanuel, 86*n.*
Psychological Abstracts, 18, 99, 126–128, 132
Ptolemy of Alexandria, 302
Ptolemy's Cosmographia, 302
Public Affairs Information Service Bulletin, 108–110, 113, 114, 200, 331
Published Library Catalogues: An Introduction to Their Contents and Use, 62
Publisher, 22
of dictionaries, 269, 284
foreign-language, 295
of encyclopedias, 137–139, 169
of indexes, evaluating, 100
of maps, 304
Publishers' Trade List Annual, 64, 66–67, 73, 295
Publishers' Weekly, 64, 69, 73, 168, 261
"Publishing: Words Never Fail Him," 283
"Purchasing a General Encyclopedia," 174*n.*
"PW Interview," 261

Questions:
directional, 11, 13
ready-reference, 11–13
in reference process, 4–5, 10–13
research, 13
specific search, 12–13
"Quick, Who Said, 'Where is the rest of me?'–and Other Memorable Questions about Forgettable Lines," 123*n.*
Quinton, Anthony, 145*n.*, 161*n.*
Quotations sources, 122–124

Rand McNally Commercial Atlas and Marketing Guide, 83, 306, 307, 317–318
Rand McNally & Company, 304, 305, 313, 314
Rand McNally Cosmopolitan World Atlas, 312, 313
Rand McNally Road Atlas: United States—Canada—Mexico, 317
Random House College Dictionary, The, 279
Random House Dictionary, The, 279
Random House Dictionary of the English Language, 269, 279, 280
Random House Dictionary of the English Language, College Edition, The, 270
Random House Encyclopedia, The, 137, 147, 148, 166, 168–169

"Random House Encyclopedia, The," 168
Random House, Inc., 269, 295
Readability of abstracts, 103
Reader's Digest Treasury of Modern Quotations, The, 123
Readers' Guide to Periodical Literature, The, 17, 23, 98, 99, 104–106, 112–113, 254
Readers' services, circulation and reference, 9–10
Ready reference, 187–226
  definition of, 187
  duplication among, 187–188
  questions, 11–12
  [*See also* Almanac(s); Directories; Handbook(s); Yearbook(s)]
Realia, definition of, 86
"Recent Canadian Reference Books—A Selected List," 39
Record of America, 177n.
Redden, James E., 287n.
Reddig, Jill, 41
Redus, Mary E., 117n.
"Reference and Subscription Book Reviews," 41, 43–45, 71n., 106n., 137n., 149, 153, 162, 163n., 174, 182, 268, 284n.. 311, 314
  Encyclopedia Supplements," 165n.
Reference books:
  bibliographic guides to, 35–41
    subject, 39–41
  negative selection of, 49–51
  reviews, 43–45
    evaluating, 45–46
    indexes to, 46–49
Reference Books for Elementary and Junior High School Libraries, 39, 87
Reference Books in Paperback, 152
Reference Guide for Consumers, 218, 221, 222
Reference process, 3–28
Reference questions, types of, 10–13
  (*See also* Questions)
Reference section, evaluation of, 8
"Reference Service with Maps," 304n.
Reference services:
  defined, 3
  direct, 6–7
  indirect, 7–8
  and the library, 8–10
  organization and administration of, 7
  and the public, 5–8
Reference Services and Reference Process, 3n., 19n., 99n.

Reference Services Review, 43–46, 334
Reference source(s), 14–26
  control-access-directional type of, 16–18
  cost of, 26
  evaluating questions to consider, 20–26
    audience, 24–25
    authority, 21–22
    format, 25–26
    purpose, 21
    scope, 22–24
  formats of (*see* Format of reference sources)
  government documents, 18
  interpersonal, 14
  primary, secondary, and tertiary, 15–16
  source type of, 17, 18
  technology and, 14
  (*See also specific types of reference sources; e.g.,* Biographical sources; Encyclopedias; *and names of individual works*)
Reference work, 3
"References to Indexes and Abstracts in *Ulrich's,*" 81
"Relationship between Time Lags and Place of Publication . . . , The," 102n.
Religion encyclopedias, 181–182
Research Centers Directory, 220
Research in Education, 129
Research questions, 13
Resources in Education, 129–132, 331
Reviewing of Reference Books, 45
Reviews:
  indexes to: of books, 105
    of nonprint media, 89–91
    of reference books, 46–49
  reference book (*see* Reference books, reviews)
"Reviews: Who Needs Them," 46
Revised Statutes of the United States, The, 212
Reynolds, Michael M., 128n.
"Rights and Permissions," 136n.
Roberts, Frank, 241
Robertson, Patrick, 205
Robinson, William C., 102n.
Roger, A. Robert, 40–41
Roget, Peter Mark, 289–290
Roget's International Thesaurus, 289–290
Roorbach, Orville, 73–75
Rothstein, Samuel, 6n.
Rough, Archie G., 16n.
RQ, 11, 43–45, 93, 123, 177n., 201n., 334

Rush, Theressa, 259
Russia, encyclopedias of, 169, 171–173
Rutsvold, Margaret, 86–87
Ryder, Dorothy, 37, 38

Sabin, Joseph, 72–74
Safire, William, 266n., 274n.
St. Paul Dispatch and Pioneer Press, The, index
    to, 117
Sakharov, Andrei D., 172n.
San Francisco Chronicle, 116
Saturday Review, 45
Scarecrow Press, 138
Scheer, George F., 318n.
Schmeckebier, Laurence F., 325
School Library Journal, 45, 47
School Library Media Center, The, 86n.
School Library Supervisors Directory, 220
"School media centers," 84
Schorr, Alan, 131n.
Schorr, Daniel, 336
Schrag, Dale R., 20n.
Schultz, Kathryn, 84n.
Schultz, Margaret E., 124
Science Citation Index, 48n., 100
Science encyclopedias, 182–183
Science handbooks and manuals, 209–212
Science reference books, guidelines for dis-
    carding, 52
Science Research Abstracts, 331
Science Year, 183
Scientific and Technical Books in Print, 70n.
Scope (see specific types of reference works, eval-
    uation of)
Scribner Bantam English Dictionary, The, 282n.
Scribner's Sons, 295
Sears List of Subject Headings, 70, 103, 131
Secretarial handbooks, 209
"Secrets of American English May Yield to
    Dialect Geography," 266n.
Selected Guide to Travel Books, 321
"Selected Reference Books of 1976–1977,"
    38n.
Selected U.S. Government Publications, 325–328,
    333, 334
Selection aids for reference sources, 41–46
    (See also Negative selection)
Selective Bibliography for the Study of English
    and American Literature, 179
Serial(s):
    definition of, 78n.
    (See also Newspapers; Periodicals)

Serial—A Year in the Life of Marin Country,
    The, 289
Serials Keyword Index, 78
Serials Librarian, 334
Serials Supplement, 332
Shabad, Theodore, 172n.
Shain, Henry, 212
Shakespeare, William, concordances to
    works of, 121
Sharp, Harold S., 237
Shaw, Ralph, 73, 74
Sheehy, Eugene P., 16, 37–42, 72, 78, 83n.,
    110, 202, 223, 233, 236, 294, 295, 303,
    314
Shell Book of Firsts, The, 205
Shenker, Israel, 144n., 166n., 167n., 244n.,
    283, 286n., 289n., 291
Shepherd, William, 317, 318
Shera, Jesse H., 4
Shipton, Clifford, 72, 74
Shoemaker, Richard, 73–75
Short Story Index, 117, 119–120
Shorter Oxford English Dictionary on Historical
    Principles, The, 279, 286
Shulman, David, 205
"Significance of Dispersion for the Index-
    ing of Political Science Journals, The,"
    101n.
Slang, dictionaries of, 288–289
Slide, 86
Slocum, Robert, 236, 255
Slonimsky, Nicholas, 232n., 262
Slote, Stanley J., 49n.
Smith, Margaret Porter, 61n.
Social science reference books:
    encyclopedias, 183–184
    guidelines for discarding, 52
Social Sciences and Humanities Index,
    106–107
Social Sciences Index, 104, 106–107, 110
Sociological Abstracts, 111
Something About the Author. Facts and Figures
    About Contemporary Authors and Illustra-
    tions of Books for Young People, 259
"Sources of Health Information for Public
    Libraries," 211
Sources of Information in the Social Sciences: A
    Guide to the Literature, 39, 40
South American Handbook, 197
Soviet Union, atlas of, 314–315
Spain, encyclopedias of, 169, 173
Special Libraries Association, 303

Speech Index, 98
Springer (publishers), 295
Standard and Poor's Corporation Records, 224–225
Standard Book Number (SBN), 33
Standard College Dictionary, 282
Standard Periodical Directory, The, 80
"Standardization of Cataloging Rules for Nonbook Materials: A Progress Report–April 1972, The," 86*n.*
State-by-State Guide to Women's Legal Rights, 212
State documents, 341–342
State libraries, 341
Statesman's Year-Book, 17, 195–198
Statistical Abstract of the United States, 189, 199–202, 333
Statistical data sources, 199–202
Statistical Sources, 202
Statistical Yearbook (United Nations Statistical Office), 199, 201
Statistical Yearbook (U.S. Department of Housing and Urban Development), 201
Statutes at Large, 339, 340
Stephen, Leslie, 249
Sterling Publishing Co., 204, 205
Stevenson, Burton E., 122–123
Stoffle, Carla J., 110*n.*
Stokes, Roy, 32
Studies in Bibliography, 36
Study Abroad, 219*n.*
Subject approach:
  to bibliography(ies), 34–35
  of reference books, 39–41
  to dictionaries, 293–294
  to encyclopedias, 173–184
  to indexes, 98
  to national library collections, 61–62
"Subject Bibliographies in Information Work," 103*n.*
Subject Collections, 61–62
Subject Directory of Special Libraries and Information Centers, 220*n.*
Subject Guide to Books in Print, 64–66, 70, 71, 73, 92, 311, 320*n.,* 329
Subject Guide to Children's Books in Print, 65, 70
Subject Guide to Forthcoming Books, 64, 69
Subject Guide to Government Reference Books, 335
Subject Guide to Microforms in Print, 90

Subject headings:
  for indexes and abstracts, 102–103, 131
  Library of Congress, 103, 131, 326, 328
  Sears, 103, 131
Subject Index of the Modern Works Added to the Library of the British Museum in the Years 1881–1900, 62, 63
Subject Index to Periodicals, 106
Suit Your Spirit: Travel Guidebooks in Review, 321
"Summary Justice," 242*n.*
Superintendent of Documents, U.S., 325, 326, 328, 334, 336
"Supplement to the 1976/77 U.S. Government Manual," 198
Supplement to the Oxford English Dictionary, A, 284, 286, 288
"Survey of Local Newspapers in California," 117*n.*
Sutherland, Earl W., 210
Sylvia Porter's Money Book, 226
Synonyms, dictionaries of, 289–291

Tallentire, D. R., 270
Tanselle, George, 75
Technical Book Review Index, 48
Technical services, acquisitions and cataloging, 9
Telephone directory, 215, 216
Television Sponsors Directory, The, 221
Texas Reference Sources, A Selective Guide, 39
Textual bibliography, 35–36
Thaxton, Lyn, 117*n.*
Thesaurus of ERIC Descriptors, 129, 131
"They Have Created the Ultimate Reference Guide . . . ," 38*n.*
Thieme, Ulrich, 255–256
Third Book of Junior Authors, 259
"This Browsing Life," 147*n.*
Thomas' Register of American Manufacturers, 222, 223
Thompson, Oscar, 262
Thorndike Barnhart Beginning Dictionary, 283
Thorne, J. O., 231
Timeliness of reference sources, 15–16, 23–24
  as guideline for negative selection, 50
  (*See also specific types of reference sources, evaluation of*)
Times, The, 115–117
  Index to, 115–117

Times Atlas of China, The, 315, 316
*Times Atlas of the World: Comprehensive 5th
    Edition,* 17, 305, 311–314
Times Biographical Service, 241
Times Educational Supplement, The, 117
Times Higher Educational Supplement, The,
    117
Times Literary Supplement, The, 45, 117, 205n.
Titles in Series, 320n.
Titus, Edna Brown, 77
Tour Book, 320
Trade bibliographies, 34, 64–93
Trade directories, 214, 222–224
Trade Names Directory, 222
Transparency, 86
Travel guides, 316–317, 320–321
    definition and scope of, 301
    guides to, 321
Trench, Richard, 284
Trends, almanacs and yearbooks indication
    of, 190
Treude, Mai, 304n.
Turabian, Kate L., 291, 292
Turtle, Mary R., 102n.
Twentieth Century Authors, 259n.
Type size:
    in encyclopedias, 146
    on maps, 309–310

Ulrich's International Periodical Directory, 77,
    79–81, 110, 215
Union list of card catalogs, 16, 56–57
*Union List of Serials in Libraries of the United
    States and Canada,* 56, 77–79
UN Monthly Chronicle, The, 197
United Nations General Assembly, 6
United Nations Statistical Office, 199, 201
United States:
    atlases of, 315–319
    bibliography, retrospective, 71–77
        book prices, 75–77
    regional dictionaries, 287
    (*See also* Government documents)
U.S. Bureau of the Census, 189, 199, 201
United States Catalog: Books in Print, 73, 75
    (See also *Cumulative Book Index*)
United States Code, 339, 340
U.S. Congress Joint Committee on Print-
    ing, 216, 217
U.S. Department of Housing and Urban
    Development, 201
U.S. Department of Labor, 206–208

U.S. Federal Trade Commission, 150–151
U.S. Geological Survey, 315–316
United States Government Manual, 195, 198,
    217
United States Government Organization Manual,
    195n.
U.S. Government Printing Office (GPO),
    316, 325
"U.S. Government Publications Acquisition
    Procedures for the Small Special Li-
    brary," 335n., 336n.
"U.S. Is Doing Well as Publisher but
    Charges More," 337n.
U.S. Office of Education, 201
U.S. Postal Service, 217
U.S. Superintendent of Documents, 325,
    326, 334, 336
"Universal Bibliographic Control" (UBC),
    55n.
"Universal Bibliographic Control and the
    Information Scientist," 55n.
Universal bibliography, 33, 55–56
*Universal Pronouncing Dictionary of Biography
    and Mythology,* 238n.
University Desk Encyclopedia, The, 168
University microfilms, 128, 129
University Society Encyclopedia, 138
Usage and manuscript style, dictionaries
    for, 291–292
"Use of the Reference Service in a Large
    Academic Library," 13n.

Vail, R. W. G., 73
Value Line Investment Survey, 224, 225
Van den Bark, Melvin, 289
Van Doren, Charles, 238n.
Van Nostrand's Scientific Encyclopedia, 182,
    183
Vaughan, Robert, 76n.
Vavrek, Bernard, 6n.
Verbatim, 287n.
Vertical File Index, 83, 84
Videorecord, definition of, 86
Vital Statistics of the United States, 211
Vocational handbooks, 206–208
Volume size of encyclopedias, 146–147

Waddell, John, 119
Wagenknecht, Robert E., 252n.
Wagner, Susan, 6n.

Wakeman, John, 259
Walford, Albert John, 37–41, 63, 72, 78, 110, 202, 233, 303
Walker, William D., 211
Wall, Edward, 111
Wall Street Journal Index, 115, 116, 226, 258
Wallace, Irving, 194
Wallenchinsky, David, 194
"Wanted More Information about Information," 6
Washington Post, The, 6
Watson, George, 273n.
We, The Americans, 201
Webster's American Biographies, 238n.
Webster's Biographical Dictionary, 234, 237–238
Webster's Collegiate Thesaurus, 289, 290
Webster's Dictionary, 269, 280
Webster's Dictionary of Synonyms, 265
Webster's New Collegiate Dictionary, 268, 280, 282, 283
Webster's New Dictionary of Synonyms, 289–291
Webster's New Geographical Dictionary, 319–320
Webster's New International Dictionary of the English Language, 272, 276–278
Webster's New World Crossword Puzzle Dictionary, 286n.
Webster's New World Dictionary, 273–274
Webster's New World Dictionary of the American Language, 280, 282, 283
Webster's Secretarial Handbook, 206, 209
Webster's Third New International Dictionary, 17, 267, 269, 270, 272–279
6,000 Words, A Supplement . . . , 276, 278
Weeding, 49–51
Weeding Library Collections, 49n.
Weekly Record, The, 64, 69, 84
Weihs, Jean, 85–86
Wellisch, Hans, 87
Welsh, Harry, 334–335
Wentworth, Harold, 288, 289
West Publishing Company, 341
What They Said in 197 . . . , 123, 124
"What's New in Documents," 335
"What's Who in Who's Who," 244n.
Whitaker's Almanack, 191–193
Whitaker's Cumulative Book List, 71
White, Carl M., 39, 40
Who; Sixty Years of American Eminence, 245n.
Who Was When, 238
Who Was Who in America, 246n.

Who's Who, 17, 21, 234, 244, 246, 247
Who's Who Among Black Americans, 256–257
Who's Who in America, 230, 232, 234, 239, 244–246, 257
Who's Who in American Art, 255
Who's Who in American Politics, 217
Who's Who in Finance and Industry, 257–258
Who's Who in the East, 246n.
Who's Who in the Midwest, 246n.
Who's Who in the South and Southwest, 246n.
Who's Who in the West, 246n.
Who's Who in the World, 247
Who's Who of American Women, 246, 257
Willing's Press Guide, 83n.
Wilson Company, H. W., indexes of, 47, 48, 64, 68, 75, 83, 84, 99, 100, 104–105, 107–109, 111–113, 117–121, 131n., 226, 255, 258–262
Wilson Library Bulletin, 38, 43–45
Winch, Kenneth L., 311
Winchell, Constance, 37
Womanhood Media, 203
Woman's Almanac, 202–203
Women, almanacs and yearbooks on, 202–203
Women Studies Abstracts, 111
Women's Movement Media, 203
Women's Rights Almanac, The, 202, 203
Worcester Public Library, 5
Word Book, The, 281
"Word King–Eric Partridge, The," 289n.
Works Progress Administration, 320–321
World Almanac and Book of Facts, The, 17, 190–193
World Atlas, Family Edition, 313
World Authors, 1950–1970, 24, 230, 259, 260
World Bibliography of African Bibliographies, A, 92
World Bibliography of Bibliographies, A, 92
World Book, 17, 138–139n., 141, 146, 149, 152, 159–161, 183, 271n.
World Book Dictionary, 283
World Book Dictionary and Childcraft, The, 138
World Book Year Book, 165
World Guide to Libraries, 220n.
World Guide to Scientific Association, 218n.
World of Learning, The, 219n.
World Publishing Company, 269, 280, 282
Wright, Andrew, 179
Writer's Handbook, The, 224
Writer's Market, 223–224
Wyer, James, 49

Wynar, Bohdan, 37–38, 40–42, 152
Wynar, Christine L., 39n., 86, 87
Wynkoop, Sally, 216n.

Yale University, 13
Yannarella, Philip A., 332
Yarborough, Judith, 129n.
Yearbook(s), 17, 188–191, 194–203, 300
  definition of, 189
Yearbook(s):
  encyclopedia, 164–165
  general, 194–195

guidelines for discarding, 51
purpose of, 189–191
subject, 195–203
Yearbook of Agriculture, 336
Yearbook of International Organizations, 198
Yearbook of the United Nations, 197
"Yellow pages, people's," 216
"Yellow pages: the Quiet Monopoly,"
  216n.
Young Children's Encyclopedia, 137
Young Students Encyclopedia, 149n., 161–
  162